FARMAGEDDON

FARMAGEDDON

THE TRUE COST OF CHEAP MEAT

PHILIP LYMBERY WITH ISABEL OAKESHOTT

B L O O M S B U R Y

LONDON • NEW DELHI • NEW YORK • SYDNEY

First published in Great Britain 2014

Text copyright © 2014 Philip Lymbery and Isabel Oakeshott
Illustrations by Liane Payne

The moral right of the authors has been asserted

Bloomsbury Publishing plc
50 Bedford Square
London
WC1B 3DP

www.bloomsbury.com

Bloosmbury is a trademark of Bloomsbury Publishing Plc

Bloomsbury Publishing, London, New Delhi, New York and Sydney

A CIP catalogue record for this book is available from the British Library

ISBN 978 1 4088 4644 5

10 9 8 7 6 5 4 3 2

Typeset by Hewer Text UK Ltd, Edinburgh
Printed and bound in Great Britain by CPI Group (UK) Ltd, Croydon CR0 4YY

To the memory of Peter and Anna Roberts

Contents

Preface

Mid-April in Pennsylvania, USA, and spring is in full swing. Birds are singing and daffodils celebrate in rampant profusion outside the front door of the white clapboard farmhouse. I gaze from the childhood bedroom window of the late Rachel Carson, the mother of the modern environmental movement, and look across the Allegheny valley where she grew up. I picture the young girl being inspired by the natural world around her: picking fruit from apple orchards, wandering nearby woods and hillsides, making countless discoveries as she went. Peering out into the morning light, I see two enormous chimney stacks belching smoke into the blue sky. Carson grew up in a world where industry and countryside existed side by side. But during her lifetime lines became blurred and industrial methods found their way into farming, with devastating consequences.

In 1962 Rachel Carson was the first to raise the alarm about the peril facing food and the countryside. Her book *Silent Spring* shone a spotlight on the effects of spraying the countryside with chemicals, part of agriculture's new industrialised approach.

I was on the last leg of a journey to see for myself the reality behind the marketing gloss of 'cheap' meat, to find out how the long tentacles of the global food system are wrapped around the food on our plate. I wanted to find out, half a century on, how things had changed, what notice we have taken, and what has happened to our food. It was a journey that had already taken me across continents, from the

California haze to the bright lights of Shanghai, from South America's Pacific coast and rainforests to the beaches of Brittany.

In the 1960s, Carson's clarion call was heard across the Atlantic by Peter Roberts, a dairy farmer from Hampshire, England. He was one of the first in Europe to talk about the invasion of intensive farming methods sweeping across from America. As he walked his fields and milked his cows, Roberts became uneasy at what was going on. He saw farm animals disappearing from the land into huge, windowless sheds, the farming press acting as cheerleader for the post-war agricultural revolution, his fellow farmers bombarded with messages ushering them along the industrial route. He felt something had to be done.

Angered by the institutionalised cruelty to animals on factory farms, Roberts approached the main animal charities of the day, urging them to get involved. He left disappointed: the charities were too busy focusing on cruelty to cats, dogs and horses. Despondent but undeterred, he shared his thoughts with a lawyer friend. 'Well Peter, at least you know where you stand,' the friend responded. 'You'll just have to take it up yourself.'

In 1967, Roberts founded the charity for which I now work: Compassion in World Farming. It was the autumn and the new organisation was run out of the family cottage; one man, his wife, Anna, and three small daughters against an industry driven by government policy, subsidised by taxpayers' money, guided by agricultural advisers and supported by a profusion of chemical, pharmaceutical and equipment companies. The odds against making any impact were huge.

The seeds of the problem were sown way back in the last century. During the 1940s, the world was at war, riven by what was perhaps the deadliest conflict in human history. The Second World War was to be a huge watershed moment, not only for global politics, but also heralding perhaps the greatest revolution in recent food and farming history. As bombs shook battlefields, the building blocks were being put in place for the industrialisation of the countryside. The means to make explosives out of thin air had been discovered three decades earlier by two German scientists who, in 1910, worked out how to convert atmospheric nitrogen into ammonia, a key ingredient in both artificial fertiliser and TNT.

During the Second World War, German scientists perfected the mass production of organophosphate nerve agents as chemical weapons, although they were never used. After the war, US companies adopted the technology for agricultural use. In the words of Carson, in 'developing agents of chemical warfare, some of the chemicals created in the laboratory were found to be lethal to insects . . . widely used to test chemicals as agents of death for man'. The scene was set for weapons of destruction to become the means for mass production in farming.

The Great Depression of the 1930s, a severe economic slump that lasted until the outbreak of war, led the US Congress to pass the first Farm Bill in 1933, a package of subsidy support for agriculture that remains to this day the federal government's main way of affecting how food is produced. It was introduced to help US farmers struggling with low crop prices due to flooded markets. It included a government commitment to buy up surplus grain, which took the brake off burgeoning production.

Some of the world's richest countries had experienced food shortages during the war years as supplies from overseas were hampered by enemy activity. It taught them a hard lesson in the benefits of self-sufficiency. When peace returned, many countries focused on boosting home-grown food supplies. In 1947 Britain passed the Agriculture Act, heralding government funding and encouragement for the new ways of mass production through the 'efficiencies' of intensification: getting more out of the same land using the latest chemicals, pharmaceuticals and machinery. In the US, the munitions plants of the American war machine were converted into artificial fertiliser factories. Pesticides derived from wartime nerve gas were used on the new enemy: agricultural insects. Plant-breeding techniques caused corn yields to take off, leading to cheap corn, and lots of it. So much so that corn became a cheap source of animal feed.

The industrialised nations had the means and the impetus for turning farming into a process of mass production, transforming food and the countryside with serious if unintended consequences. Quality was replaced by quantity as the main driver. Farmers were encouraged to meet minimum standards for the commodity market rather than trying to produce the best. Antibiotics were cleared for use in livestock, providing the means to dampen down disease arising from keeping too many animals in too small a space. The drugs came with the additional benefit of boosting growth rates which, along with hormones, helped fatten animals for slaughter faster.

Across the countryside, the old patchworks of mixed farms with their variety of crops and animals became a thing of the past, replaced by monocultures – farms specialising in the mass production of a single crop or animal. Farming in tune with nature was no longer necessary. The same crop could be grown on the same soil over and over. Artificial fertilisers provided a quick fix for flagging fields while unwelcome weeds, insects and other pests could be sprayed away with copious chemicals. Farm animals disappeared from the land into factory-like sheds; artificial fertilisers had usurped their role of replenishing tired soils through their manure in fields and orchards. There was talk of a new type of farming; of production-line methods applied to the rearing of animals; of animals living out their lives in darkness and immobility without sight of the sun. In her ground-breaking exposé of 1964, Ruth Harrison described a generation of men who saw in the animal they reared 'only its conversion factor into human food'.[1] Factory farming was born.

Successive governments saw to it that the new regime was widely adopted, blinkered to the hidden costs and investing significant resources in spreading the message. Everything became supercharged in the rush for production. Companies began specialising in fast-growing varieties of animal, like chickens that grow from tiny Easter chicks to grotesquely oversized adults in just six weeks – twice the speed of previous generations. An army of 'expert' advisers on the government payroll told farmers to get on board or face ruin. I remember Peter Roberts telling me about the day one of the farm advisers came knocking at his door. It was the early Sixties and they had a long conversation but the message was simple: if you want to boost your business, you'll have to move into intensive chicken rearing. He was told that meant specialising in chickens, lots of them, in large industrial sheds. He could buy the birds and their feed from a big company and when they were fully grown – which would not take long – he could sell them back to the same firm, which would have them slaughtered and find them a market. It would be sanitised, industrialised, integrated. All he'd have to do was sign a contract and grow the 'crop' of chickens.

Although he kept a few hundred chickens already, Roberts was uncomfortable. He felt it would mean relinquishing his power as a farmer to decide how things were done. It didn't feel right. That evening, he discussed it with his wife Anna. Her reaction was instant and instinctive: 'If you want to do this, Peter, I won't stop you, but I want you to know that I don't agree with it.' Unlike Roberts, many others succumbed to the sales patter.

Taxpayers' money was used to support farming's new direction, a legacy that lives on today. The much-criticised Common Agricultural Policy (CAP) of the European Union was set up in 1962 and now swallows up nearly half the EU's budget. Fifty billion euros a year are doled out in payments to complying farmers. Likewise, the Farm Bill in the US gives out around $30 billion[2] in the form of subsidies to farmers, with three-quarters going to just a tenth of farms – generally the wealthiest and biggest. Corn (maize) continues to be the most heavily subsidised crop, underpinning a cheap-meat culture based on the products of factory-farmed animals fed cereals and soya instead of grass and forage from the land.

Looking back, what wasn't so clear was the treadmill farmers were boarding: to produce more and more with less and less, so often for diminishing rewards. Inevitably, mass production led to a squeeze on the prices farmers earned for their work, and many farmers learned the hard way that the seductive new system was not all it was cracked up to be. Quite simply they went out of business.

Animal and crop rearing were once a happy partnership. Industrialisation divorced them. It saw the rise of 'barley barons' who would
grow cereals in great monocultures. Field sizes grew as hedges disappeared. Nature's protests at the death of diversity – insects and weeds
kept in check previously by natural means – were drowned out with
pesticides. The soil was forced to work harder and harder. Insects and
weeds were sprayed away, wildlife habitats diminished, and the growing fear of silent springs – the demise of birdsong in a desert of
industrial crops – was captured in Carson's whistle-blowing book.
Today there is scarcely a corner of the Earth that is not touched to
some extent by the spread of intensive agriculture.

In recent decades, things have changed, sometimes for the better. For
example, keeping calves in premature coffins – narrow veal crates – for
their entire lifetimes is banned throughout the EU; the toxic and hugely
damaging pesticide DDT has been banned for farm use worldwide.

But fifty years on from Carson and Roberts and their first cries of
alarm, the way food is produced again stands at a crossroads, captured
best by the proposal for a US-style mega-dairy in Lincolnshire,
England. The idea was to take 8,000 cows out of fields and to house
them permanently on concrete and sand. This was the new frontier in
the battle for the British countryside. It united local people, foodies,
celebrity chefs, environmental and civil society interests in opposition.
Eventually, the proposal was withdrawn. But the spectre of a new wave
of intensification in the countryside had been raised; was US-style
'mega-farming', with its massive scale and super-intensification, now
camped on Europe's lawn? How far had it spread already? And what
were the effects in the US itself?

I am privileged to be Chief Executive of Compassion in World
Farming, the charity Peter Roberts founded, and now the world's leading farm animal welfare organisation, with offices and representatives
across Europe, the USA, China and South Africa. In 2011, I was chal-
lenged by the charity's chairperson, Valerie James, to uncover why an
industry that started out with such good intentions – feeding nations
and the world – had gone so wrong, all too often appearing to put

profit before feeding people. How were people, animals and the planet being affected and what could be done about it? The idea for this book was born.

I set out to get under the skin of today's food system. I took on the role of investigative journalist, following leads and tip-offs; lifting the lid on intensive food production; always in my official capacity and sometimes using my Compassion in World Farming business card to dig myself out of awkward holes.

Over two years, I travelled with the *Sunday Times*'s political editor, Isabel Oakeshott, and a camera crew to explore the complex web of farming, fishing, industrial production and international trade that affects the food on our plate. I used my contacts across the world to pinpoint where to go and who to speak to. We drew up a list of countries and places to visit, based on their involvement in the globalised world of food. California was an obvious choice, not only for its cultural exports like Hollywood, but also for what some see as futuristic ways of farming. China is a rising power and the most populous country on the planet for people and pigs. Argentina is the world's greatest exporter of soya for animal feed. I wanted to see for myself how people, often in faraway lands, who provide the feed, the ingredients or the food on our plates are affected by the runaway industrialisation of the countryside. I was keen to hear firsthand from the people involved and those affected. This is their story as much as mine.

                                                            Philip Lymbery

Introduction

Old Macdonald

At the height of his powers, Chairman Mao launched a war on sparrows. On a mission to turbocharge China's productivity, the Communist leader decided that the birds were eating too much grain. One winter day in 1958, he mobilised the population of China to kill them off. The campaign was ruthlessly coordinated, as if the birds were any other enemy.

Instructions were issued, weapons assembled, and the media hammered home the importance of victory. At dawn on the specified day, young and old, in town and country, gathered to launch a simultaneous attack. Everyone had a role, from the old folk who stood under trees waving flags and banging pots and pans to terrify the birds, to the schoolgirls issued with rifles and trained how to shoot sparrows that took flight and the teenage boys who climbed trees and tore down nests, smashing eggs and killing baby birds.[1] Goaded into action by local party bureaucrats, spurred on by national anthems blasting out of Peking Radio, they threw themselves into the task.

Against such an onslaught, the birds didn't stand a chance. According to one newspaper report, by the end of day one, in Shanghai alone an 'estimated' 194,432 sparrows had been killed.[2] Across China, the sparrow population was decimated. Millions of birds lay dead.

Too late, the regime realised that the sparrows were not pests, pilfering the harvest, but vital to the food chain. When they disappeared, the bugs they once fed on thrived. The locust population spiralled out of control, the grasshoppers too. The insects devoured the crops and famine followed. So Chairman Mao called off the campaign and sparrows were once again left in peace. But it took decades for the species to recover. Meanwhile the balance of nature was so out of kilter that there was talk of having to import sparrows from the Soviet Union.

Imagine if the prime minister of Great Britain or the president of the United States tried something similar today. We would think they were out of their minds. Yet the effect of agricultural policy in Europe and the Americas in the past few decades has been almost exactly the same as Mao's purge. Tree sparrows – the same species that Mao targeted – have declined in Britain by 97 per cent over the last forty years, largely due to the intensification of agriculture. The figures for other well-loved birds like turtle doves and corn buntings are no less alarming. Modern farming has become so 'efficient' that the countryside is now too sterile to support native farmland birds. The situation is so critical that the British government is offering farmers payments to install bird feeders on their land to prevent certain species dying out through starvation.[3]

The collapse of native bird populations is just one of many disturbing consequences of an agricultural policy based on intensification. It's a process that has been under way for decades, and that some now want to deliberately accelerate in the name of 'sustainable intensification'. But where will it take us? The aim is to pound more flesh out of every farm animal, and extract ever higher yields from every acre of land, where money is poured into high-input intensive farming systems that rely on mass production to give a return on investment. The result has been the slow demise of the traditional mixed farm, on which animals and crops were rotated on grass and soil that largely replenished itself, and the ascendancy of farms that specialise in single crops sustained by fertilisers, or in livestock reared indoors.

Of course birds are not the only victims of this quiet revolution. The remorseless drive to get more for less is taking place at the expense of many other animals and insects; at great risk to public health; and often, at a heavy cost to people thousands of kilometres away.

This is not a 'poor animals' book – though chickens, pigs, cattle and fish have an appalling time on factory farms. Nor does it preach vegetarianism. It is not anti-meat, it is not anti-GM per se, and it is not anti-corporate. It dares to ask whether, in farming, big has to mean bad. It goes to the heart of the question of whether factory farms are the most 'efficient' way of providing meat and the only way to feed the world.

The insidious creep of industrial agriculture has taken place quietly, almost unnoticed except by communities immediately affected. Perhaps that's because so much of the business now goes on literally behind closed doors. Without fuss or fanfare, farm animals have slowly disappeared from fields, and moved into cramped, airless hangars and barns.

People may have a vague notion that things have changed, but they prefer to believe that farms are still wholesome places where chickens scratch around in the yard, a few pigs snooze and snort in muddy pens and contented cows chew the cud. It's a myth often peddled to children from an exceptionally young age. The fiction starts before they can walk or talk, with colourful picture books showing happy animals grazing by duck ponds in lush green fields. In these story books the ruddy-cheeked farmer and his wife are a picture of health, with a couple of bonny children and a mischievous-looking dog at their sides. At nursery school, the fake idyll is reinforced in nursery rhymes and story books. Then come the school trips and family days out to farms open to the public, where another altogether unreal image of a working farm is often portrayed. These visitor attractions offer tractor rides through meadows full of glorious spring flowers; the chance to pet newborn piglets and lambs; pony rides, donkey rides and even pig races – all in the most beautiful countryside. They are wonderful places of laughter and fun, but no more reflective of the average working farm than a schmaltzy Hollywood romance is of the average relationship.

In fact, only 8 per cent of farms in England today are 'mixed' – rearing more than one type of animal and also growing crops.[4] They face a desperate struggle to survive. They have all too often been replaced by farms that specialise in one thing only, whether it is producing cereals, eggs, chicken, milk, pork or beef. These places would make a dismal day out for anyone, and shock most schoolchildren. The Old Macdonald fallacy won't stay credible much longer.

Thankfully, Britain still has a fair proportion of farms where animals are allowed to do what nature intended: roam or graze on grass.[5] But if the policy of intensification continues unchallenged, soon the only farms rearing animals on grass in higher-welfare conditions will be tourist attractions, or rich men's playthings. Britain and Europe's farmers are still relative novices at the intensification game, but agricultural policy is encouraging them to adopt dubious and controversial practices already common in the USA and elsewhere. Without a change of tack, mega-piggeries, mega-dairies, 'battery'-reared beef and genetically engineered crops – and animals – will soon be the norm.

To anyone who travels to places where such systems are well established, the repercussions are plain to see. For the countryside, it often means a landscape so barren and depleted that little except the animal or crop at the centre of the production operation is allowed to thrive. For farm animals, intensification often means terrible suffering and results in poorer-quality produce. Some 70 billion farm animals are produced worldwide every year, two-thirds of them now factory-farmed. They are kept permanently indoors and treated like production machines, pushed ever further beyond their natural limits, selectively bred to produce more milk or eggs, or to grow fat enough for slaughter at a younger and younger age. A typical factory-farmed dairy cow is forced to produce so much milk that she is often exhausted and useless by the tender age of five – at least a decade less than her natural lifespan.

Those unmoved by the suffering might find other reasons to look again at the waste and the woefully poor-quality, high-fat meat that result from these techniques. Since farm animals are no longer on the land and have no access to grass or forage, their feed must be transported to them, sometimes across several continents. Together they consume a third of the world's cereal harvest,[6] 90 per cent of its soya meal and up to 30 per cent of the global fish catch[7] – precious resources that could be fed direct to billions of hungry people.[8]

Meanwhile the barns they are reared in are often hotbeds of disease – small wonder when so many animals are crammed into such small spaces. It's a business that depends on vast quantities of antibiotics – half of all those used in the world.[9] One consequence has been the breeding of antibiotic-resistant 'superbugs' in humans and weird and deadly new viruses that have been linked to industrial farming.

Consumers become the scapegoats, the supposed beneficiaries of a benevolent industry producing 'what the consumer wants'. Yet consumers are forced to walk supermarket aisles blindfolded, often unable to tell what is grown more naturally from what is 'fresh' from the factory farm, thanks to an industry that resists better labelling. The way food is produced has a key bearing on its quality, not just from an ethical standpoint, but also in terms of its nutritional quality and how it tastes. Feeding animals grain, rather than letting them graze grass, often results in fatty meat. In short, consumers often don't know what they're buying from an industry that wants to keep it that way.

From time to time, a food scandal will blow the lid off a shadowy aspect of what's going on. The horsemeat scandal of 2013 confirmed consumer fears that they don't always know the full story behind the food they buy, when hot breaking news quickly degenerated into a furious blame-game. Horsemeat had been switched for beef, leaving the horse-loving nation of Britain stunned and distrustful. Keen to avoid taint from the torrent of revelations, the UK prime minister David Cameron blamed supermarkets, who blamed their suppliers, who pointed to distant traders in faraway lands. Consumers were left baffled and angry.

The alarm was first raised by the Irish Food Safety Authority, which revealed the finding of horsemeat in products labelled as beef. The supermarket giant Tesco, Britain's biggest, was one of the first to be involved when an 'Everyday Value' beefburger from the store turned out to contain 29 per cent horsemeat. The offending burger was manufactured in Ireland from meat thought to be of Polish origin. Other supermarkets were affected. Within days, 10 million burgers – enough calories to feed a million people for a day – had been removed from shelves by worried retailers.[10]

What was uncovered was a fraudulent labelling scam stretching the length of Europe.[11] Day after day, new revelations involved more big-name brands. Consumers reacted by shunning frozen burgers; UK sales fell by 43 per cent. Tesco placed full-page advertisements in national newspapers with the headline 'We apologise',[12] suffering its sharpest fall in market share for two decades.[13]

'Horsegate', as it became known, was all about trust. Consumer confidence had crashed and companies licked reputational wounds. Some admitted to having lost control of supply chains which, over the years, had grown longer and more complex, as food might pass through several hands before getting to the supermarket. Some blamed the incessant pressure for low prices during the global recession that started in 2007. 'We now need the supermarkets to stop scouring the world for the cheapest products they can find,' thundered the president of the National Farmers Union (NFU), Peter Kendall.[14]

Horsegate was the biggest scandal to hit British food since 'mad cow disease' or BSE, which two decades earlier caused a ten-year ban on British beef exports. BSE, caused by turning natural herbivores – cows – into carnivores, feeding them meat and bone meal, was a real own goal for industrial agriculture. It will not be the last.

Of course there are some winners from the system, like the companies peddling products that promise farmers ever-greater yields. The new technology can be effective in the short term, but sooner or later someone pays the price. In India, for example, around 200,000 farmers have killed themselves since 1997, typically after falling into debt.

They mortgage themselves up to the hilt to buy 'magic' genetically modified seed, then belatedly discover it is totally unsuitable for local conditions. The harvest fails. In the UK, a couple of dozen farmer suicides would trigger a national outcry; in India, the tragedy has unfolded almost in silence.

In the United States, while researching this book, I stood among thousands of acres of almond trees, all in perfectly regimented rows, breathing in air so heavy with chemical sprays that it smelled like washing-up liquid. There was not a blade of grass, nor butterfly, nor insect, to be seen. In the distance was one of the many mega-dairies in the state. Thousands of listless cows with udders the size of beachballs stood in the mud, waiting to be fed, milked, or injected with drugs. There was no shortage of land; no logical reason for them not to be on grass. The system wasn't even working for the farmers themselves. At a livestock market in a nearby town, a farmer wept as he told how a friend's mega-dairy had gone out of business and the despairing owner took his own life.

In Argentina I stood in a field of genetically modified soya as thousands of mosquitoes swarmed around my head. There was no stagnant water nor any of the conditions normally associated with such high numbers of insects. Something was wrong.

In Peru I saw a malnourished child, covered in sores associated with air pollution from the fish-processing industry, hearing from doctors that she could be healthy and well fed if only she were given the local anchovies destined for animal feed in Europe's factory farms.

In France we talked to the family of a worker who had succumbed to toxic fumes as he cleared luminous green algae from a once unspoilt beach. The gunge that now blights the coast of Brittany every summer is the highly visible face of pollution from the region's mega-pig farms.

In Britain, I helped campaign against the establishment of the country's first-ever mega-dairy of 8,000 cows. It was a battle we won – but for how long?

There is a widespread and deep-seated assumption that industrialising farming – treating the delicate art of rearing animals and working the land as if it were any other business, like making widgets or rubber tyres – is the only way to produce affordable meat. For too long, this basic premise has gone almost entirely unquestioned. Governments have rushed to create the conditions in which shoppers can buy a £2 chicken, thinking they're doing everyone a favour. Yet the reality behind how cheap meat is produced remains hidden.

This book looks into the unintended consequences of putting profit before feeding people. It asks how something with such good intentions as feeding nations could go so wrong.

It questions what is efficient about cramming millions of animals indoors, giving them antibiotics to survive, then spending vast sums transporting food to them, when they could be outside on grass.

It questions what is space-saving about a system that relies on millions of acres of fertile land to grow animal feed on estates often hundreds of thousands of kilometres from the farm.

It questions what is smart about having to remove mountains of manure from concrete floors and find a way to get rid of it, when if animals were in fields, their dung would return to the earth by itself, enriching the soil in the process, as nature designed.

It asks whether it makes any sense to encourage people to eat a lot of cheap chicken, pork and beef from animals specifically selected for their ability to grow so big that they produce fatty meat.

Finally, it begs the question, is the Farmageddon scenario – the death of our countryside, a scourge of disease and billions starving – inevitable? Through the eyes of the people and animals involved, this book sheds light on what they don't want you to know and asks, could there be a better way?

I
RUDE AWAKENINGS

Every now and then, something happens to shake the very foundations of how we view our food. 'Horsegate', the scandal of a horse-loving nation waking up to find it had been quietly devouring the object of its affection, was one of those moments. The fact that horsemeat was switched for beef in our food chain on such a widespread scale served to underline for many how little we know about our food: what's in it and how it is produced. There are fears of a gulf in understanding about the food on our plate; more than a third of young adults in Britain don't know that bacon comes from a pig, milk from a cow or eggs from a hen.[1]

Much of the meat on many supermarket shelves has a dirty secret that you won't find on the label – the way it was produced. It is a matter of convenience for producers that some consumers don't know that meat or milk comes from an animal that was once living and breathing, let alone understand how the animal was reared. Some producers go to great lengths to keep it that way; to keep the veil tightly drawn. Perhaps the most extreme example are moves in the US to introduce so-called 'ag-gag' laws, that would ban the taking of photos and film of intensive farming operations without permission, thereby making it harder to expose bad practices or wrongdoing. It raises the question, what have they got to hide?

A storybook vision of farming – of frolicking animals in pristine countryside – is all too often perpetuated. I was in my late teens when I started to find out that this wasn't always the case and that this vision was in fact far removed from the reality. This realisation changed the way I thought about what was on my plate – I'd like to think for the better. Thirty years on, I travelled the world to see the role that people, in often distant lands, play in the food we eat. Where better to start than California, the land of milk and honey? I decided to push beyond the seductive glitz and glamour of the Sunshine State's hotspots and headed to the dusty valleys that yield world-renowned harvests. It was through this *Alice in Wonderland* looking glass that I was to step into what seemed like another world. For me, it begged another question: was this a curious aberration or the future direction of farming?

1

California Girls

A vision of the future?

California, USA: according to the Beach Boys, home to the cutest girls in the world. I was there to get a sense of what our planet will look like if California-style farming becomes the norm around the world. Since the legendary Sixties hit, the population of females in the Golden State has soared, but the new arrivals share none of the glowing good health and athletic physiques of the sun-kissed babes in the song. They are milk cows and their purpose in life is to churn out supernatural quantities of milk before being turned into hamburgers.

Hollywood has dipped California in gold, drawing millions of visitors to the sun-soaked beaches, twinkling city lights and luscious Napa Valley vineyards. Few tourists ever see the real powerhouse: Central Valley, the fruit bowl of America, and home to perhaps the biggest concentration of mega-dairies in the world. One and three-quarter million dairy cows are reared in California,[1] crammed into barren pens on tiny patches of land that make a mockery of the vast potential space in this part of America. They pump out nearly 6 billion dollars' worth of milk every year,[2] and as much waste in the form of dung and urine as 90 million people.[3] Through a combination of selective breeding, concentrated diets and growth hormones designed to maximise milk production, they are pushed so grotesquely beyond their natural limits that they survive for just two or three years of milking before being sent to slaughter.

The US-style mega-dairy, often twenty to a hundred times the size of the average British dairy, is on the brink of migrating to the UK and other parts of the world. For this reason, and because it has embraced intensive farming with an enthusiasm and rigour unmatched anywhere in the world, Central Valley is a vision of how the countryside elsewhere could soon look. I wanted to see it.

It would not be my first trip to an American mega-dairy. During the successful battle to block plans for the UK's first mega-dairy, an 8,000-cow facility in Lincolnshire, England, I went out to Wisconsin to look at the farm on which that proposal was modelled. It was a flying visit, the result of a pledge I made on national radio at the height of the campaign. What I found was a soulless and highly tuned milk-production operation in which the cows might as well have been Kitchen Aid machines, designed to swallow up ingredients and spew them out in another form, keeping the process going twenty-four hours a day until they ran out of steam. What I found then was depressing and gave me some idea of what to expect in California, but nothing prepared me for the sheer scale of what I was to encounter this time.

Accompanied by a small team including Isabel Oakeshott and a camera crew, I flew to California in November, hoping to see as much of Central Valley as possible in just under a week. In the event, I nearly didn't make it – thanks to a chicken sandwich that my colleague had bought from a branch of Pret A Manger at Heathrow in case the food on the plane wasn't up to scratch. She didn't eat it there, but kept it in case there was nothing to offer in the motel at the other end.

We were at baggage reclaim at San Francisco airport, waiting to pick up our cases, when an eager sniffer dog bounded over. He'd smelled the sandwich in her hand luggage. Within seconds the dog handler was on the scene and we were the focus of a full-scale security alert, the sandwich inspected like an unexploded bomb, all my colleagues' bags examined and X-rayed.

The sandwich was subjected to further forensic examination before being carted off to be destroyed. At last we were sent on our way – but not before getting a long lecture about mad cow disease. It was a sharp reminder that while the UK has very deliberately relegated BSE to an embarrassing chapter in history, America has neither forgiven nor forgotten. The incident would seem even stranger later, when we witnessed the seemingly casual disregard for public health that goes hand in hand with mega-dairy farming in California.

We didn't hang around in San Francisco, but hit the road to Central Valley. It was a five-hour drive south through drab agricultural land. Approaching the valley, we noticed a curious yellowish-grey smog on the horizon. It looked like the sort of pollution that hangs over big cities, but there were none, only the dairies, which emit so much bad stuff that the surrounding air quality can be worse than Los Angeles on a smoggy day.[4]

As well as supporting an army of cows, Central Valley coughs up an incredible annual harvest of fruit, nuts and vegetables, despite having so little rainfall that it is technically classified as semi-desert. There are fields of pomegranates, pistachio orchards, grape vines and apricot trees. There are tomatoes and asparagus, and acres of red, pink and yellow rose bushes. There are miles of orange and lemon groves. There are also enough almond trees to provide four out of every five almonds consumed in the world. It sounds like the Garden of Eden. It isn't. It turned out to be a deeply disturbing place where not a blade of grass, no tree or hedgerow grows, except in private gardens and the ruthlessly delineated fields.

The phenomenal output of fruit and veg is possible only thanks to a cocktail of chemicals and the plundering of the crystal-clear rivers that run down from the Sierra Nevada mountains. By remorselessly dousing the parched soil with fertilisers, insecticides, herbicides and fumigants, as well as diverting natural waterways, farmers have been able to pull off a multi-billion-dollar conjuring trick, extracting harvests from soil that is so depleted of natural matter it might as well be brown polystyrene.

All these chemicals make the air smell very strange. It caught in my throat and felt like it was creeping down into my lungs. In this breezeless bowl between the mountains and the coast, weed- and pest-killers from industrial sprayers can struggle to settle on crops, leaving a fine mist of toxins to hang in the air. Some days, when the temperature and air pressure combine in a certain way, clouds of chemicals can be seen hovering above the crops. All that fruit should be an irresistible draw for birds, bees, butterflies and other insects. We saw virtually none.

On this featureless chemical wasteland lie the mega-dairies: milk factories where animals are just machines that rapidly break down and are replaced. The dairies arrived in Central Valley in the 1990s, after being pushed out of the Los Angeles suburbs. Land on the city outskirts was becoming ever more valuable, and as the population expanded, farmers were finding it cost more and more to dispose of waste. Encouraged by realtors, many sold up and moved to the sticks, where they quickly discovered there was not much to stop them doing as they pleased.

At the time, agriculture was exempt from California's Clean Air Act. It was not until the late 1990s, when the cousins George and James Borba applied to build two 14,000-cow operations on adjacent properties in Kern County, in effect creating a 28,000-cow dairy, that serious attention began to be paid to the potential environmental and health impacts. The Borbas' plans were nodded through at first, but the sheer scale of the proposal galvanised people who were already worried by what they were observing in Central Valley. After a protracted legal battle, campaigners forced the authorities to undertake a full environmental impact assessment, the results of which were so alarming they changed the game for ever. Such assessments became standard procedure for subsequent planning applications, and California's exemption of agriculture from the Clean Air Act came increasingly under question.

The policy was finally changed in 2003, when a new system of permits was introduced. In theory, farmers now have to comply with tough air- and water-pollution regulations – a burden they bitterly deplore. In practice we heard – and saw – worrying evidence that many routinely flout the law while overstretched authorities turn a blind eye.

We spent several days driving around Fresno, Tulare and Kern, the three counties that generate the most agricultural produce in the whole of America. It was not long before we found our first mega-dairy, a series of towering corrugated-iron shelters set in mud pens. It was autumn 2011; the sun shone against a clear blue sky and the temperature was pleasant. Some cows jostled for space in the shade under the open-sided sheds. Others stood in the sun looking bored. There was no grass, just a deep pile carpet of earth and manure. From a distance it was hard to tell the difference between the cows and the stacks of rubber tyres in the yard.

We pulled up for a closer look. A large black beetle scuttled across the road, virtually the only non-flying insect we encountered in five days – though there were always plenty of black flies. They arrived, we were told, at the same time as the mega-dairies and are now a scourge, invading homes, schools and offices, forcing residents to install screens over windows and seals around doors.

Out of the car, we took in the scene. The stench of manure was overwhelming – not the faintly sweet, earthy smell of cowpat famil-iar in the English countryside, but a nauseous reek bearing no relation to digested grass. The cows moved very little, too engorged with milk. When they did walk, it was with a rocking gait, their legs splayed wide around their pink and grey beachball udders. We saw these farms every couple of kilometres, all with several thousand cows surrounded by mud, corrugated iron and concrete. Most of the shelters were rigged up with rusty fans, a pathetic defence against the searing summer sun. Between feed times and milking, there was little for the animals to do but wait – for food, for milking, perhaps for medication.

Near the town of Turlock we saw several mega-dairies next door to power stations, a grotesque inversion of the traditional concept of a farm. There was nothing rural about these locations: they were huge industrial estates, characterised by supersized animal feed and milk-processing plants belching out fumes. Alongside were railway tracks bearing freight trains half a kilometre long.

We had tried in vain to make an appointment for an official tour of a farm. It turned out to be unnecessary: most mega-dairies were located right by public roads. The only facilities we could not see were the milking parlours, often giant rotating carousels. Cows queue up, step onto the wheel, and are hooked to milking machines. When their udders are pumped dry they step off the merry-go-round to make way for the next animal, and return to their barren pen.

The landscape was so flat it was difficult to get a sense of scale, so we chartered a plane, a tiny four-seater Cessna, to look at the dairies from the air. It cost less than dinner for two at a London restaurant. At reception, the pilot's wife reassured us her husband had been flying for fifty years without incident. He was fond of his grandchildren, she said, and wouldn't take any risks. We showed our passports, paid up, and strolled out onto the runway with our aviation headsets. It was all strangely informal, pleasantly so. We might as well have been hopping on a city bus.

In the back of the aircraft there was barely room for two. I wedged myself behind the pilot's seat, put my earphones on and prepared for take-off. There were some cursory radio exchanges, the pilot revved the engines, and then we zoomed along the runway and were airborne. We levelled at around 600 metres. Squeezed into the front passenger seat with all his gear, our cameraman opened the window to take some aerial shots, letting in such a powerful blast of air that my colleague's contact lenses almost blew out.

When I peered out of the window it looked as if a vast steamroller had pummelled its way across the country, flattening every knoll and hillock and pulverising every plant and creature in its wake. All that remained was a vast empty canvas, carved into neat sections. Into these sanitised boxes were inserted crops, the oranges and almonds that make their way to kitchen tables all over the world. From the air, the dairies just looked like vast fields of filth peppered with black and white specks and the odd corrugated-iron roof. I could see the tops of silage mountains, their taut white plastic coats shimmering in the afternoon sun. By every dairy was a stinking pool of yellowish-brown slurry. Even up there, I could pick up the smell. What self-respecting bovine would want to be a California girl?

Back on the runway again, I stepped out feeling strangely elated – the flight had been fun. But that afternoon brought more depressing sights, including the worst mega-dairy of the lot. It was on an industrial estate, squeezed between a giant feed factory and an electrical substation. It looked run-down, the fences rusty and dilapidated, the corrugated-iron shelters unusually low, perhaps an effort to cut costs. Down the road was a huge battery chicken factory, and the acrid smell of bird droppings mixed with cow manure hung in the air.

Next door to the farm were a couple of run-down bungalows on a patch of scrubby wasteland. Piles of rusting scrap metal, old tyres and discarded plastic toys littered the yard. Just visible from the road were rows of suspicious-looking wooden crates. I went to investigate, and found that they contained around 200 cockerels. The Mexican owner spoke little English, but it was clear they were for cock fighting, an illegal but popular pastime among poor communities in these parts. I saw this neighbourhood at dusk, against a backdrop of darkening cumulus clouds. An exhausted cow stooped atop a mound of manure, silhouetted against the night sky. It was like a scene from Armageddon.

Of course that's not how the industry sees it. The California Milk Advisory Board (CMAB) claims that 443,000 full-time jobs in California are linked to the dairy industry and that it generates as much as $63 billion in economic activity a year. Apparently, a typical cow contributes $34,000. The organisation's website is a slick piece of PR, a collage of images of contented cows on green fields, wholesome-looking food, and all-American-looking farming families, their arms round each other as they pose for the camera, as if to say that being in this business makes for a happy, fulfilling life, which perhaps it does for some.

Since 1969 the CMAB has run an annual Dairy Princess competition, a beauty pageant for young women from dairy families. The twenty winners enjoy a one-year reign during which they are ambassadors for the industry, giving radio and TV interviews, talking to school assemblies and making appearances at meetings and agricultural fairs. It's all designed to put a gloss on what is a deeply dubious industry in terms of its impact on public health, the environment and animal welfare.

The mega-dairy was near the biggest single-site cheese factory in the world, a showpiece for the California industry. Above a luxurious tea shop plying a tempting array of attractively packaged cheeses, cakes and sweets is a visitor centre extolling the benefits of the mega-dairy industry. Through a window on an upper floor, you can look down at the factory floor, where workers in white coats and caps can be seen processing vast vats of bright orange cheese. Later I tried some. It was tasteless and rubbery.

Beside a display of 'educational' material about the industry, a TV screen displayed pictures of smiling farmers with their wives and children, sitting in hay-filled barns. There were touching images of farmers bottle-feeding newborn calves and cows being checked over by caring-looking vets. According to the spin, dairy farmers 'preserve water; care for the air; care for the land; care for the environment', as well as, of course, contributing to the local economy. Whoever put together the promotional film footage was not quite brazen enough to show any cows on grass.

Naturally, the visitor centre barely touched on the huge environmental and health issues presented by mega-dairies. There were a couple of information panels, with flow charts illustrating waste-disposal systems. They made it sound harmless; neat.

That is a gross distortion. A fifth of children in Central Valley are diagnosed with asthma – a consequence of air pollution linked at least in part to the mega-dairy industry. It is almost three times the national average paediatric asthma rate. Nearly a third of the 4-million-strong population of Central Valley are assessed as facing a high degree of environmental risk, both from toxic air and from water pollutants.

*

It's hardly surprising given the amount of muck being produced. One animal generates as much waste as fifty humans, meaning that a single mega-dairy of around 10,000 cows creates as much waste as a fair-sized UK city such as Bristol. According to the CMAB, as of November 2011 there were 1,620 dairy farms in California, housing a total of 1.75 million cows. Together they generate more excrement than the entire human population of the UK.

Finding somewhere to put all those cowpats is a huge headache. Most is channelled into vast lagoons attached to the farms. They let off noxious gases and leach into the ground. Even with clay liners, the lagoons are porous. The US authorities seem to accept that significant seepage is inevitable. I wanted to hear from people living near the farms about the pollution and health problems. We met Tom Frantz, a retired maths teacher who has lived in Kern County all his life. He lives in a cosy clapboard house among the almond orchards, with two energetic dogs and some noisy geese. Amid the sanitised acres of commercially produced trees his garden is a tiny oasis, a riot of brightly coloured flowers and verdant shrubs beneath towering palms.

He says that Kern County is where he will die – perhaps a decade before his time, if a recent scientific study into pollution in Central Valley is to be believed. 'I know I'll probably live ten, even fifteen years less than I would if I moved, but this is where I come from. I'm not going anywhere,' he told us matter-of-factly.

Lately Frantz has noticed he's developed a strange post-nasal drip. He is in no doubt about the cause. 'Living near mega-dairies is danger-ous. We are looking at a potential health disaster. I can see a new strain of *E. coli*, some kind of plague, breaking out in Central Valley. That is the worst-case scenario. It sounds remote, but my worry is that it's just around the corner. Nobody will care, until it is too late.'

With his unkempt wiry hair and taste for reggae music, Frantz looked like an ageing hippy, but on the subject of mega-dairies and the environment he was extremely switched on, rattling off complex facts and figures about volatile organic compounds and nitrogen organic compounds with the authority of one who has spent years poring over the evidence. Over the past decade, he has become a thorn in the side of Kern County's dairy farmers, keeping their behaviour under relentless surveillance and calling them to account when he detects evidence that they are flouting environmental regulations. Where government agencies are too busy or lackadaisical to act, he starts to file official complaints, taking cases all the way to court if need be. It did not take him long to figure out that unless lawyers are involved people don't listen. This being America, you have to sue.

There are now ten dairies within thirteen kilometres of Frantz's home. The first arrived in 1994, the rest since 2002. Officially, they house a total of 70,000 cows. However, the real total is likely to be far higher: dairies are only required to submit the number of cows being milked at any one time, meaning they do not have to count animals that are being rested during their 'dry' (non-lactating) period. According to Frantz, what folk first noticed when the mega-dairies arrived was an influx of flies. Hardest hit was a school just over a kilometre from the first mega-dairy that opened. Teachers used to keep the doors and windows open in summer because the place had no air conditioning. These days that's out of the question. 'There were swarms of black flies in the classrooms. It was difficult for the kids to work with them buzzing around. That first year, they used rolls of sticky tape to catch them. Later, they installed screens on all the windows and sealed the doors.'

What bothers Frantz most though is air pollution. For much of the year, the smog is so thick and heavy that the Sierra Nevada mountains, 3,000 metres high, are invisible from the valley floor. Hardly anyone lives here, but air quality-wise, it might as well be Beijing. Of course there are many factors involved, from the exhaust fumes that pour from trucks carrying agricultural and other produce up and down the highway, to emissions from the industrial animal feed processing plants. They are a blatant source of pollution. The impact of mega-dairies is less visible but just as insidious, because of noxious gases from manure and silage.

Frantz and other concerned locals hold monthly meetings to discuss what to do. They work with sympathetic lawyers who take cases pro bono. Victory can mean multi-million-dollar fines for companies found responsible for environmental breaches. There's no money in it for the campaigners: the payouts are given to environmental groups.

For many small communities in Central Valley it is not air quality but water quality that is the most pressing issue. Studies have also shown a direct correlation between intensive dairy farming and contamination of water wells, especially with *E. coli* bacteria and nitrates.[5] During our trip, we spotted a well located within a few metres of the perimeter of a mega-dairy. It supplied local communities with their domestic water. Little wonder that so-called 'boil notices' – letters from local authorities ordering residents not to drink water out of their taps unless they have boiled it – are a way of life here.

Maria Herrera, a mother of four, runs the Community Water Center in the city of Visalia in the heart of the San Joaquin Valley. The organisation campaigns for universal access to safe drinking water. In a nation as rich as America, you'd have thought that people could take it for granted. Yet in parts of Central Valley it has become a luxury. In the small Hispanic communities that have sprung up to provide farm labour, it seems few dare to drink from the tap. Herrera told us:

> Ground water here is heavily polluted, mainly with nitrates, though there are also concerns about arsenic, which is linked to some fertilisers and is sometimes used as an additive in cattle feed. The meetings we hold with residents are always packed. The dairy farmers and their lobbyists come along and deny it has anything to do with them, but the evidence proves otherwise.

A permit system for farmers is supposed to keep water pollution within safe limits. In practice, it has proven impossible to prevent seepage from the Olympic swimming pool-sized lagoons of slurry attached to mega-farms. 'The lagoons aren't properly lined, and so the effluent leaks,' Herrera told us. 'It's crazy – we treat human waste so that it doesn't pollute water supplies; yet effluent from cows is allowed to get into the system. It makes no sense.' When nitrate levels in the water supply get too high, letters arrive from water companies advising folk not to drink from the tap. Herrera took us to meet some of the families affected who lived in a small trailer park surrounded by fields of citrus trees, a few kilometres outside Visalia. We stood amid the simple wooden bungalows, some so basic that the toilets were outside. Despite the obvious poverty, it was a welcoming place. The trailers and car ports were painted in pretty pastels; children and kittens scampered about; everyone knew everyone.

I was introduced to Luis Medellin, a handsome twenty-five-year-old who works at a mega-dairy but hates what the farms are doing to his community's water supply: 'To tell you the truth, our water here doesn't smell good. It looks cloudy and smells of chlorine. You can't trust it. From time to time, I do drink it right out of the tap, knowing it is contaminated, but mostly we buy bottled. I think there are Third World countries with safer water than we have here.' Every week, Medellin sets off with two giant plastic bottles the family keeps in the kitchen to replenish them with filtered water. It costs about four dollars a go, not a trivial sum for a family whose living conditions – an overcrowded trailer with little ventilation, lit by a few bare bulbs hanging from bare wires – would shock most well-heeled Americans.

According to the Community Water Center, there are at least six settlements within a few kilometres of Medellin's home where water quality is a serious issue. He has been campaigning for clean water since he was at high school. The irony that he earns his living from the very business that is responsible for polluting the supply does not escape him: 'I am not happy that I have to work there. The dairy has two huge lagoons full of crap – there's no other way to put it – and I am always thinking about what it's doing to the water.' He sticks it out because he is lucky enough to have a good boss, who looks after his workers and seems to care for the cows. His father has been working at the same dairy for fourteen years. It is the way of life here, but that doesn't mean people do not aspire to better or care about the damage the business is doing.

We were told about a growing body of scientific evidence about the health risks associated with living near mega-dairies. A recent study found that people living near factory farms have their life expectancy shortened by as much as a decade. We interviewed Kevin Hamilton, a blunt-talking registered respiratory therapist, at the Clinica Sierra Vista, in Fresno. His experience on the medical front line prompted him to become a committed activist against mega-dairies:

We're talking about heart disease, birth defects, and stunted lung development among children who spent a lot of time outside playing sport. We're talking about high blood pressure and increased risk of stroke. We have the second-highest level of child-hood asthma in the whole of the US. Fifteen years ago, I couldn't have said any of that with confidence. Now the evidence is over-whelming. It's terrifying.

The most vulnerable groups are children and pregnant women who can suffer long-term medical consequences as a result of even short exposures to dairy-related pollution. People over the age of sixty-five are also disproportionately affected. These high-risk groups make up a high percentage of Central Valley's population. Other groups heavily affected are the farm labourers who are exposed to noxious gases daily. 'They literally never escape the assault,' Hamilton said. 'They live in sub-standard houses, where the doors and windows are not sealed, and on the farms they are working very hard. The harder they breathe, the more stuff they take in. These workers are poor and disempowered. A lot of them are here illegally. Word gets round that if they make a fuss, they will be deported. It happens.'

Hamilton told us that one of his doctor colleagues recently moved away from the area because her son had developed bad asthma. 'She went to live in Colorado. I had a postcard from her six months ago, saying that since leaving this place, her son hadn't needed any medica-tion.' Hamilton believes mega-dairies are a repellent symbol of a grotesquely unnatural agricultural food production system.

You have to use a phenomenal amount of chemicals to push multiple crops out of the soil we have here. If you look at the official data on the amount of pesticides applied per square mile, the figures would stun you. I don't think people have any idea. These pesticides are capable of penetrating the human body to genome level – meaning they can affect the very building blocks of the body.

My family is from Kansas, and we had one crop a year, and were really grateful for that. Some people would argue that CAFO [Concentrated Animal Feeding Operations] systems feed the world. I would argue that the world was feeding itself pretty well before we did all this. We've taken agriculture out of fields where it should be, into places where we have to farm against nature. If we have to have mega-dairies at all, why have them in a place like Central Valley, an airless bowl? We have loaded them in at a totally unsustainable rate. It's got way out of hand.

I left Hamilton's offices feeling drained and wondering who wins from this system. It would be easy to blame the farmers, but it's not as if they are all making fortunes. Most seem to feel under siege by environmental activists and regulation on a scale they never anticipated nor signed up for when they abandoned their small farms on the outskirts of LA.

Mega-dairy farming is a high-risk business exposed to global price hikes and price volatility. Evidence suggests they cannot weather recession as well as smaller pasture-based systems. Between 2011 and 2012, feed prices almost doubled, driving some dairies to the brink of financial collapse. According to one report, produced by the farming industry itself in the UK, mega-dairies only become more competitive in a hypothetical situation in which the price of milk is fixed for ten years. As this is impossible, the report states that pasture-based farms are more likely to turn a profit. It seems the system is not working brilliantly for anyone.

It was not until the last day of our trip that I fully appreciated what an unhappy business mega-dairying can be. We were in Turlock,

Stanislaus County, visiting a livestock market. I wanted to see what cows from mega-dairies look like at the end of their lives. I had a pretty good idea what to expect: sad black and white bags of bones with saggy, dried-up udders and the exhausted demeanour of animals five times their age.

Known as the 'Heart of the Valley', Turlock was a depressing place, just a sprawl of dilapidated houses and stores interspersed by gas stations, downmarket food joints and the odd tattoo parlour and palm-reading salon. The surrounding area was scarred by the towering concrete and steel apparatus of intensive agricultural production. Locating the market was a step too far for our satnav GPS, and I was twice forced to stop and ask for directions. There were few friendly faces and folk struggled to understand my accent. I wondered whether we would witness blatant cruelty and how the locals would react when we pitched up. Experience taught me they were likely to be suspicious. The Humane Society of the United States, America's biggest and most effective animal protection charity, has a high profile among those in the livestock industry, most of whom are primed for unwelcome visits. In the event it was okay. Though the owner Chuck Cozzi was wary, he was sufficiently intrigued by his unexpected English visitors to usher us in. Not only did he agree to show us round, he also allowed us to film, a highly unusual concession in this type of facility.

The auction house had the feel of a small-town football club, with a dog-eared office and a greasy-spoon café selling a daily breakfast special of two eggs any style, two bacon strips, two sausages and two pancakes, all for $3.99. The salesroom was like a little theatre, with rough wooden benches for customers, a small ring for the animals, and a raised kiosk at the back, where the auctioneer sat.

I sat down, feeling painfully out of place among the weather-beaten men in Stetsons. The sale began, and I listened in amazement. It was not the sight of the animals that was remarkable but the auctioneer's breathless sales patter which, to the untrained ear, was curiously captivating, like someone singing the popular country song 'Cotton-Eyed Joe'. It turned out he had just qualified for the world livestock auctioneer championships.

I hung around until I'd seen a few depleted-looking dairy cows stagger into the ring. A pair of workers armed with plastic paddles swatted them out as the auctioneer sold them off for cheap meat to the slaughterhouse. Outside, a cowgirl on a paint horse cantered up and down corrals, herding animals towards the ring, her long blonde hair streaming out behind her. A prominent wooden sign in the lorry park warned farmers not to show up with animals too sick to walk. To my relief, there was no obvious sign of cruelty.

My film crew interviewed Cozzi, anticipating familiar complaints about low milk prices and the rocketing cost of animal feed. So it was completely unexpected when Cozzi, a 6ft 4in all-American guy, suddenly broke down in tears. He spoke of a close friend who owned a large dairy, but could not cope with the financial pressures. 'You know, he had enough. I think he shot himself, you know, leaving families behind. You know, kids. It's so sad.' He welled up and turned away from the crew, embarrassed. Composing himself, he said: 'You know I think maybe that guy was just so far in debt, he just gave up you know. Just got no more drive. I don't think anything could be that bad that somebody would want to do that, but it must have been for him.' It was a poignant moment. My crew and I felt hugely sympathetic to his account and thanked him for his honesty.

It is a reminder that it's not just California's milk cows who are suffering from this bizarre perversion of farming. Yes, the dairy cattle are dying young, but so all too often are the people who live and work with them. Everyone is struggling to survive – even the farmers who should be raking in their share from California's billions of dollars-worth of milk a year.

In the complex mesh of economic pressures and corporate interests that have given birth to factory farms, nothing is black and white. One thing does seem clear. In the land of the mega-dairy – a land that is inching perilously close to home – humans, cattle and the environment are dancing to a grim tune of extraction and depletion. Each is just an asset to be milked dry.

2

Henpecked

The truth behind the label

It was a perishing winter day, and I was pounding up the motorway to Northumberland in my old Renault hatchback to view some brand-new luxury homes.

According to the publicity, the development boasted cutting-edge fixtures and fittings and a wonderful location in Tyneside, on the rugged northeast English coast. I knew the area well – a place of stiff breezes, salty air, fish and chips, and cheerful folk. I'd often been there to visit the Farne Islands, a twitchers' paradise teeming with puffins and seabirds of all sorts. Out on the water, on birdwatching trips, they always provided a breathtaking interactive display, whistling past so close you could touch them. There would be a heavy smell of nesting birds and rotting fish, and you'd get the odd peck to the back of the head.

This time however, I was not going out in a boat. I was in the area to see birds of a different variety – hens – and more specifically their state-of-the-art accommodation. I'd been invited by a UK government advisory body, the Farm Animal Welfare Council (FAWC), to see an innovation: battery cages with perches. Officials were excited by the new features and wanted to know what I thought.

After hours on the road, I finally made it to the farm, where I was welcomed by a tall man with a thick Geordie accent. We shook hands, he offered me coffee, and I was introduced to the FAWC committee members who had also come to inspect the new cages. Among them was a government vet with thin greying hair, wearing a green anorak.

Coffee finished, we set off round the farm, a series of hangars crammed with battery cages: tiers of tiny, barren cages so small the hens couldn't even stretch their wings. Groups of five hens were usually crammed into each cage, where they could do little else but lay eggs and survive. The special ones we had come to see were really no different to the standard model – except that each contained a little wooden perch. We were told the hens loved the perches and that the new design made a huge difference to their lives. I resisted the temptation to roll my eyes. Anything was better than a bare wire cage, but it was hardly revolutionary.

Tour completed, we regrouped for a discussion. There was much debate about the ins and outs of what we'd seen. Eventually my moment came. I reeled off all the reasons why keeping hens in cages the size of an A4 piece of typing paper is dreadful, perch or no perch. Then I sat back and waited. The room was quiet. The government vet fixed me with a quizzical stare. 'Philip, I agree with much of what you've just said, but how can you say that hens *suffer*?' he asked incredulously. It sounds incredible, but back then in the early 1990s when my trip to Tyneside took place, the view that hens could not feel pain and suffer was commonplace. At the time, I had a fairly junior job with Compassion in World Farming. At first the work was mostly administrative, but soon I became involved in campaigns. As my knowledge grew, I was increasingly asked for my views by various organisations including government bodies. People often questioned whether farm animals could suffer. Along with colleagues, I spent a lot of time amassing scientific evidence to prove what seemed perfectly obvious to me: that hens and other farm animals are wired much the same as people when it comes to a nervous system, and can experience pain, fear, pleasure and excitement much in the way that we do.

As many as half a million people in Britain now keep hens in their garden, and I doubt that many of them would question this.[1] They can see that what happens to these complex creatures matters to them. They can see how much it means to them to feel the dust under their feathers, the sun on their wings, the soil beneath their feet. I am certain this isn't just sentimentality. People who keep chickens and other animals for pleasure, like our pet dogs and cats, often have an instinctive connection with their animals. I certainly don't feel the need to be anthropomorphic – to project human feelings onto animals, hens or others – because it's quite obvious that they are neither human nor automata, they're sentient creatures in their own right.

Our own little flock arrived one summer day in 2010, after my wife paid a visit to the local farm shop. We'd been talking about getting hens for months, but nothing had been agreed. In the end, I wasn't consulted. The assistant in the farm shop told Helen that their hens were soon going for slaughter. Without further ado, she grabbed a cardboard box, punched some air holes in it, popped three birds inside and brought them home. The first I knew of it was when I came home after a long day in the office and was relaxing outside with a cool drink when an unmistakable clucking broke out.

The hens spent a few days confined to barracks – a makeshift pen we constructed – before we released them into the garden. They burst out excitedly, running and flapping, and began rearranging our garden. They particularly liked pecking about underneath bushes, just as their ancestors must have done when they first evolved in the Asian jungle. It was obvious how much they valued scratching and foraging, being able to stretch their wings and feel the earth under their feet. I could see that each was an individual with her own personality, likes and dislikes. By winter, we had four and they had names: Hetty, Henna, Honey and Hope.

One particularly cold January afternoon, they were outside scrubbing around, when I heard an awful screech. It was a sound I recognised from childhood, when my mum and I kept bantams. Occasionally they were stalked by a cat and we'd hear a sudden cry of alarm, followed by an explosion of wings and frantic squawks. I would be sent to the rescue, by which time they were often in someone else's garden. This time the stalker wasn't a cat, but a fox. I felt a flash of panic. I rushed downstairs, shouting, arms flailing, and burst out of the back door, just in time to see the interloper making a run for it, hen in mouth. He tried to jump the 2-metre fence, then dived into the bushes, before tearing off towards the neighbour's shed, with me in hot pursuit.

At some point during his great escape, he dropped the hen, though I didn't know where. I was pretty sure she'd be dead, or fatally wounded. The rest of the hens had taken refuge by the house. They stood flicking and shaking their heads with stress. I counted them: one by the gate, a second by the table, a third at the back door . . . and the fourth? There she was, sitting on a wellington boot.

Hardly able to believe it, I counted again just to be sure, then scooped her up to check for injuries. To my surprise, apart from some superficial blood on her leg, she was in one piece. I attended to her wound and put her back on the grass. She hurried over to join the others. She seemed almost indignant at having been kept from her business of scratch and search. I felt ridiculously happy and relieved.

It was the first time I'd kept poultry since being at school. I never really liked classes. I was often told off for staring out of the window looking at birds when I should have been looking at the blackboard. However, one day I did sit up and pay attention. It was a Friday afternoon, I was eighteen years old and we'd all trooped into the lecture theatre to hear the latest in a long line of weekly visiting speakers.

It was the early 1980s and I remember that we were all excited because Kajagoogoo, a pop band from our town, had just made it into the charts. My neighbour Stuart Neale was on keyboards. Even back then, I was fascinated with birds and their freedom, and used to keep homing pigeons. I loved watching them fly over our neighbourhood, but sometimes they'd decide not to come back home, and would roost on Stuart's dad's guttering instead. I can see him now shaking his fist at them, as they peered down nonchalantly.

In the lecture theatre, I remember messing around until the teacher told us to shut up. Eventually, the hall went quiet and the speaker was introduced. He was a man called Chris Aston from Compassion in World Farming, and the teacher said he was going to tell us where our dinner came from. I remember being horrified at the pictures of pigs and calves in factory farms. I was particularly upset by the hens in battery cages and how they couldn't flap their wings, never mind fly. I thought about my pigeons and the wild birds that mesmerised me. The hens crammed into cages seemed a crime. It was a moment that changed my life for ever. I resolved to do something about it, which is how, a decade or so later, I found myself sitting in that farmhouse in Tyneside, listening to a government vet question whether hens could suffer and wondering why the Farm Animal Welfare Council existed, and why its members were interested in the perches, if they didn't think hens could feel anything anyway.

Fortunately, attitudes were about to change. In 1997, Labour swept to power after a landslide victory at the general election. A few weeks later I was in Amsterdam for a demonstration, the culmination of a long campaign by Compassion to change EU legislation. We wanted animals to be classified as 'sentient beings', an official recognition that they can feel pain and suffer. It was baking hot as we marched with colourful flags and banners, but the sweat was worth it, because the protest marked a watershed.

Later that day, European leaders agreed to our call, giving animals basic legal status as 'sentient beings'. We were now swimming with the tide. No longer were animals just 'goods' or 'agricultural products'. At last, it appeared their welfare was being taken seriously. The legal recognition won that day has gone on to become a dedicated 'Article', a core text to the European Treaty, giving it more weight. The wording states that 'since animals are sentient beings', the EU must 'pay full regard to [their] welfare requirements'.

Nothing much changed overnight. There was no sudden end to cruel practices like taking animals on long, unnecessary journeys for slaughter or caging them like units of production. Yet for those who cared about animal welfare, the new legal status changed the game for ever. Finally, EU law reflected both the scientific evidence and the message of common sense: that animals will suffer if they are badly treated, and experience a sense of well-being if they are well kept. It strengthened our calls for reform and meant I was unlikely to be hearing the sort of views expressed by that vet in Tyneside again – at least not from a government figure.

Two years later, in 1999, I was travelling all over Europe trying to persuade the EU to ban battery cages. It was an uphill struggle. Britain, the Netherlands, Germany, Austria and Sweden were in favour of reforms, but France and southern European states were deeply opposed. We had a battle on our hands, and we pulled out all the stops. We treated MPs and MEPs to breakfasts with free-range eggs; we delivered cakes made with cage-free eggs to embassies and governments on all sides; we locked celebrities and supporters in human-sized cages; and we organised marches all over Europe. Our protests were always colourful and carried out with a smile: we wanted people to join us, rather than turn away because they'd rather not know.

It was a huge effort, and right up until the last few days before crunch EU negotiations, we were staring at defeat. The southern member states simply would not budge. Then a young Italian called Adolfo Sansolini went on hunger strike against battery cages. It's not a tactic I'd advocate but it proved a turning point. Sansolini had contacts in the Italian government. Within days their position had changed; they supported the ban. It prompted a domino effect, resulting in one of the most significant victories in the history of animal welfare: barren battery cages were to be banned.

It takes a gargantuan effort to get production systems outlawed, especially when they dominate an entire industry providing a staple product. Yet we did it, by waving banners, writing letters, buying better eggs and articulating what was by then widespread public concern. I will never forget the overwhelming sense of elation when we heard the news. I had travelled to Luxembourg for the announcement, not knowing which way it would go. I remember standing on the steps of the European Council building, waiting for the UK minister to emerge and explain what had been agreed. It was a hugely proud moment for everyone who had worked so hard to make it happen.

The new law was far from perfect. For a start, there was a painfully long 'phase-in' period: twelve years for the industry to adapt. Furthermore, a clause allowed so-called 'enriched' cages: marginally bigger cages with perches and some pretty pathetic provisions for nesting and scratching in dust.

In summer 2011, my team was granted access to the facilities of the UK's largest egg supplier, Noble Foods, a company that introduced the new enriched cages well before the 2012 deadline. Getting permission was quite a process, involving extensive form filling and security checks. Having thoroughly checked our credentials and established that we were not animal rights protesters, the company eventually offered us a tour of their Nottinghamshire plant.

The Compassion team drove through lovely countryside – rolling fields of ripening wheat and shady lanes along which trundled lorries laden with fresh produce. The egg farm was a series of giant sheds clad in corrugated iron. Inside were a million hens. Throughout their short seventy-two-week lifespan (chickens can live eight to ten years), they would never see daylight. They lived in cages around 5 metres long, known in the business as 'colonies'. Suspended lights brightened and dimmed at particular times to create the impression of night and day, all geared toward regulating the egg-laying process.

Each colony cage contained four laying areas, with flaps to keep the hens' heads in the dark and a central scratching area for the birds to keep their claws short. Though the cages were less than half a metre high, the birds also had small perches. Their beaks had been severed by a laser to prevent them pecking each other, an almost universal feature of cage farms. The process appeared to have been carried out fairly clumsily: some beaks were of unequal length, and others cut diagonally. All perfectly legal – which raised the question of how far we've really come.

Nonetheless the ban on battery cages marked a sea change in attitudes, both public and corporate. Several of the world's biggest companies, including McDonald's in Europe, Sainsbury's, and well-known Unilever brands like Hellmann's mayonnaise in the EU, now sell or use only cage-free eggs. Yet while Europe has moved on, around 60 per cent of the world's egg-laying hens remain in barren cages. In the last decade I've travelled all over the world with my job and witnessed the unpalatable truth about how most eggs, meat and milk are produced.

A trip to Taiwan, which has 30 million laying hens, sticks in my mind. My fixer and companion was a Buddhist monk. He wore flowing white robes and had the classic shaved head. We would drive around together without a map, trying to find farms. Every now and then our local driver would stop to allow the monk to wind down the window and shout at a passer-by. The passer-by would shout back with equal fervour. We would drive on. This went on for a fortnight, as we made our way round the island, looking into how food is produced on this much-disputed territory. There were two key types of egg farm, one known as 'traditional' and the other known as 'controlled environment'. Sadly, on both types, the hens were caged. On the 'traditional' farm, row upon row of cages, covered by a tin roof, were otherwise open to the air. The wire cages were barely bigger than the hens crammed inside and were completely featureless. The hens had nothing, except access to a food trough and water, the very basics of life. Conditions on 'controlled environment' farms were little different, except that the barns were entirely enclosed, with temperature and ventilation controlled by computers and fans.

The spin about these sealed units, which exist all over the world, is that they are somehow safer and healthier because the birds are not exposed to agents of sickness and disease outside. The lie that this improves disease control was exposed in Britain years later when an intensive Bernard Matthews turkey plant was hit with highly pathogenic avian influenza.[2] It showed that merely to be 'closed' to the outside world and run by computer does not make a shed immune from the obvious laws of nature.

One traditional farm we visited in Taiwan was slightly different to the rest, in that it was open to the air. The birds were still crammed into the most appalling tiny cages, but at least they got natural light and felt a cooling breeze in what was often intense heat. I remember watching as a woman in blue slacks, pink blouse and a wide-brimmed wicker hat pushed a rusting cart along the rows of cages, collecting the eggs.

I soon found that eggs weren't the only thing being collected. Two perforated plastic bins stood by the cages, overflowing with chicken corpses. Beside them was a sealed plastic bag. It appeared to contain more bodies. Suddenly, something caught my eye: the white rubbish bag moved. Horrified, I tore it open, and a chicken's head popped out. She was panting for dear life. After a while the bird got to her feet. Then she gingerly clambered out of the hole in the bag and crept away. This, I learned, was how dying birds or those that didn't produce enough eggs in Taiwan were all too often killed: they were simply put in a bag and suffocated, then emptied into the bin.

I visited several farms in Taiwan's Miao Li province, and almost all the birds I saw were caged. Some were crammed as badly as I'd seen anywhere in the world, with a hand-span of space. It was a depressing experience. I also visited what was in 2002 Taiwan's only 'organic' egg farm. It wasn't what I expected. In Europe, organic production is tightly regulated. Hens must have outdoor access and be kept in fairly natural conditions. In Taiwan, far from seeing a few hens happily scratching around small huts in the middle of a field, I found myself looking at 300,000 birds, in cages stacked seven high, in four industrial buildings. The word 'organic' simply related to the feed they were given; and I doubt even that would have withstood scrutiny.

There was a further shock in store. On most intensive farms in Britain and Europe, laying hens are slaughtered after a year. Their commercial lifespan is largely determined by the fact that they renew their feathers every year, during which period they stop laying eggs for a few weeks. In Taiwan, I discovered that the hens were typically kept for two years. To minimise the drop in egg production linked to the feather-renewal period, they were 'force-moulted': shocked into shedding their feathers quickly. This involved starving them for ten days, a treatment that appeared – rather surprisingly – to accelerate the moulting and refeathering process, and get them laying again as fast as possible. A year in a barren cage, then ten days without food, then another year before slaughter? I couldn't help feeling that the lucky ones were those released early through death and piled into those perforated black bins. Thankfully, 'forced moulting' is now banned in Europe, although it is still allowed in the United States.

My time in Taiwan is peppered with bitter-sweet memories. Though much of my visit was shocking and depressing, there was also a hint of change in the air. Interest was growing in healthier food from animals not routinely treated with antibiotics or fed growth-promoting drugs. When I delivered a lecture at a livestock research centre in Heng Chung, I was encouraged to find that both the goat and cattle farmers in the audience were keen to switch from rearing their livestock indoors to pasture-based systems.

Yet there is still a mountain to climb. A decade or so after my trip to Taiwan, I found myself in the middle of a cluster of battery chicken farms in Argentina. We were in South America to look at soya production and cattle. It was a sunny autumn day in Marcos Paz, about 50 kilometres outside Buenos Aires and a pleasant enough area. We drove past a centre for veterans of the Falklands war, still a highly sensitive issue in Argentina, particularly at the time of our visit, the thirtieth anniversary of the invasion. There was a children's playground with swings, a slide and a basketball hoop; a miniature football pitch; a brown horse in a paddock. We rumbled down a very bumpy lane where there was a sprawling bakery. It looked like any factory; you would not have known its business from the outside. Apparently it was where many of the eggs from the nearby battery operations ended up.

Soon we were among the farms. Set a little back from the road, there were seven or eight, looking much the same. We were told that once upon a time this had been an isolated area, but the town had grown, and the farms were now very near houses. Exasperated by the flies and smell, apparently locals had been trying to get them shut down for years. I got out of the car to explore. Though it was surrounded by a high fence, the gate to one of the farms was wide open. I walked in.

I noticed that there was a cottage right next to the barns. The family living there had strung up their washing between two trees on either side of the battery sheds. The air was thick with ammonia and dust – foul to breathe. Three small children and a dog peeped out of a window, eyeing me curiously. I hated to think what state their health must be in, living in such a place.

A worker, perhaps their father, approached. He wanted me off the property so I turned and left, he locked the gate behind me, and we went to try somewhere else. A number of the farms were deserted, the cages empty but for sad clumps of feathers caught in the wire. I walked into one open-sided barn, some 300 yards long, with empty cages stacked high from one end to another. Rusting ventilation fans were shrouded in thick cobwebs. A forlorn-looking pair of worn-out trainers lay abandoned on a cage. The place was silent. It looked as if the hens had been cleared out fairly recently. Suddenly there was a shout. A chap in shorts and a baseball cap wanted me out. He picked up a large stone in case I didn't get the message. I didn't hang around.

I moved on to another farm. This time I was able to get very close to the birds. A teenager was pushing a galvanised metal trolley up and down between the rows of cages under a corrugated-iron roof. Each cage contained about seven birds, with barely enough room to stand. The boy was dispensing feed. The speed of the trolley flustered the hens into panicked squawks and attempts to flap. It was clear that in summer the heat would be unbearable. The hens had big blood-red 'combs' – crowns – making them look like cockerels. This is a way to deal with overheating. Some combs were so big they flopped down over one eye. The feathers on the hens' necks and backs were sparse. Bald patches were rife and their tails were like fistfuls of quills.

Their beaks were stumps, cut short in an attempt to stop them pulling each other's feathers out in frustration. A decaying corpse was trampled into the wire floor of one cage, rotting and grey. The survivors stood on it. They had no choice. Flies swarmed. Ash-grey droppings built up below. The birds cried with woe. I hated it. I focused on the eggs rolling off the back of the cages. Some people claim hens wouldn't lay 'if they weren't happy'. If ever there was proof of what nonsense that is, it was here. It's hard to see how anyone could witness birds in these conditions and still believe such a thing.

As I stood there among the cages, the stench catching in my throat, listening to the dismal squawking, I thought about the clean sanitised eggs, sold in nice little boxes, on supermarket shelves under 'fresh eggs'-type labels. They are so far removed from their filthy origins. From thousands of miles away, my wife was sending me cheerful text messages about what she was up to, in particular about how Hetty, Henna, Honey and Hope were doing. Compared with what I was seeing, the occasional threat of a fox seemed like nothing.

II
NATURE

Nestled among hedges and mature trees, the little village of Nocton in Lincolnshire seems an unlikely setting for a battle for the countryside. Life for the six hundred or so inhabitants revolves around a small post office, village hall and a primary school. There isn't even a pub, as an old by-law forbids such revelry. Those wanting a quiet pint must head down the country lanes to the nearest hostelry a kilometre or so away. Not so long ago, Douglas Hogg, Britain's former government agriculture minister, opened a guided trail of Nocton's historic features dating back to Roman times. Henry VIII apparently visited in the sixteenth century, planting a chestnut tree that still stands today.[1]

In 2009 this quiet hamlet was thrust into the media spotlight when it was chosen as the site for an 8,000-cow mega-dairy, planned to be the first of its kind in Britain and modelled on large-scale dairies in the USA. Angry locals were joined by MPs, environmentalists and a wide spectrum of campaigners worried about the impact of so many cows together, and all their dung, in such a small space. On local radio, the man behind the proposal suggested that: 'Cows do not belong in fields.'[2] His words came back to haunt him. Children from the local school drew pictures in protest; local buses carried advertisements insisting that cows belong in fields; questions were raised in the House of Commons. So loud was the public outcry that the plans were scrapped, the death-blow delivered by the Environment Agency and serious concerns about pollution. It was the first skirmish in what threatens to be a lengthy war.

The countryside is shaped and tended by the people who work the land. Three-quarters of the UK's land is farmed, providing a rich and varied landscape. The past sixty years have transformed it. Successive governments have presided over the uptake of industrial farming techniques often developed in the US. Now there are signs of damage. Sights once common are growing rare – the stunning aerobatics of huge starling flocks, the flutter of butterflies like the Brown Hairstreak, the buzz of previously abundant bumble bees.[3] Wild-flower meadows have vanished and areas of outstanding natural beauty are at risk as never before. Hedgerows that once criss-crossed the entire country have been disappearing along with woodlands. Large parts of the countryside are being built upon. Farms are getting fewer and bigger; farmers are struggling to survive.

The proposed Nocton mega-dairy may have been defeated, but the impetus behind it grinds on. Dairy cows are not the only farm animal affected in a new wave of industrialisation, this time conducted under the seductive language of 'sustainable intensification' and dubious justifications of feeding the world. It threatens to take the countryside, its wildlife and many of those who live in rural areas to breaking point.

3

Silent Spring

The birth of farming's chemical age

For more than three decades, I harboured a nagging sense of inadequacy, a puzzling feeling that I just couldn't see things in quite the same way as others. I remember how it started. It was the late 1970s when, as a young teenager, I read a book that would fire my imagination for the rest of my life. It led to years of gazing out of windows, a habit that got me into trouble with a string of teachers. It was a Sixties wildlife classic called *The Peregrine*, by J. A. Baker. I was enthralled, inspired, filled with a sense of nervous wonder. As I read his vivid and meticulous descriptions of the falcons he watched near his home in Essex, I dreamed of seeing them too. With eyes filled with awe, I scrutinised every kestrel I saw, just in case.

It would be some years before I saw my first peregrine falcon. Majestic, enthralling, and when they close their wings in a stoop, said to be the fastest animal on the planet, hurtling at speeds of 200 kilometres per hour. Since then I've seen many all over the world, as well as on my very doorstep at home in the South Downs of England. But that sense of inadequacy never quite went away. You see, after countless encounters, I've just not been able to see them so vividly, so close or for so long as Baker did. What was the matter with me? Was I doing something wrong? For thirty-five years that question remained unanswered; until now.

I was on my annual winter trip to North Wales with my wife, Helen. We love to call in at the wonderful nature reserve at Conwy. Situated on the banks of the estuary, with magnificent views of Snowdonia and Conwy castle, it is a spectacular place to while away an afternoon. The weather was foul, which meant more time in the shop and café surrounded by wildlife paraphernalia. Out of the bookshelves a title leapt out at me: *Silent Spring Revisited*, by Conor Mark Jameson. It explored the legacy of Rachel Carson, who first raised the alarm over the perils of pesticides sweeping across Britain and America and the demise of songbirds.

What happened next came as a bolt from the blue. Standing, book in hand, I started to read: 'In a book about the dawn chorus, about songbirds and birdsong, the Peregrine Falcon might not be the obvious place to start, but bear with me.' I had to agree, and was intrigued. Turns out both the writer and I had a love affair with *that* bird and *that* book by J. A. Baker. Both bird and Baker were described as having achieved 'almost mythic, prophet status'. Memories came flooding back of how much better, faster, closer the peregrines looked through the lens of Baker's eloquent prose. But then a twist: what I hadn't quite appreciated was that others were quietly questioning what Baker *really* saw. Through forensic analysis, the author suggested that Baker might not have been looking at wild peregrines, but instead at escaped falconers' birds, hence why they were so tame. Indeed, in some cases, they might not even have been peregrines at all, but some closely related escapee!

Okay, it's only a theory, but in that moment, decades of inadequate feelings, of wondering why I couldn't quite see what he saw, were lifted from me. The relief was so real that I ran round the shop telling anyone that would listen! You see, way back in the 1960s, when Baker was writing in southern Britain, peregrines had pretty much been wiped out. Agrochemical pesticides were poisoning wildlife, including those at the top of the food chain like birds of prey. People still remember how chemicals persisted in the food chain, accumulating in predators like falcons, causing nests to fail. What is less well remembered is how the countryside was littered with dead or dying birds. Foxes were affected by a mysterious illness where they lost their fear of people.[1] Those were extraordinary times in the countryside on both sides of the Atlantic; a time of dramatic demise.

When Rachel Carson published *Silent Spring* in 1962, it carried an introduction by Lord Shackleton, a member of the UK House of Lords, who declared: 'we in Britain have not yet been exposed to the same intensity of attack as in America, but here too there is a grim side to the story.' Things were bad in Britain, but worse in America. The US had given birth to techniques that treated the countryside like an industrial site, with unforeseen but devastating consequences. Half a century on, history is repeating itself; mega-farms are using the latest industrial practices pioneered in the US and now being exported to Britain and beyond.

I was in America and the car ride from our hotel was surprisingly short. Before I knew it, my cameraman, Brian, stopped the hire car and I was looking up at the childhood home of Rachel Carson. I had come to find out what inspired her to kick-start the environmental movement and how well we had heeded her warning. I stepped out into the chill air and reticent sunshine of the morning in suburban Springdale, Pennsylvania. A small black and white woodpecker clattered the branch above me. A simple white-boarded farmhouse stared imposingly toward the leafy street. It seemed isolated now that the once surrounding farm had gone. Instead, its natural appearance was bordered by the neatly manicured lawns of its neighbours. It was mid-April and the anniversary of Carson's untimely death less than two years after *Silent Spring*.

I walked up the raised driveway and banged on the back door. Peering in through the glass I could see Carson artefacts in an otherwise empty house. There was no answer, but then I was a bit early. The house was sheltered by mature trees: oak, maple, pine. A cluster of low wooden benches, set out theatre-style, where visitors would sit and learn. A sign welcomed the curious to the 'Wild Creatures Nature Trail', where

Carson began her lifelong fascination with the natural world. It was inscribed with her own words as a fourteen-year-old: 'The call of the trail on that dewy May morning was too strong to withstand . . . It was the sort of place that awes you by its majestic silence, interrupted only by the rustling breeze and the distant tumble of water.'

Back then, it clearly led to endless woods and fields. I followed the trail a short walk up the hill and peeked over the brow only to find an office and car park strewn with cars. I felt mildly disappointed, but then it has been over eighty years since the Carsons sold up.

Robert Pfaffman, a fifty-eight-year-old building architect, emerged welcoming and enthusiastic. He was on the board of the trust now running the Carson homestead as an official museum. He showed me round the five-room Pennsylvania German farmhouse which overlooks the Allegheny River valley. It came originally with sixty-five acres of orchard way back in 1900 when Carson's parents bought it, until bits of land got sold off to meet the expense of the children's education.

Pfaffman and I scaled the narrow staircase and entered a small bedroom complete with fireplace, low ceilings and pastel-pink walls. I felt a connection: the room was strangely similar to my own bedroom back home in my tiny eighteenth-century English cottage. This is where Rachel as a young kid would look out and daydream. I gazed out of her window to see the tree-covered beauty of the Allegheny valley, interrupted by two great chimney stacks dissolving smoke into the atmosphere. Coal-fired industry sits alongside agriculture in this community today, very much as it did during Carson's formative years. She was no stranger to the realities of life and landscapes. Perhaps this helped her to spot the blurring of lines between industry and agriculture that went on later in her lifetime. It was the insight I came for.

My plan was to drive from Pennsylvania and Rachel's former home and head across to historic Chesapeake Bay. I wanted to see whether the countryside would offer clues to Carson's legacy. Along the way, I called in to meet my fellow Brit Bill Sladen, ninety-two years old, a former professor at Johns Hopkins University in

Baltimore, where Carson studied zoology. He greeted me playfully with an impeccable old English accent: 'We've not met before have we? Why are you so bald?!'

Sladen is one of a distinguished band of 'bipolars': intrepid individuals who have travelled on icy journeys to both north and south poles. After training in the Second World War at London's Middlesex Hospital, Bill travelled to the Antarctic with the Falkland Islands Dependency Survey and United States Antarctic Research Program. It was during one of these expeditions that Bill discovered the first evidence of chemical pollution having gone global. During studies of Antarctica's Adélie penguin in 1959, the samples of six penguins and a crab-eating seal that he sent back for analysis in the US were found to have minute traces of DDT contamination, revealing that chemical pesticide pollution had reached all the way to the Antarctic.[2]

Sitting back, relaxed and reflective in a traditional leather chair, he told me of another of his ground-breaking projects: training goslings to learn historic migration routes by following a microlight plane. His long-standing dream was to re-establish the historic migration routes of the trumpeter swan to the nearby Chesapeake Bay, a vast estuary 320 kilometres long. But it was geese that grabbed the limelight, starring in a film, *Fly Away Home*, that documented the exploits of Sladen, his Canadian pal, Lichman and their microlight.[3]

I watched jauntily coloured American goldfinches and a wren behind him on the tasteful decking patio as he told me: 'Rachel was the pioneer of modern conservation. Her legacy is in having started a movement of concern for the environment.' But has it helped save Chesapeake Bay? I asked. He told me that the bay has declined, not just because of pesticide pollution, but perhaps even more because of manure run-off from the chicken industry. That was the clue I needed for the next part of my journey.

A farm tractor clanks along with what looks like thick red smoke belching from the back of a long green trailer and billowing across the adjacent road. Reddish-brown lumps spray out onto the field behind.

This is poultry manure being blown mechanically into the air and spread across the soil. 'The stuff along the ditches and field edges, if it rains, could run off and end up in Chesapeake Bay,' warns the local waterkeeper Kathy Phillips. 'The pungent smell of chicken manure being spread is a familiar part of spring here.'

Kathy has taken me on a 'muck safari' across Maryland. She moved here with her husband in the 1970s to live the beach life. After running for County Commissioner on a clean-water ticket, Kathy became local waterkeeper, charged with enforcing federal law protecting the coast of Assateague. 'CAFOs are everywhere in this area,' she told me, using her favoured acronym for Concentrated Animal Feeding Operations, better known as factory farms. 'They only grow corn and soya in these parts to support the area's poultry industry.'

Poultry manure is used as cheap fertiliser to spread on the fields growing the corn and soya that will end up as chicken feed. At first glance, it's a virtuous circle: the chickens eat the corn and their droppings replenish tired soils. The only flaw is the vast number of chickens in such a small area. Chicken manure is heavy in nitrogen and phosphorus, precious nutrients in the right amounts, but too much or at the wrong time and the rain washes it into waterways where it becomes a serious pollutant.

Kathy drives across a patchwork of woodlands and crop fields, tall pines and pasture, and pretty homes of pastel blue and white, painted using the 'coastal palette'. 'Smell that?' she asks, waving her arms. 'They're spreading manure out there.' This area used to be big on producing timber, orchard fruit and vegetables like tomatoes and cucumber. Now the dominant 'crop' is chickens. They try to portray massive industrial agriculture as family farms, she tells me, but it just won't wash. 'Family farms own and make all the decisions about the farm, that doesn't happen on these factory units.'

We cross the Pocomoke River, then drive past a great pile of manure, big and brown. It's not long before we pass another muck heap, then another. Some of the piles are so big that they look like small mountains. 'These fields have had manure newly spread on them; you can see clumps of it.' The smell filled the car. Then we found a 'muck shelter': sheds purpose-built to protect the manure from the elements before spreading. Kathy pointed out how local communities are often 'buffered' by lines of trees and shrubs to protect them from the emissions of dust and ammonia blown from the factory farms with their huge extractor fans.

I asked Kathy if she buys cheap chicken. 'No, I don't. Buying chicken in the supermarket is cheap food all right, but what people don't see is the hidden cost. It's their taxpayers' money that's being used to put up manure sheds, vegetative buffers around poultry houses to catch the dust and ammonia emissions. State money also goes into moving the manure out of the watershed.' We stop alongside the farm of a former secretary of agriculture. We can see a large 'muck shelter' with farm equipment standing inside; great piles of chicken manure stand outside. 'It's a great example,' Kathy says, 'of how Maryland's nutrient management programme isn't working, and it's in the Chesapeake watershed.'

We spent a morning seeing chicken sheds aplenty and mountains of manure, but not a single bird until we drove up behind a slow-moving articulated lorry stacked high with cages. Each one was crammed with hapless chickens on their way to the processing plant. Feathers flew from the battered and rusting crates. A couple of chickens managed to squeeze their heads through the bars, beaks open, eyes straining in distress.

Soon we were at Ocean City airport and keen to see the countryside from the air. The piping chatter of oystercatchers – noisy birds, all black and white with long carrot-like beaks – told me we were close to the beach. The quiet little airfield advertised scenic rides. A friendly-looking fellow in Hawaiian shirt and sun-strip cap sat inside the aerodrome talking into his Bluetooth headpiece while tapping into a computer. He spotted us and wrapped up his conversation. Neil Kaye, a medical doctor and helicopter pilot, had offered to take us up in the air as part of an initiative known as Lighthawk, specialising in helping environmental causes for free.

Soon we were strapping ourselves into Kaye's four-seater chopper. The rotors fired up, shaking the plane as they whirred faster and faster. I felt a little nervous. The chopper floated, swung round, tilted forward and my head went with it. We rose 150 metres, the same height as a passing bald eagle. It was like sitting in a tiny version of a London Eye capsule wobbling frantically side to side. We juddered along, following the river over expanses of woodland. We weren't up long before the forest gave way to fields. Then our first 'CAFO'. 'Twenty thousand birds per house in those,' Neil announces into my headset. We swoop over eight long, low-slung warehouse-like buildings, each accompanied by a huge feed silo. More sheds are scattered in other fields, perhaps run by different farmers. We see another two, then four more, then they are everywhere. Chickens are big business here.

The chopper tilts and we circle. 'This one disturbs me,' says Kathy over the headphones. 'Nine massive poultry houses, and directly to its right is a particularly sensitive tributary.' Any overflow from the meagre storm-water arrangements go straight into the creek. Kathy explained how it used to be a small farm, just crops. A CAFO like this takes as much ground as a small shopping centre. The difference is that a proposal for a shopping mall goes through a lot of planning processes. CAFOs, on the other hand, are treated a lot more lightly: 'Often the first you know about it is when it's being built.'

We fly on. I can see a mass of grey in the distance, like a lake surrounded by forest. As we get closer, I couldn't be more wrong. 'It's a big operation,' warns our pilot. Thirty huge factory-like sheds, each one covering perhaps 2,000 square metres, arranged in rows with massive extractor fans to keep alive the chickens crammed inside. Fast-growing trees shroud the site from the ground. The storm water from this CAFO, I'm told, runs into the Manokin River and then on to Chesapeake Bay.

It feels spooky to look down on what could be three-quarters of a million chickens and not see a single bird. I run the numbers and speculate: this site alone could produce upwards of 5 million birds a year. This is how 'premium fresh young chicken' is produced.

*

Chesapeake Bay is the largest estuary in the United States and has a rich history of battles. It is here that the British Royal Navy was defeated by the French in 1781 during the American War of Independence. A century of violent disputes over shellfish raged in the bay until the 1950s during the so-called Oyster Wars.

Today, the bay's vast watershed, which touches six states, is home to 17 million people as well as more than 3,000 species of plants and animals. Its skies are patrolled by the mighty bald eagle, while the beaches and mudflats swarm with some of the largest populations of shorebirds in the Western hemisphere.[4] However, the bay's latest and biggest battle is now against birds of another kind: chickens, and the muck they produce.

The sun is blazing on Shady Side, where I'm due to meet with people at the forefront of the battle to save Chesapeake Bay. A spectacular fish-eating osprey quarters the sky. Brown turns to white as the bird banks and hovers briefly before folding its wings to dive. A powerful plunge, a momentary pause, then broad, fingered wings lift bird and fish from the surface and away with a shake.

Betsy Nicholas, the executive director of Chesapeake Waterkeepers, waits by the jetty. We take a boat ride across the bay. A group of ruddy ducks with their comical plastic-blue bills bob ahead of us. A cobalt-blue belted kingfisher darts along the bank. A young bald eagle fixes us from afar with beady eyes. Chesapeake is well known for its oysters, but they're in trouble: less than 1 per cent of former numbers, thanks to overharvesting and pollution. 'The three biggest problems with pollution in this area are agriculture, agriculture, agriculture,' Betsy tells me. 'There are huge problems here with algal blooms, times when there are complete dead spots in the bay.' Folks are reluctant to address the pollution issue because they don't want to be seen to attack family farmers. 'But factory farms are a different matter. It's really become an industrial pollution source and really needs to be addressed as such.'

Betsy's main worry was the lack of accountability, the veil of secrecy that seems to be drawn around anything to do with agriculture. 'Until we can get through that, we can't address the problems, or separate the good from the bad actors.' Water-management targets have been agreed to try to reduce pollution from nitrogen and phosphorus run-off, but: 'I don't think we've done enough; no one wants to be the one responsible for making the changes.' The different interests and different states along the watershed would rather blame each other than take action.

In Baltimore I met Bob Martin, senior policy adviser at Johns Hopkins University. He echoes concerns about the extraordinary growth of the region's poultry industry and its effect on Chesapeake Bay: 'There are now nearly as many chickens being produced in the States surrounding the bay as there were across the entire country sixty years ago.' The vast majority of these are factory-farmed. Bob goes into greater detail about the effects on the local wildlife: 'The pollution from the chicken factory farms is causing a reduction in natural seabed grasses, making it harder for the oysters to grow. Local crabs are growing bigger and eating the oysters. Periodic fish kills involve thousands of dead and stricken creatures through nitrogen-induced oxygen starvation. Things are out of balance.'

Bob sees industrial agriculture as the biggest threat to environmental damage and public health in this area. 'I enjoy eating meat,' he confesses, 'but there needs to be some common sense in what we do.'

Farmland covers a quarter of the Chesapeake Bay watershed and is the largest single source of pollution, much of it relating to poultry manure.[5] The Bay lies on the eastern edge of the United States 'Broiler Belt' where many of America's chickens are reared. For want of a safe place to put it, excessive amounts of chicken waste are spread on the surrounding farmland, from there to wash into the Bay. Environmental authorities are slowly waking up to the crisis, and Chesapeake Bay has been placed on an unprecedented 'pollution diet'. Several states together with the Environmental Protection Agency (EPA) are working hard to reduce the nutrient flow into the water. However, despite best efforts, targets for reducing pollution have yet to be met. In environmental terms, more than half of the streams in the Chesapeake watershed are described as 'poor' or 'very poor', stripped of the snails, insects and other waterborne wildlife essential for a healthy aquatic environment.[6] Although agriculture isn't solely to blame, farming, and poultry litter disposal in particular, is the main culprit.[7] Nor will the problem go away in a hurry: the backlog of nutrients already built up will likely pollute the bay for years to come.

In *Silent Spring*, Rachel Carson focused on the overuse of chemical pesticides in the mid-twentieth century. I met with Ruth Berlin, executive director of the Maryland Pesticide Network, who told me that despite fifty years of reform, pesticide pollution is still a threat and found widely in Chesapeake Bay. The problem is far from unique to this area. Ruth told me how a cocktail of chemicals has been found in drinking water and fish samples. She sees agriculture as by far the biggest user of pesticides, affecting wildlife and implicated in serious public-health issues. Her verdict: pesticide overuse is probably 'a bigger problem now than fifty years ago'.

During my travels from her childhood home to the banks of Chesapeake Bay, I found people talking about the tremendous legacy of Rachel Carson in raising awareness. At the same time, there was a great deal of concern that the central message in *Silent Spring*, the threat from treating the countryside like just another industrial process, had been ignored. Yes, there have been some reforms – the banning of the infamous organochlorine insecticide DDT for farm use worldwide is a key achievement. The skies around my homeland are once again filled with buzzards, sparrowhawks and the like. Sometimes I also see the powerful pointed wings and black 'moustache' of the peregrine, thankfully restored to the skies over much of Britain and elsewhere. However, industrial agriculture is still linked to devastating effects, and Chesapeake Bay is far from unique. Wild bird populations are seen by the British government as an indicator of our quality of life, a yardstick for the health of the countryside. The sad fact is that half a century on from Carson's epic book, once common farmland birds still suffer heavy declines on both sides of the Atlantic.

4

Wildlife

The great disappearing act

NO FLY ZONE

It was the mid-1970s and the age of punk rock. I was eleven years old. When not hanging out with friends listening to the Sex Pistols, I was discovering birds. I liked the raw energy and anti-establishment lyrics of the bands at the time, but I was also drawn to the quiet of the countryside. It started when we went on a family holiday to a cottage in rural Norfolk, England. My grandad gave me a copy of the *Observer's Book of Birds*, and I remember thumbing through it trying to match the birds I could see out of the window to the pictures in the book. I was delighted when I figured out that the twittering dots in the sky were skylarks, and excited when two exquisite partridges came and sat on our window ledge and peered in at us.

It was the start of a lifelong passion. Back from holiday I joined the RSPB's Young Ornithologists Club, went to their local meetings and became an avid follower of nature programmes on TV. After school and at weekends, I would disappear into nearby woods and roam across farmland, inspecting the hedgerows and scanning the trees and skies for species I hadn't seen before.

One weekend, the Young Ornithologists Club organised a day trip to Tring Reservoirs in Hertfordshire. They were built in the early nineteenth century against the backdrop of the Chiltern Hills and act as a magnet for birds. Grebes dived, ducks bobbed and herons loafed in the reedbed. That's when I got really hooked. I spent pretty much every spare teenage moment cycling through the English Home Counties countryside, usually ending up beside the reservoirs. The bike ride would take me past farms and hedges full of yellowhammers and other birds. I used to love the sound of the corn buntings as they sat on telephone wires. I remember thinking they sounded like jangling keys.

Little did I know that just as my interest in birds was awakening, the objects of my fascination were disappearing almost before my eyes. Ten million breeding individuals of ten species of farmland birds disappeared from the British countryside between 1979 and the end of the twentieth century. And the problem was not confined to Britain. According to a group of scientists led by Oxford University, 116 species – a fifth of all the bird types in Europe – were at risk. Warning of a 'second Silent Spring', they described as 'damning' the evidence that agricultural intensification was the culprit.[1]

Nor was it only birds that disappeared – farm animals followed. The two are linked. About half a century ago, pigs, poultry and to some extent cows began vanishing from fields to be reared indoors on factory farms. Mixed farms, where crops and animals were rotated around hedge-lined fields – working with nature – began to be a thing of the past. Hedges disappeared – 100,000 kilometres of them between 1980 and 1994 – and farmers began concentrating on just one type of crop, using more and more chemicals to fertilise tired soil and wipe out pests. The industrial revolution had hit the countryside and it wasn't pleasant.

I remember the late Chris Mead of the British Trust for Ornithology speaking at our local bird club. He'd just published a book, *State of the Nation's Birds*, and talked of heavy declines in birds familiar from literature and folklore – skylarks, turtle doves, peewits. I remember him saying that intensive farming had created a 'wildlife desert', a view that resonated with me. His book highlighted the devastating loss of seeds on arable land – just a tenth remains of what birds could choose from half a century ago. Chemical insecticides do likewise for insectivorous birds.

Fast-forward a decade and the figures are shocking. According to the British Trust for Ornithology, the last forty years or so have seen the population of tree sparrows crash by 97 per cent; grey partridges by 90 per cent; turtle doves by 89 per cent; corn buntings by 86 per cent; skylarks by 61 per cent; yellowhammers by 56 per cent; even common species like starlings and song thrushes have fallen by 85 and 48 per cent respectively.[2] In 2010 the UK government published its own bird census which revealed that the population of farmland birds overall had more than halved since 1966. Their research revealed a sharp decline between 1976 and the late 1980s,[3] a period when farming in the UK was going through massive change, from traditional mixed farms to intensive operations.

This bleak picture is replicated in Europe and America. The European farmland bird census, which covers thirty-three species, found that the overall population fell by 44 per cent between 1980 and 2005. The sharpest drops once again took place between the late 1970s and early 1980s, a period of rapid agricultural intensification.[4]

In America, the 2011 edition of a multi-agency report called *The State of the Birds*, concluded that a quarter of the 1,000 bird species in the US were 'threatened, endangered, or of conservation concern'. In the States, farmland birds are often described as 'grassland' birds. The study noted that more than 97 per cent of publicly owned wild grassland in America had been lost, 'mostly because of conversion to agriculture', as a result of which grassland birds have declined far more than any other group of birds.[5] In 2009 it warned that some of the US landscape's most iconic species, like short-eared owls, which hunt during the day as well as at night, and the beautiful yellow-breasted meadowlark, which has a very distinctive melancholy whistle, are in deep trouble. It noted that ranchlands are 'often overgrazed, causing desertification' and that when migrant birds fly to South America for the winter, they often find conditions even worse, because grassland there is being converted to agricultural production.[6]

I spend a lot of time trying to convince governments and the food industry that factory farming is unsustainable. All sorts of arguments are put up to defend the system. Sometimes I'm told it's better to farm some land intensively so that we can save other areas for wildlife. An interesting idea – but in practice we don't save much land for wildlife.

Others try to claim that the blame lies elsewhere, usually abroad. I remember talking to a group of farmers on a rural leadership course who tried to blame the shocking decline of Britain's tree sparrows – the dapper and much rarer rural cousin of the city house sparrow – on factors in the bird's migratory wintering grounds. Just one problem: tree sparrows don't migrate.

Yet even the biggest apologists for intensive farming struggle to deny the impact. The evidence is just too overwhelming. In both the UK and Europe, farmland birds have declined more than those found in other habitats like woodlands or wetlands.[7] Tellingly, scientists have managed to reverse the decline of four species, at least on a local scale, by experimental changes in farming. Grey partridges – plump game-birds with cheerful orange faces – did better when pesticides were reduced and more nesting cover provided. Cirl buntings, which are pretty little European birds related to the yellowhammer and already have a tough time with the climate here, seemed to like it when farm-ers left fields as stubble in winter rather than immediately re-sowing, and left bigger grass margins around crops. The secretive little corn-crake spends most of its time hiding in tall vegetation; it responded well to extra nesting cover and delayed harvesting of the grass it likes to forage in. Stone curlews, with their spindly yellow legs and big eyes, visitors to southern England in summer, seemed to appreciate mixed farmland, with spring crops planted next to grazed pasture.[8]

It's not all bad news: various initiatives by the EU and US federal government have helped slow the decline of some species. Under the EU Common Agricultural Policy, farm subsidies are no longer based simply on how much a farmer produces. There has been an enthusias-tic uptake of various environmental stewardship schemes. Fertiliser application levels have dropped from around 150 kilograms per hectare in 1987 to just under 100 kilograms per hectare in 2009;[9] an indication that soils and the creatures that depend on them are being better protected. For example, artificial fertilisers tend to create acid conditions, which can be fatal to earthworms[10] – and quite a few British birds eat worms. In 2011, a study found that there are between double and quadruple the number of worms on organic farms as on conventional arable farms, probably because of the use of organic manure, as opposed to artificial fertilisers, and the lack of pesticides.[11]

In America, the US Conservation Reserve Program is a lifeline for millions of birds, because it pays farmers to leave some land out of production. However it is under threat from the government's decision to promote biofuels, which is likely to entice farmers to use their set-aside to grow corn for cars.[12]

Farming and wildlife can, and often do, go hand in hand. I talked to Richard Owen, a lifelong farmer now in his sixties, who works at Bickley Hall Farm in Cheshire. It's a demonstration farm to show that food production and nature can coexist to everyone's benefit. He runs 350 hectares of permanent pasture and hay meadows grazed by cattle and sheep. The talk here is of 'relearning traditional wisdom'; of farming sympathetically with the land, using fewer chemicals and rotating animals around the farm to preserve soil health. 'Farmers are often blinkered by what they're doing and the amount of money they owe,' Owen told me. 'Once they try this system of farming without inputs, with different breeds of livestock, that brings communities and people back to the farm, they become enthusiastic.'

Some of the local farmers have started to adopt this model. It's just one example of farming in tune with the countryside. As we talked, we walked up a steep bank overlooking a reed-fringed mere with lapwings nesting in an adjacent field, serenaded by skylarks. We peered into bushes and saw a blur of brown wings: tree sparrows; rare in Britain nowadays, but doing well here.

People care about birds – the Royal Society for the Protection of Birds (RSPB) has over one million members. That declines have been less steep in recent decades is probably due to growing public awareness of the damage done by industrial farming. Popular TV programmes like *Springwatch*, where birds are the soap-stars, can only help.

Almost every day I'm out with my binoculars scouring the South Downs, where I live. I've led birding expeditions to countries including Costa Rica, USA, Turkey, Israel and the Seychelles. I still 'twitch' when a really rare bird gets found in Britain, I've seen over 470 species so far, and have often driven overnight and sometimes squeezed into six-seater planes to chase rare birds on far-flung places like Scilly in the southwest and Fair Isle in Shetland.

I try to do my bit; feeding in the garden, supporting charity work and buying organic food when I can. One bird touched me like no other. I was at home in Hampshire one day when I got a phone call from a stranger asking for help. It was the kind of call I was used to, having been a volunteer 'ambulance' driver in my spare time for a local wildlife hospital. We'd just had a heavy storm, and the caller said they'd come across an injured bird. They didn't know what type it was. They gave me an address, and I jumped in my car and set off. On arrival, I found a young man and woman and a beautiful, if somewhat dishevelled, kestrel – a small falcon that you sometimes see hovering over fields and motorway verges. The bird had no obvious bone break but had clearly done something bad. I popped it in the back of my car and deposited it at the local Brent Lodge wildlife hospital, where experts were on hand.

A few weeks later I received a call to say the kestrel was ready for collection. The idea was to take him back to the place where he'd been found. It didn't go well. Weeks of rehab hadn't sorted him out. My heart sank when I released him, and he dropped to the floor. I tried hard to get him to fly, to no avail. With a combination of hopping and flapping though, he could move pretty fast. And he did; across the field, down a lane, up a bank and down again, all with me in hot, panicky pursuit. He might have been covering ground, but he would stand no chance against predators, and would most likely have met his end in the jaws of a fox. Eventually I snaffled him, and returned him to his box, and then to the wildlife hospital.

Months went by before I got the call to come and pick up him up again. This time I was told straight out that if he didn't 'go' when I released him, they'd put him down. I took him back to the field near to where he was first picked up, and wished him luck, urging him on with all my heart. I held out my hand and we both looked to the sky. He opened his wings, reluctantly launched himself forwards and then just dipped towards the floor, with my heart plummeting after him. Suddenly, as if by some guiding hand, his wings found strength. He flew in level flight away from me before gaining height and more height till he was above the treetops and away. Soon he was just a speck in the distance. As he disappeared, I leapt and cheered. I cannot describe the feeling. Even now as I write this, I can feel the surge of joy at having helped bring freedom and a new chapter to the life of a creature as amazing as a kestrel.

In the introduction to this book, I described Mao Zedong's war on sparrows as part of the Great Leap Forward in the late 1950s. Mao's war on nature was lost and people starved.[13] Looking back, it sounds absurd. Yet the same war is being waged – albeit in a far less visible fashion – every day in every country where vast swathes of land are given over to single types of chemical-soaked crops. It is rare to see a tree sparrow in the UK today: owing to changes to the countryside and intensive use of chemical sprays and fertilisers, they have effectively been wiped out, with less fanfare than Mao's war, but for the sparrows and other farmland birds, the result is the same.

BUZZED OFF

For fire chief Kenny Strandberg, 10 July 2011 started like any other Sunday in Island Park City, Idaho. Weekends in his part of the world are usually peaceful affairs, especially in summer, when the meadows are full of yellow and blue wild flowers, the sun shines against an azure sky, and for a few glorious months there is no need to battle the snow. It is a time for cowboys to hang up their boots and relax on the porch, taking in the mountain air. On Henry Fork of the Snake River, fly fishermen try their luck for trout, while elk and antelope roam through the high mountain pastures. The silence of the pine and aspen forests is rarely broken except by the occasional holidaymaker hiking out from a log cabin or guest ranch.

At the last census, Island Park had a population of just 215. It bears no likeness to a town, never mind a city, but back in the 1940s the owners of the many lodges along US Route 20, the highway that cuts across the state, somehow persuaded the authorities to call it a city so that they could dodge draconian liquor laws banning sales of alcohol outside city limits. Island Park now boasts the most extended and sparsely populated main street in America – a full 53 kilometres long.

As always, Strandberg was on call. Forest fires and car crashes are the usual trouble in these parts, but the day passed uneventfully until 4.30 pm, when his pager went off. There had been an accident on Route 20, and the sheriff's office was being bombarded with 911 calls. Details were sketchy, but Strandberg learned that an articulated lorry had veered off the road and partially overturned as the driver fought to steer his wheels back onto the highway. Apparently the vehicle had shed a large part of its load. The fire chief dropped everything and headed for the scene, where he met an extraordinary sight. Hundreds of beehives were strewn across the tarmac, and a giant swarm of bees – 14 million strong – was buzzing angrily overhead.

I tracked Strandberg down and managed to talk to him over the phone about what happened next.

'It was just a black cloud of bees,' he told me. 'You didn't dare open your window. You didn't dare get out. You didn't dare do anything.' The fire chief pulled alongside the driver's cabin, to check he was okay. 'He was suiting up. I didn't get out either. We just waited a few minutes until he got out. He grabbed the hose.' Clad in protective clothing, the driver and fire crews first tried spraying the bees with water to calm them down. Frantic calls were made to bee experts, who suggested dousing the swarm with fire foam to kill them, so that workers could approach the truck and begin the clean-up operation.

Strandberg was worried about something else: grizzly bears. A. A. Milne, author of *Winnie the Pooh*, was not wrong to claim that bears love honey. They find bees tasty too. The highway was covered in honey, and with many bees still buzzing around, it would offer an irresistible lure. Bears on the highway would have been pretty danger-ous, so the crews worked all day to remove the stuff, receiving a number of stings for their pains. Strandberg admits that he and his team were ill prepared: 'We train for fires and extrication, but we have never trained for bees. We have learned a lot. Next time it happens, if it happens again – hopefully not – we will know what to do.'

Which is just as well, because he and his colleagues could easily find themselves fighting escaped bees again. At certain times of the year, three or four trucks carrying beehives rumble along Highway 20 every week. Their destination: California, where the bees are required for pollination services. During my time in California researching mega-dairies, I learned about an extraordinary conse-quence of intensive farming taken to extremes: industrialised pollination – a business that is rapidly expanding as the natural bee population collapses. In certain parts of the world, as a result of industrial farming, there are no longer enough bees to pollinate the crops. Farmers are forced to hire or rent them in.

Both wild bumble bees and domestic honey bees are under severe threat. In the UK, which has around twenty-four types of bumble bee, two species have gone extinct in the last seventy years. Six are consid-ered seriously endangered,[14] and half the rest are considered at risk.[15] The British Beekeepers' Association fears the UK could lose all of its bees within the next decade.[16] In the United States, several species that were common as recently as the 1990s have disappeared. It's the same story in other parts of the world.

The potential implications of the decline are mind-boggling. Most fruit and vegetable crops are dependent on pollination by bees. It means the future of around a third of global agricultural produce is at stake. Governments have been slow to wake up to the problem. In 2007 the US House of Representatives held an emergency hearing on the status of pollinators in North America and set aside $5 million for honey bee research, but the amount was later cut by half.[17]

Farmers can't afford to sit and wait, so they are taking their own desperate measures, hiring commercially reared bees by the truckload, at vast expense. It's desperate measures for desperate times. Wild bees, so essential for natural pollination, have been driven out by chemical-soaked monocultures, industrial farming methods that have robbed them of the varied habitats they need to survive. In their place is the business of bees for hire, at least for now.

Some clue as to the scale of this bizarre new industry lies in the fact that the accident in Idaho was not unique. Just a year earlier, in another American state, there was a similar crash near Minneapolis, Minnesota, involving a flatbed lorry carrying 17 million bees in 7,000 beehives. Hundreds of hives were jolted free.[18]

Arriving at the scene, Lakeville fire chief Scott Nelson opened his door and immediately got stung in the face – 'It was a black haze. Never seen anything like that.' The driver of the lorry told reporters that he felt a bang, looked in his wing mirror and 'saw boxes and beehives exploding'. Rescuers were forced to stay inside emergency vehicles until the swarm dispersed. Three hours later, they were still trying to clear bees from the area.

Many beekeepers now make more money from pollination services than from honey production. The load that fell off the lorry in Island Park, Idaho was worth an estimated quarter of a million dollars. Charges for bee services are soaring. Prices have tripled since 2004, with hiring a hive now costing as much as $180.[19] These runaway prices have been enough to push some farmers out of business.

Nowhere is the problem more pressing than in California, where the almond industry is so in need of bees that vast numbers of US honey-bee colonies are joined by bees flown in from as far afield as Australia.[20] Here, the industrial production of a single crop, or mono-culture, has been taken to new extremes.

Every year, in late winter or early spring, some 3,000 trucks drive across the United States carrying around 40 billion bees to California's Central Valley, which houses more than 60 million almond trees. The orchards cover around 240,000 hectares of land, stretching the best part of 600 kilometres and producing 80 per cent of the world's almond crop – the largest pollination event in history.[21] Buying in these services is costly: Californian growers now spend $250 million a year on bees.[22] It is yet another sign of how nature's support systems are breaking down in the wake of unsustainable farming techniques.

China has a different answer to the same problem. Every spring, the pear orchards in Sichuan province blossom, transforming the hills into a snowy white fairyland. Each flower carries the promise of a juicy fruit. For centuries, farmers had only to sit back and wait until bees and the summer sun worked their magic, delivering a bumper crop in autumn. Fast-forward to the twenty-first century however, and nature has stopped providing these services free. Instead, thousands of villagers troop up to the orchards and perform the task themselves, armed with simple pollination sticks made of chicken feathers and cigarette filters. They climb the trees and dip their sticks into plastic bottles of pollen, then dab the pollen onto each individual blossom.[23] With a huge population willing to toil long hours for little reward, this may be a reasonable solution. It's hard to see such a labour-intensive operation proving viable in the West, where labour costs are much higher.

While I was in California investigating mega-dairies for this book, I came across a commercial beekeeper who told me what it's like being in this business. The plight of the cows in the mega-dairies and that of the wild bees are linked; both have become victims of the industrialisation of the countryside.

Mike Mulligan, a third-generation Californian beekeeper, and probably the most cheerful person I've ever met, invited me and the team to his home. Isabel, my camera crew of two and I set off for our breakfast invitation. From the moment we arrived at his farmhouse Mike was virtually hopping with excitement about his English visitors. Every now and again he would exclaim 'hot *dog*' and slap me on the back, grinning from ear to ear as he zipped around his kitchen preparing a magnificent breakfast feast. There was pumpkin pie and a plate piled high with freshly fried cinnamon bread. The kitchen counter heaved with bowls of fruit, supersized jars of Nutella, peanut butter and maple syrup. There were plates of biscuits and English breakfast tea. He was a born-again Christian and his company was called Glory Bee.

His home – a luxurious detached property, tastefully decorated, with a glorious garden amid the sanitised almond orchards – suggested that business was good. Behind the property was an extensive backyard with various open-sided barns storing the paraphernalia of beekeeping. On a patch of scrubland, bordered on one side by almond fields and on the other by a field of commercial rose bushes, stood a couple of hives. At very short notice – our visit had been arranged over the phone less than twenty-four hours earlier – Mulligan had somehow arranged the hives especially for us to see: he explained that his own bees were currently 'overwintering' on the central coast of California where conditions were warmer. It was November and they were effectively on holiday, conserving energy for the busy season ahead. They would stay on the coast until late January or early February. By Valentine's Day, they would be home earning their keep. After providing pollination services for almond farmers, they would be moved on to the orange groves and from there to pollinate buckwheat and sage in the so-called 'chaparral', a heathland scrub in the Californian hills. They return to Central Valley in mid-July, to work on cotton and alfalfa, before their annual holiday by the sea.

It all sounded rather lovely, but Mulligan was blunt. 'There's nothing romantic about it,' he told me. 'It is a difficult business.' Though his father and grandfather were both beekeepers, he is the first in the family to hire out bees for pollination services: previously, the money was in honey. He owns 6,000 hives, each containing between 30,000 and 50,000 bees. In 2011 he rented them out for between $150 and $160 a hive. It might sound a lot, but the bees are fragile, vulnerable to parasites and chemicals, and he has had some close shaves, like the time he took them to another state.

That year, there had been a drought in Central Valley, and business wasn't great. He'd heard there was a better market in the Midwest. Mulligan and his bees travelled by lorry to North Dakota, the heart of

American's honey-producing industry, where he rented a house. From the start, it was a nightmare. He and his staff arrived in early spring, and were dismayed to discover that there was still snow on the ground, dangerous conditions.

They had not brought the right equipment to care for the bees in cold weather, in particular the pollen and nectar supplements they need. Mulligan was worried they would go hungry. Slowly the weather improved, and in May he began unloading the hives into the wild-flower meadows. One by one, his bees died.

> Before going, I'd been having all these fantasies about getting rich out of honey production. I got quite carried away. Then my bees started dying – thousands and thousands of them. We had no idea what was going on. I was embarrassed to admit to my family that we were having problems – I felt a fool. But it got to the point I couldn't keep it from my wife – I had to tell her what was going on. I was almost crying, begging her to pray for me. I could see our whole livelihood going.

It turned out that the bees had been feeding from a musky flower called Zigadenus, otherwise known as death camas. It proved deadly to a large number of his bees. In the end Mulligan didn't lose them all and the trip wasn't the financial disaster he'd feared. However, by the time he returned to Central Valley he was deeply shaken, and behind schedule with an important annual health treatment for the bees. The 'varroa' mite, a parasite around the size of a pinhead, is one of many threats to his livelihood. If it gets inside the hives and reproduces, it's deadly. He says he has little choice but to spray the hives with chemicals. 'I don't like doing it, but I can't afford the risk. When you see the accumulation of pesticides our bees are exposed to, it is a worry.'

In fact commercial bees suffer a near-continuous chemical assault, and Mulligan worries about the consequences. 'It is possible that we could build up lethal doses of chemicals in our hives, without even knowing it,' he believes. His bees are also at continual risk from pesticides, to which they are highly sensitive. He explains that citrus trees are sprayed just after they have bloomed, and that bees can be severely damaged by the toxic material. His contracts with farmers specify time lags between any spraying and the installation of hives among the trees. His bees are also registered with Kern County authorities, who hold a copy of their proposed itinerary. In turn, his clients and other farmers who hire bees submit their spraying schedules to officials, theoretically enabling beekeepers to avoid sending bees into recently treated crops. It is an inexact science: in certain weather, pesticide spray drifts to neighbouring fields, affecting bees working there.

On the morning of our visit, Mulligan received 100 queen bees through the post. They cost $16 a head and came all the way from Hawaii housed in tiny cardboard boxes with mesh screens at both ends. Apparently the queens are particularly vulnerable to chemicals. 'The queen is exposed for months and months,' he told us. 'We are noticing that they are under stress – their economic life is being shortened.'

There is still some debate over the cause of collapse of the bee population, but most experts attribute it to agricultural intensification, particularly the use of chemical pesticides.[24] Research suggests that what has been dubbed Colony Collapse Disorder (CCD) is linked to the use of a group of pesticides called neonicotinoids. These are water-soluble, nicotine-like chemicals which, when sprayed onto the ground, are absorbed by the entire plant, turning it into what has been described as a 'poison factory'.[25] Plants grow extremely toxic to insects and, of course, to bees.

In 2013, the EU voted to ban the use of neonicotinoids on crops attractive to bees. The UK voted against the measure, arguing that the science was inconclusive. Speaking after the vote, EU Health Commissioner Tonio Borg welcomed the ban: 'I pledge to do my utmost to ensure that our bees, which are so vital to our ecosystem and contribute over 22 billion euros [£18.5bn; $29bn] annually to European agriculture, are protected.'[26]

Dave Goulson, a professor of biological sciences at Stirling University and a world expert on bumble bees, also believes that intensification of farming has been critical to their decline:

> Bumble bees are major contributors to pollination of crops and wild flowers throughout the temperate northern hemisphere. Many species have declined, contributing to fears that we might face a pollination crisis . . . In Europe, the primary driver is thought to be habitat loss and other changes associated with intensive farming. In the Americas, declines of some species are likely to be due to impacts of non-native diseases.[27]

Artificial nitrogen fertilisers mean there is no need for the old-fashioned rotation of crops, most importantly clover, that bees used to forage on, and herbicides have eliminated most of the wild alternatives. Their nesting sites have gone too. Some species live in dense grass above ground; others prefer underground cavities – typically abandoned rodents' nests. The removal of hedgerows and unploughed field margins has put paid directly to the upstairs bees and indirectly to the downstairs ones by starving out the voles and mice that create their homes. Any that do find nesting places are likely to have them smashed by farm machinery or zonked by pesticides.

Bees have become just as much a victim of agricultural intensification as the pigs, chickens and cows crammed into factory farms. The industrial rearing of animals goes hand in hand with intensive crop production, often grown to feed incarcerated animals.

In the developing world, where small producers cannot afford to hire hives or pay for hand pollination, there are fears that reduced yields will cause malnutrition. The UN estimates that around 70 per cent of crops that together provide 90 per cent of food supplies depend on bee pollination.[28]

Dr Parthiba Basu, an ecologist at the University of Calcutta, has carried out a number of studies that show a link between falling bee populations and poorer crop yields. Basu became an international bee expert almost by accident, after stumbling on the connection during a different project. He was originally investigating whether it would be commercially viable for farmers in India to turn their backs on intensification, a policy that is being aggressively promoted by the Indian government. The answer was a resounding yes. His research involved eighteen farms in sixteen different regions of India, from the Himalayan foothills in the far north to the swampy southern tip of the subcontinent. The farmers who took part previously focused on just one or two types of crop or livestock production and typically used high quantities of pesticides and fertilisers. They were persuaded to experiment with mixed farming, rearing several different types of live-stock and several different crops in the same location. Although they did not go 100 per cent organic, they were gradually weaned off their dependence on chemical inputs. At the end of the year-long experi-ment, almost every farm involved had made more money, partly because diversification enabled them to be productive all year round rather than only during the fertile monsoon season.

The results were exciting enough in themselves, confirming Basu's suspicions that Western-style agricultural intensification, championed by the Indian government as the key to riches, does not translate well to India's unique and highly varied ecological conditions. However, there was another interesting finding: crops that were highly depend-ent on bees for pollination were not doing as well as expected.

I met Basu while he was briefly in London in autumn 2011 to attend an international bee conference in Sheffield. Deeply worried about the bee crisis and its implications for poorer people in India, he told me: 'It was particularly striking in Bengal, where they grow a lot of a vegetable known as painted gold. It's a highly pollinator-dependent crop. They have been hand-pollinating it for a while now, because there are just not enough bees left. The plants are not very high and grow in dense rows, so you see a lot of children doing the job. They can squeeze between the rows and don't have to bend down to reach the flowers.'

India produces about 7.5 million tonnes of vegetables a year – about 14 per cent of the world's total – and has undergone an agricultural

revolution since the 1960s. Half a century ago, the subcontinent was
heavily dependent on food imports. Now it produces more than
enough to feed its own population, though there are still distribu-
tional problems, and malnutrition remains rife. Buoyed by this success,
the government is trying to go further faster. Recently, Basu has begun
to look at bee problems in other developing countries and has found
a link between declining populations and deforestation: 'Forest cover
is essential for maintaining pollinator services. Bees need trees to
survive. If you mix the two factors – pesticide use and loss of forest
cover – you see a very strong link.'

He is in no doubt that agricultural intensification is to blame:

I had hoped that pollinator loss would not be nearly as serious in
developing countries as it is in the West, but that does not seem to
be the case. It is very sad. It is going to take a lot of effort to turn
this around, but unfortunately the developing world is going down
the opposite route right now, embracing Western-style intensification. That means more mono-cropping and chemical fertiliser and
pesticide use, and more loss of the wilderness habitats on which
bees depend.

Achim Steiner, director of the UN's Environment Programme, believes
that as a society, we are labouring under the illusion that in the twenty-
first century we have the technological prowess to be 'independent of
nature'. In a world of close to 7 billion people, as he has put it, bees
'underline the reality that we are more, not less dependent on nature's
services'.

THE ETERNAL SUN DANCERS

Catching butterflies sounds a cruel and old-fashioned hobby, but in
the United States these days it's quite the thing. In the nineteenth
century, the Victorians would snare the insects in delicate nets, then
kill them with a drop of opium on the head. The drug kept the

butterfly flexible long enough for the wings to be opened and set out neatly without breaking. The collector would then mount his specimen on a board with a pin through the thorax and display it proudly in a glass case.[29] These days, the aim is not to kill butterflies and turn them into works of art, but to attach a tiny tag to their wings, then set them free.

It's hard to imagine that a creature so fragile could survive being trapped and handled and still have the strength to fly away. Yet if they are treated gently, it can be done, and as thousands of proud American owners of butterfly nets will testify, it's not only worthwhile, but fun. This game is Monarch Watch, an extraordinary conservation programme involving enthusiasts of all ages in northern states in the US.[30] Every autumn, in gardens, schools, colleges and country parks, butterfly lovers head out with nets to try to catch and tag as many monarchs as possible. The aim is to track their unique annual migration, a phenomenon that is now under threat because of the industrialisation of farming.

The monarch is an emblematic species in America, the only type of butterfly that the average North American knows. More importantly, it is the star of one of nature's most spectacular shows – an international migration that takes it thousands of kilometres from the northern states of the US to Mexico and back again. En route, these delicate creatures with wings like orange and black stained-glass windows face incredible challenges. Fluttering along at around seven and a half miles an hour, they negotiate motorways and chimney stacks, railway lines and pylons, and power stations belching noxious smoke into their path. They navigate over rivers and mountain ranges, through towns and cities, weathering storms and downpours. Millions die en route, blown apart in the slipstream of aeroplanes, splatted on car windscreens, drowned in puddles and birdbaths, burnt in bonfires and trapped in webs. Against all the odds, millions of others make it, and the cycle continues.

Every year, tens of millions of the butterflies embark on this incredible journey, always starting on the same date: the autumn equinox, when night and day are the same duration.[31]

Every year, they end up in the same place, the high-altitude pine and fir forests of the Neovolcanic Plateau, some 390 kilometres from Mexico City. This is where they spend the winter months, surviving on little more than water. Not one who makes the journey across the continent has ever done it before; nor has a single one of those that return to America when spring comes ever previously travelled north. Each butterfly embarking on the migration in either direction is a member of a new generation. Yet they are guided by some kind of internal navigation system, and they all end up in the same place.

How they do it is one of the world's great natural mysteries that scientists have yet to grasp fully, and time may be running out to do so. Monarch butterflies are in decline and their migration is under threat. The population is currently the lowest on record. The finger points at pesticides.

Because monarchs all hibernate together in the same part of Mexico, scientists have been able to assess the strength of their population by measuring the area of forest covered by the colonies. According to the WWF (World Wildlife Fund) in Mexico, the current colony size is just 1.92 hectares, down from the previous low of 2.19 hectares in 2004 and far down from the recorded high of 21.6 hectares in 1995.[32] Though there is no danger of the monarch going extinct, experts fear the numbers are becoming so sparse that the migration will either disappear altogether or no longer bear any resemblance to the magnificent spectacle it is today.

At the heart of the problem is an unremarkable-looking plant called milkweed, with clusters of pale pink flowers. It used to be very common on arable farms. Monarchs love it, and won't lay eggs on anything else. Unfortunately, however, it is a weed, and farmers don't like it. The use of genetically modified crops, engineered to resist super-strength herbicides that destroy pretty much everything else, including milkweed, has all but wiped out the plant in many areas.

Dr Orley 'Chip' Taylor, an insect ecologist at the University of Kansas, is a director of Monarch Watch and a world-renowned expert on butterflies. I rang him to ask him what he believes is going on. He told me that the tagging programme run by Monarch Watch is now very large, but the number of butterflies volunteers can find to tag has dropped by almost a third in the last eight years. He is in no doubt that pesticides are to blame, describing the evidence as 'solid':

Monarchs are dependent on milkweed plants, and milkweed plants are weeds. They used to be controlled by tillage – farmers would mechanically till to get through the weeds, and milkweed would survive the process to a certain extent. There would be a small number of plants per acre that would survive in corn and soybean fields. I've got pictures of those types of situations and you can see clumps of milkweed here and there within the corn and soybeans. These turned out to be extremely productive areas for monarchs. But in 1996 they developed a herbicide-tolerant soybean, and then they came up with herbicide-tolerant corn . . . Eventually what they did was eliminate the milkweed. At the same time as herbicide-tolerant corn and soybeans have been adopted, we've seen the decline of milkweed and a very strong decline in monarch populations.

Monarchs are the only butterfly species to migrate like this. Nobody even knew about their amazing journey until the 1970s, when the full wonder of their behaviour was revealed by a biologist who devoted his life to figuring out where they went.

Fred Urquhart began trying to track the movement of individual monarchs in 1937. At that stage very little was known about their migration, except that thousands headed south each September. Urquhart's day job was as a curator of insects at the Royal Ontario Museum, although he also had a position at the University of Toronto. At his home in the 1940s and 1950s, he and his wife Norah, who also worked at the university, reared monarchs by the thousand, and studied them in the hope of safeguarding their future. Their positions in the faculty of zoology gave them much-needed access to a laboratory and equipment to step up their research.

The Urquharts decided to try to track the monarchs on their autumn journey by marking and releasing individual butterflies, then plotting the distances and locations where they were seen or found. The couple spent several years experimenting with different tagging systems before they found something that worked, a sensitive adhesive label that would not come off in the rain. The tags were easy to apply by gently squeezing them to the wing. On each tag were the words 'Send to Zoology University Toronto Canada'.

In 1952 Norah wrote a magazine article appealing for volunteers to help with the tagging programme and twelve people responded. It was enough to start up an organisation, which they called the International Migration Association. The volunteers were given tags and instructions, and monarchs were soon being caught, tagged and released. Not long after, little boxes began arriving from all over Canada and the United States, containing tagged monarchs. It was proof that the creatures really could fly hundreds of kilometres.

By 1971, 600 volunteers had joined the association, with thousands more taking part every year. The Urquharts were now amassing a great deal of information, and were able to establish that the monarchs were migrating northeast to southwest. However, where they ended up for winter was still a mystery. Desperate to identify the butterflies' final destination, the couple went on numerous field trips to search for the hibernation site. Their travels took them from New England to the Californian coast, and from southern Canada to the Gulf of Mexico, with no luck.

The following year, 1972, Norah wrote to newspapers in Mexico about the project, appealing for volunteers to report sightings and help with tagging. It led to a breakthrough. A young American engineer called Ken Brugger who was working in Mexico City at the time saw the article. He didn't know much about monarchs but he was an amateur naturalist and keen to help. Over the next two years, he spent his weekends and holidays driving around the mountains of Mexico, searching for the monarchs' secret winter destination. In 1974, Brugger married a woman called Cathy, herself a butterfly lover, and together they continued the search, taking their clues from tattered monarch remains they came across along the roads in a certain area. When they showed some specimens to a group of Mexican loggers, they were told there was a place in the mountains where many such butterflies could be found.

On 9 January 1975, all was finally revealed. An overjoyed Brugger rang the Urquharts to say that he and Cathy had at last tracked down the butterflies' roosting site – 'We have found them – millions of monarchs!' He was breathless with excitement and no wonder, because the colonies are a truly amazing sight. Great clumps of butterflies coat entire tree trunks and branches in what looks like jagged orange and black fur. Most of the butterflies rest, wings folded, on the pines, but others swirl between the trees in dizzying masses. People who have witnessed this amazing sight say the biggest surprise is the noise of all the beating wings. It sounds like rushing water.

Understandably, the Urquharts were eager to see this extraordinary spectacle for themselves. They arranged to travel to Mexico the following winter. Despite being in their sixties, they were determined to climb the 'Mountain of Butterflies' – their reward for forty years of research.

Seeing the colonies of monarchs they had spent a lifetime seeking must have been an amazing moment, but there was one further magical surprise. While the Urquharts were staring in wonder at the fluttering masses, a pine branch collapsed under the weight of the insects, scattering a huge cloud of butterflies. Among a cluster that spilled at their feet, the Urquharts found one bearing a white tag. The butterfly had been tagged in Minnesota by one of their volunteers before setting off on its journey to Mexico. It was the final proof they needed. There could no longer be any question that the monarchs seen in North America were the same butterflies that spent the winter over three thousand kilometres away in Mexico.[33]

Since then, large monarch populations have been found at thirteen overwintering sites spread over five mountains. But the destruction of milkweed raises serious questions over their future, and it is only one of several threats they face. The other serious danger is illegal logging, which is destroying their winter habitat in Mexico.

Five hundred years ago, the Aztecs believed that the souls of the dead returned as butterflies. They called them 'eternal sun dancers', and treated them with care. Today, though the roosting sites are ecological reserves protected by the Mexican government, trees are still being felled. The pines and firs provide shelter for the butterflies, protecting them from fluctuations in temperature. If the canopy becomes too thin, they are exposed to storms and cold blasts that are often fatal.

The Mexican government has ploughed several million dollars into protecting the colonies, running campaigns to persuade locals in the 50,000-hectare area where the colonies spend the winter that the butterflies are worth far more as a tourist attraction than the trees are as wood. In the first year of the campaign, which began in 2007, the WWF reported a 48 per cent drop in illegal logging, but the decline of the colonies has continued.

When I spoke to Taylor about what is happening, he was deeply worried: 'Here we have one of the world's most magnificent biological phenomena, and to lose this would be absolutely drastic. I mean, this is one of the most spectacular events that happens on the planet.' He believes it is crucial to keep working with the Mexican authorities: 'Maintaining the conditions in Mexico is extremely important, and becoming more so as the population of butterflies goes down. These populations down there in Mexico can suffer seventy to eighty per cent mortality under extreme conditions as they overwinter, and if the population becomes really small, it will be tough coming back from a mortality event like that. Recovery is going to take several years.'

I was lucky enough to see the monarch migration myself while leading a wildlife tour in Cape May, New Jersey. We were there to watch the birds of prey that pass over those skies in September on their way back south. The bushes were full of tiny warblers who were also on the move, a marvellous sight. But the clouds of beautiful orange and black butterflies were simply breathtaking. A month later, I was on the Isles of Scilly off southwestern England. As I picked my way round a little airfield bordered by the Atlantic Ocean searching for migrants of the feathered variety, to my amazement I saw a monarch fluttering strongly over the grass. It must have come all the way from America, probably blown off-course. It is just mind-blowing to think that something so delicate could make it thousands of kilometres across the ocean.

Yet these superb migrants are under threat; and it's not just monarch butterflies that are suffering as a result of intensive farming. In the UK, farmland is the main habitat for three-quarters of butterflies, but according to a report by the Butterfly Conservation Trust, Natural England and the Farming and Wildlife Advisory Group, 'Typically, they now survive only on relatively small areas.' The organisations describe wild-flower meadows as vital. Such areas provide habitats for up to twenty-five different species, including those that are rare and declining. The advice is that no fertilisers or pesticides should be used in these pastures.[34]

In a recent report, the government-funded UK Butterfly Monitoring Scheme, which tracks the well-being of fifty-four types of butterfly, found that thirty had declined over the last ten years. A total of twenty-one species declined by more than a quarter, while twelve species declined by half or more. Victims include iconic British species such as the red admiral, painted lady and holly blue.[35]

One of the landmark extinctions in Britain when I first became interested in wildlife was that of the large blue butterfly. Decades of conservation effort came to a bitter end in 1979 when the species was declared extinct. Intensive farming was blamed for destroying much of its habitat.[36] It was particularly regrettable because the species is threatened globally. Not to be deterred, conservationists reintroduced the large blue to the British countryside in what was described as 'the world's largest-scale, longest-running successful conservation project involving an insect'. Twenty-five years later, its delicate pastel-blue wings can be seen again over more than thirty former sites.[37] It goes to show that declines can be reversed; but how much better to avoid them in the first place.

As for the monarch, there are large, non-migratory populations in other countries, so the future of the species seems assured. Yet its decline is symptomatic of a far deeper malaise. It would be devastating if the migration, a great natural wonder of the world, disappeared. As Taylor puts it:

> It's not that monarchs are important in themselves, it is that monarchs are symbolic of how we're doing. It's an iconic species that is symbolic of the biodiversity problems throughout the United States. If we can't support the monarch butterflies, it means we're not supporting a lot of things, because monarchs share habitats with virtually all pollinators in the US and they share habitats with a lot of small mammals and birds.

Like the proverbial canary in a coal mine, warning of impending danger, butterflies, like birds and bees, are the hallmarks of a healthy environment. Their plight is part of the complex web of life that underpins food and farming.

5

Fish

Farming takes to the water

PLAYING SCALES

It was one of those moments when everything seems just right. I was on the front deck of a glinting white catamaran, soaking up the sun with my new wife Helen. We were sailing through the turquoise seas off Mauritius, enjoying the tropical clear waters, seductive white beaches, cold drinks and cocktails. It was a heavenly experience and the honeymoon I'd dreamed of. The skipper turned the boat towards Ile aux Cerfs, a tiny island said to boast Mauritius's most beautiful beach. There was a party atmosphere. We were aboard with several other honeymooners, sipping beer and bottled water, sharing wedding stories and laughing about how you can spot male newly-weds because they fiddle compulsively with their wedding rings.

There was a splashing in the water. Dolphins! Everyone stopped talking and turned to look at the frolicking bottle-nosed dolphins swimming ahead of us. I was so excited I almost spilled my drink. Helen and I had been desperately hoping we'd see some on this trip. Just then, Helen spotted something strange in the distance: 'What's that over there?' she asked. I peered through my binoculars. It was a fish farm. In an instant, I was back in work mode, staring at the green pillars and white railings of the floating pontoons. They jarred on the landscape, a bum note in an otherwise perfect symphony. No doubt thousands of fish were caged in giant net-bags beneath the surface. I thought about the inevitable outpouring of muck from thousands of caged fish and how this might affect the pristine waters.

Mauritius has become a hot spot for fish farming, with twenty or more sites chosen for development by the island's Ministry of Environment.[1] Locals are all too aware of how this might affect the water. Mauritian environmentalists have voiced concerns that the feed and toxic chemicals used in intensive fish rearing will cause pollution, foster disease, and might even attract sharks, seriously jeopardising the all-important tourist industry.[2] There are also concerns for the health of coral reefs. Dr Deolall Daby, Professor of Marine and Environmental Sciences at the University of Mauritius, fears the effect could be fatal: 'We have to be very careful. It is because of corals that there are beaches. They are so important in the whole functioning and protection of the shores.'[3]

A tropicbird flew past our catamaran like a sharp-dressed gull, gleaming white with its long tail streaming like a ribbon stiff on the breeze. We'd had a wonderful day, one that I would never forget. But I couldn't suppress a nagging sense that the fish farms we'd seen were just plain wrong. The wildlife and environment in Mauritius have already taken a ferocious battering. The carpet of sugar cane throughout the countryside is a hint to why the native birdlife has its back to the wall. Some of the rarest birds on the planet are to be found here but are on the brink of dying out. The Mauritius Kestrel and Echo Parakeet, for example, are down to their last few hundred. That Mauritius still appears so idyllic is testimony to nature's resilience. I learned something on that otherwise perfect day: that industrial farming had taken to the seas in paradise. Until then, it was something that I associated much more with salmon farming on the remote coasts of Scotland.

In the shadow of snow-capped mountains, surrounded by bracken and Caledonian pines, lies Loch Maree Hotel, on the pebbly shores of one of the world's loveliest lakes. Ever since Queen Victoria stayed there in 1877, the hotel in Wester Ross, Scotland has been a popular destination for tourists drawn to the wild and lonely scenery.

The loch itself, the fourth-largest freshwater lake in Scotland, has long been thought to have special powers. In the late eighteenth and early nineteenth centuries, it was thought to hold some kind of magical cure for lunacy. The mentally ill were brought to the water as a last resort. The ritual involved tying the patient into a boat, which then set off for a small island in the loch called Isle Maree. The boat would circle the island three times – always clockwise – and on each lap, the unfortunate patient would be plunged into the freezing water. The vessel would then dock at the island, where there would be a further ritual by the remains of an ancient chapel, graveyard and holy well, thought to date back to Pictish times. It involved the patient drinking water from the well, and an offering made by nailing a rag or ribbon to an ancient tree. A visitor who witnessed the rites in 1772 told how the patient was forced to kneel before a crumbling altar and sip from the well, in a process that was repeated every day for several weeks in the desperate hope of a cure.[4]

In modern times, Loch Maree's star attraction has been something rather more tangible: fish. Every summer, thousands of adult sea trout and salmon used to swim back to the loch from the sea. They gathered in huge numbers in the bays, providing phenomenal angling. The loch developed a reputation as the world's finest sea-trout fishery,[5] a place where it was possible to land a trout weighing close to 9 kilograms. The record salmon landed in Loch Maree weighed in excess of 13 kilograms.[6] Loch Maree Hotel was a thriving business with ten boats and a team of Highland fishing guides or 'ghillies'. During high season, it employed as many as nine full-time ghillies. After sundown, a throng of anglers would gather round a roaring open fire in Ghillies' Bar, a glass of malt whisky in one hand, comparing notes about the day's catch. Now the hotel is deserted, because the fish have gone.

These days you'd be lucky to land a trout weighing more than one kilogram – as a recent expedition to test the state of wild fish stocks showed.[7] On 17 September 2010, around a month before the end of the fishing season, three boats set out from Loch Maree Hotel, each with an experienced ghillie, to assess a sample catch. According to a report by the Wester Ross Fisheries' Trust, which organised the trip: 'The day was cold, with showers and NW breeze. 21 trout were retained for measuring (all trout were subsequently released) and scale samples were taken to confirm identity. Andrew Ramsay caught the largest sea trout, a fish of 875g, nearly 2lb.'[8] In other words, tiddlers are all that remain. The sea-trout fishery in Loch Maree and nearby Ewe River has collapsed, leaving the owners of the hotel forced to find other ways of attracting guests, and the people whose livelihoods used to depend on the angling industry out of work.

Nick Thompson, who owns the hotel lease, says he barely gets one angler a week. The hotel is currently closed for renovation: his latest idea is to turn the place into a beauty spa. He's clear it has no future as a paradise for those who love the rod and line. When fish stocks vanish, the usual story is overexploitation, but at Loch Maree it seems anglers who got so much pleasure from landing one or two prime specimens every season are not to blame. The real culprit? Fish farms – there are two nearby.[9] One way or another, it appears these intensive fish-production operations have driven wild fish stocks to destruction. It is a picture that is being replicated all over the world.

Tucked along remote coastlines and river valleys, fish farms are the forgotten factory farms under the water, and one of the fastest-growing sectors of intensive animal rearing. Around 100 billion farmed fish are produced globally every year, 30 billion more than all the chickens, cows, pigs and other terrestrial farm animals reared worldwide.[10] Looking at it in terms of volume of flesh generated, in 2009 the world produced just over 80 million tonnes of chicken meat from an estimated 55 billion chickens; fish farming, known as aqua-culture, now produces about 70 per cent of that amount – using twice the number of animals.[11]

As natural fish stocks all over the world reach critical levels of deple-tion, there is a widespread assumption that fish farming is a happy solution. However, far from helping preserve wild fish stocks by taking pressure off the sea, fish farming requires ever more plundering of the oceans for the smaller fish fed to carnivorous forms of farmed fish, like salmon and trout. Bluntly, these kind of fish farms waste fish, rather than generate a net gain.[12] The figures speak for themselves. According to industry data, it takes between three tonnes[13] and five tonnes[14] of small fish to produce one tonne of farmed fish like trout and salmon. Supplies of wild fish are in danger of running out; according to the FAO (Food and Agriculture Organization), over half of all wild fish populations are already 'fully exploited' while almost another third have been overexploited.[15] In 2008, 23 per cent of the total global fish catch was small pelagic fish of the open ocean used to make fishmeal and fish oil, largely for farmed fish. In other words, around a fifth of the world's fish catch is effectively being wasted feeding other fish.[16]

Worryingly, a very significant proportion of this ground-up fish – around one-third of the total – is quietly being fed to other farmed animals,[17] usually chickens and pigs. So if your chicken nuggets or pork chops have a strange aroma, that could be why. Over the last few decades, the production of fishmeal and fish oil, mostly to feed farmed fish,[18] has removed around 20–30 million tonnes of fish from the sea.[19] It is usually made from pelagic fish like anchovies from the southeastern Pacific Ocean, and herring, mackerel and sprat species. Contrary to popular belief, fishmeal largely doesn't come from off-cuts and processing waste that isn't any good for anything else. In fact, most fishmeal is made from highly nutritious stuff that could happily be eaten by people. Indeed, the type of fish involved already provides half the fish for direct human consumption in over thirty countries.[20]

The use of pelagic fish for animal feed contributes to overfishing of other species, and thus to the current overfishing crisis in the oceans. It's not even as if the supply of pelagic fish is unlimited. According to the FAO, the two main stocks of anchoveta in the southeast Pacific, Alaska pollock in the north Pacific and blue whiting in the Atlantic are fully exploited. So are several types of Atlantic herring, while stocks of Japanese anchovy in the northwest Pacific and Chilean jack mackerel in the southeast Pacific are also running out.[21] Either way, it is clear that fish farming is a very inefficient use of limited resources, with a poor ratio of 'fish in:fish out'.

The industry is slowly beginning to recognise that it's unsustainable to continue feeding wild fish to farmed fish. Alarmingly, some people are suggesting the use of livestock meat and bonemeal as a possible alternative. Indeed, in areas where aquaculture is growing rapidly – China, Vietnam, Bangladesh and India for example – farmed fish are already being fed on 'cakes' that contain manure from intensive terrestrial animal feedlots.

At the Global Conference on Aquaculture in Thailand in 2010, scientists highlighted the threat to pelagic fish stocks and warned of a 'crisis in feed qualities' for farmed fish. Looking ahead to 2050, they predicted increasing use of material like chicken slaughterhouse waste and chicken manure to feed farmed fish.[22] In other words, the fish-farming industry may increasingly take to feeding fish with chicken muck. It is hard to see how this would be acceptable to Western consumers. I suppose it would depend how much they were allowed to know.

Like other factory farms, fish farms involve animals kept in intense confinement – up to 50,000 salmon in a single sea cage. Often suffering from blinding cataracts, fin and tail injuries and body deformities, and infested with parasites, they are forced to compete for space and oxygen. Salmon are reared in stocking densities equivalent to a single bathtub of water per 75-centimetre fish. Packed this tightly, these natural wanderers of the ocean swim as a group, or shoal, in incessant circles around the cage, in the same way that frustrated zoo animals pace their enclosures. Fins and tails are rubbed sore as the fish press against each other and the sides of the cage.

Life for farmed trout is even worse. Generally reared in freshwater 'raceways' or earth ponds, they can be kept at densities of 60 kilograms of fish per cubic metre of water. It's the equivalent of twenty-seven trout, each measuring the length of a ruler, being allocated a single bathtub of water. More normal rates are 30–40 kilograms of trout per cubic metre of water. The stress of crowding and confinement makes the fish highly susceptible to disease. In recent years, salmon farming has been hit by a number of serious outbreaks of illness, killing millions of fish. Mortality rates among farmed salmon are particularly alarming, with average losses in sea cages ranging from 10 to 30 per cent.[23] This kind of death rate would raise serious alarm bells in other farm animal species, but for some reason people care less about the welfare of fish. There is a sense that because they're not mammals or birds, it doesn't matter as much if they suffer.

I remember an experience that illustrated this attitude quite vividly. I was invited to Strasbourg, Alsace, to the Council of Europe, which promotes cooperation and human rights among European governments. Officials were drafting common standards for fish farming and I was there to observe. I spent a lovely couple of days in Strasbourg's narrow cobbled streets and half-timbered buildings. I marvelled at the famous Gothic cathedral that towers up in the city centre and enjoyed the varied local cuisine, making sure to avoid the ubiquitous foie gras made from force-fed geese. However, most of my time was spent inside the rather less aesthetically pleasing Council building, a modern whitish affair flanked by colourful flagpoles of member countries. On my way to and from the building, I liked to look out for the white storks in the nearby park.

The meetings were long and intense. European government officials in grey suits would pore over complicated texts, arguing over whether a sentence should read 'shall' rather than 'should'. 'Should' was a wishy-washy guideline, whereas 'shall' meant something had to be done. Sometimes, as 'expert' observer, I would talk into the microphone and get the right result: I wanted as many 'shalls' as I could get. That way, I felt we were at least beginning to get some protection for a kind of animal that frequently gets none at all.

Strasbourg sits within the Rhine Valley straddling the border with Germany in wonderful wine country. Our itinerary involved a day trip to look at examples of inland fish farms, presumably a rewarding break for staying the course of the interminable, bureaucratic discussions that occupied most of our time. I assumed EU officials in our party must surely have seen them many times before, or they wouldn't have been in a position to draw up legislation on the sector.

Along with thirty or forty government officials, advisers and vets, I boarded a coach for the day trip. Our first stop was a carp farm in the Rhine Valley. It had two types of pond, one for fish, the other for the tiny organisms – or zooplankton – that young fish like to eat. Apart from their early life, when the 'fry', as they are known, are packed tightly in tanks, the carp were generally reared in a fairly relaxed way, in unremarkable-looking earth ponds where they were left to grow by eating whatever they could find.

Our next stop was a farm rearing trout in rectangular concrete ponds surrounded by grass. The water came from a local spring and flowed through successive ponds, each one lower than the next. Each pond had bigger fish than the last. They seemed in reasonable condition, as did the water. You could see the bottom easily, though by the time it finished going through the farm, it was probably less pleasant. The fish were fed by hand twice a day every day except Sunday. I wondered whether the Sunday fast was for the benefit of the fish or the owner.

Our third and final stop was billed as a 'modern raceway site'. As I could probably have guessed from the euphemism, this was the factory-farm version of trout rearing. We were told that it came complete with automatic oxygen injection systems. It certainly needed them. Compared with the previous farm, three times as many fish were being reared in the same space. The water was a murky brown. The fish were barely visible, let alone the bottom.

I stood incredulous as government people, vets and other experts watched fish in obvious distress without a word of criticism or alarm. Lots of the fish had worn tails from rubbing the sides of the tanks and each other. Some had raw red flesh exposed above their tails; others had no tails at all. They were crowding round the water inlets, desperate for oxygen. The grids across the inlets churned the water, allowing oxygen to dissolve more readily. Schools of larger fish swam in tight lethargic circles, their backs reaching high out of the water. They were clearly not happy. One expert told me that this was probably due to 'clogged gills', which made for 'uncomfortable fish'.

I chatted with the farm owner, a tall amiable man in workaday wellington boots. He said he was happy to answer any questions and let me take photos. I took pictures of this stark factory-style place in the open air. It was very different to the two farms we'd seen earlier that day.

I saw fish with their eyes apparently popping out. A fish vet who was standing beside me said that they were probably suffering from 'impact damage' or infection. I took photos, much to the distaste of one of the other vets. He asked in a voice that barely concealed his anger whether I would use the photos publicly. He repeated the question a couple of times. I wasn't willing to give him any reassurances. He didn't like the idea that the pictures might be used to show what goes on in such places.

In the end, I never did use the photos. The water was so murky you couldn't really see anything. Yet ten years on, the memories of that day remain vivid. I can still see those fish in my mind's eye, with their missing tails and bulging eyes, swimming in appalling conditions. I can see a huddle of vets and legislators looking down, and saying nothing. I can remember how odd it felt getting back on the bus, with no one else concerned by what we'd seen. Vets are seen by many as the animals' champions; that some seemed unfazed by such poor rearing conditions really shocked me. I couldn't help wondering whether the veterinary profession was failing somehow to properly stand up for animal welfare, instead following and thereby supporting the status quo. In the complex moral maze presented by farming on land or water, it is easy to get lost in the profit bottom line: to lose sight of the patient – the animals – when dealing with the customer – the farmer. It's a theme we'll return to in chapter 6.

Since my trip to Strasbourg, the fish-farming industry has boomed. By 2009, nearly half of the total supply of fish on the global market came from fish farms. Between 2004 and 2009 alone, production tonnage increased by almost one-third. Regionally, Asia accounts for almost 90 per cent of global production, followed by Europe (4.5 per cent) and Latin America (3.3 per cent). In Asia, fish farms mostly produce carp and tilapia, though species of prawn and shrimp, as well as largemouth black bass, catfish and turbot, have also been introduced. In the West, the fish-farming industry is primarily driven by demand for salmon and trout.[24] Scotland's west coast is jam-packed with fish farms. It's a highly concentrated industry. Two-thirds of the market is reportedly controlled by the 'Big Four' fish-farm companies, the largest of which is Marine Harvest. Like its competitors, Scottish Sea Farms, Lighthouse Caledonia and Grieg/Hjaltland, it's owned by companies listed on the Oslo stock exchange.[25]

But for wild fish, such as salmon in Loch Maree, fish farms often pose a grave danger, primarily because they are hotbeds of sea lice.[26] These parasites, which look like tiny tadpoles, are one of the single biggest problems for salmon farms.[27] When they latch on to fish, they eat away at the skin and scales. The effect around the head can be so corrosive that the bone of the living fish's skull can be exposed – a condition known as the 'death crown'.

Wild salmon get rid of the lice naturally, because they drop off when the fish migrate into fresh water. Mature wild salmon also have a covering of mucus that repels the lice.[28] Farmed salmon don't have these advantages. Ridding them of lice often involves bathing them in powerful chemicals. Because farmed fish are kept in such high concentration, it doesn't take long for lice to multiply and spread. Young wild fish can tolerate brief exposure to sea lice, but when they migrate past salmon farms, they are often exposed to sea lice for several weeks, allowing the lice burden to accumulate to fatal levels.[29]

According to The FishSite, a fisheries industry news and information website, when wild salmon swim from the open ocean back inland to spawn, they have to pass through river mouths and inlets 'clogged with salmon farms'. Some wild salmon carry parasites, which don't bother them. However, when they swim past the cages, the parasites can jump ship. Due to the high density of salmon in the cages, once sea lice enter they reproduce like mad. Essentially, according to The FishSite, they become 'a reservoir of infestation'. The next generation of tiny smolts juveniles face this infestation with none of the mucus, scales or other armour against the sea lice of adult salmon, and many do not survive.[30]

According to the Atlantic Salmon Trust, in the Highlands and Islands of Scotland wild salmon are outnumbered by farmed salmon by a ratio of more than 700:1, creating more than 61 million potential hosts for parasites and pathogens.[31] Guy Linley Adams, an environmental lawyer employed by the Salmon and Trout Association, told me:

> The problem is when you've got a fish farm with 400,000 to 500,000 adult fish, all of which have a couple of female lice and all of which are producing eggs, then you can imagine the wild juvenile fish that are coming down the rivers have got to swim right past these cages, and are faced with this subsurface cloud of sea lice. And if you're a five- or six-inch-long wild smolt and you get ten lice on you, that's enough to kill you.

The evidence that sea lice from fish farms are to blame for the catastrophic decline of wild fish stocks is long established. Back in 1999, a study by the Scottish Environment Protection Agency (SEPA) concluded that in relation to salmon, the link should be 'accepted as beyond reasonable doubt'.[32]

A study carried out in British Columbia, published in 2006, looked at how lice affected juvenile wild fish on three different migration routes, each containing several fish farms. The farms were the primary source of lice throughout the entire migration route. The scientists concluded that if outbreaks of sea-lice infestation continued in British Columbia, 'local extinction of wild salmon is certain, and a 99% collapse in pink salmon population . . . is expected in four salmon generations'.[33] In 2009, the industry body, the British Columbia Pacific Salmon Forum, accepted that more needed to be done to protect wild salmon.[34]

A review for the industry that same year acknowledged that it would be hard to 'find anyone who would claim that lice from the farms *aren't* a factor in wild salmon survival' and that the industry needed to tackle the problem.[35] Peter Cunningham is a biologist at the Wester Ross Fisheries Trust, an organisation that is trying to restore the wild fisheries in Loch Maree and surrounding waters. I talked to him about what has happened to wild fish stocks and the role played by fish farms. 'There's been no fish over five pounds [2.3 kg] since I've been here, and in the old days, they were common in Loch Maree,' he told me. 'In the 1980s, something like 12 per cent of the sea trout over 1 pound [0.5 kg] were over 4 pounds [1.8 kg]. We see nothing like that nowadays. The fish aren't surviving as long at sea as they used to. There are a few one- or two-pounders around, but we find they have quite high numbers of sea lice on them most years.' Cunningham acknowledges that other factors have played their part in the demise of Loch Maree's natural fish population. However, Wester Ross Fisheries Trust believes that if the lice issue were resolved, there would be a 'substantial recovery' in the sea trout population.

As part of these efforts, some years ago the farms were moved a few kilometres further north up Loch Ewe. However, according to Cunningham it has not resolved the problem:

> It's helped a bit, but it doesn't seem to have made a difference yet in terms of getting the big sea trout back again. We're still getting some quite heavily affected sea trout when we sample them each year. Some of the fish may be going outside the Loch and picking up lice from other areas – it's hard to be specific about whether all the lice are coming from a single fish farm. There may be some drifting in from other areas.

Of course, fish farming is not just about trout and salmon. An article in the scientific journal *Nature* in 2008 pointed out that as the industry expands into other species, such as cod and halibut, 'the same concerns over disease and parasite transmission, and other impacts, will certainly apply to these species too'. The piece concluded that it is vital to assess the potential environmental costs and reduce them before the introduction of very large-scale farming of these new species.[36]

Fish farms pose another major threat to wild stocks: escapees. An incident in Scotland one icy November evening shows what can happen. As they were being hauled out of the water and off to market, 24,000 Scottish salmon had a lucky escape. The net ripped and the captives lost no time in breaking free and swimming off into the blue-black waters of Loch Ewe, never to be seen again.[37] For the escapees, it was a stroke of good fortune. But for wild fish in Loch Ewe and the surrounding area, the sudden influx of 24,000 farmed fish was a potentially deadly threat. As the company that owned the fish publicly acknowledged at the time, the great escape was deeply regrettable, and not just because of the wasted money.

Escapes from fish farms happen regularly as a result of careless handling or damage to nets and cages by storms and predators. Occasionally, farms deliberately release economically unviable young salmon. Farmed trout are also capable of mass breakouts – in 2000 there were six reported escape incidents from Scottish Rainbow Trout farms involving over 63,000 fish.[38]

Farmed salmon have been selectively bred since the 1970s to develop certain 'desirable' traits, such as faster growth rates and later sexual development. Large-scale escapes mean that former farm fish compete with wild stocks for limited food and places to spawn. Some anglers who accidentally catch farmed fish in Scottish rivers have discovered that the animals have salmon eggs and parr (young freshwater salmon) in their stomachs – suggesting they are preying on their wild counterparts.[39]

There are also worries about interbreeding. In 1991, the UK Salmon Advisory Committee expressed concern that interbreeds may result in offspring with a reduced ability to cope in the natural environment. This is because wild fish are genetically adapted to their surroundings. Even moving a salmon to a different river can reduce its ability to survive. This suggests that mixing wild and farmed salmon genes may make wild fish less robust. In 1999, SEPA declared that such 'genetic pollution' should be recognised as a 'real and present danger'.[40]

It certainly seems that farmed fish can be woefully ill-adapted to the real world. There have been a number of sightings of farmed salmon apparently stranded or caught out by the tide. Commenting on this odd state of affairs, the marine biologist James Mortimer told the *Orcadian* newspaper that it was 'unheard of for wild fish to be ignorant of the phenomenon known as tide'.[41]

Because of these concerns, fish-farm escapes are now closely monitored. Companies must immediately report accidents to the authorities. The Scottish government reported five escapes in 2009, in which a total of 88,000 fish broke free from seawater Atlantic salmon sites. The situation may be improving. For 2010, the Scottish Salmon Producers' Organisation, which represents 95 per cent of the industry, reported that around 15,000 fish had escaped, the lowest figure since statutory reporting began in 2002, and just 0.1 per cent of the total number of salmon farmed. Most of the escapes seem to have been due to 'human error or holes in the nets'.[42] It remains to be seen whether these far lower figures are just a blip, or the result of genuine improvements in the system.

The impact of the fish-farming industry on wild fish stocks might be less depressing if farmed fish were as tasty and wholesome as the organic alternative. Unfortunately that's not the case. Farmed salmon and trout, for example, contain significantly more fat than wild alternatives. Figures from the US Department of Agriculture show that farmed Atlantic salmon has more than twice the fat content of its wild cousin, and farmed rainbow trout is up to 79 per cent more fatty, while protein levels are comparable.[43] A study of chemicals in farmed fish led by Ronald Hites, a professor of environmental and analytical chemistry at Indiana University, in 2004 caused widespread alarm after it exposed worrying levels of contaminants. Hites's team analysed over two metric tonnes of farmed and wild salmon from all over the world and found that concentrations of chemicals were 'significantly higher' in the farmed samples. The conclusion was damning: 'Consumption of farmed Atlantic salmon may pose health risks that detract from the beneficial effects of fish consumption.'[44]

Chemicals are also used to make farmed fish an attractive colour. Wild salmon and trout eat crustaceans and algae, which make their flesh pink. To achieve this complexion in farmed fish, colourants are added, otherwise their flesh would be grey. Synthetic pigments – canthaxanthin and astaxanthin – are used, either individually or in combination.

Like other types of factory farming, the fish-farming business is designed to extract as much flesh as possible with minimum input. In the early 1990s scientists began exploring ways of getting round the fact that fish stop putting on as much flesh once they hit puberty. The problem was that they were maturing before they reached market size. The answer? A technique called triploidy, now widespread on trout farms. It's a procedure that involves creating fish that are sterile; technically neither male nor female.

Trevor Whyatt, an avid sea angler who runs a trout farm in Dorset, has been in the vanguard of triploidy since the 1990s and is a staunch defender of the practice: 'The problem is that maturing fish lose their appetite, and put all their energy into their reproductive system. The environmental benefits of fish that do not mature in this way are massive – you reduce your dress-out [gutting] loss from twenty-five to sixteen per cent. At the same time you gain back nine per cent of the food that would have been used.'

The process itself is relatively simple and can be performed by farmhands. Eggs and milt (fish sperm) are collected from the trout and artificially fertilised under heat. The raised temperature prevents a natural process taking place in which a second set of chromosomes present in the egg disappears. Instead, that second set of female chromosomes is retained, along with a set of chromosomes from the male, resulting in offspring with three sets of chromosomes instead of two. These fish are infertile. It's a defect that sometimes occurs naturally; the technology is designed to guarantee it.

Whyatt believes that in some ways it's better for the fish, though he admits it makes them more vulnerable to temperature changes. 'They tend to be slightly more placid. It makes for a more harmonious population, which are easier to manage,' he said.

There is one distinct advantage: any escapees can't breed. For this reason, the Environment Agency has ruled that from 2015, all farmed brown trout in UK rivers must be triploid, to protect wild fish stocks. Whyatt, who is passionate about protecting wild fish stocks, has been pushing for this since the 1990s:

> I first saw the potential benefits of sterile fish a long time ago. There's a wonderful lake in the West Country with a great stock of brown trout, but there are only two small streams feeding into the lake. The problem was that all the fish wanted to spawn there at once, and the nests of those that spawned earlier were being destroyed, because the population was too dense. If half of the fish in the lake were sterile, they would not destroy the nests. Productivity would rise and mortality would fall.

He sees it as an opportunity to use a viable industry tool to enhance and restore the genetics of wild fish. It is always welcome when new technologies are used to solve environmental problems, rather than create them. However, there is evidence that triploid fish have higher levels of deformities, breathing difficulties, low blood haemoglobin levels and a lower ability to cope with stressful situations.[45]

The industry is all too often bad for other marine life, an issue highlighted when two decapitated seals were washed up on a beach on the Isle of Skye. It was a gruesome discovery that prompted a public outcry and the attention of the police.[46] Nigel Smith, a Skye businessman who runs award-winning wildlife-watching cruises in the area, found the carcasses – a pregnant female and a juvenile – as he was walking along the beach near a fish farm. 'Their heads had been blown off,' he told me. He has grown used to coming across grisly finds involving seals. The incident, in May 2008, threw the spotlight on one of the most unedifying and emotive aspects of the fish-farming industry: its impact on seals.

Huge numbers of fish in one place present an irresistible temptation to seals, as well as to birds, otters and other wildlife. Some farms see shooting these creatures as a legitimate way to protect their stock. In 2008, both common and grey seals were officially protected in Britain under the Conservation of Seals Act 1970. However, the legislation only applied during the breeding season and excluded fish farms, so that operators could kill seals all year round to protect their cage nets from damage.

For a long time, seal culling by fish farmers was largely unregulated. All that was required was a high-calibre rifle and a gun licence. Now, under new legislation, it is supposed to be a means of last resort, but there is considerable evidence that some in the industry continue to regard a bullet as the cheapest and easiest way to get rid of the problem.

John Robins, an animal welfare campaigner in Scotland, argues that many salmon farmers do not bother to invest in alternatives like protective nets to keep predators away from the fish:

> I first learned about this back in the 1980s when I got tip-offs from people in the industry. At that time, we worked out – and it had to be a rough estimate because there were no official figures – that roughly three thousand seals minimum were being killed by fish farmers every year. That was a guesstimate based on about ten seals per year per farm. I'd been told by one group of farm workers that they had killed over sixty seals at one unit in one year, and we had other information that made us think that 3,000 was probably a rather conservative figure.

In 2006, fish were given official recognition under the Animal Health and Welfare Scotland Act, a move that animal welfare campaigners such as Robins backed. It obliged fish farmers to take adequate steps to protect their stock from predators. Some in the industry have seen this as a green light to get out their guns. There is another way: anti-predator nets. Robins believes these are far more effective than bullets at keeping seals out: 'You'd have to be shooting seals twenty-four-seven to fully protect the fish. You really do need anti-predator nets.' The legislation makes it clear that shooting a seal should be the last resort.

The problem is that anti-seal nets are expensive to buy, install and maintain. Using the Freedom of Information Act, Robins has discovered that 80 per cent of Scottish fish farmers do not have anti-predator nets and even fewer use them. 'That does not make shooting a seal a last resort, it makes it very much a first or second resort,' he said. The Scottish fish-farming industry denies using shooting as a routine method of controlling seals, arguing that a single rogue seal can cause enormous suffering and kill thousands of fish.

The Scottish government claims that the number of seals being shot has fallen dramatically in recent years. However, in March 2011 it gave the go-ahead for the culling of more than a thousand seals, issuing sixty-five licences to kill up to 1,298 seals in total that year. The shooting goes on in remote areas, the government relying on the honesty of the shooters to provide accurate records of how many seals they kill. Robins believes: 'It's a true saying that when you buy a Scottish salmon you pay for bullets to shoot seals.'

PLUNDERING PERU

I was heading into the Peruvian desert when I discovered that my local guide and fixer for the week had a loaded gun in his pocket. Stefan Austermuhle, a German zoologist who runs wildlife expeditions and bird-watching tours out of Lima, turned out to have a rather more buccaneering lifestyle in mind: he was about to ditch the green frontline and become a gold prospector, at least for now.

His impending shift of status from penniless conservationist to potential kidnap target focused his mind on his personal security. Experience in this country had apparently taught him that carrying a pistol at all times was just basic self-protection. His investigations into environmental destruction in Peru had made him the target of death threats, a concern not lost on the police here, who gave Stefan a special gun licence and training to boot.

I did my best to hide my surprise as I made some rapid mental adjustments about both Stefan and Peru. He was clearly no mild-mannered ecologist, and my trip might be more of an adventure than I'd bargained for. It was the first of many unexpected developments on my expedition to investigate the impact of one of Peru's biggest businesses: exporting ground-up fish to China and Europe to be fed to farm animals.

Fishmeal is one of the filthiest secrets of the factory-farming industry, an environmental catastrophe that involves sucking millions of tonnes of small fish out of the sea and crushing them into fish oil and dry feed for farmed fish, pigs and chickens. The process deprives millions of larger wild fish, birds and marine mammals of their natural prey, drastically depleting stocks of important species. It also pumps vile fatty waste into ocean bays, creating 'dead zones'; pollutes the atmosphere around processing plants, causing widespread human health problems; and diverts what could be a highly valuable source of nutrition for people to industrially farmed animals.

There is nowhere better to see it in action than Peru, the second-largest fishing nation in the world after China. The country makes upwards of a billion pounds a year from a single species of fish, the anchoveta or anchovy, which is ground into fishmeal.[47] It has the biggest commercial fishing fleet in the world geared towards the exploitation of a single type of fish and exports more than a million metric tonnes of the stuff every year, making it the leading global fishmeal supplier.[48] The UK consumed 135,000 tonnes of fishmeal in 2010,[49] a third of it imported from Peru.[50]

Stefan was my fixer – a highly experienced biologist based in Peru for thirteen years. He had witnessed the impact of the fishmeal industry on marine life and birdlife for himself and seemed an ideal person to accompany me. He had worked with many international documentary makers and had the contacts I needed to delve beneath the surface

of the industry. As I was to discover, after more than a decade struggling to secure funding for conservation projects, he now wanted to
make serious money for his green campaigns by setting up what he
described as Peru's first ethical and environmentally friendly gold mine.
Until that was up and running though, he was available as a guide.

My primary destination in Peru was Chimbote, capital of the fishmeal industry and a port that lands more fish annually than the entire
Spanish fishing fleet.[51] I flew into Lima from Buenos Aires and spent
a few hours in the city getting my bearings. Perched on a cliff between
the desert and the Pacific Ocean, Lima seemed an odd mixture of a
place: ugly but cheerful, the city centre dominated by an entertaining
mixture of Sixties, Seventies and Eighties architecture.

I wandered downtown from our hotel, to find myself in a buzzing
backpacker district of cheap shops, money changers and juice bars. It
was Sunday and the vibe was relaxed, no one moving faster than a
stroll. The soundtrack was low-volume Europop from tinny old ster-
eos, interspersed with the odd 'poop' from battered-looking 1970s
local buses. As I made my way down to the seafront I found myself
amid concrete flyovers, multi-storey car parks and grey municipal
buildings. Overlooking the sea was a long strip of high-rise flats, their
blue- and black-tinted glass façades glinting in the sun. I stood at the
cliff edge and looked at the sea. There was no beach to speak of, just a
thin fringe of dark pebbles and grey-black sand. Some kilometres away
at the end of the curving bay was a barren hill shaped a bit like Cape
Town's Table Mountain, covered in pylons. I must admit that I was
disappointed. Peru had been high on my list of 'must-see' places, but
the capital was a let-down.

Before we left for Chimbote, Stefan offered to take me to Asia
Island, a rocky outcrop off Lima that once teemed with birds. Apparently the birdlife had been devastated by the anchoveta industry. He
told me it was a 'guano' island, uninhabited, with a dull white coat
consisting of thousands of years' worth of bird droppings. In some
places, the guano used to be 90 metres thick, evidence of the extraordinary number of seabirds that once lived there.[52]

In the nineteenth century, when cormorants, boobies and pelicans covered the rocks, the bird muck was a valuable commodity. By the 1850s it was Peru's biggest export and the government's principal earner. Some 20 million tons were shipped overseas between 1848 and 1875, half of it to Britain, where it was prized by farmers as a rich organic fertiliser.[53] It was an industry fuelled by abundant marine life, not least the anchoveta, which provided food for tens of millions of seabirds. Then the fish stocks were plundered; Stefan told me that most of the birds were now gone.

We picked up a 4x4 hire car in Lima and headed for Pucusana, a traditional fishing village not far away, where Stefan kept a motorboat. It's renowned for a good day out and its cebiche: salads of fresh raw fish. Dozens of little fishing boats were busy around the harbour, sorting their nets or unloading fish at the local market. People, dogs and birds wandered between market stalls and crates of newly landed fish. Pelicans flapped at the harbour edge looking for scraps.

I walked down the slipway, where the smell of seafood mingled with fumes from the boats. A wizened woman in a wide-brimmed hat stood under a blue gazebo, pulling huge lobster-coloured crabs out of a bucket. She and others were busy preparing food for sale: cockles, mussels, mackerel, a single tuna next to a small shark.

Stefan was worried that fog was rolling in and wanted to get going, so we clambered into his twin-engine motorcruiser and chugged out of the harbour. Almost at once we passed our first commercial fishing boat, about 30 metres long, its rusty black hull piled high with black nets. It was a purse-seine vessel, using a net to surround shoals of fish before the bottom is drawn shut like a purse. The mass of wriggling silver fish would then be lifted aboard by two elongated crane arms, which stood like idle sentries.

We passed independent fishermen bobbing their lines from rocks. The fog was closing in. I marvelled at the seabirds dancing above. Inca terns bounced on buoyant wings, their exquisite markings like sooty sea swallows. Through my binoculars I could see their waxy-red beaks, bright yellow at the base, and what looked like a curly-white pencil

moustache. Gulls swirled about the boat. I saw two types of cormo-
rant, and a rare Humboldt penguin standing high on some rocks.
Gannets known as Peruvian boobies plunged and dived.

It thrilled me when a huge, shiny brown body, thick whiskers and
bulldog-like face burst out of the water: a sea lion. In the mist, it all
seemed other-worldly. A playful pod of bottle-nosed dolphins
joined the boat, their back-combed fins glistening. They stayed
close, swimming diagonally across our path, as if to say we weren't
going fast enough. Stefan cranked up the speed and the dolphins
kept the pace, four side by side, bow-riding; sometimes breaking
the surface, sometimes dancing below. They were so close I could
almost touch their smooth silver-grey bodies. I could see the scars
and notches on their fins. Local biologists use pictures of these like
fingerprints.

Small fish leaped, sprinkling the water like a handful of corn, probably trying to escape the dolphins. And then we were at Asia Island,
now protected as a national nature reserve, uninhabited but for guards.
As we approached, a warden on the rocks gestured at us to come closer.
He'd received a tip-off of trespassers on the sanctuary's no-go zone and
wanted help to investigate. As a thank you he allowed us to spend a
few minutes ashore.

After the exhilaration of the boat ride, it was a depressing experience. The protected status had clearly come much too late: though
there were still a few birds round the perimeter, it was unrecognisable
from the place described in historical records. I saw rotting pelican
carcasses, and a booby too ill to move. The strong smell of guano –
dry, musty ammonia – was the only clue that it had once teemed with
thousands of birds.

Today, guano is still harvested, but in much smaller quantities. The
state-owned company that collects the deposits is said to be struggling
to survive. Stefan told us: 'Around the middle of the last century, there
used to be forty million seabirds across twenty-eight islands off the
Peruvian coast. Now they have only 1.8 million birds. The decline in
bird numbers correlates with the rise of the fishmeal industry. All these

seabirds feed on anchovies. Since the anchovy industry, there has been a ninety-five per cent drop in bird numbers in sixty years.'

Seabird population crashes in this area are nothing new. Oceanic shifts in currents can have devastating effects on food sources for marine birdlife, leading to sharp but temporary declines. The waters on the Peruvian coast are not warm tropical seas but cool upwellings known as the Humboldt current, which are highly favourable to marine life.

During El Niño years however – a climatic pattern that occurs across the tropical Pacific – the ocean shifts and warmer waters reach the islands, causing the marine food chain to break down. Plankton disappears, along with the anchoveta that feed on it, and seabirds starve. After each natural crash, populations recover. They were hit hardest in 1957–8 when numbers declined by 70 per cent. Five years later, they'd pretty much sprung back. Lasting decline is something else. It seems that overfishing, primarily of anchoveta for fishmeal, is preventing recovery.[54] 'The island is now empty,' Stefan said. 'The guano workers of days gone by would lift clouds of birds into the air; so many, they would darken the sky for hours.' He described the current picture as a 'permanent El Niño low'.

Peru learned the perils of overfishing as long ago as 1970, when the industry collapsed. It prompted the government to introduce a quota system to ensure that some fish are left to spawn.[55] The quotas seem to be preventing anchovy stocks from further decline, but numbers remain at a base level compared with sixty years ago – hence the desperate state of marine birds. The Peruvian government would like the outside world to believe the anchovy fishery is now well regulated and sustainable. Others tell a different story.

Back in Lima after our boat trip, I met Victor Puente Arnao, a forty-three-year-old marine lawyer based in the capital. He told me that in 2010 his law office won a public contract to work on 12,500 cases of fishery violations. They had a combined fine value of US$200 million. I was not surprised when he added that the government ended up following up on less than half of these. Apparently the breaches all involved anchovy vessels. 'The authorities are not capable of regulating the quotas. The people that work in the ministry are involved in the fishing industry themselves. This leads to a very soft treatment of the companies concerned,' he alleged.

The 1970s fisheries crash also saw the start of dolphin hunting, a practice that has since been officially outlawed. However Stefan's own investigations suggest that between two and three thousand dolphins a year are still being killed illegally for human consumption.

Earlier in the day, while still on the boat, I had spotted a broiler-chicken farm on the mainland, one of many in Peru; the birds possibly being fed fishmeal. Whether it be here or oceans away, it was a reminder of the big picture: marine life sacrificed for factory farms.

Next morning we set off for Chimbote. I had been promised spectacular views along the 400-kilometre route, but it was a long time before they materialised. Lima's suburbs sprawled on and on along the traffic-choked highway. We ground along at a snail's pace through congestion worse than rush hour on the M25. All along the road, packed stiflingly close together, were flats and houses, many of them little more than shoebox-shaped brick sheds, stacked two or three high. Billboards with scantily clad women advertising who knows what loomed above them. Hawkers plied cigarettes, grapes and oranges. Children careered on rusty bikes. It was chaotic and colourful, exciting and slightly intimidating, teeming with life.

Finally we shrugged off the city and found ourselves in an arid semi-desert. Strings of pylons marched up scrubby hills. There was the odd hut, matchbox-small and rudimentary, though little sign of anyone at home. Some of the hills on the outskirts of the city had been turned into free advertising hoardings: scraped into the sand were names of politicians in huge letters, presumably carved out in the run-up to elections and never removed after polling day. A few kilometres beyond the city limits, we passed a new settlement, thousands of colourfully painted low brick huts, huddled close together. Stefan said it had sprung up within the last five years, a giant squat created by speculators. He explained that the inhabitants were bussed in by mafia types who illegally staked out the land and sold people 'leases'. For a while, he said, the settlement was entirely run by armed thugs who controlled entry and exit. It became a refuge for criminals on the run. Eventually the government moved in, built a police station and legitimised the place.

A few kilometres further along the highway we came across the first of scores of broiler-chicken factory farms. Rearing chickens for meat, from the outside at least they were are all the same: rows of long low sheds with saggy black or grey canvas roofs and black plastic tarpaulins slung haphazardly over the sides, presumably to provide shade. We didn't attempt to poke around: Stefan's gun was evidence enough that angry Peruvians can't always be relied on to waste time with words when they want you off their property. Further along the road we passed a field of burning sugar cane. Dark red and orange flames leapt 6 metres high, billowing yellow-black smoke over the plantation. The fire made a snapping, crackling sound. We passed through occasional small green valleys, heavily irrigated, with scrubby palm trees, tropical flowers and fields of maize.

And then, 200 kilometres out of Lima, we entered another world: the Peruvian desert, an extraordinary lunar landscape, desolate and endless. We were in the foothills of the Andes, but the mountains were made of sand. The different hues and textures were beautiful: no longer just barren brown scree, as outside the city, but undulating hulks in subtle shades. Some were great smooth dunes that looked as if they were made of soft brown sugar; others were more solid, rubbly, gunmetal-grey, pinkish-orange or ancient red. On the flanks were occasional hard ridges where rich seams could be found: of gold. It was a landscape unlike anything I'd seen before. We stopped to film. That's when I spotted some shells in the sand. The ocean was far away. Shells in the Andes: surreal.

Clinging to the road were occasional signs of life: the odd rustic shack, the walls just flimsy canvas, like those fold-up sun shelters that holidaymakers use on the beach, the most rudimentary of family dwellings. Now and again we passed roadworks, monitored by men clad in full-body protective clothes like chemical warfare suits, the labourers fully masked as they stood by the road, waving red or green flags. They were an eerie sight, but the heavy gear was vital in these conditions: every passing lorry threw up a wave of sand and grime in its wake.

As we drew nearer Chimbote, the dry mountains to the west fell away into smaller softer dunes, and suddenly we saw the South Pacific. The juxtaposition of desert and sea, the ocean stage-lit steely grey-blue by shafts of sunlight breaking through great puffy clouds, was a dramatic sight.

The journey through this ethereal scenery was exhilarating, which was just as well, because our destination most certainly was not. On reaching the outskirts of Chimbote, the largest town in the Ancash region of Peru, we were greeted by a polluted marshland strewn with litter and occasional pools of filthy stagnant water crusted with yellow algae. A sun-bleached sign over the main road welcomed us to the capital of the fishing industry. The air was humid, laced with the sharp stink of fish. My heart sank as we drove in.

The hotel where we would spend the next few nights looked quite promising from the outside. Built on the seafront, away from the bustle of the town centre, it had a cheerful pillar box-red façade, fancy white wrought-iron lamps and a mosaic porch, and it enjoyed spec-tacular views over the bay to a number of small guano islands. Behind the façade, however, was a much bleaker prospect. It was like a deserted government institution or student hall of residence, with long soulless corridors leading to desperately drab rooms of the kind you would expect in a backpacker hostel. Mine had dim strip lighting, brown curtains and dirty lino flooring. Its crowning glory was a portable fan which, when switched on, was so loud it sounded like an aircraft revving for take-off. A jaunty sticker on the stand said 'High Velocity Cozy Air'. It was no match for the suffocating heat. Night was falling.

I wandered down the corridor feeling uneasy. I seemed to have the whole floor to myself. Dark staircases led to more deserted accommo-dation. On the ground floor, several unlocked doors led to an unlit car

park. Stefan had made no secret of Chimbote's reputation as a dangerous place. However, the hotel was the best the town had to offer, so I
shut out negative thoughts and hunkered down for the night.

Next morning, after breakfast served by a middle-aged waiter who
appeared to be deaf and wore the expression of a man who had just
swallowed a rancid mussel, we headed to the harbour. We had
arranged to meet some local shellfish divers who were going to take
us out in their boat. They wanted to show us the contrast between
the rich pickings on the seabed a kilometre or so out in the bay, and
the toxic sludge towards the shore where the fish-processing factories
spew waste.

In the bay were perhaps a thousand fishing vessels of differing
shapes and sizes, all tied up. During the season, commercial vessels
typically head out to sea for several days at a time. Few if any have
refrigeration facilities on board, so that fish caught at the start of the
voyage are often rotting by the time the ship returns with its haul.
Boats dock at floating platforms equipped with pumping machinery
that sucks up the catch and pipes it over to the factories. The process
of turning it into fishmeal is complex. It involves steam-heating the
raw fish to sterilise it and squeeze out the liquid; separating out the
valuable oil from the rest of the fluid; and drying the heated fishmeal
into pressed cakes. The drying process is highly energy-intensive; the
waste – blood, guts, scales, fat – is repulsively discarded. The leftovers
are disposed of in rudimentary ways; typically it seems by pumping
the raw filth into the sea. The pipes through which the sludge flows
quickly clog up, like fatty arteries. Some processing factories are said
to use caustic soda to flush them out at the end of the season – a toxic
chemical that also ends up in the water. The effect of all this is a seabed
without oxygen: a dead zone.

At the harbour, a small market was in full swing, attracting a posse
of pelicans. The birds stood in a neat little row on the edge of a warehouse roof, their eyes fixed on some rusty blue barrels that contained
fish guts. Every time a trader flung offcuts into the bins there would
be a great flapping of wings. Out of the noisy melee a victor would

emerge with a slimy piece of flesh in its long beak and waddle round the corner to devour it.

We found the sea-clam divers, who led us to their boat, a basic affair with a small motor and no life jackets. On the bow was a huge fisherman's knife, so thick with rust that you could not tell it was once another colour. The benches were sprinkled with gull droppings. I sat on an empty fishmeal sack and we set off out of the harbour. The water was mercifully flat as we headed towards L'Isla Blanca, a guano island not far from the shore, where the seabed remains in reasonable condition.

Out in the bay, pelicans flew low over the boat, showing us their white bellies, and neotropical cormorants swooped and dived for fish. Through my binoculars I spotted a blue-footed booby, common on the Galapagos Islands but not so much around here, and an American oystercatcher. An empty fishmeal bag bobbed past us on the water. The midday sun was ferocious. There was no escape from its unforgiving rays.

As we approached the island, the divers cut the motor. I noticed a greasy film on the water. At first, I assumed it was pollution from our own boat, but the divers told us it was fat from the fishmeal factories. It shimmered gloopy yellow in the sun like the top of a bad takeaway meal. The diver, wearing an old black wetsuit, prepared to go overboard, carrying a small black bucket in which to collect what he could find on the seabed. He would get his oxygen through a plastic pipe leading to a motor on the boat. He plunged in, emerging a few minutes later with his bucket. In it were several dozen small crabs, clams and black snails, as well as a creature that looked like a rubbery yellow snooker ball coated in mucous slime. The diver poured them all onto the floor. The point was made: plenty of life on the seabed here. I signalled my appreciation, then scooped up the crabs and snails, managing to avoid being nipped, and dropped them back into the water. Trying not to wince, I also picked up the mucus-covered thing and sent it on its way too. We headed off towards the bay lined with fishmeal factories.

As we neared the shore, we came close to a number of deserted docking platforms and anchored commercial boats with names like *Susana* and *Mary Carmen*. The diver plunged back in, emerging this time with a bucket full of black gunge. I ran my hands through it, feeling the sludgy, slimy texture. It smelled of sulphur – rotten eggs. I poured it back. I was told that the muck is several metres deep here – too thick to allow life on the seabed any significant recovery when the boats are tied up. It was a total dead zone.

Until the 1990s, nobody bothered collating any data on this environmental disaster. The Peruvian National Fisheries Research Institute now carries out some research. An acoustic study of Ferrola that it undertook in 2008 concluded that there were around 54 million cubic metres of organic matter – toxic sludge – in the bay.

The National University of Santa in Chimbote also has an ongoing research programme. Romulo Aguilar, Dean of the Faculty of Biology at the university, has spent years studying the impact of effluent from fishmeal factories on marine life. We met him at his faculty, where he told us about his work:

> To the south of Chimbote is another bay, called Samanco, which is exactly the same shape and size as the Bay of Ferrola [lined by fishmeal factories]. Geologically, it is so similar as to be an excellent yardstick for how Ferrola could, or should, be. Our tests show that Samanco is still an extremely rich ocean system, with wonderful natural shellbanks and fish, crustaceans and algae. It is very high in biodiversity. In Ferrola, all this is gone.

Aguilar's team has measured what are termed oxygen-demand values in Ferrola Bay. It's a standard way of assessing water-pollution levels. The results showed oxygen-demand values of 56,000 micrograms per litre. I asked him what that meant. 'It shows pollution levels are off the scale,' he replied. Aguilar claims the bay is in such bad shape that even the tiny organisms normally seen as an indicator of high pollution cannot themselves survive. 'We see no sign of life, nothing,' he lamented.

The government has attempted to force the companies to clean up their act, to little effect. While a few are said to have improved their sewage-disposal technology, according to Aguilar most continue to operate much as before, discharging raw waste directly into the bay. Speaking about the use of caustic soda to clean out pipes at the end of each fishing season, he said: 'I have had several rows with the companies at meetings, where they have emphatically denied doing it. However our analysis of the water shows pH values at a level that clearly indicate it's being discharged. I am in no doubt it is going on.'

So thick and raw is the waste as it is pumped out to sea that it has spawned a cottage industry: fat collection. On a beach near some of the processing plants, desperadoes have made holes in the sewage pipes and can be seen siphoning the effluent into a network of vats. When the fat floats to the surface they skim it off and sell it for the equivalent of a few dollars. It sounded a foul and desperate way to make a living. We went to see.

Stefan and our cameraman had been to the beach before with a documentary team from Norway and had never forgotten the experience. They warned me that once I'd been there my boots were likely to be unwearable, so we went to a local market and bought the cheapest footwear we could find before setting off.

The approach to the beach was down a ramshackle lane in the suburbs. We took the car as far as we could and walked the final stretch, through hot sand strewn with bits of concrete, broken bricks and discarded tyres. To either side were fishmeal factories, hidden behind high walls with jagged broken glass along the top and watchtowers at each corner. As we reached the beach, the smell of decaying fish hit me like a punch in the stomach.

A gang of workers sat on a wall and eyed us warily. In front of them was a rudimentary system of tanks and vats, full of yellowy brown liquid. Every surface was coated in sticky black slime. A turkey vulture swooped low over the vats of fat. A pile of rotting fish lay abandoned on a bin bag. It was a squalid place.

The workers were hostile, wanting money. Officially what they were doing was illegal, but their facilities were well established. Far from anyone challenging them, it seemed to us that their operation was actively supported by the fishmeal companies. After lengthy negotiation the foreman agreed to talk to us. He told us that he and his team paid the companies for the right to 'treat' their water. He argued – with some justification – that he and his men were performing a public service by reducing the amount of fat pumped into the sea. He told us more than a thousand people were trying to make a living this way.

We asked whether fishing would be preferable to this dirty work and he laughed bitterly. 'Everything has gone. It's no longer possible.' He was pessimistic about the future, saying that he and his team would all leave Chimbote if they could. 'It is not possible to clean up the bay. This is all we can do. We need help to get out of here. Our children are suffering; they are being poisoned. The only reason we don't leave is because we can't afford to.' His claims of sickness and poisoning of children might sound exaggerated but are well supported by the evidence. Life expectancy in Chimbote is 20 per cent below the national average.

Dr Wilber Torres Chacon works for the department of health in the region. We met him at a nursery school not far from the beach, where he carried out health checks. It was a cute little place, with lots of bright wooden and plastic toys, colourful foam matting on the floor, and a lovely bed for naps under a spotless white mosquito net draped from a pretty hoop. The children wore coloured bibs according to their age. They looked healthy and happy, but Chacon told us all was not as it seemed: 'The fishmeal production activity here causes several health problems: severe respiratory infections, asthma, acute diarrhoea, malnutrition, parasitic diseases . . .' He examined some of the children, pointing out unusual-looking lesions on their skin. 'These children are constantly exposed to fumes from the factories. You can see the blemishes on their skin.'

Malnutrition is widespread in Peru, but rates in the Ancash region are particularly high, at between 20 and 30 per cent of the population.

Though the government has been attempting to tackle the problem for several decades, Chacon said progress was slow. In the last two years, despite increased efforts, rates of malnutrition have dropped by just 2 or 3 per cent.

Among other nutritional programmes, health chiefs and NGOs are trying to encourage locals to eat more fish – a habit that seems to have died with the rise of the fishmeal industry. As little as 1 per cent of the highly nutritious anchoveta caught off Chimbote is likely to end up on dinner plates,[56] a shocking fact, given how desperately the local population needs the protein. 'The population here consumes excessive amounts of carbohydrate, and not nearly enough protein,' the doctor informed us. 'Officials here on the coast are providing the infant population with fish to boost their nutrition, especially anchovies for the protein and non-saturated fats.' He told us that seven out of ten children in Chimbote suffer from skin conditions, with the figure rising to 90 per cent among those living next to fishmeal factories.

Such is the scale of concern about the health problems in Chimbote that some officials now believe the only solution is to move the entire fishmeal production industry out of the city. Chacon spoke of relocating all the factories to an industrial zone, 'far away from the population'. Chimbote's failure to provide adequate nutrition for its own population – a quarter of Peru's infants are malnourished,[57] while the country exports millions of tonnes of fish – is an irony not lost on everyone in the industry. Javier Castro Zabaleta, general secretary of the local fishing trade union, believes that the government needs to educate Peruvians in the value of eating fish instead of turning it into fishmeal for farm animals: 'We don't have a culture of eating fresh fish such as anchovy, even though it's so high in protein and we have it in such abundance. Peruvians are not used to eating darker flesh-coloured fish – we prefer white fish, chicken and other meat. We need to convert the anchoveta industry step by step into an industry for human consumption.'

We met Zabaleta at the union's headquarters on a main street in Chimbote. He sat behind an old wooden desk under a poster of Che

Guevara. Now in his sixties, Zabaleta was a weather-beaten man of the sea. Next to his desk was a ponderous bookcase that looked as if it might keel over at any moment. An old portable fan in the corner barely ruffled the air. It was hot in the room. A fisherman served us Coca-Cola in plastic cups and offered us biscuits.

Zabaleta told us his union represented 1,700 fishermen. In its heyday it had 5,000 members, but many big fishmeal companies now have in-house employee associations. He echoed what the fat collectors had told us about how hard it now was for independent fishermen to make a living: 'Before the fishmeal industry arrived, we used to fish for anchovy four or five miles off the coast. It was very productive and we did two trips a day. Now seventy to eighty per cent of the fishing here is industrial.' Because of overfishing, to find anything 'you need to fish two, three or even five hundred miles offshore. That is illegal for artisanal fishermen – they are only allowed to operate a maximum of fifteen miles offshore.'

He described illegal fishing as a persistent problem, though he said things were improving. In the last five years, the quantity of fish landed in breach of quotas had fallen from 3 million tonnes a year to 600,000 tonnes. 'The authorities don't enforce quotas. Some companies cover up the real weight of fish they unload. Either they don't register it when they bring it into port, or they fix the scales.' He claimed the most disreputable operators hired professionals to beat the system, deliberately underweighing catches by as much as 40 per cent.

Our last meeting in Chimbote was with a local heroine, Maria Elena Foronda Farro, who enjoys celebrity status among many ordinary folk in the town. She has campaigned against the corruption and environmental damage associated with the fishmeal industry in Chimbote since the 1990s. For her pains, she spent a terrifying spell in prison after being falsely accused of belonging to the Peruvian terrorist organisation Shining Path. Convicted and sentenced to twenty years behind bars in 1994, she was released after thirteen months following an international outcry spearheaded by Amnesty

International. Few doubt that her incarceration was due to her outspoken activism.

In 2003 she was awarded the prestigious Goldman Environmental Prize,[58] an international award for outstanding grassroots activists, but it took her two attempts to collect it: the first time she tried to get into America she was turned away at immigration because of her 'terrorism' conviction. Despite offers of asylum from eight countries she has never left Chimbote, where she was born and raised. Her home is two blocks away from a fishmeal company.

Now in her early fifties, Foronda continues to campaign through her organisation Natura to raise environmental standards in the fishmeal industry. She works on a shoestring budget out of a run-down little office in town, helped by a dedicated and loyal team of volunteers. I met her there and we went to a local restaurant to talk over lunch. 'Our first victory was forcing a number of the fishmeal companies to relocate out of the centre of Chimbote,' she told me. 'We managed to get an order against them in 2009, and in 2010 they began to move. It was a big thing – they had to build entirely new plants.' One of the biggest companies reportedly spent £27 million moving its premises. Foronda shrugged off the figure as insignificant relative to industry profits – 'In one season the combined fishmeal industry here makes 1,800 million US dollars profit. There are two fishing seasons a year, so annual profits are double that. Building a new plant is really no big deal. In any case, when they install new technology, they improve their yields.'

According to Foronda, twenty-six companies already located in the industrial area were given until the end of 2010 to clean up their technology, but as of March 2011 only eight had done so. She told me cheerfully that campaigning often meant two steps forward, one step – sometimes two – back. 'Just when we thought we were getting somewhere, the regional government started authorising the building of new low-grade fish-processing plants, arguing that it would create jobs. The national government turned a blind eye when factories opened that were dirtier than ever.'

Her hope is that the industry cleans up its act and begins to reinvest some of its huge revenue in the town and its citizens. 'The fishmeal business has left us without much to live on, plundering our natural resources and failing to put anything back into development in Chimbote. The bay used to be considered the pearl of the South Pacific. Look at it now.' As we talked, a cheerful procession was snaking its way through the streets outside the restaurant. At the front was a brass band, dressed in glorious red and black uniforms. Behind was a raggle-taggle bunch of people of all ages, carrying banners and balloons and tooting klaxons. It was a protest against a local oil company, accused of damaging fish stocks. In Chimbote, it seems, the fishmeal processors were not the only ones seen as villains.

I was so glad to see the back of the place that as we got back on the road to Lima later that afternoon, I was singing. We cranked up the volume on a CD of Eighties rock songs, and I was giving it gusto, only wishing I had my guitar. Chimbote symbolises all that is wrong with factory farming and its long tentacles that reach out across the world. I never wanted to set eyes on the town and its godforsaken industry again.

As dusk fell, we reached the desert. It looked so eerily beautiful it took my breath away. The sun slowly disappeared, turning the sandy mountains rose-purple. The moon hung in the sky. Soon there was nothing to see from the car window but inky black. I was monumentally relieved to be on the way home.

But Peru had one last surprise in store. On the outskirts of Lima, as we pulled away from a road tollbooth, there was a sudden jolt accompanied by a sickening crunch. Somebody had driven into the back of our hire car. Exhausted and overwrought after five hours dodging kamikaze lorry drivers in the dark on the winding desert road, Stefan was in no mood to be messed with. He leapt out of the car, flagged down the offending driver, and an angry confrontation ensued. It soon turned out that the other driver was drunk and refusing to supply us with his details or to stick around. For his part, Stefan was keen not

Selected examples of trade routes linked to industrial farming

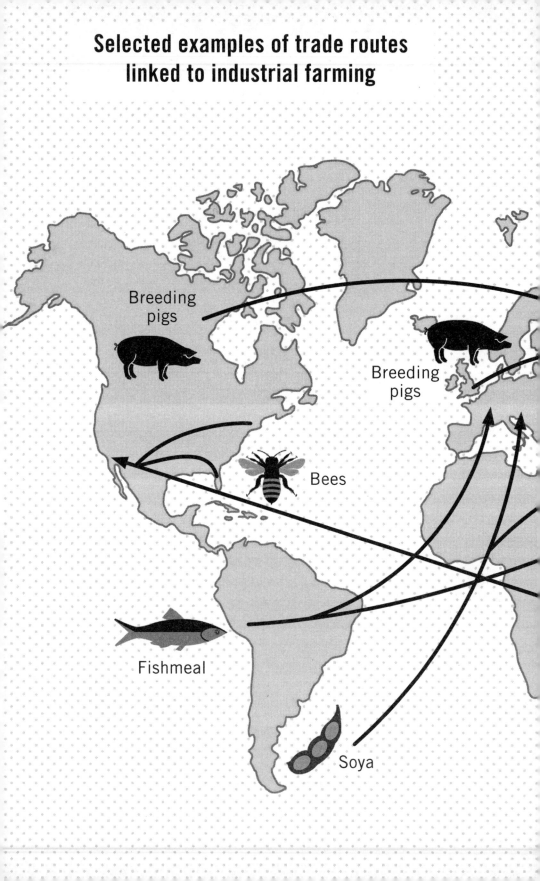

Breeding
pigs

Breeding
pigs

Bees

Fishmeal

Soya

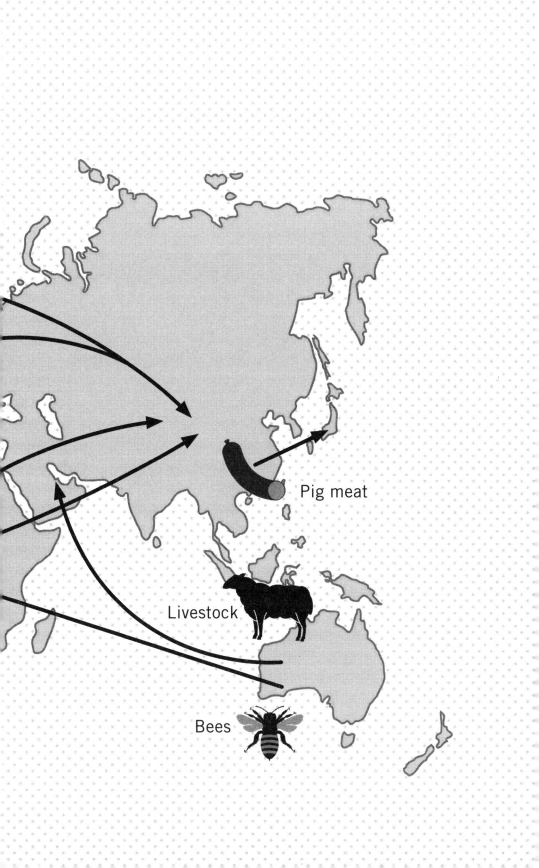

Pig meat

Livestock

Bees

to let him escape, aware that we stood to lose a hefty deposit we'd paid to the hire-car company, Europcar.

In what seemed like a masterstroke, our cameraman was able to swipe the drunk driver's car keys, which he'd left in the ignition while he was talking to Stefan. It looked like we had him cornered. We all hung around waiting for the police. It was almost midnight, and as time ticked by with no sign of the officers, both Stefan and the drunk were getting increasingly angry and impatient. I was horribly aware of the loaded gun in Stefan's pocket. The atmosphere was volatile and tense. I sat in the back of the car, figuring I was best keeping out of it. With no Spanish, there was not much I could do to help. Meanwhile Stefan was on his mobile, trying to get through to Europcar. The drunk, a small, heavy-set, unkempt man in his fifties, kept going back to his own car, disappearing for a few moments, then emerging in a worse temper than before.

It never occurred to us that he might have been attempting to hot-wire the vehicle, until he finally succeeded and roared off down the motorway in a puff of exhaust smoke. Despite it all, we had to laugh. At least Stefan's gun was still in his pocket. It was the last we saw of the drunk, and of the deposit. The only consolation was that we still had his keys.

6

Animal Care

What happened to the vet?

It started with James Herriot, the hero of the best-selling book and TV series *All Creatures Great and Small*. Everyone was charmed by the antics of the handsome young vet as he trundled about in his classic car tending to stricken animals in the Yorkshire Dales. The novels were written decades ago, but the public relations job they did for the veterinary profession was truly extraordinary. The image of the bright-eyed young man ready to battle through snow and floods, wade through manure, be kicked, knocked over and bitten by ungrateful animals and still be polite at the end of it all to their even less grateful owners stuck firmly in the public consciousness, and has never quite gone away.

Yet there is a darker side to the veterinary profession, which is rarely seen by those outside the industry. A growing army of vets do not work in small town surgeries microchipping pet dogs and patching up injured cats, but on farms that bear no resemblance to the picturesque homesteads of Herriot folklore. They often work in dimly lit sheds and in abattoirs, where they prop up the factory-farming system. In these grim settings, the aim is to keep animals alive long enough for profitable slaughter or ensure they continue churning out enough milk or eggs to justify their existence, then to dispatch them with as little ado as possible. The role played by highly respected and supposedly animal-loving professionals in this business reflects the less romantic side of the veterinary profession.

Few vets begin their careers intending to work in such environments, but slaughterhouse jobs have regular hours and the work involves more observation and inspection than physical intervention, meaning that it suits older practitioners and those with bad backs or other work-related ailments. Furthermore, there is a genuine chance to do good, an opportunity to minimise suffering for tens of thousands of animals in the hours before slaughter, a time when they are at risk of pain and suffering.

Jean-Claude Latife, a vet from Brittany, spent nine years working in UK abattoirs. He finally quit in 2010 after being threatened with a butcher's knife by a drug-crazed slaughterman who objected when he paused a production line because of a hygiene concern. I first met him at an animal welfare conference in Brussels. We chatted over dinner and my jaw dropped when I heard his story. Because the incident is subject to ongoing legal action, I'm not using his real name or any details that could identify where he worked. However, in his experience, UK slaughterhouses, widely assumed to boast the highest welfare standards in the world, are riddled with untrained workers who pitch up for work drunk or twitching for the next tea break when they can take another fix of drugs. Not surprisingly, vets are frequently pressurised or intimidated into turning a blind eye when they witness these dangerous men mistreating animals.

It's a far cry from what Latife imagined when he first moved to the UK. As a small-animal vet in France he had developed various medical problems and was advised by doctors to look for a less stressful job. He and his family had fallen in love with the English countryside on holidays, so when a position came up in a slaughterhouse in one of the most beautiful parts of the country, he jumped at the chance: 'The conditions were good – there was no work at the weekends, and there were decent career opportunities. It might sound like the last sort of place a vet would want to work, but I realised that caring for animals isn't just about looking after cats and dogs.'

By law, abattoirs in the UK must have a vet on-site. Their job involves witnessing animals arriving and being unloaded, checking that they are in a fit state to be transported, and that conditions on the lorry are acceptable. Abuses can be reported to the enforcement authorities.[1] They also keep an eye on how animals are handled before they are killed and whether they are properly stunned before slaughter. So-called 'missed stuns', which even in the UK can run at between 5 and 10 per cent at badly run abattoirs, are a huge source of suffering and can also be reported. The other part of the job involves leading a team of meat inspectors who monitor cleanliness and the processing of carcasses to rule out any risk to health and hygiene.[2]

Latife soon adapted to his new line of work in what he describes as a 'very very hostile environment'. 'You are surrounded by death, noise, shit and concrete, but it's something you get used to after a while. I felt I was playing an important role in a place where there is a huge risk of animals suffering, at every stage of the process.' It was the behaviour of rank-and-file workers that shocked him:

It's the same in most slaughterhouses. Monday mornings are the worst. That's when new foreign workers arrive. Often they don't have a clue what an animal is, and have had no training at all for the job.

As the vet, you have the power to stop the production line if you're not happy with anything you see, but it is a huge responsibility, and it's not easy to do. You might have fifty people working on the line, and if you stop it for some reason, delaying the kill for an hour or two, it's not just the workers who are upset, it's also the inspectors, the managers, even the supermarkets, who are waiting for their delivery of meat. The workers hate it because it means they lose money, or get a shorter break, and the bosses hate it because any delay in production has financial implications. The result is that you are under a lot of pressure and are pushed to accept situations that are far from ideal.

Latife grew quickly hardened to being insulted by workers frustrated when he questioned procedures and caused delays. He says he has a good sense of humour, realised there was no point in complaining, and just let it wash over him. However, when a slaughterman who had previously served six months behind bars threatened to kill him, he knew it was time to quit:

> In this particular slaughterhouse, around half the staff were British; the other half were eastern European, mostly Polish. The Polish workers were often drunk, and many of the British workers were on drugs. One day, a guy I normally got on well with went crazy. I knew he took drugs, and that day he took something during his tea break. When he came back, I noticed that there was not enough space between two carcasses, which raises a risk of cross-contamination. It meant stopping the line. When I told him we had to stop the line, he got very mad, I think because it delayed his next fix. He started insulting me and threatening me with a knife, and threatening to hurt my wife and children. At the same time another guy came at me with a knife. It was terrifying. I stopped the line anyway and reported the incident. I realised it was no longer a safe place for me to work.

Latife's account of the calibre of UK slaughterhouse workers, and the shameful way some incentivise staff to cut corners in animal welfare by paying them 'per kill' rather than hourly rates, is a damning insight into an aspect of meat eating that most people prefer not to think about: the way animals are treated when they come to be killed. What he experienced was not an isolated incident. Undercover filming in nine British slaughterhouses between 2009 and 2011 revealed evidence of cruelty and alleged lawbreaking in most of them, including animals being kicked, beaten and burned with cigarettes.[3] An exposé of twenty-five abattoirs in France uncovered rough handling and poor stunning practices.[4]

Given their professional status, vets are uniquely positioned to make a positive difference. Latife's experiences suggest that many are cowed into keeping their mouths shut about routine abuses, only intervening over the most flagrant breaches of standards. And the questionable role of vets in propping up factory farming is not confined to the end of the process. They play a vital part at every stage, often treating and preventing disease, but also acquiescing in a system in which suffering is inbuilt. Vets who are uncomfortable with factory farming and choose to have no part in it accuse colleagues who make a living on such premises of becoming institutionalised, seeing the animals they treat as little more than production units. These vets may have started their careers with ideals, but industrial farms are often big businesses where the bottom line is what counts. In time, some vets who work on such farms are affected by this culture, approaching sick farm animals as if they were faulty machines. A quick and dispassionate judgement is often made by farmer and vet together, much like car mechanics sizing up a broken-down car: either the machines are worth fixing, and they are treated; or they are not, and they are written off.

The harder farmers push animals beyond their natural limit, and the more closely animals are confined, often the greater the risk of disease and the heavier the reliance on vets to keep herds alive. Their weapon of choice is antibiotics. According to Dil Peeling, who qualified as a vet in the UK but spent much of his career working in developing countries:

> A vet's worth is now measured by his or her ability to deliver on production and animal health – not welfare. It is difficult to persuade vets who have invested so much of their careers in propping up intensive farming to turn their back on such systems. You're asking the high priests of the livestock ministry to reject everything they know. As far as they're concerned, this is how things have always been done.

Now working for Compassion in World Farming, Peeling believes that the industry is geared towards rewarding vets who focus on farm animal health in terms of how it relates to production, rather than seeing the welfare of the animals as an end in itself.

No vets ever produce scientific papers on anal glands in dogs, though one of the commonest things they see in their surgeries is dogs with itchy bottoms. It's not sexy and it isn't going to get them international recognition. Vets are scientists, and scientists are rewarded for writing scientific papers and presenting them at symposiums. Certain diseases are more fashionable than others, and the sexiest of all are diseases like foot-and-mouth disease, which impact on animal exports.

All seven of the UK's veterinary colleges incorporate animal welfare into the curriculum, as has been compulsory in the EU since the late 1970s.[5] The vast majority of vets who work on farms in this country genuinely care about the animals they work with and are upset when they witness suffering. They would alert the RSPCA to flagrant welfare issues.

Alastair Hayton is one of the UK's leading cattle vets and works on a variety of dairy farms in Somerset, some with over 1,000 cows. He insists that large farms do not necessarily go hand in hand with poor welfare and argues that the quality of management is more important than the scale of the operation when it comes to welfare. He kindly arranged to show my co-author, Isabel Oakeshott, around two very different dairy farms in Somerset where he works: one organic, the other one of the largest indoor dairies in the UK, with 1,000 cows, that I would later visit personally. He is happy with conditions on both: 'I am convinced there is no right or wrong system, only right and wrong management. Big is not necessarily bad. I have seen some very bad practice on small farms. The key is the individual farmer – how well they manage their farm, and whether their facilities are appropriate for the number of animals being kept.'

Hayton is adamant that most UK farmers genuinely care about their livestock, and have a strong vested interest in keeping them in prime condition: 'I have seen plenty of farmers cry when they've had to have a sick cow shot. A healthy herd is a productive herd.' However, he acknowledges that intensive farming is highly fine-tuned and that some farmers are increasing the size of indoor-reared herds without extending their barns:

> It's like these animals are on a mountain ridge. The higher the yield farmers are going for, the harder it is to keep the animals from falling off that ridge. A lot of farmers know that the housing they're providing is inadequate, but don't have the money to invest in something better. They know they need to sort it out, but financially it can be very difficult. But there are also welfare compromises with cows on grass.

I agree with Hayton that good husbandry and management is the key to getting the best out of any system. However, the reality is that some systems have only very limited scope for decent welfare. Take barren battery cages; they generally provide each hen with only enough space to stand on. They spend their entire lives standing on bare wire and can never flap their wings. The system is so intrinsically limited and restrictive that the birds are bound to suffer frustration and ill health. The fact is that no amount of stockmanship will create decent welfare in those cages. In short, it is a system with appalling low welfare potential.

By contrast, free-range systems for hens have high welfare potential. The birds have room to flap about; they feel the sun on their backs and the ground beneath their feet. The system provides scope for the hens to lead decent lives. Of course the human element is still important in unlocking the basic potential. If standards of husbandry and management are poor, or the birds are neglected, then they could still suffer. However, at least there's a chance for the animals to have a decent life.

I've spoken to vets who categorically reject the notion that colleagues working on factory farms in the UK perform a disservice to the animals they treat. However, others tell a different story. I recently talked to a young vet who decided to go into the profession after working on a small organic dairy farm as a teenager but was shocked by the realities of large-scale agriculture that she observed when she began her training:

I saw things that really upset me: calves castrated without local anaesthetic; animals prescribed antibiotics without proper diagnoses. A lot of the older vets, the men, have different attitudes that just aren't right today, but they're the people you're working under, and there's a lot of pressure to do things their way. Then there's the farmers who don't want to pay for blood tests or extra visits and might just keep a bottle [of pills] on the side . . .

She gave up practising as a small-animal vet two years after qualifying, in order to campaign for better farm animal welfare.

Katherine Jennings, a Norfolk vet who completed her studies at London's Royal Veterinary College a couple of years ago, agrees that the reality 'can be a bit grim'. She has dealt with pneumonia outbreaks in cramped, poorly ventilated veal sheds and flu epidemics among chickens, both with extremely high mortality rates, but doubts she has seen the worst of it. 'I don't go to the big farms because it's cheaper for them just to have their own vet on-site,' she told me.

There are other so-called experts working on factory farms whose role raises welfare issues, like the unqualified technicians many farmers use to perform routine tasks such as foot trimming and artificial insemination. They are cheaper than hiring a professional, are common in the US, and are becoming increasingly popular in the UK. Then there's the army of 'nutritionists' who ply their trade on factory farms. Although some are independent, most are linked to animal-feed companies, and have a close financial interest in recommending particular diets for livestock.

While there is an enduring tension between business-minded older vets and more animal welfare-conscious recent graduates, progress is slowly being made. Dr Anabela Pinto, a Research Associate in Animal Welfare at St Edmund's College, Cambridge, believes the demographics are helpful, but cautions that more vets are now coming to the UK from overseas. 'Vets have more compassion now. Older vets tend to be male and quite stiff-upper-lipped, but now the majority of veterinary students are women drawn to the job because they love animals. But there are foreign vets working in some of the more industrialised processes who won't necessarily have come from the same background.'

Some vets believe that animal welfare is hampered by the attitude of veterinary colleges towards organic farming. Some organic techniques could be used by non-organic farmers to reduce vet bills and dependency on drugs. Forward-thinking vets promote so-called herd health programmes, encouraging farmers to consider lighting, medication, rations, pasture and a range of other factors as part of a holistic approach to animal health. However, vet colleges do not appear to see any of this as a priority. Though students are taught not to overmedicate, they say lecturers often give the impression that organic farming is primitive. It seems there is an inbuilt bias towards intensive farming within the veterinary profession – hardly surprising, perhaps, when it provides so much employment.

Addressing the issue is as much about understanding what 'animal welfare' actually means as it is about changing the nature of farming or what it means to be a vet. It's not the same thing as simply animal health. Take battery hens again. Apologists often claim the birds wouldn't lay eggs if they weren't happy. Yet the truth is they're genetically programmed through selective breeding to lay about 300 eggs a year, and will do so whatever conditions they are kept in, so long as there's food and water. The mere fact that farm animals continue to function does not mean that they are 'happy' or well.

So where does farm size fit in? Does big have to mean bad? In principle, the answer is that it is not the scale that matters, but the nature of the operation. I've seen backyard farms in China that were just as awful as any mega-operation. Yet when farming becomes divorced from the land, problems are far more likely to arise.

Mega-dairies are a case in point. No farm animal works harder than the high-yielding dairy cow. In peak lactation, her body is being forced to work at a similar rate to a human jogging a marathon every day. No wonder their lives are so short. The average high-yielder often lives only for three lactations before being culled.

Thirty years ago, the average UK dairy cow was producing 5,000 litres of milk a year – no mean feat when you consider that beef cows, milking at a more natural level, produce only a thousand litres or so. However, average dairy cows today yield more like 7,000 litres a year. They need to be fed high-energy concentrated food to avoid 'milking off their own back' and growing weak and emaciated. Higher-yielding cows are under even more pressure. They churn out an incredible 10,000 litres or more a year. At this level, they simply can't survive on grass, can't possibly graze enough to keep up with the demands of such heavy lactation. So their diet is geared towards very high-energy food – grain, not grass.

It becomes unprofitable to turn cows out to pasture where they simply cannot take in nutrients fast enough. The result is the 'zero-grazing' system, in which cows are kept indoors for much of their lives. Once they're confined indoors, all their food is brought to them, and the system is disconnected from the land. If the herd size then rises from the UK average of about 100 animals to 'mega-dairy' proportions of thousands, this takes things beyond the carrying capacity of the land that the herd started out on. And from there, there's no way back.

In essence, the vets involved have become servants of the industrial farm machine, the technicians called in to fix things before they break down, to patch things up and keep the system going. Their job is to keep the animals healthy enough for long enough to be productive. They cannot afford to antagonise their clients by accusing them of cruelty, albeit institutional. To do so would be professional suicide. And so the system remains self-reinforcing.

A whole industry has grown up around factory farming, from breed companies developing the latest types of animal, to the feed companies with their latest formulas, the pharmaceutical companies with their wares advertised so prominently in farming journals, and the equipment manufacturers. Scientists are employed to build the evidence base to support the new way, often paid for by vested interests. I remember a leading member of the US egg producers' association beating his breast at a London conference, pronouncing that there were cabinets full of evidence to show that battery cages were best for the welfare of hens. It was a defensive statement made just after Europe had voted to ban the system due to animal welfare concerns. With so much behind it, it is not surprising that industrial farming has taken off with the momentum of a juggernaut.

Among the casualties are rank-and-file farmers who are often forced to produce more for lower prices. In any other industry, oversupply with plummeting prices would elicit a curb on production. In intensive farming, falling margins all too often trigger the next round in expansion; units get bigger and so too does the amount of suffering and damage to the environment, in the hope of maintaining income; and so the treadmill moves on, yet faster, often with greater debts to service. The inevitable outcome is that many farmers can't keep up and have gone out of business.

Alternative voices and approaches are often pigeonholed as being for niche markets, or they get shouted down. The status quo is further reinforced by the difficulty of making meaningful comparisons between the economics of different systems. After all, the industrial system is all too often supported by the distorting effect of agricultural policy, with its subsidies and incentives. And so the juggernaut hurtles on.

Fast-food chains and supermarkets have grown up and prospered in the wake of industrial agriculture: they sell cheap and plentiful ingredients from animals 'processed' through fewer but bigger slaughterhouses within a system increasingly geared around centralised supply and distribution. The industrial way has no doubt suited companies looking to trade at scale with standardised products. There can be no escaping their dominance in the marketplace; in Britain, five supermarket companies account for four out of every five pounds spent on food. The US retail giant Walmart is the world's number one supermarket, while Britain's biggest, most widespread store, Tesco, ranks third. In the restaurant business, McDonald's is the world's number one by a big margin. Yum! Brands, the owner of KFC and

Pizza Hut, is runner-up. Farmers are drawn to the massive markets that these companies represent, yet complain about their buying power and ability to drive a hard bargain.

How often have I heard commentators talking about the latest revelation in the food industry saying: 'I blame the supermarkets.' Yes, their business is commercial success – making profits for shareholders and investors. But that doesn't mean a company must, by definition, do bad things. John Mackey, CEO of Wholefoods Market, believes that most modern economists continue to see the purpose of business as being to transform factors of production into profit for the benefit of the investors. As he puts it: 'Corporations are probably the most influential institutions in the world today and yet many people do not believe that they can be trusted.'[6] Each time another scandal comes to light, be it in the oil, banking or food sectors, this feeling of mistrust is reinforced.

In the UK and Europe, the horsemeat scandal of 2013 saw consumer confidence and share prices hit hard. It also drove home the message that the world of business has become a much more sophisticated place, that businesses have to take account of interdependencies, be they societal or ecological. Writ large was the need to take the integrity of supply chains seriously if company bosses wanted to sleep well at night. Integrity doesn't stop at the basics: knowing where products come from and what they contain. It also requires being sure of the quality of products, be they meat, milk or fish; that there are no nasty surprises or questionable ethics lurking within and waiting to be found out. It is something that leading businesses are increasingly coming to recognise.

I saw this firsthand when Compassion in World Farming launched a new league table of food companies aimed at investors, based on how seriously they take farm animal welfare. As I rose to my feet in the heart of London's financial district, I wondered whether hard-nosed financial types would get it. Would they not ask what animal welfare has got to do with good investment decisions? I needn't have worried. Riding on the back of Horsegate, no one in the room needed convincing. They could see the danger in not addressing serious issues of public interest and transparency. The launch of the league table made headline news in the UK's *Financial Times* newspaper. Minds had been alerted to the perils of cutting corners.

The big supermarkets, restaurant chains and the like have become society's 'super-consumers'. They are seldom tied to some particular system or way of producing food. They themselves can be much more fleet of foot, able to choose what best suits their business and their customers. It is no accident that in the twenty-first century, 'super-consumer' companies are increasingly taking the lead by changing their policies for reasons like the environment or animal welfare. At Compassion in World Farming, I have made it a priority as CEO to assist businesses looking to do good things by changing policies. That is why we run an awards scheme that celebrates companies pledging to cut out whole swathes of cruelly produced food – committing to selling or using only cage-free eggs for example. I am proud that my organisation works with companies who have changed their buying habits in a way that brings better lives to hundreds of millions of animals. Rather than taking the one-dimensional view that business, big or small, is the cause of the problem, I see business as a key component in achieving change from the industrial model that has gone way too far down the track of putting profit before feeding people properly.

Governments will continue to have a role in shaping how things are done, be it through legislation or how they dole out public subsidies or incentives; but businesses can move far more quickly and decisively than governments. While leading businesses offer the scope to be part of the solution and governments in Europe have banned some of the worst forms of farm animal cruelty, the sad truth is that industrial agriculture still has a stranglehold in much of the developed world. And with industrial farming often comes an attitude that animals are mere units of production, a means to make a profit. James Herriot once said he hoped to help people realise how 'totally helpless animals are, how dependent on us, trusting as a child must that we will be kind and take care of their needs . . . [They] are an obligation put on us, a responsibility we have no right to neglect, nor to violate by cruelty.'[7] One can only wonder what he would make of what has happened to the British countryside in the last few decades, as pigs and chickens disappeared from fields into factory farms.

III
HEALTH

The Tower Wing at Guy's, London, is the world's tallest hospital building. Its thirty-four floors look down over a labyrinth of hospital wings and office blocks connected by long whitewashed corridors. The bustling reception area throngs with patients and staff. It is one of the country's oldest teaching hospitals: the in-house cafés teem with medical students relaxing after lectures.

Guy's Hospital stands in the heart of the capital like a monument to Aneurin Bevan's National Health Service, now a much-loved national institution, founded following the landslide Labour victory after the Second World War.[1] It is now the largest publicly funded health service on the planet and employs a staggering 1.7 million people, said to be second only to the massed ranks of employees of the Walmart supermarket chain, the Chinese army and the Indian railway. In 1948 it was launched with a budget of £437 million – equivalent to £9 billion at today's value. Today its budget is more than £100 billion a year. Since Bevan's day, life expectancy has increased dramatically,[2] and many deadly diseases can now be prevented or cured.

Yet new threats to health have emerged. Certain potentially fatal conditions – cancer, diabetes and cardiovascular disease – are far more prevalent. Over coffee in the shadow of the Tower Wing, Dr Michael Antoniou, a molecular biologist involved in developing gene medicines, speculated on the possible causes of this new wave of illness. A scientist with a wide-ranging interest in human health, he singled out cancer as a particularly interesting case. One in three people now get this awful disease. 'This is not just down to people living longer or to better detection,' he suggested. 'The incidence is going up due to environmental factors.'

So what has happened since the middle of the last century to trigger such a change? Antoniou believes that farming is partly – even largely – to blame, having become dominated by an industrial approach reliant on chemical pesticides and fertilisers.

Meanwhile there is an obesity crisis, epidemic in developed countries. Some blame diets high in saturated fats, such as cheap red meat, as well as lack of exercise. At the same time, more and more antibiotics are being deployed to prevent and treat disease in animals on factory farms. Evidence continues to emerge on the link between this dubious practice and the emergence of drug-resistant superbugs and new killer diseases.

The big question is: are factory farms making us sick?

7

Bugs 'n' Drugs

The threat to public health

PENICILLIN FOR PIGS

There was only a small audience for the health minister as he rose to his feet to tell the House of Commons about an exciting new discovery in America. It was midweek, 7.35 pm on 13 May 1953, and as usual at that time of day, most honourable members were otherwise engaged enjoying a pre-dinner tipple in the Houses of Parliament bars or smoking cigars on the Terrace. Winston Churchill was prime minister, Ian Fleming had just published his first James Bond novel, *Casino Royale*, and everyone was looking forward to the coronation of Queen Elizabeth II.

It's probably not surprising that a debate on a new piece of legislation, the Therapeutic Substances (Prevention of Misuse) Bill, attracted little interest among MPs. Aside from two government ministers, just six members spoke in the debate that night – probably the only ones who bothered turning up – and the bill was nodded through to its next stage after just fifty minutes. For health minister Iain Macleod, the poor turn-out was not unwelcome. He and his colleague George Nugent, a junior agriculture minister, didn't think the legislation they were presenting was particularly controversial, describing it as a 'little bill'.

The first part was designed to give the government more control over an array of promising but potentially dangerous new medicinal drugs that were being developed at the time. The part Macleod was more excited about was the second clause – dubbed 'penicillin for pigs'. It proposed to give farmers a new right to feed antibiotics to farm animals. He told MPs the Americans had discovered that putting a tiny amount of antibiotics in pig feed could have a 'most remarkable effect' on their growth. 'The amount of antibiotic is minute – a proportion between two and twenty parts in a million,' he said excitedly.

The health minister saw little to worry about. He had been assured by the Medical Research Council that there could be 'no adverse affect whatsoever upon human beings'. This was, he felt, 'mainly an agricultural matter'. Some of those present were more prescient. Hugh Linstead, the then MP for Putney, felt that allowing farmers to give their animals antibiotics to promote growth was 'entering into unknown country'.

> We have not been doing it long enough, I feel, to know what effect it will produce in the long term in herds and on meat, and indeed, on human beings who eat the meat . . . This drug has acquired a reputation as an efficient and magic cure-all, and particularly in the veterinary field, there is a real danger that if farmers can get hold of penicillin without having to pay the fee of a veterinary surgeon, they will be tempted to use it carelessly and in a widespread way on their flocks.

He wasn't the only politician to warn of the risks associated with giving one of the most important and powerful medicines available for human use to farm animals. Dr Barnett Stross, MP for Stoke-on-Trent Central, saw the potential for disaster:

> We are really treading into strange country. If pigs are fed in this way, new types of bacteria may evolve and thrive which are resistant to the penicillin, which the pigs are eating regularly in their food . . . Should that arise, it would mean first that we should lose the benefits that we are now about to gain . . . if there be migration

of the bacteria to humans we may find ourselves in trouble. I do not want to frighten anybody, but these are matters we may look at.

He sounded a further alarm bell:

We should remember an experiment in America which gave the lead to so much of this work nowadays. They found that another chemical substance, an oestrogen – a type of ovarian hormone – could be used to fatten table poultry. It produced birds with large breasts which were very succulent and they made a much greater delicacy on the table. What they did not know, of course, when they offered those birds to people in expensive restaurants, and no doubt to Senators and Congressmen, was that the oestrogen remains in the breast of the chicken and causes, in men only I am glad to say, sterility, which is a very serious matter.

The official parliamentary record, Hansard, records that Stross's warning was greeted with guffaws.[1] What a pity that the MPs who attended the debate did not take him more seriously. Fast-forward sixty years, and events have unfolded almost exactly as Linstead and Stross predicted. Antibiotics, the 'wonder drug' of the medicine cabinet, are now so widely used and abused on farms that they are losing their potency in human medicine. And just as Stross foresaw, science is struggling to keep pace with the speed at which bacteria are adapting to resist them.

In his annual report in 2008, Sir Liam Donaldson, the UK's then chief medical officer, warned that bacteria were becoming so resistant to antibiotics that 'In some diseases . . . the last line of defence has been reached.'[2] So acute is the situation that the Director General of the World Health Organization (WHO), Dr Margaret Chan, warned on World Health Day in 2011 of a 'post-antibiotic era, in which many common infections will no longer have a cure and once again, kill unabated'.[3] In such a scenario there would be no effective treatment for a range of killer diseases, such as typhoid, tuberculosis, pneumonia, meningitis, tetanus, diphtheria, syphilis and gonorrhoea. Of course, the misuse of antibiotics in human medicine is a big part of the problem. Nevertheless, the excessive use of antibiotics on farms is helping to bring this medical Armageddon closer.

Penicillin, the first mass-produced antibiotic, was first used experimentally in farm animals in 1942, before it was widely available to doctors. Studies showed that hens fed low doses of the drug laid more eggs and sows produced more surviving piglets.[4] No wonder farmers were so keen. For a while, it seemed there was no dark side to the magic. The first warning sign cropped up in the 1960s, when there were several serious outbreaks of salmonella. Thousands of people were hospitalised and at least four children died. It was the world's first recorded 'superbug' resistant to a range of drugs.

It was clear by now that every dose of antibiotics given to a person or animal was a chance for resistant bacteria to develop. The greatest risk came when people or animals were given low doses of the drug, as was happening on farms. These were the ideal conditions for bacteria to fine-tune their resistance, and there was every probability that the powerful new bacteria were being transferred from animals to people.

In 1968 the UK government launched an official inquiry into the problem, led by a distinguished biologist, Professor Michael Swann.[5] His committee clearly wanted to ban all non-essential use of medically important antibiotics in agriculture.[6] Little came of it. The then government succumbed to industry pressure and allowed farmers to carry on as before. Swann's committee also called for a ban on advertising antibiotics to farmers, pointing out that if drug companies could persuade farmers that their livestock would perform better with certain pills, farmers would put pressure on vets to prescribe the drugs. That recommendation was also blocked by industry lobbying. Four decades on, the UK remains the only country in the EU to allow direct advertising of antibiotics to farmers.[7]

People have been sounding the alarm about this for years. The world's public-health experts, from the EU, the US and the WHO, agree that resistant bacteria from food animals are being transmitted to people. High-level public-health authorities including the European Medicines Agency and the European Food Safety Authority have issued stark warnings about the danger, arguing that it is essential to curb antibiotic use in farming before it is too late. Yet the veterinary drugs industry and factory-farming lobby continue to dispute the science and resist any clampdown.

The quantity of antibiotics used by the livestock industry is enormous. By the turn of the century, approximately half of all antibiotics produced in the world were destined for food animals.[8] According to one estimate, 80 per cent of antibiotic use in America is on farms, 70 per cent of the total to boost growth or prevent disease rather than to treat it.[9] In theory, the use of antibiotic growth promoters is now banned in the EU – though some farmers have found a simple way round the law, using low doses to ward off disease, whilst also boosting growth. In America and elsewhere the practice stays legal and widespread.

Of course antibiotics and other veterinary medicines should be used to treat genuine illness in farm animals; few would argue with that. But the fact is that precious antibiotics are being squandered to prop up an inherently bad and disease-ridden system. Intensive farms are breeding grounds for disease, because they keep legions of animals in very close proximity. The European Medicines Agency has described factory farms as places that provide 'favourable conditions for selection, spread and persistence of antimicrobial-resistant bacteria'.[10]

Factory farms actually promote disease. When pathogens – both bacteria and viruses – can find an endless supply of hosts to infect among crowded animals, they do not die out. Viruses can mutate as they infect a succession of different animals, growing more virulent, and potentially developing the ability to infect people and be transmissible between people. To make matters worse, because of the miserable conditions in which they are reared, factory-farmed animals are typically stressed, depressing their immune systems. Being trucked and shipped around heightens the stress. Studies have shown that when animals are moved, they shed increasing amounts of bacteria and virus particles,[11] meaning that more are infected at the end of the journey than were infected at the outset. If the journey is to a slaughterhouse, the pathogens can migrate to meat.

As chickens, cows and pigs are housed in ever-closer confinement and pushed further beyond their natural capabilities, farmers have grown more and more reliant on antibiotics to prop up the system. This usually involves giving low, sub-therapeutic doses of drugs to animals through their feed or water. Treatment often lasts for several weeks. The aim is to compensate for the sickly environment the animals are kept in.

Dairy cows are prime targets. In a practice known as 'dry cow therapy', they are routinely given antibiotic infusions in their udders to prevent them getting mastitis. 'Blanket' dry cow therapy, in which all dairy cows are treated this way during the two-month period that they stop producing milk ahead of calving again, is widespread in Europe, with the exception of organic operations. Dairy cows receive an average of two courses of treatment a year.

Pigs receive similar treatment. On factory farms, they are typically separated from their mothers at four weeks old, so that the sow can conceive again quickly. Under more natural conditions, sows would wean their young at three to four months of age, when their immune systems are more robust. Pigs weaned at one month old, the minimum age under EU law, are far more vulnerable to serious infection, so many intensive pig farmers start adding antibiotics to their feed once they are weaned. Often they continue to be given medicated feed of one sort or another at intervals throughout their six-month lives.

Not all livestock farms are hooked on antibiotics, and a strong lobby within the community itself argues for drug-free farming. I talked to Richard Young, a farmer with an encyclopedic knowledge of antibiotics and the perils of not using them wisely. His farm is in one of the loveliest parts of the Cotswolds. His cattle graze on rich pasture under oak trees over six hundred years old. He is in no doubt that farming can kick its drug dependency:

There has been little public scrutiny of farm antibiotic use for over a decade, yet during that time we have seen farmers dramatically

increase their use of antibiotics . . . critically important in human
medicine, and we have also seen the development of several serious
antibiotic-resistant bugs in farm animals which are passing to humans
on food and in other ways. It is high time that the government took
this problem seriously. Organic farmers have shown it is entirely
possible to raise healthy animals with minimal use of antibiotics. We
could immediately start a Europe-wide programme of change to look
after animals in ways that naturally keep them healthy.

Where antibiotics are used on farms to treat sick animals, this usually
involves administering high doses of drugs for relatively short periods.
On many intensive farms, if a few animals are ill, the whole flock or
herd gets the drugs, sick or not. The cross-over between the classes of
antibiotics used on farms and those used by doctors has serious implications for public health – as those who catch so-called 'superbugs'
discover.

Simon Sparrow was just seventeen months old when he died in the
US in 2004 of the killer superbug MRSA. Unlike many victims of
methicillin-resistant *Staphylococcus aureus*, he didn't contract the bug
during a hospital stay. The day before he passed away, the toddler
woke up with a fever and was disorientated. His parents took him to
the paediatric emergency room at their local hospital to have him
checked over, but the doctors weren't that worried.[12] According to his
mother, Dr Everly Macario, they ran a few standard tests and thought
he might be asthmatic.[13] She was not reassured:

I could tell something was really wrong given how irritable Simon
was . . . he truly was inconsolable. When my husband came to
pick us up, [he] noticed Simon's lips were blue . . . We went back
in and pointed this out to the doctors. They once again measured
his oxygen level and informed us he was within normal range. We
went home and gave Simon some albuterol [a treatment for
asthma] via an inhaler. When we did this, Simon's eyes rolled back
in his head in a way that really alarmed us. But we said to ourselves:

'He'll be fine – he's just sick like any other kid his age gets sick; he'll be fine . . .'[14]

When Simon's breathing began to change, Dr Macario, herself a Harvard-educated public-health expert,[15] called a paediatrician friend, holding the phone to her son's nose and mouth so that the friend could hear. Her friend told her to call the emergency number, 911, straight away. Simon was rushed back to hospital. 'As soon as Simon was wheeled into the ER, doctors hooked him up to everything imaginable. And I kept hearing: "Your child is very, very sick. Your child is very, very sick." At this point, I became almost hysterical,' Dr Macario recalled.[16]

Simon's condition deteriorated fast. His heart raced, his blood pressure crashed, and his lungs filled with fluid. He was pronounced dead at 12.45 pm the following day. No cause of death was given.

Two months later, an autopsy informed Dr Macario and her husband that their son had died from MRSA, probably 'community acquired'. In her words: 'It seems unfathomable that a healthy, hearty and beautiful little boy could have such a bacterium – one that attacked his organs by releasing lethal toxins – and in less than twenty-four hours was gone. MRSA took my son swiftly and totally.'

Following Simon's death, Dr Macario launched a campaign for action to combat the spread of MRSA. She is now the public face of Moms for Antibiotic Awareness, an American-based pressure group, as well as co-founder of the MRSA Research Centre at the University of Chicago. Moms for Antibiotic Awareness is sponsored by the Pew Charitable Trust, an organisation that has highlighted the damage done by factory farms, including their role in rendering antibiotics less effective.[17]

Every year 25,000 people die in the EU from infections caused by drug-resistant micro-organisms. The European Commission estimates it costs the EU economy at least 1.5 billion euros a year. The Commission has described antibiotic resistance as 'an important, largely unresolved issue in public health'.[18]

If a disease is antibiotic-resistant, it means initial treatment is less likely to be effective. The consequence is more severe illness, more hospitalisation and higher death rates. Doctors are forced to use more expensive and complicated drugs that may have worse side effects. Young children are particularly vulnerable.

It is easy to imagine how antibiotic-resistant bacteria can be passed from animals to humans through their meat, but that is only one of the ways it happens. The bacteria can be passed on to people who work with infected animals, through manure or even in airborne particles. The bacteria can then spread further from person to person.

Of the so-called superbugs, MRSA is the most notorious. Until a few years ago, it was found almost exclusively in hospitals. They have responded vigorously to the threat through better hygiene, and infection rates on wards are now falling. However, the bug is now striking people who have had no contact with hospitals, like baby Simon. There have been outbreaks of so-called 'community acquired' MRSA in many countries, including the UK, US, France, Germany, Switzerland, the Netherlands, America, Canada, Australia, New Zealand and Japan.[19]

A Soil Association report tells how in 2004 a previously unknown strain of MRSA, called MRSA ST398 (or NT-MRSA), was identified in pigs and began to spread to people. The first recorded cases of human colonisation by 'pig' MRSA were in a Dutch baby girl and her parents, who were pig farmers. Now half of all Dutch pig farmers are thought to carry the new strain – 760 times the average rate in the wider population.[20] Tests suggest MRSA is often present in raw meat. It was in 35 per cent of turkey samples inspected in the Netherlands, and at least 10 per cent of chicken, pigmeat and beef.[21]

It's no surprise that factory-farmed pigs are generating superbugs. They get more frequent doses of antibiotics than any other farm animal. The European Food Safety Authority believes MRSA ST398 is probably 'widespread' in the food-animal population, 'most likely in all Member States with intensive animal production'.[22] Dutch scientists and government officials have no hesitation in pointing the finger at the intensive pig industry and its reliance on antibiotics for the rise and rapid spread of farm-animal MRSA.

In June 2011, the respected medical journal *The Lancet Infectious Diseases* published findings of the first-ever documented cases of MRSA in British farm animals. Scientists found fifteen cases of a completely new type of MRSA in milk from English dairy farms. It's already infecting people in England and Scotland – though not from drinking milk, as the pasteurisation process kills bacteria.[23]

MRSA is just one threat to human health created by antibiotic use on factory farms. Rising numbers of food-poisoning cases are now antibiotic-resistant, which means that catching these bugs can threaten life. Just how many people fall victim to food poisoning every year is hard to assess; as most people don't bother reporting it, official statistics represent only a fraction of the true number of cases. The UK government department Defra (Department for Environment, Food and Rural Affairs) estimates that there are between five and nine times as many cases as officially recorded.[24] In 2009, there were almost 200,000 reported cases of campylobacter in the EU and around 109,000 cases of salmonella.[25] The main sources were poultry meat, pigmeat and eggs. The real annual figure for campylobacter and salmonella cases in the EU may be more than 2 million.

Across the EU there were also 3,573 cases of dangerous toxic strains of *Escherichia coli* (*E. coli*), such as *E. coli* 0157. Defra has said that *E. coli* 0157 is 'widespread in cattle in the UK'.[26] Other types of *E. coli* now offer greater resistance to antibiotics; in the UK, 12 per cent of all cases of blood poisoning caused by *E. coli* are resistant to almost all antibiotics.[27]

In the US there are around 9.4 million cases of food poisoning every year. Of those leading to hospitalisation around a third are due to salmonella and 15 per cent to campylobacter.[28] Between March and September 2011, ground turkey processed and distributed by the meat production giant Cargill and contaminated with salmonella was reported to have infected 119 people in forty-two states.[29] Cargill recalled over 16 thousand tonnes of the ground turkey produced at one of its plants. The strain of salmonella involved was multi-drug-resistant.[30]

The peak of the scandal over salmonella in eggs in Britain was in the late 1980s, when over 90 per cent of British hens were kept in cages[31] and the cabinet minister Edwina Currie famously lost her job for claiming that 'most' British eggs were infected. Now, almost 50 per cent of laying hens are either free-range or organic,[32] and salmonella rates have plummeted to 0.25 per cent.[33] The reduction may be partly due to testing, vaccination, and culling of infected flocks, but it may well also be linked to more free-range conditions. A study of salmonella in British laying hen flocks published in 2010 found that smaller flocks and non-caged flocks were much less likely to carry the bug: over 18 per cent of caged flocks tested positive for *Salmonella enteritidis*, the most common strain causing food poisoning, compared with less than 3 per cent of non-caged flocks. The largest flocks, of 30,000 birds or more, were seven times more likely to carry salmonella than the smallest flocks of 3,000 hens or less.[34]

It has been estimated that two-thirds of bacteria, viruses or other micro-organisms that can cause human disease are zoonotic, meaning they originate from animals.[35] The aggressive viral diseases like bird flu and swine flu have strong links with intensified farming. Intensive animal production has provided a new route for the likes of swine flu and bird flu to develop and spread. Highly pathogenic bird flu such as the H5N1 virus emerged during a time of massive expansion of the poultry industry in the Far East. It was first spotted in Hong Kong's live-bird markets and chicken farms in 1997. Six people died. From 2003 it spread across east Asia, at exactly the time when the poultry population was soaring and poultry production growing more intensive. China reared three times as many meat chickens in 2005, when bird flu was rampant, as it did in 1990.[36]

The H5N1 virus spread across Asia, the Middle East, Europe and Africa. It has been found on chicken, goose and turkey farms, and in some wild birds, mainly swans and geese. By August 2011, 564 people were confirmed to have been infected, of whom 330 died – a fatality rate of almost 59 per cent.[37]

Most people who caught it lived cheek by jowl with chickens or were involved in killing them. However, an outbreak of a different strain of bird flu, H7N7, in the Netherlands in 2003, during which a vet died, showed that such viruses can be transmitted from poultry workers to other people. Tests found that eighty-six poultry industry workers and three family contacts were infected with the disease during the outbreak, and around thirty more family contacts were also probably infected, although tests were inconclusive.[38]

Factory farming was always bound to cause a disease backlash by pushing nature way beyond its limits. Keeping massive numbers of poultry on intensive farms worldwide appears to have come back to bite us in the form of potentially fatal strains of avian influenza. Luckily, at the moment H5N1 is not easily transmitted between people. The big fear is that every time someone is infected, the virus gains more ground to mutate in, raising the prospect that it will become far more contagious. This could lead to a global epidemic.

Recently, scientists have shown that just a few mutations would allow H5N1 to become as infectious as seasonal flu.[39] An editorial in the *New Scientist* described the risk of a pandemic as 'fact, not fiction'.[40] Public-health experts writing in *The Lancet* have estimated that such a flu pandemic could kill as many as 62 million people, mostly in developing countries.[41]

I remember Peter Roberts, former dairy farmer and founder of Compassion in World Farming, sharing with me his conviction that factory farming would have to end because of the vast tide of disease coming from it. The fact that pigs, humans and birds can exchange flu viruses or elements of viruses raises the nightmare prospect of a highly contagious and lethal flu strain that starts out in animals transferring to people. These worrying new mixes of human, bird and pig viruses are likely to be very hard to treat.

A key element in the spread of diseases originating on farms is long-distance transport of animals for fattening and slaughter. As well as being a major welfare issue, it allows diseases to 'hitchhike' their way to new places and populations. I was reminded about this issue when

I went to Ghana in 2011 for the Commonwealth Veterinary Association conference in Accra, where there were representatives from the UN, the European Commission and the World Organisation for Animal Health. Several eminent speakers talked about the role of global travel and international trade in agricultural products, including live animals, in the emergence of disease. The slogan 'one world, one health' was widely bandied around by vets in the conference hall, summing up the general view that animal and human health are intertwined. It seems to highlight the folly of the live-export trade, in which millions of live animals are trucked and shipped long distances across the world, just to be slaughtered at the end of the journey.

Many scientists still seem reluctant to speak out about the role of intensive farming in antibiotic resistance and the rise of aggressive strains of viral disease. The science is complex, pressures from the industry are intense, and it takes a long time to track specific antibiotic-resistance problems all the way through the food chain. It can be hard to be precise, because the bacteria usually changes slightly during the process. Naturally businesses benefiting from the system seize on any holes in the evidence. Some have even tried to suggest that the wire or slatted floors typical on factory farms reduce disease and increase food safety for consumers, because the animals are separated from each other's faeces and isolated from infections circulating in the outside world. There may be some truth in this, but any protection farm animals get from being reared indoors is far outweighed by the health risks associated with being in such a confined and artificial environment.

Disturbingly, some have tried to scapegoat wild birds as responsible for avian influenza and use this as an excuse to support greater farm intensification. They claim that keeping poultry inside protects them from wild birds carrying disease. What this argument conveniently overlooks is that low-level avian flu is a perfectly natural disease in wild birds. It's only when it enters the pressure-cooker environment of an intensive farm that the disease tends to mutate dangerously. Once a virus gets into an intensive poultry shed it can move quickly through the flock, constantly replicating itself. Any 'errors' or changes to the genetic code during replication don't get repaired: this is how the virus mutates and new variant strains emerge. The tragedy is that while intensive farms provide ideal conditions for the emergence of new aggressive disease strains, wild birds can then become infected too.

Experience from the 2005 outbreak of highly pathogenic avian influenza (AI) H5N1 suggests that the disease is more likely spread along major road and rail routes than on the flight routes of migratory birds. Also, the overwhelming majority of wild birds found infected with H5N1 were dead, preventing them from carrying the virus over long distances. When H5N1 hit a Bernard Matthews turkey farm in Suffolk in 2007, there was no evidence of highly pathogenic AI in wild bird populations in Britain. Defra reported at the time that over 4,000 wild birds had been tested over the previous six months; only 0.4 per cent were found to be infected with AI, of which none were highly pathogenic strains.

Blaming wild birds is an excuse for doing nothing about the dominant source of the problem: the factory-farming system itself. Dr Aysha Akhtar, a neurologist and public-health specialist and Fellow of the Oxford Centre for Animal Ethics, sums it up like this: 'By confining billions of animals on factory farms, we have created a worldwide natural laboratory for the rapid development of a deadly and highly infectious virus.'[42] Akhtar works for the Office of Counterterrorism and Emerging Threats of the US Food and Drugs Administration. She points out that human terrorists don't have a monopoly on killing and causing chaos. Factory farming, she fears, has as much potential as, and probably more than, any terrorist to do the job.

MEXICO'S 'GROUND ZERO' FOR SWINE FLU

High in the mountains of southeast Mexico is an unassuming little town with a very unfortunate reputation. La Gloria in the Perote Valley is a cheerful place where children play volleyball on the dusty roads and the streets are decorated with yellow bunting. Lying

8 kilometres from one of the biggest concentrations of pig farms in the world, it was at the epicentre of one of the biggest-ever health scares linked to factory farming. It was here early in 2009 that people first started falling sick with a previously unknown disease, a new and highly contagious virus containing genetic material from a mix of pig, bird and human influenza.

Soon the virus had ripped across the world, leaving thousands of people gravely ill and La Gloria notorious as the 'ground zero' of swine flu. The spotlight has long moved away from this place and the surrounding area, where a company called Granjas Carroll de Mexico (GCM) owns a network of pig farms. Now the immediate panic is over, most people have stopped worrying about catching swine flu, just as they have stopped worrying about contracting bird flu. Yet there is every chance that the combination of conditions that created these strange new viruses will sooner or later throw up another patho-logical monster. In the meantime the daily battle goes on between communities like La Gloria and industrial farms on their doorstep.

I visited Perote Valley in November 2011 just before the annual festival to mark Revolution Day, commemorating a long armed strug-gle that began in 1910 and resulted in the overthrow of Mexico's autocratic ruler and the creation of the Constitution of 1917. I wanted to see the supposed birthplace of swine flu and find out whether what happened was still affecting people there.

Starting our journey in the bustling city of Xalapa, capital of the state of Veracruz, my camera crew and I hired a car and headed for the hills through uplands that could have been English, except that the light was so bright the grass looked greener than I'd ever seen. Small groups of black and white cows dotted a rolling landscape. We were on the lower slopes of an ancient volcano looking towards the Sierra Madre mountain range, shrouded in the morning mist. In the distance, a city winked in the sunlight. After an hour or two talking with dairy farmers in the area, we pressed on to the high mountain plateau, at 2,500 metres. Here we found an entirely different land-scape – a scrubby desert littered with great fat cacti. The occasional dusty village sat amidst vast open terrain on which people strove to grow anything that could survive on such dusty land. Growing crops here was clearly a struggle – though there was a fair amount of maize – but factory farms were another matter.

In hangars scattered over a few square kilometres in the valleys of Perote and Guadalupe, GCM (a partnership between a Mexican animal-feed corporation and US-based Smithfield, the world's largest pork producer) rears more than a million pigs a year here.[43] As with the mega-piggeries we saw in China, the animals spend their whole lives indoors in cramped concrete pens, their manure flushed into open-air lagoons.

The first time we thought we'd spotted one of GMC's establishments it turned out to be a prison – factory farms and jails can look very similar. It wasn't long before we came across what we were looking for: a huge industrial piggery made up of eighteen long corrugated-iron hangars. Next to each one was a giant steel bin, most likely an automated feeding cylinder. The farm was surrounded by an electric fence topped with barbed wire. From the outside there was nothing else to see: no pigs, no farmers, no signs of life; just a series of grim metal structures that looked as if they'd been more or less dumped at random on the countryside. With its forbidding locked gates and high fences, the perimeter screamed 'Keep Out!' and so we did. There was no one around to ask if we could see inside, and it's hardly likely they'd have let us, so we drove on through the valley.

Our first stop was the village of La Tlalconteno, where a vibrant market was in full swing. Shoppers and customers mingled under bright awnings that gave some respite from the intense sun. Standing among the brimming stalls was a man holding a colander piled high with crackling golden-brown snacks: fried pig skin. He tipped them onto a tray and piled more on top, till the stack nearly spilled onto the floor. Eager hands reached out and the pile was gone. A small boy danced to the music as his dad watched proudly.

The boy was a picture of health, with a cheeky smile and glossy black hair, his little feet shuffling to the beat in tiny buff-coloured cowboy boots. His name was Alan, and he was not quite five years old. His father offered him a toy from a nearby stall. He told us he was thankful for this day, because back in 2007 he almost lost his son. Alan was less than one year old when he fell sick with a mystery illness. Doctors offered different diagnoses, ranging from a nasty cold to pneumonia, but it was no ordinary sniffle. Alan developed severe breathing difficulties and became so sick that he was hospitalised for almost three weeks, a long time for an infant.

His father, Gerardo Praxedis Serrano Diaz, firmly believes that the child's illness was linked to pollution from nearby pig farms. His symptoms were uncannily similar to those suffered by victims of swine flu, but the family will never know. At the time, Diaz was asked by doctors if he kept pigs at home. He doesn't. However, he lives less than 100 metres from a slaughterhouse.

He was keen to show us more piggeries, so we piled into the car and set off. We passed several livestock transporters being cleaned in an area just off the road. Diaz explained that this was where the lorries were usually disinfected. Past a hump in the road, the valley opened up, industrial pig farms strewn in all directions. We passed an access road with a pig-farm sign; then another and another. In all we could see a dozen or more pig farms, each with a row of factory-like sheds and giant metallic feed bins. Our car stank of slurry.

We pulled up next to one of the farms. The smell was overwhelming. Around us was semi-arid landscape. Diaz told us that dead pigs from the valley were taken to La Gloria for disposal. GCM claims that carcasses from pigs that have died from 'stress or old age' are disposed of using biodigesters or composting,[44] but there are persistent complaints from locals that carcasses are left lying around, attracting wild dogs.

We drove on, and could see more farms: another fifteen. They looked like clusters of low aircraft hangars or military installations. The steel, concrete and electrified boundary fences warned us off. Articulated lorries trundled in and out, ferrying huge quantities of feed. The finished product, fattened pigs, would be loaded onto huge transporters for their final journey to slaughterhouses nearer the city.

I knew from past experiences that these closed farms rarely welcome casual visitors; being in a place once caught in a media hurricane made it even less likely that we'd be allowed through the firmly shut gates with our cameras. My suspicions of sensitivities were confirmed when we passed a pickup truck, presumably from one of the pig farms. The driver wound down the window and asked what we were doing in the area. No sooner had we started to move off than he was on his walkie-talkie, most likely alerting others to our presence.

We parked near a lagoon beside the road. Not a picturesque lake, but a slurry lagoon full of liquid effluent from the pig farms. I scrambled up a bank for a better view, doing my best to avoid being skewered by cacti. The smell told its own tale. Just behind it was another piggery. A figure in white overalls walked between the barren buildings. I could hear pigs squealing. It was all surreal: the heat, the dust, barbed wire over a 3-metre boundary fence. None of it bore any resemblance to the traditional image of a farm.

Diaz wanted us to talk to his father, who lived in La Gloria and was a key figure in a local protest group opposed to the expansion of industrial pig farms. On the outskirts of the village we passed a graveyard; a colourful riot of stone and wooden crosses and miniature monuments to loved ones. Bright pink and orange ribbons, ornately arranged into crucifix shapes, stood proud over graves. A gecko wiggled up a tomb, casting a tiny shadow in the morning sun.

The village of La Gloria has a population of less than 3,000. It is sheltered by tree-lined mountains that bring water to the area. The wind swept dusty streets, children scampered in the road, and a red scooter drifted by with a megaphone booming a recorded voice to advertise *tamales*, a traditional maize mixture wrapped in banana leaves. The bunting was up for Revolution Day; the walls of a hacienda were peppered with bullet marks from the historic battles of that time. A century on, a different type of civil war continues: between people and pigs.

Diaz's father, Guadalupe Gaspar, a charismatic man with a deep tan and a white Stetson, was sixty-eight years old but seemed younger. He was a farmer and a leading member of the local campaign group Pueblos Unidos (People United). He welcomed us warmly into his modest home. Next to the blue front door, a little shrine stood in a bay window. The sitting room inside was painted mauve, with quintessentially Mexican light blue and pink curtains. By an empty cabinet, a collection of statuettes attested his religious faith. Gaspar seemed a proud man of strong beliefs.

Sitting with his feet tapping the tiled floor, he explained that La Gloria had long been a farming community, growing corn, beans, potatoes, barley and wheat. He told us that as a child he had spent happy days walking in the countryside with his dad. In those days, he claimed, there were no water shortages in the area. Now it is a different story. He blames deforestation in the mountains and the mega-piggeries. Locals must now compete with swine for scarce water in the dusty valley. He talked of a lack of jobs, a real concern for families, particularly young people, many of whom are moving away. It is already said to be common for villagers to commute to work in Mexico City, 200 kilometres away, returning at weekends.

The arrival of multiple industrial pig farms could have been the answer to villagers' prayers, providing jobs and opportunities. In practice, Gaspar claimed, few locals were being employed. Most farms seemed to be staffed by outsiders. We heard the familiar story of pollution, strong smells, contaminated drinking water and flies. Since few locals have any economic stake in the piggeries, it was little wonder they were seen as the enemy. Gaspar told me he felt cheated. 'We were deceived. They said some companies were coming that were going to give people jobs. They never said anything about coming here to pollute.'

His account may not be entirely fair. According to GCM's website, it is the main source of employment in the Perote Valley, generating more than 3,000 direct and indirect jobs[45] – though that is not to say that the people it employs come from local communities. The company points out that it also pays a lot of tax, contributes 2 per cent of its payroll to support Veracruz's infrastructure, and has funded reforestation and irrigation. It also says it provides free medical care to eighteen communities in the states of Puebla and Veracruz.

Whatever the true costs and benefits, soon after the first pig farm arrived near La Gloria, villagers say they noticed a change in the quality of the groundwater. There was widespread concern and they began writing letters of complaint to the federal government, the state authorities and the town council. In 2007, when they heard another farm was planned, closer to La Gloria than the first, they organised a protest. Several hundred demonstrators tried to close the road, a common form of protest in Mexico. They managed to partially block traffic onto the federal highway and annoy the authorities.[46] One morning, around a month after the protest, there was a knock at Gaspar's door. He opened it to find three federal policemen, together with a man in civilian clothes. He was told he was being charged with launching an 'attack' on a federal highway. 'They caught me and arrested me as if I was a drug smuggler.' He claims he was forced to sell his corn crop to defend himself, and that every fifteen days for a year he was forced to make a two-hour round trip to Puebla, the nearest big town, to check in with the authorities.[47]

Two years after these early protests, more than a quarter of the population of La Gloria – 28 per cent – went down with swine flu or something like it.[48] Mexico's government first reported the outbreak in La Gloria to world health authorities in April 2009. A week later, clusters of pneumonia were reported in Mexico City. At the same time, California identified a novel influenza virus. On 23 April, Mexico confirmed cases of infection with the same virus, newly named as H1N1 influenza A. It spread far more quickly than anyone anticipated: within a week, ten countries were affected; 180 countries by the end of August.[49] Within a year, according to the World Health Organization, the virus was linked to over 18,000 deaths worldwide.[50] It was traced back to La Gloria, where a young boy, Edgar Hernandez, was the first confirmed case. He later became known as 'kid zero' or 'patient zero'.[51]

In a small park in the middle of La Gloria is a lifesize statue of Edgar on a podium surrounded by a strange waterless well. The paint around it has begun to peel, but the statue makes it difficult for anyone in La Gloria to forget what happened.

What was unusual about the viral strain was that it had a mix of genetic material from two different swine influenza viruses as well as from human and avian strains of flu. It was suspected of having been spread by people arriving from affected areas in Mexico.[52] Since then, question marks have been raised over the scientific link between the emergence of the new virus in La Gloria and the neighbouring piggeries.

Naturally GCM has highlighted doubts over the evidence. It says that Mexican public-health authorities inspected its facilities, particularly farm 113B, the nearest to La Gloria, and certified the absence of 'any sign associated with the flu in our animals'. Their website[53] states that 'the company requested [the authorities to] collect new samples to certify the state of health of our swine.' The tests were conducted by the National Health Services, the authority responsible for animal health. The website states: 'There is no scientific evidence that links GCM with the A/H1N1 flu virus.'[54] It goes on to say that these reassuring findings were endorsed by another government agency, the Federal Commission for Protection Against Health Risks. Apparently they carried out an extensive study in La Gloria, which concluded that the firm had 'no diseased pigs or sick people, nor any respiratory or diarrheic problems'.[55]

Maybe it's just a coincidence that a novel strain of flu, a key component of which was two different strains of swine flu, was first diagnosed right by some mega-piggeries? Either way, the focus of local protests about the farms shifted from pollution, smells and flies, to disease. 'When we realised what was happening, all the villages came together to demonstrate,' Gaspar recalled. 'People were dying. That is when we got up and started to fight; to make demands, so that the farms knew we didn't want them here.' They marched along the main road to make their point to the authorities, but according to Gaspar they were 'treated like troublemakers'. He claims he has effectively lost everything as a result of speaking out, and that many locals are too frightened to stick their necks out or have been bought off.

At the time of my visit, it was almost three years since the swine flu outbreak, but the anger and fear in the community burned as powerfully as ever. Gaspar said it felt like 'living in a time bomb'. 'We don't know when something else bad is going to happen to us. The government must get rid of the farms because while they remain, the pollution will continue and I am sure there will be more new diseases.' Locals say that while La Gloria was in the global spotlight, they were quietly assured that no new farms would be built. Now the world is no longer watching, and they doubt the pledge will be honoured. Indeed, there are already signs of new pig farms arriving.

Having said goodbye to Gaspar, we went to meet a local elected official who had agreed to talk to us on condition of anonymity. He took us in our car down a dusty, cactus-lined track. We passed through fields of maize growing in corn-dolly pyramids, stopping 2 kilometres outside La Gloria. The sixty-year-old official was taking us to see what he claimed was the future site of a new industrial pig farm.

The first signs of development were already in place: concrete foundation posts wrapped in barbed wire and a well for drawing water. A white cross, 6 metres tall, towered over the plot. It was not a religious symbol but one of a line of identical posts that stretched as far as the eye could see, erected to carry power or communications to the place.

The anonymous official told me he was sad and angry at the way companies had moved in offering jobs when so few people in the community benefited. It would be much better for the community if money were invested in traditional agriculture, which generates more jobs. As a civil servant, his particular concern is for the future of the valley's young people. 'So many are leaving. We need job creation here in the countryside so they aren't forced to go. If more farms are built, they are going to cause problems for our grandchildren and great-grandchildren in years to come.' He wants communities faced with similar proposals to act quickly. 'Don't allow them to build more farms, because we will never rid ourselves of the pollution,' was his message to others.

We returned to La Gloria, where we went to speak to a thirty-year-old mother of two girls, who gave her name as Hortensia. When we arrived she was standing in the doorway of her brightly coloured home. She beckoned us inside, where she felt she could talk more freely. It was more evidence that people were uneasy about speaking out. Hortensia told me she had lived in La Gloria nearly all her life. She sat underneath a painting of a child wearing a hat with sad blue eyes and tears rolling down his cheeks. It was a strange picture to choose for your wall, but seemed symbolic of the sadness and fears of the community. Hortensia was one of the protesters against planned expansions of the industrial pig-farming area. She described the people who took part in blocking the road as ordinary folk, worried about the environment and their children. She said strong winds blew bad smells over the village.

I asked her about polluted water, and she looked resigned:

People have got used to it. They say that once these farms are established, there's nothing they can do. Even if they complain, nothing will happen. The water that supplies our village comes from the forest, but sadly it is being cut down illegally, so you can imagine the concern we feel, knowing that it is being felled, and a business is going to be established that uses thousands and thousands of litres of water every day. It is a huge worry.

Like others we talked to, she was sceptical that any new pig farms, like the one apparently already rising just out of town, would create jobs for locals: 'They have promised, as they always do, to provide jobs for the men here. It is the same every time. I don't believe it.' She thinks the new farm will be the biggest yet. From what we observed, the company had already bought the land and dug wells.

I asked her if the village would benefit from the pigmeat produced. She told me that it was normal for people in La Gloria to have their own pigs at home, which they feed on leftovers. They don't need pork from a mega-farm. It turns out that the pigs from these industrial farms are sold live for slaughter in Mexico City and other mainly urban places.

I asked about the swine flu episode. She told me that the first villagers knew of it was when journalists arrived and then it was all over the television. She was frightened for her children and relatives. Her mother went down with the illness and the family feared everyone would catch it. She said it was blamed on the pigs at first, but acknowledged that nothing has been proven.

I left her house and walked past the hacienda. I remember thinking that the pockmarked walls of the crumbling citadel fortress were no match for this new type of enemy. It doesn't have to be like this – as we could see when we visited a very different type of farm in the same area. We stopped for a breather outside a village called Acajete which had beautiful views over the Sierra Madre mountain range. The slopes were shrouded in morning mist. A farmhand was walking up a hill carrying three white buckets. He spotted us, waved in a friendly sort of way, and beckoned us over. We explained what we were doing in the area, and were treated to an impromptu tour of the farm.

The farmer, Ana Maria Frauzoni Hernandez, also a vet, took us round, first through a cluster of modest flat-roofed buildings – the farmhouse and dairy – and then into the fields. There was a faintly pleasant smell in the air of baby-sweet dairy mixed with a slight hint of manure. Hernandez explained that the farm belonged to her brother. She talked about respecting the cow as a noble animal. We walked past a few trees and found twenty calves loafing in the sun. I stood in the inevitable cowpat.

The place turned out to be one of thirty-four farms in a local dairy cooperative. It was a pretty big farm by European standards: 500 cows in all, but you wouldn't have known it. They were well dispersed, grazing happily on the hillside. We watched as forty Friesians were milked out there in the fields. The animals and a couple of farmhands stood among a cluster of silver milk-churns. Hernandez explained that they were milked twice a day. Her father used to milk them three times a day but the cows got stressed. When milking was over, a horse carried the churns up the hill. The cows followed along behind. It was wonderful to see them walking naturally, without the bloated, bulging udders and splayed back legs we'd seen in California's mega-dairies.

The cows on this particular farm were kept outdoors all year round. No chemicals, preventative antibiotics or hormones were used, though a bit of supplementary feed was offered when the grass was short. Hernandez told us they had an average lifespan of twenty years – around four times the life expectancy of cows in intensive dairies.

Towards the end of the tour, she started talking about the battle to get a decent price for the milk. It's a familiar theme on both sides of the Atlantic, with farming systems big and small. The milk from this farm was sold under the name 'Joyalat' – *joyal* means jewel in Spanish. Hernandez said she saw the milk as 'white gold'. She shared some customer feedback about how good the product is, apparently because the cows graze naturally on grass full of nutrients.

Before we left, I tasted the yoghurt. I found it full of flavour, very smooth, with no hint of sharpness: delicious. A poster in the dairy window proudly proclaimed that 'The best milk in the world is produced in Mexico.' Looking around me, at that moment, I had to agree.

I went to southeast Mexico looking for answers. I hoped to trace swine flu to its origins, and find out whether the virus was really linked to the piggeries. I left with no definitive answer: nobody seemed to know. There is speculation that the virus may have been circulating in the US pig industry long before it showed up in remote, dusty La Gloria. Standing in an arid valley surrounded by many thousands of pigs, without seeing a single animal, was an eerie experience. What I did gain was an insight into the reality of life for communities near factory farms. It's an issue that would have received far less public attention had it not been for swine flu. However, as always, once the immediate panic was over, the media caravan moved on, leaving the community to fight on alone.

8

Expanding Waistlines

Food quality takes a nose-dive

The fattest man in the world lives in a small ground-floor flat in north London, and spends his life sleeping or sitting propped up in his reinforced bed. Keith Martin has not ventured outside for more than a decade, except for the odd visit to hospital, and the time he moved house, which involved an uncomfortable journey in the back of a van.[1] At 368 kilograms (812 pounds), the forty-two-year-old is too large to go anywhere or do anything other than eat, drink, read, play on his games console or watch his enormous plasma TV. He is so fat he can't even roll over in bed by himself. His girth is greater than his height.

Every day, seven carers working in shifts arrive to wash and change him. On alternate days he is visited by two nurses who tend his bedsores. Last time he left his flat to go to hospital after falling over, it took a specialist team and a £90,000 ambulance designed for morbidly obese patients to transport him. He had to be dragged across the floor to the vehicle in a special bag. That's nothing compared with the practicalities involved in taking the world's fattest teenager to hospital. Also from the UK, Georgina Davies weighs 400 kilograms (880 pounds), and getting her out of the house involved pulling down two walls.

Martin began to binge at the age of sixteen, when his mother Alma died. He left school that year, with poor qualifications, and went to work as a warehouseman and labourer until he got too fat to do the job. He continued to overeat and every year his weight ballooned: 'I let myself go. I just didn't care. I got so bloated on sausages, bacon and roast dinners. I just ate whatever I felt like.' Now he is desperately trying to change the habits of a lifetime, knowing that his weight will soon kill him. Doctors have warned him that unless he succeeds, he will be dead by the age of fifty.

For years, he has started the day with eight hot dogs and four slices of bread, or a stack of ham sandwiches washed down with sugary coffee. For lunch he gorges on chocolate bars, cakes and biscuits, while a typical dinner has been two entire roast dinners with all the trim-mings, or sixteen sausages, plus a family-sized bag of oven chips. His target is to slash his daily calorie intake from 9,000 to 2,500, the recommended amount for men.[2] To stand a chance, he will have to overcome his addiction to cheap processed meat. The sausages and hot dogs he loves provide little nutrition for the calories.

Martin is an extreme example, but on current trends, by 2030 half of American adults will be obese. The projections for the UK popula-tion are almost as bad. Annual obesity-related health costs are expected to soar over the same period by $48 billion in the US, and nearly £1.25 billion in the UK.[3] The availability of low-cost factory-farmed food has played a key role in the global obesity epidemic. Scoffing roast chicken and sausages might seem healthier than guzzling cake, but evidence shows that factory farming has stripped away much of the nutritional value of the meat on offer in supermarkets and fast-food joints. At the same time the fat content has soared. Intensification has had so severe an impact on meat quality that some scientists claim you'd have to eat four entire factory-farmed chickens to benefit from the same level of some nutrients as you would have got from a single organic chicken in the 1970s.

'The intensification of animal farming has virtually destroyed the nutritional quality of our food,' according to Professor Michael Craw-ford of the Institute of Brain Chemistry and Nutrition in London. Crawford visited my office in Godalming, Surrey, on a lovely summer day in June. As we talked about his decades of research into this issue, we strolled along the banks of the river Wey, which meanders through the town. He pointed out the strange appearance of the trees on the grazing marsh, which had been browsed by cattle that graze there in summer. The leaves had been chomped to exactly cattle-head height, giving them a sort of bobbed-haircut look. The professor predicted that the meat from those cattle would taste good as well as being nutritious. His research suggests that the best-quality meat comes from animals allowed to forage for food as nature intended, grazing on grass and browsing on trees and hedges. Confinement to 'improved' pasture – grassland with little variety – reduces the quality. Feeding intensively on grain, an unnatural diet for ruminants, makes it even worse.

In a presentation to my staff team at Compassion in World Farming, Crawford talked about his study published in *The Lancet* more than half a century ago highlighting the huge difference between the fat content of farmed animals and their 'wild' counterparts. The research revealed that the ratio of 'bad' to 'good' fats in farmed animals was 50:1, compared with less than 3:1 in their wild counterparts. Since then, the picture has dramatically deteriorated.

Crawford describes modern industrial chicken-rearing as 'fat production, not meat production'. He argues that intensively reared farm animals are effectively 'selected for obesity' and get virtually no exercise. The result is meat 'marbled' with excess fat. 'If you eat obesity, you become obese' is the way he puts it. According to UK government nutritional advice, most people eat far too much saturated fat, a large proportion of which comes from fatty cuts of meat and products like sausages and pies. Diets high in saturated fat are associated with high cholesterol and heart disease. According to one study, if the UK population reduced its intake of saturated fat from animal sources by 30 per cent, rates of coronary heart disease would fall by 15 per cent, and the number of premature deaths would fall considerably.[4]

The science on this subject is complex and mainly relates to the balance of 'good' and 'bad' fats in factory-farmed meat, specifically amounts of polyunsaturated fats, known as omega-3 and omega-6 (good), versus saturated fats (bad). The life-or-death difference between 'good' and 'bad' fats in the human diet was first identified in the 1970s, when Danish doctors noticed that Greenland Inuit had exceptionally low rates of heart disease and arthritis, despite an apparently high-fat diet. Their good health was traced back to high levels of omega-3 in fish, which was their staple diet.[5] Scientists believe that people evolved to eat roughly the same amount of omega-6 fat as omega-3.[6] Current recommendations allow for a bit more of a tilt: up to four times as much omega-6 as omega-3. Yet the average Western diet ranges from ten to twenty-five times more omega-6 than omega-3.[7] There is compelling evidence that this is linked to the seismic shift from natural grazing on farmland to rearing animals on grain.[8] Unlike grain, grass is full of omega-3.

The link between the nutritional value of meat and the animal's diet is now well documented. According to an American study published in 2010, fresh forages (plants, grass and leaves eaten by grazing farm animals) have ten to twelve times more ALA – an important building block for omega-3 fatty acids – than grain. The study showed that when the amount of grain given to animals on a basic grass diet was increased, the concentration of omega-3 in the meat fell. It concluded that 'grass-finished beef consistently produces a higher concentration of n-3 FAs [omega-3 fatty acids], resulting in a more favourable n-6:n-3 ratio. The amount of total fat found in a serving of meat is highly dependent upon the feeding regimen.'[9]

A Bristol University review of grass feeding versus grain feeding in cattle found that beef cattle given a diet of fresh grass between the ages of fourteen and nineteen months had much higher levels of omega-3 than steers given grass silage – and very much higher levels than steers fed on concentrated diets that include high levels of grain or soya, as happens on feedlots (cattle factory farms).[10]

A major review of the literature found strong evidence to show that animals kept in higher-welfare conditions – not reared in highly intensive factory farms – provide more nutritious food. It looked at data from over seventy-six studies and found that meat, milk and eggs from higher-welfare farms often contain less fat and higher levels of key nutrients than their factory-farmed alternatives. As compared with factory-farmed produce, pasture-reared beef has 25–50 per cent less fat, and free-range and organic chicken up to 50 per cent less fat.[11]

The difference in omega-3 levels is striking: compared with factory-farmed produce, pasture-reared beef is on average 2.7 times higher in these essential nutrients; higher-welfare chicken is from 20 per cent to five times higher; meat from higher-welfare pigs is 40 per cent higher; free-range eggs are 30 per cent higher; and milk from pasture-raised cows is 100 per cent higher. These are important health benefits given that the chronic lack of omega-3 in the modern diet is linked to heart disease and cancer.[12]

Antioxidants in our diet are vital to good health and help fight diseases like cancer. Keeping animals in better conditions has been found to provide benefits here too. Free-range eggs can have up to double the amount of vitamin E, a powerful antioxidant, vital in fighting disease. It may play a role in preventing cancer by blocking the formation of certain carcinogens and boosting the immune system. It is also thought to prevent cataracts. Keeping hens so that they are free to roam outside also produces eggs with nearly three times as much beta-carotene. The human body converts beta-carotene into vitamin A, key to maintaining healthy eyesight, bone growth, reproduction and cells. It also helps promote healthy skin and a strong immune system. Whether it is beef, pigmeat or milk, keeping the animals in better conditions where they have a more natural diet has been found to produce better-quality food; free-range pigmeat has, on average, 60 per cent more vitamin E; higher welfare milk has 180 per cent more beta-carotene.[13]

Perversely, some nutritionists and health experts seem to think that the solution is to supplement animals' diets with additives and continue to feed them grain, rather than the more obvious and simpler option of letting them live and eat as nature evolved them.

There is a widespread assumption that chicken is a high-protein, low-fat choice. Recipes involving steamed or poached varieties frequently feature in weight-loss programmes. But factory farming has dramatically changed the nutritional quality of chicken: it is no longer as healthy as it should be. Up to a fifth of the weight of broiler chickens is now fat.[14] It's partly genetic – decades of selective breeding for plump birds – and partly diet. In any case, factory-farmed chicken contains around 40 per cent more fat than protein.

In 2005, Crawford's team published the results of an analysis of modern chicken meat. His study revealed that a typical supermarket chicken today contains almost three times more fat than a typical chicken in 1970, and a third less protein.[15] All this means that a portion of chicken today contains 50 per cent more calories than it did in 1970. Crawford also discovered that modern meat chickens contain only a fifth as much DHA – another of the omega-3 fatty acids – as is found in 'wild' chickens.[16]

Crawford attributed these huge changes in the nutritional content of chicken to factory farming, pointing out that traditionally reared chickens used to be active and eat vegetation and seeds, whereas modern, intensively reared birds are fed on high-energy foods and can barely move: 'Such chickens are no longer a protein-rich food, but a fat-rich food. The explanation is simple, namely that they are fed largely on cereals.'

That fast-food restaurants risk peddling obesity and ill health every time they sell extra-large burgers made with factory-farmed beef and supersize portions of chicken nuggets made from factory-farmed broilers is so glaringly obvious that they find themselves taken to court more and more often. In 2010 the former manager of a McDonald's outlet in Brazil was reported to have successfully sued the fast-food giant after claiming they made him put on 20 kilograms (45 pounds) during the twelve years he worked there. The thirty-two-year-old man, whose name was kept anonymous, ballooned from 70 kilograms (155 pounds) to 105 kilograms (231 pounds) while McDonald's employed him. He blamed it on the company's policy of mandatory food sampling and free lunches of burgers, fries and ice cream. He was awarded $17,500.[17]

Other cases have been more complicated, and some have yet to conclude. In 2002, a man from the Bronx, Caesar Barber, filed a class-action lawsuit in New York against a number of fast-food companies, claiming that eating regularly at the restaurants had made him obese. In the first action of its kind, he sued the companies for failing to warn him of the health risks associated with regularly eating their food, blaming them for his two heart attacks and diabetes. The fifty-six-year-old weighed 120 kilograms (266 pounds) and had been eating fast food up to five times a week. He claimed that until a doctor pointed out the dangers of his diet, he was misled by deceptive advertising suggesting the stuff was healthy. 'Those people in the advertisements don't tell you what's in the food. It's all fat, fat, and more fat. Now I'm obese. The fast-food industry has wrecked my life. They said 100 per cent beef. I thought that meant it was good for you,' the *Guardian* reported.[18]

Barber's lawyer Samuel Hirsch claimed that the main aim of this lawsuit was to 'get the chains to inform customers that their food is guilty of expanding their waistlines'. Hirsch subsequently dropped the case. According to some reports, he felt he stood more chance with a case involving children.[19] He later took on a nineteen-year-old client, Jazlyn Bradley, who, at just 1.70 metres (5 foot 7 inches) tall, weighed 122 kilograms (270 pounds); and a fourteen-year-old, Ashley Pelman, who weighed 77 kilograms (170 pounds) despite being only 1.47 metres (4 foot 10 inches) tall. This particular litigation was aimed solely at McDonald's, and originally included several other teenagers, all of whom, according to *Time* magazine, claim that 'as [a] result' of eating Happy Meals, McMuffins and Big Macs for several years, they became obese and developed diabetes, coronary heart disease and high blood pressure.[20]

It was this case that inspired Morgan Spurlock to make his famous 2004 film *Supersize Me*. It charted what happened to his physical and mental health when he spent thirty days eating only at McDonald's. During the experiment, he dined at the chain three times a day, trying every item on the menu. His average daily calorie consumption was 5,000 – double the recommended amount. The result was that he piled on almost 11 kilograms (24.5 pounds); his body mass increased by 13 per cent; his cholesterol level rose and he experienced mood swings, sexual dysfunction and fat accumulation in his liver. It took him fourteen months to lose the weight.

Hirsch argued that McDonald's child-focused advertising and toy promotions portrayed the restaurant as child-friendly, making his clients think it was fine to eat there regularly – sometimes as often as two or three times a day.[21] In September 2003, New York District Judge Robert Sweet dismissed the suit, saying the allegations were 'vague' and 'insufficient'.[22] But litigation has continued.[23]

It's not just Americans with less access to education and food choices whose health is being compromised by high-fat diets involving too much meat. There is now abundant evidence from public-health scientists that what has become a 'normal' level of meat consumption in industrial countries is excessive in terms of individual health. An overview of the global obesity pandemic published in *The Lancet* blamed the public-health crisis on 'changes in the global food system',[24] a reference to factory farming, which has made animal products, especially animal fats, too cheap. Average meat consumption in rich countries is currently around 200–300 grams per person per day. According to a group of public-health experts from Cambridge University in the UK, the London School of Hygiene, the Australian National University and the University of Chile, this needs reducing to a global average of 90 grams per person per day, for both environmental and public-health reasons. These scientists argue that limiting meat consumption to 90 grams a day would bring 'important gains to health' for people who currently eat more than that, including a likely reduction in the risk of colorectal cancer, breast cancer and heart disease, as well as the poor health linked with overweight and obesity. They argue that the reductions in heart disease would be mainly due to reducing the consumption of saturated fat in meat.[25]

Factory farming is behind the very high level of meat consumption in the most industrialised countries these days. Grain or other specialised high-protein and high-energy feed is used to raise yield per animal and maximise 'food-conversion efficiency' – in other words, the amount of meat produced relative to the amount of feed used in rearing the animal. Animals are kept in highly concentrated and confined conditions to reduce labour and feed costs. These conditions limit the amount of energy the animals 'waste' by limiting their movement; reduce the effects of temperature fluctuations by keeping them indoors; and cut the amount of time and energy 'wasted' by farm labourers who do not work in open fields. Specialised high-yielding livestock strains are used, selected because of their ability to grow and mature faster, put on more muscle or produce more milk, and requiring specialised feed, veterinary drugs and housing in order to reach maximum productivity. These methods meet – and arguably fuel – the huge demand for meat.

However, the conversion of potential human food like grain into meat in factory farms remains fundamentally inefficient: more calories go into the farm animal than come out in the form of meat, milk or eggs. When farm animals were first domesticated, ruminants like cows and sheep would eat grass that people couldn't eat and turn it into food. The conversion rate didn't matter because the animals weren't competing with people for food. Similarly, pigs and poultry were kept to eat scraps and leftovers and to forage; again, providing a useful service where they didn't compete with people for food. On the factory farm, potential human food – grain – is now absurdly fed to farm animals in a process that produces unhealthy meat and other products.

There are encouraging signs that meat consumption in the West may already have peaked or be on the verge of doing so. Euromonitor International, the world leader in consumer market research, predicts that sales of alternatives to meat will rise by 15 per cent in value between 2010 and 2015, and has highlighted the 'massive potential' for growth in demand for non-meat-based food of all types.[26] In September 2011, Rabobank, the international agricultural bank based in the Netherlands, released a report called *Where's the Beef?* claiming that meat consumption per head in America 'appears to have peaked' and that the industry should no longer rely on increasing domestic demand to get them through 'over-production situations'.[27]

In December 2011, the Values Institute at DGWB, a California advertising and communications company, predicted that one of five 'health and wellness trends' Americans are most likely to embrace in 2012 is 'flexitarianism' – the reduction of meat consumption for health reasons, without eliminating it altogether. One example of this trend is the growing popularity and social media following of so-called 'Meatless Monday', an initiative promoted by Johns Hopkins Bloomberg School of Public Health.[28] However, the trend is exactly the opposite in rapidly developing countries, particularly China. Rabobank predicts continuing rising global demand for meat.[29]

IV
MUCK

The old saying 'Where there's muck, there's brass' meant that there was money to be made from dirty jobs. In the twenty-first century, livestock farming has turned this adage on its head: disposing of mountains of animal muck is costing the earth.

In 2002 there was an outcry among UK farmers when they were banned from dumping manure wherever they wanted. New EU legislation was introduced to tackle a mounting environmental crisis linked to excessive quantities of animal waste and fertiliser spread on fields leaching into ponds, rivers and lakes. Desperate to overturn the new measures, the agricultural industry launched a scare campaign, suggesting that up to 10,000 farmers could be forced to cart millions of tons of manure across the country. They stoked up fears of congestion and disease, not to mention the inevitable stink. 'There will be manure criss-crossing the countryside from livestock areas to arable areas,' said a consultant to the National Farmers Union. The NFU's president wrote to the government claiming that the restrictions on spreading manure and fertiliser in sensitive areas would cost farmers about £100 million.[1]

The row highlighted just how serious the consequences of separating animals from the land had become. As animals have been moved off fields into barns, the age-old nutrient cycle of manure from grazing cattle and pigs replenishing tired soils has been broken. When too much manure is produced for any given areas, as happens on mega-farms, rivers and lakes are all too often polluted.

Britain's farm animals produce 80 million tons of muck a year. An average-sized dairy herd of a hundred cows can produce as much effluent as a town of 5,000 people. Across the country, there is a total of 1.8 million dairy cows,[2] not to mention many millions of pigs, chickens and other farm animals. Disposing of all this manure has become a phenomenal and increasingly costly battle. The muck presents the single gravest threat to our waterways, as Britain's farms account for the lion's share of water pollutants like nitrates and sediments.[3] Fertilisers and manure spread on the land can be washed into waterways; the excessive nutrients suck oxygen out of the water, choking aquatic life. Eventually, the water can become a dead zone, in which nothing can live.

The trend toward intensification of livestock farming, with more animals on fewer farms, is likely to make things worse. Manure, once a valuable commodity in the natural process of growing food from farm to fork, is now a problem. From the beaches of Brittany to the rivers of North Carolina, we find stark warnings of the perils from mountains of muck. But is anyone listening?

9

Happy as a Pig

Tales of pollution

BRITTANY IN BLOOM

Minutes before they collapsed, Vincent Petit and his horse had been happily galloping along the beach. When they set out for a long ride along Brittany's rugged northern coast, both the young man and his fifteen-year-old mount had seemed in perfect health. As a vet, Petit would have been better placed than most to spot anything wrong with his thoroughbred, and there had been nothing to trouble him as they thundered along the sand.

Coming to a rocky stretch, Petit pulled the horse up and dismounted, to walk the animal along a rough beachside road. It was here that they slipped, plunging into a hidden pool of algae that had accumulated on the shore. The sludge was so deep it reached to the horse's withers. Panic-stricken, Petit yelled for help. Struggling not to sink further himself, he battled to hold his horse's head out of the sludge, but within seconds the animal was dead. 'I cried for a man on a tractor to throw a rope, and then I looked at my horse and saw that his nose was falling into the sludge. I held his head up for him, but a few seconds later, he went into respiratory arrest, without even a fight. It was incredibly fast,' Petit recalled.

The horse was not the only victim. Moments later, the vet too lost consciousness. He was rescued by passers-by, who prevented him from drowning in the algae. Initial veterinary reports suggested that the horse had died from asphyxiation. An autopsy told a different story. The horse hadn't drowned: it was poisoned. Both animal and rider were overcome by toxic gases from the algae.

The tragedy happened in summer 2009, casting the spotlight on the environmental disaster unfolding on Brittany's beaches. Once upon a time Saint-Michel-en-Grève, the quaint seaside resort where the accident took place, attracted thousands of tourists. Now the beaches in the area are no-go zones, and hotels are struggling. Sunbathers and sightseers have deserted the picturesque inlet and coves. Holidaymakers have been replaced by workers in bulldozers battling to clear the unsightly and potentially lethal algae that have been washing up on the shore.

Commonly known as sea lettuce, the weed-like algae, resembling lettuce leaves, are naturally present in small quantities all along the littoral. But in certain conditions, when the warm summer sun hits the calm shallow waters of some of the prettiest bays in the region, they proliferate, spurred by an excess of nitrogen carried downstream by polluted rivers and waterways. The algae sweep in with the tides in what is described by locals as mighty green swells and amass in stinking piles on beaches. As they dry up and begin to decay, they release hydrogen sulphide, otherwise known as 'sewer gas', and other toxic fumes that get trapped in pockets under a fine white crust of residue.

Apart from their reek (they smell of rotten eggs as they putrefy), the algae were long believed by locals to be harmless. According to Yves-Marie Le Lay, a philosopher who heads up a local conservation group, though dogs occasionally went missing on the contaminated beaches, the owners simply assumed they'd drowned.

However, in recent years a series of fatal accidents, beginning with the death of two large dogs on the Saint Maurice beach in 2008, have left little doubt that the algal blooms pose a threat to all forms of life in the water and on the shore. In summer 2011, the corpses of thirty-six wild boars, a badger and a river rat were found washed up on the Saint Maurice beach near the mouth of the Gouessant River, all within days of each other. Autopsies revealed lethal doses of hydrogen sulphide in the tissues of all but one of the animals. Despite the weight of evidence, it was nearly a month before the authorities confirmed publicly that the animals had been killed by the noxious algae.[1] 'It must not be said that the green tides kill,' Le Lay told us when we went to Brittany to investigate. He was referring to the way that this crisis is being hushed up by local government, for fear of what it could mean for tourism.

The Saint Maurice beach has since been closed; a sign in French blocking the way simply reads 'Access Prohibited'. On the brushy headland next to the beach, a small chapel bears witness to the monster on the beach. Local activists have nicknamed it 'Notre dame des algues vertes' (Our Lady of the Green Algae).

As life ebbs from areas contaminated with the green algae along Brittany's northern shores, elsewhere in the region business is booming. For just beyond the windswept vistas of the Côtes d'Armor and quaint cobbled summer resorts that draw in tourists from around the world lies a very different kind of landscape: an ugly vista of industrial pig farms. Not far from the bay of Saint Brieuc is a dense network of highways and roads that link together a thriving industrial hub. There are warehouses, factories, processing plants and superstores, all connected to the region's most important economic sector: the production of pork, eggs and milk.

Brittany produces 14 million pigs a year.[2] The region is France's top pork producer: over half of the nation's pigs are reared here.[3] There are as many pigs produced annually in these parts as there are people in London. Despite the number, you'd be hard pressed to spot a single one rooting in a field or farmyard. Here, pig farming is heavy industry, driven by modern machinery, cheap labour, biotechnology and metrics that demand the highest output at the lowest cost.[4] In France, this type of farming is known as 'hors sol' or off-land.

Ask a local environmentalist about the green algae crisis and you'll invariably get a history lesson that begins just after the Second World War. It was then that 'les Américains', helping to rebuild the country after the war and keen to develop new export markets for their own agro-industry, brought factory farming to France. As André Ollivro, head of a local environmental campaign group, told us when we visited, no one could have anticipated the consequences. 'A farming model was developed but no modelling or trials were ever carried out,' he said gloomily.

Brittany's landscape was transformed. Le Lay describes how massive monoculture cereal plantations replaced the graceful rolling pastures of clover or alfalfa that animals once grazed on. Farm animals were sent indoors into feedlots, industrial triumphs of productivity that measure their performance with terms like 'stocking density'. According to Le Lay, cereal crops now harvested on Breton lands are processed into animal feed, alongside other crops sourced from around the world, including soya, often from deforested land in Brazil. Access to the global commodities market means there is never a shortage of food for the ever-growing herds.

And the pigs themselves contribute to their own nourishment. They are housed on perforated concrete floors above massive containers that collect their waste. The liquid manure is then spread heavily as agricultural fertiliser, largely on the corn plantations that now cover most Breton farmland. Corn is a resilient crop which can withstand doses of pig slurry as fertiliser that would flatten other crops such as wheat. The fields are said to be doused in treble or quadruple the amount needed to optimise yields. 'Where else are they to put it?' Le Lay told us with a French shrug.

According to André Pochon, a pioneer of sustainable farming in the region, Brittany's corn fields have become a 'dumping ground' for pig manure: 'Local authorities have aggravated the situation by allowing farmers to spread the slurry when the land is bare [of crops]. When it rains, the slurry drains into the rivers and aquifers. It's nonsensical; these practices defy the most elementary laws of agronomy.' The result is that massive quantities of phosphates and nitrates sweep into the region's aquifers and waterways, ultimately draining into the Atlantic. There they feed the spread of algal blooms that deplete the water's oxygen level and suffocate fish and marine life. In the end, there are dead zones that can no longer sustain life. 'Nothing lives in the bay of St Brieuc any more,' said Le Lay. 'Everything has died. We used to be able to fish periwinkles and clams from the rocks. The sand is black now; it's saturated with hydrogen sulphide.'

When the weeds finally make their way through the tides onto dry land, they pose a potentially fatal health risk. Thierry Morfoisse worked for one of the local companies charged with cleaning some of the beaches contaminated with green algae. In 2009, having unloaded a final load of seaweed at a treatment centre, he passed out and was found dead by the foot of his truck at the roadside. Paramedics took a blood sample onsite; his body, its darkened skin showing signs of suffocation, was taken straight to a funeral home. His family was told he had died of natural causes.

The affair might have been kept quiet were it not for the horse that died days later on the beach in Saint Michel-en-Grève, raising alarm bells at the Elysée and prompting a visit to the region from the then French prime minister François Fillon. An autopsy carried out two months after Morfoisse's burial, unknown to his parents and against their wishes, revealed that the forty-eight-year-old algae worker had died of cardiac arrest,[5] possibly resulting from a pulmonary oedema, the often fatal signature of hydrogen sulphide poisoning.

Understandably, the authorities appear to have been all too well aware of the public alarm that this was likely to cause. Apparently, Morfoisse's death was reported to have been linked to basic poor health and his smoking habit. His family is now suing for involuntary manslaughter. They believe his employers were negligent, failing to protect him from the poisonous fumes. 'He was well and truly taken to the gas chambers,' is how his father Claude put it. They are still waiting for the case to be heard before Parisian courts:

There were no gas masks, no metering devices [used to detect the presence of hydrogen sulphide], no automated boxes [to unload the algae], nothing at all. My son had to come out of his truck to unload the containers; he was caught between two fires – the gases at the treatment centre and those coming from the truck. I keep saying, I don't want my son's death to be in vain. Something has got to be done.

His wife Jeanne, a small, gentle woman, speaks of her concern for the children playing on the beaches. She sees them scrambling on the rocky shores of the Côtes d'Armor, where perhaps her own son once played. They are rough-and-tumble playgrounds where seaweeds naturally accumulate, beyond the reach of the bulldozers sent to clear the beaches. 'If a child dies on these beaches, there will be no other name to call them but murderers,' she told us, referring to the local authorities.

Experts agree that the green algae crisis is just the most visible aspect of the pollution from pig farms. Dr Claude Lesne, who specialises in pollution at the University of Rennes, told us that the pig manure contains traces of pesticide and cadmium, a carcinogen that can disrupt the endocrine system and is added to zinc supplements to speed up growth, as well as residues of the antibiotics routinely given to the pigs. There are many public-health implications when these wash off the fields into the water supply. In the dark, rank sheds where the animals are reared, the air is filled with toxic gases, faecal germs and bacteria. Both animals and the farmers in this area frequently suffer from chronic respiratory disorders and other health problems.

Were it not for the powerful ventilation system required to keep the animals, to the untrained eye the pig farms would be fairly indistinguishable from any other warehouse. According to Thierry Dereux of the pressure group Côtes d'Armor Nature Environment, the reach of the gases is so extensive that residents of Lamballe, a small city in the hinterland of the Côtes d'Armor, are forced to breathe higher than normal doses of ammonia.

Few things in the region seem untouched by the industry. When we visited in August 2011, locals were celebrating the annual mussel festival. The celebration will soon become history. We were told that the water pollution is so bad that harmful bacteria including *E. coli* are rife, and by 2015 the EU is expected to impose a ban on the sale of mussels from the area. People are doing their best to put a brave face on it. There is a solidarity that local activists prefer to call denial.

'*Dieu merci*, there will always be smokers,' a woman who runs a small tobacco shop and news-stand told us as we scanned the latest headlines about the wild boars that died on the beach. She voiced fears that the dead animals would finish off many local businesses. Le Lay believes most folk in the area are still in denial. 'The stakes are too high,' he said. Tackling the problem 'would mean radically revisiting the agricultural model. But when thirty-eight animals die, it's time for emergency measures.'

Campaigners in the area have modest demands: an information campaign to raise public awareness of the risks and a more thorough clean-up of the shores. I couldn't help feeling that such measures would be no more than a sticking plaster over a gaping wound. It's clear that the problem won't go away until it is stopped at source. This means starting to restore the balance between land and animals, and recognising that there are now far more pigs than the land can sustain.

There are about fifty pig farms in the region now using what is called the Pochon system, a more sustainable form of pig farming where the animals are fed mainly from what is grown on the farm and live happily on straw beds.[6] Alternatives to industrial farming exist and are successfully being practised by some farmers, but they are still considered mavericks by many of their peers in these parts.

PINK LAGOONS IN AMERICA

After giving a quarter of a century of service to his country in the United States Marine Corps, Rick Dove was looking forward to a gentler way of life as a fisherman on the river Neuse near his home in North Carolina. Snaking its way right across the state, the waterway, 442 kilometres long, has a proud history. It is said to have been named by two of Sir Walter Raleigh's scouts, Arthur Barlowe and Philip Amadas, who found it while exploring the New World in 1584. They named it after the American Indian tribe known as Neusiok, who lived along its reaches.

Dove's childhood dream was to make a living on the river, and when he left the forces in 1987 he bought a boat and set to work. For a while it was all that he hoped it would be. He caught enough to make a good living, and his son went into business with him. Between them they owned three boats. They crabbed and net-fished, selling the catch both retail and wholesale. They opened their own seafood store in the local town.

Just a few years later, however, father and son were forced to abandon the business after the fish began to die and they themselves fell seriously ill. Their livelihood and health were under threat from a deadly organism. The second element of its name, *Pfiesteria piscicida* (PP), is the Latin for 'fish killer'. It's often referred to as the 'cell from hell'. Between 1991, when it was first detected in the Neuse, and 1999 when it peaked, this single-cell organism is thought to have killed more than a billion fish in North Carolina. It also made many fishermen sick.[7] Its arrival in the Neuse was traced to pollution from pig manure.

The commercial hog industry in North Carolina is huge. It is worth around $2 billion a year to the economy,[8] and at any one time there are around 10 million pigs being raised on factory farms in the state.[9] That number of pigs makes mountains of poo: in one North Carolina county alone, 2.2 million pigs generate as much untreated manure as central New York City creates sewage.[10] Like the manure produced on every factory farm, it has to be disposed of somewhere – and all too often it ends up in the wrong place.

The state of North Carolina is no stranger to factory farm-related disasters. In 1995 it was the scene of a catastrophic spill when the dike of a 10,800-square-metre lagoon filled with liquid manure belonging to a pig-farming company ruptured. A torrent of pig waste – 117 million litres – poured into the headwaters of the New River. At the time it was the biggest environmental spill in US history, more than twice the size of the *Exxon Valdez* oil spill six years earlier.[11] Almost two decades on, environmental legislation in North Carolina is tighter but the potential for manure-related disasters persists. Huge lagoons of pig sewage, upwards of 3,000 of them,[12] dot the North Carolina landscape. Each can hold vast quantities of faecal matter, urine and other obnoxious by-products: blood, excrement, afterbirths, even still-born piglets. The liquid is pinkish brown. Anyone who falls in is almost certainly doomed.

In an exposé of the pig-farming industry some years ago, *Rolling Stone* magazine described the perils of trying to save a person who falls in. The article cited a case in Michigan involving a worker who passed out while repairing a lagoon, overcome by the fumes, and toppled in. His fifteen-year-old nephew dived in to save him but was likewise overcome. The worker's cousin went in to save the teenager and suffered the same fate. Almost unbelievably, two further relatives died the same way that day trying to rescue the others.[13] It sounds too incredible to be true, but pig manure is ten times more water-polluting than untreated domestic sewage.[14]

Inevitably the lagoons sometimes overflow, allowing the noxious soup to flood over fields and seep into groundwater. Campaigners claim that major floods turn entire counties into 'pigshit bays'.

To stop this happening, farmhands sometimes reduce the level of the lagoons by pumping out some of the stuff and spraying it over nearby farmland. Unfortunately the process is not always carried out in moderation, which brings what the industry calls 'over-application'. The land becomes saturated with pig waste, which festers in stagnant toxic pools. Scientists attribute to this the devastating attack of *Pfiesteria piscicida* in the Neuse. It appears to have caused eutrophication of the river, a process in which phosphorus and nitrogen (high concentrations are found in livestock waste) over-enrich water, distorting the ecosystem. The excessive nutrients create the ideal conditions for algae like PP to flourish, sapping oxygen levels in the water till eventually there is too little oxygen to support any other life, and leading to so-called 'dead zones'.

Dove shudders at the memory: 'Between 1991 and 1999, we lost billions of fish – certainly a billion and a half. I know that because I was on the river. I watched. These fish had huge holes right through their body. They'd get sores, these bleeding, ulcerating sores, and fishermen get the same sores.' He said the problem was unknown in North Carolina before the swine industry arrived. It was not long before Dove himself got sick, as did his son. As they would no longer eat fish from the river themselves, he says they couldn't possibly have continued to sell it to others. He described PP as a 'vampire' because of the way it eats away at fish flesh. In humans, prolonged exposure has been linked to brain scarring, central respiratory problems and memory loss. Dove's memory was impaired, his respiratory system was damaged, and his immune system remains weak.

Dr JoAnn Burkholder, the biologist from North Carolina State University who first identified PP, experienced its corrosive effects herself. One day early in her research, while pouring the algae into a flask, she recalls how she became disorientated and began to suffer from stomach cramps. Her eyes became so bloodshot that for a few hours she could hardly see. She also suffered short-term memory loss. The research was moved to a secure room, but not before another colleague had to be hospitalised.

After he gave up fishing Dove did something else for a while, but he pined for the water. When an opportunity arose to be river keeper on the Neuse in the mid-1990s, he leapt at the chance. That's when he began investigating who was to blame for wrecking the river. 'I've been trying to pay them back ever since,' he said. Now retired, Dove regularly takes to the skies above North Carolina in a beat-up old Cessna. From the air, he documents the environmental impact of large-scale industrial pig farming. Over the last sixteen years he has compiled a dossier of more than 80,000 pictures and hundreds of hours of film footage exposing the pollution caused by the farms, most of it linked to manure.[15] He uses the material he has gathered to fight for better standards, particularly from the meat giant Smithfield, the largest pork conglomerate in the world. The company owns most of the pigs in North Carolina, but as Dove explains, likes to claim it doesn't own their poo: 'Smithfield tries to contend that when the poop comes out the back end of the pig they no longer own that – that belongs to the grower who's going to grow the pigs for them.'

After years of legal battles, things are looking up. There are new regulations in North Carolina governing the disposal of pig waste. Pricey Harrison, North Carolina's Democratic member of the House of Representatives, has also introduced a bill to make all hog operations compliant with new air and water-quality standards by 2016.

Yet the environmental and public-health nightmare created by the seas of manure from factory farms is not unique to this place. Wherever there are factory farms, there are all too often problems with disposing of the manure they produce. For fly-by-night operators, the temptation is huge to cut costs by 'accidentally' allowing lagoons to leak, or by breaking regulations on the quantity that can be spread on fields. Even conscientious operators make mistakes. On a typical factory farm, the amount of manure is simply so enormous that disaster is rarely more than a cowpat away. According to the US Government Accountability Office, an independent non-partisan agency that works for Congress, a very large hog farm rearing 800,000 hogs – of which there are at least two in America – could generate more than 1.6 million tons of manure annually, or more than 150 per cent of the urine and faeces produced by the 1.5 million residents of the city of Philadelphia, Pennsylvania.[16]

On traditional mixed farms, manure is a valuable fertiliser. The trouble with factory farms is they produce far too much, too far away from land that could benefit. All too often, it ends up in the wrong place. According to a review by American and Canadian environmental scientists, releases of phosphate into the environment now exceed 'planetary boundaries' – they have overloaded nature's means to cope.[17] The result is widespread eutrophication of lakes and rivers, something I witnessed myself in China. There are now dead zones across the world, devastating fishing and tourist industries as well as contaminating drinking water.

Repairing the damage is costly. In Kansas alone, scientists have put the cost to taxpayers at $56 million. As Kansas is not one of America's major dairy or pig-producing states, the bill in other states must be far higher. Based on data put together by the Union of Concerned Scientists, a not-for-profit environmental pressure group, a rough estimate of the total cost of cleaning up after American pig and dairy factory farms could approach $4.1 billion.[18] No wonder factory farmers are so careless about the waste they produce. Disposing of it properly involves big money.

The US Department of Agriculture believes it would cost around $1.16 billion a year to spread manure over farmland in an environmentally friendly way.[19] The trouble is that many arable farmers would refuse to accept it as fertiliser anyway – even if it were free. One reason is the stench. The large tanks and lagoons in which it is usually stored create chemical conditions that make it smell far worse than it does when it initially emerges from the animal – like rotten eggs.

The scene is little better in Europe. Under EU law, large pig and poultry facilities are now classified as 'industrial installations' for pollution purposes. It means they are bound by the so-called 'Pollution Prevention and Control regime'. This requires each 'installation' to have a permit setting out emission limits and various other conditions on the release of pollutants. In theory, the rules imply a minimum 'spreadable land area' available per animal. A 1991 EU directive on nitrates set out certain limits to the amount of manure that can be applied to land and when it can be spread. However, Brussels admits the effects have been limited, saying recently that member states need to 'step up their efforts regarding monitoring, identifying pollution hot spots, and tougher action programmes'. The European Commission has noted that 'storage capacity' for manure remains a 'frequent problem', suggesting that factory farmers are failing to cater for periods when applying manure to land is banned or impossible because of bad weather.[20]

Throughout my travels, the muck issue has always come up, from Lake Taihu in China, where pollution has ruined the drinking water, to California, where rivers have been stripped of fish. It's probably no coincidence that a proposal for Britain's first US-style mega-dairy was dealt a death blow by the Environment Agency's concerns about water pollution. Near and far, the effects are being felt.

10

Southern Discomfort

The rise of the industrial chicken

After an idyllic childhood in rural Georgia, USA, Janisse Ray never doubted what she would do for a living. As a little girl, she spent endless happy days with her grandparents Arthur and Beulah on their farm, roaming around, building dens and eating crab apples, pomegranates and muscadines, a delicious type of purple grape. She remembers her grandfather's mules, her grandmother's chickens, fields of vegetables and sprawling watermelon vines, and granaries full of corn. During her pre-school years, her grandmother milked a cow.

The post-Second World War years brought the so-called Green Revolution in the USA, and agribusiness began to woo farmers towards a new dawn. It marked the start of a long slide from agrarian to industrial life. American farmers began using heavy machinery and fertilisers; the face of the countryside was transformed.

When Ray was six, her grandfather died. Soon after, farmers in the area began to grow subsidised tobacco and douse their crops with Roundup weedkiller. 'Then came monster combines, terrible erosion and the invasion of privet,' Ray recalls. The cane grinder was sold, the smokehouses fell, the last hen wasn't even eaten. Her grandmother sent the milk cow to the livestock auction. Ray remembers the final pea patch. On that same farm where she spent her childhood, the fields are now sown with genetically modified soyabeans. The fences have been torn down, the wax myrtle has gone, and the wild cherry trees have been felled. The mockingbirds and cardinals have fallen silent. The sassafras tree her grandfather carefully skirted with his harrows is long dead.

In the neighbours' field are two industrial chicken houses, lit day and night, where tens of thousands of birds are fed grain with antibiotics until they are fat enough for slaughter. Whoever is in charge is not a farmer but a 'contract grower', rearing the birds for some distant corporation. Sometimes the smell of burning chicken corpses fills the air. Sometimes the air is acrid with the smell of chicken litter being spread on fields. Everyone hates it, but something must be done with the muck.[1]

Today Ray lives in a beautiful old farmhouse with forty-six acres of land in southern Tattnall County Georgia, in the delta of the Altamaha and Ohoopee Rivers. Despite the ugly transformation of the agricultural industry in Georgia, she never gave up her dream of becoming a farmer and now makes a living growing organic vegetables, pecans, fruit and seeds, as well as producing meat and eggs from grass-fed animals free from growth-promoting antibiotics and hormones. Her farm shop sells homemade sodas – birch beer, ginger ale, root beer, raspberry and cream – as well as jams, jellies, woodcut note cards, granola and cakes. She also runs workshops on cheese making, fermentation, backyard chickens and other modern homesteading and sustainability skills.[2]

It could not be more different from the dominant type of farming in the state of Georgia today: industrial chicken production. Chickens are the most populous farm animal on the planet. Worldwide, 55 billion chickens are reared for meat each year; nearly three-quarters are factory-farmed.[3] The US produces nearly 9 billion broiler chickens for meat a year on some 27,000 farms.[4] A typical farm will raise 600,000 birds a year.[5] And with that number of chickens comes an awful lot of chicken muck. The chickens in Maryland and Delaware alone generate 42 million cubic feet of litter – enough to fill the US Capitol dome nearly fifty times over.

Down the years, I've visited many chicken farms rearing broiler birds for meat. From Britain to Beijing, they're all much of a muchness. Commercial chicken production is dominated globally by just two or three breed companies responsible for supplying the genetic strains of an estimated 80 per cent of the chicks. The white-coloured fast-growing broiler chicken, together with its health and welfare problems, has become a standardised global product.

In hotter countries like the Philippines, there are often slightly fewer birds packed into each building and the sheds are frequently open-sided with natural light. In the EU, the birds are most often kept in fully enclosed industrial buildings. In the Peruvian desert, they were housed in what looked like long low tents. These differences are mainly cosmetic: the conditions inside the buildings are all along the same industrial lines. Europe recently passed new legislation designed to protect the welfare of meat chickens, but it did little to help. In fact, Britain's chickens can be packed even more tightly into sheds than under government guidelines in the 1990s.

Georgia is the largest producer of meat chickens in the United States, rearing 1.4 billion meat chickens every year.[6] If it were a country, it would be the sixth-largest poultry producer in the world.[7] The heart of the industry is in the foothills of the Blue Ridge mountains in a place called Gainesville. It enjoys a dubious status as 'poultry capital of the world'. Georgia's chicken industry started to evolve as early as the Great Depression, when Jesse Jewell, a feed salesman from Gainesville, was struggling to keep his business afloat. Millions of Americans were out of work, some on the brink of starvation. Bread lines were a common sight. Farmers were desperate and had little money to buy feed or chickens. Jewell came up with a plan to sustain sales: he started selling baby chicks to Georgia farmers on credit. The farmers raised the chicks and then sold the fully grown birds back to him for a profit. Eventually Jewell had enough farmers producing broilers for him that he was able to invest in his own processing plant and hatchery.[8] He was a pioneer of so-called 'contract farming'.

In 1939, there were fewer than sixty chicken farms in Hall County. With the onset of the Second World War, the poultry industry in Georgia began to grow. The US War Food Administration, which administered food reserves during the conflict, snapped up all the chicken processed in North Georgia, giving poultry farmers a guaranteed buyer. The industry boomed. Within a decade, Hall County had over 1,000 chicken farms.[9]

Jewell's own business expanded. In 1954 he added a feed mill and rendering plant.[10] Eventually, J. D. Jewell Incorporated had the resources to manage every phase of chicken production, from hatching to processing, distribution and marketing. His 'vertically integrated' production model, in which he controlled a chain of companies managing every step of the process, set a new industry standard, as did his trademark frozen chicken. His approach to hiring was also innovative: he was one of the first employers in Gainesville to take on black workers.[11]

For the next couple of decades, broiler production in Hall County continued to thrive. Sensing a quick buck, everyone piled in. Competition drove down prices, but through the 1970s and 1980s Americans were acquiring a new taste for poultry over red meat, and there was no shortage of demand. During the 1990s the number of companies involved in the business fell, but not because there was any less appetite for chicken. It was simply that the industry consolidated, with fewer and bigger operators, serviced by an army of contract growers, who continued to expand. Within less than a decade, the number of chicken farms fell by half.[12] Today, just a few companies dominate the industry. In 2006, Gold Kist, an Atlanta-based company founded during the Great Depression, merged with Pilgrim's Pride Corporation to form the world's largest poultry company.[13] These food giants are vertically integrated and continue Jewell's practice of contracting out to farmers the business of turning chicks into broilers.

In 2012, Compassion in World Farming expanded its work beyond Europe into the US. One of its first initiatives, led by US director Leah Garces, was to set up a coalition of concerned organisations under the banner 'Georgians for Pastured Poultry'. A detailed study was commissioned of the broiler chicken business in Georgia, where conditions and practices are fairly typical of those in the industry worldwide. The findings exposed the grim realities of this type of farming, not only for the birds themselves, but for many of those who make a living from the industry.[14]

For the big companies who pull the strings, it's a business that continues to bring in megabucks, but for the farmers – or rather 'contract growers' – it's a stressful line of work to be in, characterised by the constant threat of being cut loose by their sole customers: the companies who employ them to fatten the birds. The chickens remain the property of the firms, who set out their expectations in legally binding contracts and pay according to targets and performance league tables.[15] Growers have little negotiating power, and anti-competitive behaviour by those who hold the purse strings appears commonplace.

Carole Morison, an award-winning broiler farmer whose contract was terminated after twenty-three years, has told how she was constantly bullied by the companies she worked for. 'I can't count the many, many times that I have heard in one shape or form that our contract was going to be terminated if we did such and such. That's no way to communicate with people who are your business partner,' she told a public workshop.[16] This is the way that 99 per cent of broiler chickens in America are reared,[17] not by farmers on homesteads using generations of acquired knowledge about livestock and land, but by producers at the beck and call of company bosses in far-off offices who issue instructions and targets.

For the chickens themselves, it's a grim existence, with virtually no legal protection. All farm animals are exempt from America's Federal Animal Welfare Act. Despite comprising 95 per cent of farm animals reared in the US, for some reason chickens are not even protected by the Humane Methods of Slaughter Act.

No other farm animal has been as selectively bred as the meat chicken to reach an unnatural size so quickly. Over the last fifty years, growth rates have quadrupled.[18] Getting the birds to target weight now takes no more than seven weeks.[19] At this age, they are still very young; chickens don't reach puberty and start laying eggs, for example, until about eighteen weeks old. This rapid growth has allowed for mass production of cheap meat, but the chickens pay a heavy price, from leg problems to heart disease and a condition colourfully dubbed 'flip-over syndrome', characterised by sudden frantic wing-flapping, shaking and loss of balance, sometimes accompanied by a shrill clucking. Within a minute or so, birds fall onto their backs or sides and die.

Like other factory-farmed animals they are kept in extremely crowded conditions. The typical 'grow house' for a flock in Georgia is reported to be 15 metres wide and 150 metres long,[20] and contains more than 30,000 chickens. Each bird has what has become the customary floor space, the size of a sheet of standard typing paper.

Because of cramped conditions and obesity, leg disorders are common. In fast-growing breeds, the development of birds' bodies cannot keep pace with their weight gain, making walking painful. Most move around only when absolutely necessary to reach food or water. Towards the end of what the industry calls their 'growth cycle', or just before slaughter, they spend most of the time sitting or lying down. Some are in such poor shape they can barely walk.

Leg problems are just one of many health problems associated with the system. Heart and lung disorders are another, linked to the sheer size of the birds' bodies. Not surprisingly, an estimated 42 million chickens in Georgia every year die before they get to slaughter weight.[21] Because it makes them eat more, and therefore grow faster, they are typically kept in continuous, or near-continuous, light. This has become a major welfare issue, disrupting their natural bodily rhythms.

When they are ready for slaughter, chickens are manually caught for taking to the slaughterhouse. Catchers grab up to seven chickens at a time – three in one hand and four in the other – before pushing them into crates for loading onto trucks. It's an unpleasant process, usually carried out in the dark in an attempt to reduce stress. According to the Southern Poverty Law Center, a civil rights organisation based in Alabama, supervisors require catchers to grab and crate birds at the almost unbelievable rate of around 1,000 an hour.[22] On arrival at the slaughterhouse, where as many as 200,000 birds a day are processed,[23] they are typically taken out of their crates, loaded onto conveyor belts and shackled upside down by their legs. They may be stunned – rendered unconscious – before having their throats cut, but unlike in the EU, it is not a legal requirement in the US.

On welfare grounds alone, there is clearly a case for changing the way meat chickens are reared, but it isn't only the birds who suffer. According to a 2010 report by the US Bureau of Labor Statistics, poultry processing is among the industries with the highest rate of non-fatal occupational illness.[24]

Georgia offers a depressing insight into the working lives of the 47,000 people employed in the industry, a high proportion of them female and Latino.[25] Many of these workers, especially those in the lowest-paid roles, face daily hazards and have few rights and protections.[26] Being a catcher is particularly unpleasant. Workers are contracted by poultry companies to round up birds for transportation to slaughter. They are typically paid per truckload filled, at rates that work out at less than the minimum wage.

Tom Fritzsche, from the Southern Poverty Law Center, has interviewed many catchers. 'One thing that is really noticeable about many chicken catchers is how their hands look,' he reported. 'They are swollen to double the size of a normal hand and some workers even shrink back from shaking hands, because it's so painful. There's even a condition that people refer to as "claw hand", that some chicken catchers develop from gripping so many chickens so tightly over the years.'

Catchers tend to be divided into crews of seven or eight workers, and have limited contact with the companies that ultimately pay their wages. It's a fly-by-night business. Investigations have suggested as few as 5 per cent of workers have clear employment conditions and many travel from job to job in unlicensed, unsafe vehicles. Fewer than 15 per cent of crews keep proper records to ensure that workers are paid properly for the hours they do.[27]

Jobs at processing plants fall into three broad categories: slaughtering, deboning and packaging. Specific roles include live hanging, a task that involves removing birds from cages when they arrive and hoisting them by their feet onto moving shackle lines; wing folding – twisting and tying carcass wings into position for cutting; wing cutting – using scissors to remove chicken wings from carcasses; and deboning – cutting meat from dead birds. There are also many unpleasant cleaning jobs.

Of these jobs, live hanging is among the worst. To keep the birds calm, they stand on hard floors in almost complete darkness, lifting each bird by its legs to hang it on hooks, at shoulder or head level, attached to moving conveyor belts. They may hang up to twenty-six birds per minute, a process that often strains workers' upper shoulders and necks.[28] Here's how one worker described the experience:

> I hung the live birds on the line. Grab, reach, lift, jerk. Without stopping for hours every day. Only young, strong guys can do it. But after a time, you see what happens. Your arms stick out and your hands are frozen. Look at me now. I'm twenty-two years old, and I feel like an old man.[29]

According to official figures, around one in seven workers is injured on the job, more than double the average for all private industries. Poultry-line workers are forced to keep pace with speeding conveyor belts, repeating the same finger, hand, wrist, arm and shoulder movements as many as 20,000 or even 30,000 times a day.[30] The result is that they are fourteen times more likely than other workers to suffer repetitive strain injuries.[31] The speed of the conveyor belt is directly correlated with company profit. Workers are under constant pressure to perform faster, and fear of retaliation pervades processing plants.

I wish I could say that US-style industrial meat-chicken farming was confined to North America. Sadly, it's how four out of five chickens are reared in Britain too. The system is dominant in Europe and has spread across the world.

Some years ago I was invited to be an after-dinner speaker at a gathering of poultry producers. I was pretty sure the entertainment value would be in me entering the lions' den, rather than anything I was going to say. And once I'd finished, they didn't hold back. Some of the remarks from the floor are unprintable. Others were very defensive. I was asked: 'How can you criticise my farm if you've not seen it?' It was only a matter of time before someone invited me over. Their tone was confrontational: 'I challenge you, Philip, to visit my farm . . .' To this day, I'm still not clear why that was seen as such a big deal. I accepted the invitation without a flicker of hesitation. After all, I'd been to plenty of chicken factory farms before then, and many more since.

When the meeting was over and I was sportingly given a case of English wine as a thank you, the chairman had the task of organising my 'Challenge Philip' visits. It was not straightforward. It turned out that the ones reluctant to let me come were the very individuals who'd thrown down the gauntlet in the first place. It hadn't taken them long to have second thoughts. To avoid the club's embarrassment, Andrew Maunder and David Lanning of a company called Lloyd Maunder filled the breach and the visit was arranged. I'll never forget Maunder's face when I told him bluntly that modern broiler chickens were genetically selected to suffer. We were sitting in his farmhouse kitchen, having a chat. He looked surprised – almost wounded. We spent the day looking round farms, standing in huge sheds thick with top-heavy white birds. I'm sure he'd already seen the potential in moving away from the intensive system. A few years later, his business changed the way they reared their chickens, giving them more space and attaching far greater priority to welfare.

The state of industrial chicken farming in Britain was exposed in 2008 by an investigation commissioned by Compassion in World Farming. Grainy footage from inside dimly lit warehouse-like sheds showed tens of thousands of birds, packed so close together they looked like thick white carpets. They would have more room in the oven. Some were limping or lifeless. Outside were dustbins full of dead chicks; the ones that didn't make it to six weeks old. We didn't know where the chickens were bound. What we did know was that this was the kind of production system supplying major supermarkets with cheap chicken. At the time, 95 per cent of Britain's 800 million meat chickens were kept like this.[32]

The subsequent outcry, spearheaded by the celebrity chefs Hugh Fearnley-Whittingstall and Jamie Oliver, made so-called 'battery' chicken a high-street talking point. People in unprecedented numbers started demanding higher-welfare chicken. By 2010, despite the economic recession, nearly a quarter of fresh chicken sales were from farms keeping their birds in better conditions: free-range, organic or RSPCA Freedom Food standard.[33] Some supermarkets responded strongly to customer concerns. The volume retailer Sainsbury's is moving all its fresh chicken to a new higher-welfare standard, dumping what the media have dubbed the 'battery' bird. That one commitment alone means that nearly 100 million birds a year face the prospect of better lives. The Co-operative, Marks & Spencer and Waitrose have committed to similar things.

On a recent trip to America, I found myself in a retail park in midtown Atlanta, Georgia, home of civil rights leader Martin Luther King. Slap bang in the centre was a Whole Foods Market store, a food emporium if ever there was one. On chilled shelves lay neat rows of chicken products complete with animal welfare ratings. Signs extolled the virtues of the produce – 'Raised with care', or 'Great tasting meat from healthy animals' – and a chalkboard listed local farmers supported by the store. I recognised some of the names. They were part of a new group, Georgians for Pasture Reared Poultry, which recently exposed the dark side of the state's industrial chicken business. Even here, in the epicentre of the global industrial chicken phenomenon, the signs of a better way are starting to show.

V
SHRINKING PLANET

A police motorcade with outrider bikes and flashing lights sweeps into the East Anglian town of Ipswich, making for the docks. A helicopter buzzes overhead, keeping a watchful eye on the crowd gathering below. It's a blustery September evening. In the fading light, a horde of cameramen scramble for a picture. Yet this is no celebrity exit from the country. Flanked by police vehicles are six livestock transporters carrying sheep destined for slaughter on the Continent. It's the latest skirmish in a twenty-year war of attrition between live-animal exporters and opponents of the trade.

Banner-waving protesters yell into the night as the four-tier juggernauts disappear into the gloom. A former Soviet tank carrier waits by the dockside for its live cargo. It's the first shipment of live animals for slaughter out of Britain since the exporters were thrown out of another port following an incident involving two arrests and the death of over forty sheep.

Many people, myself among them, have spent much energy trying to stop animals being transported on horrifically long journeys simply to be slaughtered at their destination. Today this notorious trade is but a stubborn rump of its original shape: fewer than 100,000 animals exported live from Britain every year, compared with 2.5 million two decades ago.

Yet in ports across the globe, another trade linked to the questionable treatment of animals is booming. It's the import and export of grain and soya for animal feed, much of it destined to feed animals on factory farms. It takes place day and night, without fanfare or protest, and in many ways is just as insidious as live animal exports. As I discovered on a personal journey to bear witness, producing and transporting all this soya and cereal to feed animals is a dirty, thirsty business, ruining many lives.

Over the coming decades, the world's livestock population is set to near-double in the face of rising global demand for meat. It comes at a price. Much of the predicted increase is from industrial farms that use vast quantities of water, oil and land to churn out meat, milk and eggs of dubious quality. The resources required are in diminishing supply. Many of the world's best brains are now focused on solving an increasingly vexed question: the mismatch between growing global demand for food and the world's ability to deliver on a shrinking planet.

Land

How factory farms use more, not less

NO MAN'S LAND

Deep in the forests of northeastern Argentina live the last survivors of a once proud tribe. For centuries, the American Indian Toba Qom were feared and revered by outsiders. So remote and inaccessible was their terrain that it was known as the Impenetrable Forest. According to early Spanish settlers, the nomadic hunter-gatherers were fierce and unforgiving, hardened by their inhospitable surroundings. Today just a handful of Toba Qom remain in the Chaco and Formosa provinces. Theirs is a hot, humid lowland, stretching from the banks of the Paraná River to the Andean foothills and across international borders into Paraguay and Bolivia.[1] Once it was a rich and spacious hunting ground with all the natural resources needed to support their primitive lifestyle. Now, far from being impenetrable, much of the ancient woodland has disappeared, the elegant quebracho trees felled for their fabulous hardwood timber and the land carved up by anonymous speculators whose business is growing genetically modified soy, some of it for biofuels, some destined for factory farms, in the UK and elsewhere.

For the hard core of Qom who have doggedly refused to leave the Chaco, life today is a bitter struggle. Shockingly, in a country whose economy has boomed, in recent years some are reported to have starved to death.[2] Without land on which to hunt, grow and forage for fruit, gnawing hunger has become the norm. The traditional cotton cultivation in Chaco, which provided seasonal work, has disappeared to make way for the less labour-intensive soya production. There are few if any jobs left. The Qom manage as best they can, eking out a living from the little land they have left and turning to witchdoctors when they fall sick, but herbal remedies and rituals are proving no match for the scourge of malnutrition.

In 2011, five Qom made a drastic decision. Carrying little more than the clothes they were wearing, they left the Chaco and embarked on a 1,000-kilometre journey to Buenos Aires, where they set up camp at the intersection of two of the capital's main avenues and began to stage a hunger strike. The aim was to secure an audience with government officials, to demand the 'immediate return' of land they claim is rightfully theirs and has been appropriated by the provincial government. A few months earlier, two Qom had been killed in a violent clash with police in Formosa, after they blockaded a road in protest at the disappearance of their land. They manned it for four months, during which tensions with local authorities rose. Finally it seems both sides opened fire, with tragic consequences. The Qom were not the only victims: a police officer was also killed.[3] As each year goes by and the Qom feel more oppressed, the stakes for the last survivors rise. Many have abandoned what appears to be an ever more hopeless battle to preserve their heritage and, against their instincts, left Chaco for a new life in the city.

The Qom are just one group among many who have become victims of factory farming's appetite for land. In a disturbing form of modern colonialism, land in developing countries is being carved up by richer nations to guarantee a steady supply of cheap meat. The flow can only be maintained if there is enough grain and soya on which to fatten the animals, no matter how far it is grown from where they are reared.

The notion that factory farms save land is a widespread misconception, yet an argument commonly deployed in their defence. I remember a prominent figure in the poultry industry insisting factory farms were space-saving and scoffing at the idea that all chickens could be reared free-range. 'There wouldn't be a mountain in Scotland or a valley in Wales or any spare business land in any town, city of village that would not have a chicken on it,' he claimed. Free-range for all chickens was, in his words, 'absolutely ludicrous and impossible to achieve'.

In fact, if all chickens in the UK were reared for meat free-range, they would take up an area around a third of the size of the Isle of Wight – not so ridiculous after all. The entire global population of meat chickens – about 55 billion birds – could be kept free-range on an estate the size of Hawaii.[4] And though it is hard to imagine all 70 billion of the world's factory-farmed animals being reared in such a way, the idea becomes less ludicrous when you consider how much land they already require, including a third of the world's entire cropland.

Intensifying farming, getting more crops or animals out of the same land, may seem like a space-saving idea, but in practice it encourages more land to be used, not less.[5] Scientists from Argentina, the US, Canada, France and Belgium found that agricultural intensification between 1970 and 2005 was accompanied by cropland expansion. Part of the reason is that the intensive farming of animals is fuelled by the industrial production of animal feed crops. So much land is used for industrially farmed animal feed that if it were all in one field, that field would cover the entire surface of the European Union, or half the surface of the United States.[6] A third of the entire global cereal harvest goes to livestock; even more – 70 per cent – in rich countries.[7] In addition, about 90 per cent of the world's soya meal is destined for industrial livestock. If that food wasn't diverted to feed animals in factory farms, the land could be used for something else. Every year, an area of forest equivalent to half the UK is cleared, largely to grow animal feed and for cattle ranching.

So factory farming actually uses a vast amount of land or 'ghost acres' – it's just that the animals themselves are often no longer on it. The concept of ghost acres was invented in the 1960s by Georg Borgstrom, a professor of food science and geography at the University of Michigan.[8] He used the expression to describe the difference between the amount of food a country consumes and the amount it grows on its own land, a gap filled by imports. Half a century ago, he was warning that this gap was too big. Factory farming has dramatically increased it. According to one calculation, the amount of land used worldwide for agriculture has increased by almost 500 million hectares – ten times the size of France – in the last forty years.[9]

This might not matter if the supply of fertile land was infinite, but it is not. Estimates vary widely of the amount of remaining virgin land in the world that is suitable for cultivation. The most optimistic figure is 15.6 million square kilometres of rain-fed land – roughly equal to the existing cultivated land area.[10] But this is likely to be a gross overestimate of what might be realistically available, because much of it is forested. The World Bank has come up with a far more modest figure that excludes forested areas: 4.45 million square kilometres.[11]

It may sound like plenty. The trouble is that rising population, urbanisation and erosion are swallowing up fertile land at a ferocious pace. And much of it is in Africa and Latin America, which means that wildlife will likely be bulldozed to make way. The result is a global land grab on a phenomenal scale. It is the twenty-first-century equivalent of the scramble for Africa in Queen Victoria's reign. Though it is being driven by a number of factors, particularly the global demand for biofuels, the insatiable demand for animal feed to supply factory farms bears much of the blame.

In Argentina, 200,000 hectares of woodland are believed to be lost each year to make way for soy.[12] Genetically modified soya now covers at least 19 million hectares[13] of the country – 65 per cent of the entire farmland[14] – much of it for export. The level of soy planting is causing disquiet as yields stagnate due to high inflation and lack of crop rotation needed to maintain healthy soils.[15]

Carlos Vicente works for GRAIN, a small international organisation that campaigns to safeguard land for local communities to manage their own food production. I met him at his home outside Buenos

Aires, where he told me about the devastating impact of 'land grabbing' for soya production in his country:

> What we're looking at is a new breed of food colonialists. In Argentina, the stark reality is that we have stopped producing food for ourselves. Fruit and vegetable production has fallen drastically – they now have to bring it into Buenos Aires from a thousand kilometres away. More than fifteen thousand dairy-producing farms have gone out of business in the last fifteen years. Milk production has declined so dramatically that at times there's been talk of having to import it from Uruguay.

I asked him how all this had affected ordinary people.

> The single-crop model does not really need people. In Argentina, the authorities themselves have said that it takes only one person to work five hundred hectares of soya. So we can produce twenty million hectares of soya with a few thousand individuals, and the rest of the people – rural folk who used to be farmers – are simply left over.
>
> The impact on biodiversity and public health has also been huge. For example, we have had outbreaks of dengue fever, caused by mosquitoes. They have been extremely precisely mapped and occur where there are soya plantations. Why? Because those areas are now monocultures, where the natural habitats of the animals that controlled mosquitoes have been destroyed.

Land deals in Argentina and other parts of South America are often highly complex, involving multiple countries based in different parts of the world. Speculative buyers pool finance with hedge funds, investment funds and pension funds. 'It's impossible to get a clear picture of who is buying the land to hoard and produce food,' Vicente said, 'though we know Saudi and China are both trying to strike these deals with the government here.'

Naturally there are winners from the system, like Gustavo Grobo-copatel, CEO of the agriculture giant Los Grobo. In Argentina, he is known as '*el rey de la soja*' – 'the soya king'. His company controls more than 250,000 hectares of soya.[16] 'He boasts about being the most successful farmer with no land,' Vicente told me.

During a trip to Argentina I went to talk to some Qom people who had lost their land to soya. It was a sad and troubling experience. Most of those who abandoned the Chaco now live in a poor suburb of Rosario, an industrial town 300 kilometres northwest of Buenos Aires. Arranging an audience with them was a delicate task and involved lengthy negotiations. Instinctively suspicious of outsiders, they had grown cynical about sharing their story, feeling that they had often given their time and energy for no immediate tangible return.

My co-author, Isabel, and I enlisted a local anthropologist, Laura Prol, to speak on our behalf. Over a period of weeks, she talked to the Qom about our work, gently persuading them of the case for drawing wider attention to their experiences. A meeting of community leaders was held to discuss our request. Finally they agreed to see us, but it was clear it had not been a straightforward nor a unanimous decision. We were keenly aware of the sensitivities, anxious to make it clear that we came neither as voyeurs nor as wealthy benefactors bearing material gifts.

We found their neighbourhood in a rough suburb of Rosario, down a bumpy dirt road lined with weeping willow trees. We had been warned that the area was a hotbed of crime; rife with car-jacking and theft at gunpoint. We left our valuables in our hotel.

The Qom houses were solid and weatherproof but extremely basic, with perhaps two rooms for sleeping and eating, and outdoor toilets. Out in yards, families cooked over real fires and chickens pecked in the dust. Stray dogs roamed the streets and children played in the dirt. Our meeting was at a community centre. We arrived to find about ten men sitting around a table in a small, poorly lit room. It was full of antiquated IBM computers – like the old Amstrads of the 1980s – which had been donated by well-wishers. Though none of the machines were switched on, we were told they all worked and were used for computer literacy classes. The men – there were no women – were drinking maté, a bitter herbal tea made from the yerba plant. As is traditional in Argentina, it was served in a communal cup through a curved nickel straw, and offered to everyone present. They eyed us warily.

It was a difficult few hours, complicated by the fact that the Qom have their own language, an additional challenge for our Spanish–English translator. The secretary of the group introduced himself as Abel Paredes, a name he described as having been 'imposed' on him by white people. What he meant was that it was not his indigenous name, which he did not seem to want to give. He wore a sporty fleece and cargo trousers and looked in his late forties. As he told his story he became emotional, his voice dropping and breaking:

> I came to Rosario with my brother and cousin, who live in a shanty town. My parents stayed in Chaco and are now dead. Over the centuries, our people have been pushed into smaller and smaller territories. Then some years ago a multinational came in and bought our land. The provincial government sold our land, with us included in the price, because we happened to be there. We had no value of course. We used to live in the forest; hunting for alligators, honey, iguanas, fish, and we tilled the land, growing vegetables and cotton. When the multinational arrived to grow soya, they fenced off the land and installed armed guards. What could we do? We are peaceful people, and so we decided we would try our luck here in Rosario.

For Paredes and his family, it had clearly been a desperate decision. 'We didn't want to come here and live on the edges, as beggars, but we were driven out,' he said. The displacement of the Qom from their ancestral land began long before soya cultivation took off. However, the huge sums to be made from growing soyabeans have accelerated the process.

Paredes said that when they first arrived in the city, they were treated as foreigners. They faced a bitter fight for the most basic services, including education for their children, and were ostracised by the local community, who accused them of bringing parasites and diseases like tuberculosis to the city. Now they have their own school in Rosario, where pupils are taught in the mother tongue. However, they claim that their access to healthcare services and other public services remains extremely limited.

Others had similar stories. The vice president of the community centre, Domingo Lassaro, whose elderly parents are still in Chaco, said he came to Rosario five years ago, after a company bought 40,000 hectares of his ancestral land. They fenced it off and installed sophisticated surveillance systems, leaving his family destitute.

We asked the men what their message would be to the outside world, a question that prompted lengthy debate. It boiled down to a demand for the same rights as the rest of the population, particularly in terms of access to healthcare and secondary and adult education, as well as reservations for Qom still in the Chaco. 'We don't want handouts, just recognition of our rights,' Paredes said finally.

> There is a healthcare centre just a block away from here, but all it is, is a building, with a sign outside. There was an election recently, and the candidates promised they would get it up and running, but it is still empty. We want to preserve our identity as indigenous people, but we also want to get on in this city. It would be good to have a government teacher to help us with literacy. Even our houses here are not our own – we could be evicted at any point.

We left the community centre feeling drained. It was a truly moving experience. We owed the Qom something for talking to us, but it was hard to see what we could deliver, given the scale of the difficulties they face. They show how the poorest and most disempowered people in the world are being cast aside to ensure a steady supply of artificially cheap, poor-quality chicken, pork and beef for people thousands of miles away. For that is where much of the soya meal ends up: feed for industrial livestock.

Just as it was in the nineteenth century, Africa is the other target for rich land-grabbers. A 2009 UN study of land transfers in five sub-Saharan countries – Ethiopia, Ghana, Madagascar, Mali and Sudan – found that 2.4 million hectares of land had changed hands in such deals since 2004.[17] A separate study the same year by the International Food Policy Research Institute put the figure for Africa between 2006 and 2009 at 9 million hectares, about three-quarters of the total amount 'grabbed' worldwide.[18]

More up-to-date studies dwarf these figures. A report by the World Bank found evidence of 'large scale land acquisitions' of 45 million hectares in 2009 alone. Many of these ventures have yet to get off the ground – the WB described more than half as in 'initial development' stage – but the general (upward) trend is undisputed.[19] An international conference on Global Land-Grabbing held in London in 2011 estimated that more than 80 million hectares of land were acquired in this way in 2008–9[20] – an area nearly twice the size of California, the USA's third-largest state.

It's a phenomenon driven by speculators, such as the UK investment management company Chayton Africa. Glancing at its website, you might think its business is luxury travel. There are glorious photos of pink sunsets over fields of sunflowers; rainbows over rushing waterfalls. In other images a patchwork carpet of luscious green pasture rolls out under a vast skyscape and a huge sprinkler quenches fields of ripening corn.[21] It could be France but in fact it is Zambia, and the firm's line of work is making money for Western investors from rich African soil.

The firm's founding partner, Neil Crowder, a former Goldman Sachs man, believes there are substantial returns to be made from growing food crops in this part of the world and has snapped up thousands of acres in Zambia for maize, soya and wheat. He is using Zambia as a guinea pig before launching similar ventures across sub-Saharan Africa.[22] 'We have identified Botswana, Malawi, Mozambique and Tanzania as target markets for our investments,' he has said, boasting that once his firm's huge agribusiness in Zambia has taken root, it will have 'numerous competitive advantages'.

For the hordes of international investors now piling into agriculture in Africa, this sort of financial adventure is little more than an experiment with what Crowder calls 'a new asset class'.[23] So far, there is no evidence that his project has upset or disadvantaged the local population. However, if it does not it will be the exception rather than the rule. In Africa there are multiple examples of both warlords and legitimate governments blithely selling land to foreign companies, at the expense of local people.

The Ethiopian government appears to be a particularly enthusiastic seller and has set aside 3 million hectares to lease to foreign and local companies for food crops.[24] In 2008, it signed a deal with an Indian-based multinational, Karuturi, involving 311,000 hectares in a remote part of the west of the country – a tract of land larger than Luxembourg. Karuturi's usual line of business is cut flowers, mostly roses grown in giant greenhouses in Ethiopia, Kenya and India.[25] Every year the company produces 555 million stems which are shipped across the world to luxury markets in places like Hong Kong, Muscat, Dubai and Japan. Now they are diversifying, as their website says, into 'agribusiness' and have taken up cultivation in Ethiopia 'on a mega scale'.[26]

The Ethiopian government believes that partnerships with companies like Karuturi are good for the people, 85 per cent of whom are smallholder farmers. Berhanu Kebede, Ethiopia's ambassador to the UK, has dismissed the amount of land involved as 'relatively small' compared with the 76 million hectares of arable land in the country, saying that investors such as Karuturi bring 'huge benefits, not just the jobs, houses, schools, clinics and other infrastructure, but knowledge transfer, skills training, tax revenue and other benefits to the workers and country as a whole'.[27]

However, by their own admission officials have sometimes been too hasty to sign deals. Karuturi's original concession ran right through a national wildlife reserve, which had been created in 1974 to protect an endangered species of antelope. The Ethiopian government belatedly realised that Karuturi's venture was located dangerously close to the antelopes' migration route, and the boundaries had to be redrawn.

Officials later admitted they had 'signed an agreement without any coordinates or delineation of the land . . . a mistake'.[28]

Meanwhile the catalogue of benefits for the people has been slow to materialise. Previously, locals earned a living by farming or fishing. More recently, they have been reported as being employees of Karuturi, earning less than the World Bank's $1.25 per day poverty threshold.[29] The Ethiopian press has carried various reports of exploitation, and child labour appears rife. Local people say they were not consulted about the deal. Karuturi says that things will get better, and that it pays at least Ethiopia's minimum wage. Bosses claim they are 'very very cognizant' of the fact that the company is dealing with people who are 'easily exploitable', and have grand plans to build a hospital, cinema, school and a daycare centre in the settlement.[30] Yet the reality is that locals have lost control of their own land and with it their destinies, perhaps for the sake of cheap burgers thousands of miles away.

The near-miss for Ethiopia's rare form of antelope underscores the future threat of a world where wildlife is forced out. There is already intense pressure for land, bringing wildlife into competition with people. Over the next few decades, climate change is likely to increase this competition. Witness what has happened at Titchwell RSPB bird reserve in Norfolk. One of my earliest memories of this magical place was a night I spent on the reserve when I was eighteen years old. It was 3 am on a warm spring morning and I was sitting in a makeshift dugout looking out over an expanse of marshland glowing silver in the moonlight. Every now and then the gulls would spook themselves, taking to the air and filling the hush with harsh cries. The glimmering white of a barn owl sometimes hovered overhead like a ghost. But this was no ordinary birdwatch. I was a volunteer on the night watch. My vigil was to protect the nest of the rare wading bird the avocet, famous as the emblem of the RSPB, and returning from the brink of extinction in Britain. It was nesting for the first time on Titchwell's brackish marsh, a wonderful shallow lagoon where fresh water and salt water meet.

These days, the primary threat to birds is habitat destruction, but anachronistic as it seems, rare species still face a threat from egg collectors. It's a strange throwback to a bygone age when it was commonplace for schoolboys to collect birds' eggs. Although it is now illegal, a small number of offenders persist. They will go to great lengths to steal the eggs of target species, and the avocet was definitely on their hit list. The warden of Titchwell marsh, a nature reserve owned by the RSPB, was very worried. 'Eggers', as we called them, had been reported at other sites along the coast, so my fellow volunteers and I organised a rota to keep watch.

When it came to my turn, I sat through the night in my dugout a mile or two from the nearest help. It was long before the days of mobile phones. It was a privilege to see the natural world at this hour. I felt drunk through lack of sleep but purposeful and resolute. Every now and then, I wondered what I'd do if the eggers came. And then the moment I'd been dreading happened. The wind suddenly whipped up, the gulls spooked, and against their eerie cries, I could hear what sounded like boots on gravel – 'scrunch, scrunch, scrunch . . .'

The sound was distant at first, but it grew louder. My heart pounded as I considered my options. Grabbing a stick, I leapt out of my dugout to do my duty – only to discover that my foe was water lapping on gravel. The rest of the night passed without incident and I felt a bit foolish. Several days later as dawn broke on another night watch, I peered out to catch sight of avocet chicks. The first Titchwell avocets had hatched, and on my watch! I was elated. All the efforts of the warden, us volunteers and the support of people far and wide had paid off.

That was 1984 and the early years of the RSPB's tenure at Titchwell Marsh. It has since gone on to become one of the most popular and best-loved nature reserves in the country. Some 90,000 visitors flock there every year. It is famous for its breeding bitterns, bearded tits and marsh harriers, the latter among my favourite birds.

Now the reserve is under threat from rising sea levels. The brackish marsh that I watched over as a volunteer all those years ago is to be sacrificed to save the rest of the reserve. The RSPB wants to save the freshwater haunts of the bitterns and harriers, and that means realigning coastal defences, at the expense of the marsh. The magical expanse on which those first avocets hatched will slowly be claimed by the sea. New islands have been created to tempt the avocets to other parts of the reserve.

While the threat from the sea at Titchwell is part of a natural process of coastal erosion under way for many years, climate change is making things worse. The work to strengthen sea defences in this part of Norfolk should save these important freshwater marsh habitats for the next fifty years, but I can't help wondering what happens after that – especially as the reserve is hemmed in by farmland and village. Will we face a future where wildlife has nowhere to go?

The submerging of the Norfolk marshes is a reminder that climate change is not a theoretical problem for faraway countries to worry about. Its effects in places like the UK are very real. By the middle of this century, wildlife and many millions of people are likely to be displaced by rising sea levels. This will intensify competition for land, and is likely to cause profound difficulties, particularly as so many major cities are close to the sea.

Experts differ over the extent to which sea levels will rise over the next century. Unless the scientific consensus is completely wrong – probably a forlorn hope – then over the next few decades, millions of people will be forced to move away from the coast onto land previously used for agriculture. Planet Earth has reached 'peak land', the point in present history where land will begin to disappear as sea levels rise. It seems that a two-degree temperature rise this century is fairly inevitable; it would bring with it a one-metre rise in sea level.[31] This would have profound consequences as the rising tide laps at coastal cities and farmland alike.

A more modest sea-level rise of 0.7 metres this century would affect around 150 million people living in low-lying coastal areas, including some of the world's largest cities. Almost half of the world's top fifty cities are at risk, including Tokyo, Shanghai, Hong Kong, Mumbai, Calcutta, Karachi, Buenos Aires, St Petersburg, New York, Miami and London.[32]

The UN predicts that the growing appetite for meat, particularly in developing countries, will lead to a near-doubling of the current global livestock population. If this happens on an industrial basis, more land will also be needed to produce extra feed crops. It seems that human demand for land and other resources could well be on a collision course with global warming. Sea-level rises threaten to swallow up land, affect crop yields and cause widespread disruption.[33] To keep pace with the food demands of a growing population, experts suggest that an additional 2 million square kilometres of land will be needed by 2030.[34] That's the same amount of land that would be lost to the sea if the planet warms by two degrees.[35]

SCORCHED EARTH

Sundown on a cattle ranch, Argentina. Three gauchos in cowboy boots and berets leap and lunge, swinging their lassos at galloping calves. From a distance it's a curiously beautiful dusty dance, the animals bucking and ducking, their rusty hides rich red in the setting sun. Their hoofs kick up clods of mud as they hop and swerve to dodge the ropes. Hobbled, they crash to the ground, legs flailing, the thud of rumps throwing up great puffs of dirt. On the corral fence there's a box of Philip Morris cigarettes, the classic cowboy vice.

In a slick air-conditioned office, a rancher is mulling over whether to let us take a closer look. He is a lean fellow with a quirky moustache and the rich complexion of a man who has spent most of his life in the sun. He wears expensive-looking shoes, tight-fitting black trousers, a luxury watch, and a pair of Ray-Bans hooked into the top of his crisp white open-necked shirt.

He sits at the head of a long boardroom table. Behind him are a dozen silver-framed photos: three generations of his family. Before him is a neatly arranged stack of business cards, a sheaf of invoices and a large calculator.

On a couple of dozen acres in the Argentine pampas, the rancher's twenty-five-strong team of workers rear and fatten 4,000 beef cattle in conditions designed to maximise profit by getting the animals to market weight in the shortest possible time span. He has invested US$10 million in this feedlot facility, and by the looks of it he's making a handsome return. Soon he hopes to double the size of his beef herd. 'There are no limits. There's no roof out there,' he shrugs, gesturing at the corrals outside. This rancher is a typical Argentine feedlot operator. He also owns about 3,000 hectares southwest of Buenos Aires. For generations, this land would have been used for cattle grazing. Today only a fraction of the estate is for livestock. Like many other landowners in Argentina, the rancher now uses much of his estate for something else: cultivating genetically modified soya beans. His cattle live on little more than a patch of mud, while his most fertile fields are devoted to crops. 'That's where the real money is,' he told us with a knowing smile.

Soya production is a little-known but vital part of the factory-farming system, meeting the colossal demand for high-protein animal feed for industrially reared animals. Much of the soya produced on the pampas, the plains of Argentina, is ground into soya meal and shipped to Europe and the UK, as well as China, where most is used to fatten pigs and chickens.

Though the destructive effects of soya production for biofuels have been widely documented, particularly in relation to deforestation, the devastating environmental, social and health impact of soya production for animal feed has largely escaped the spotlight. In terms of overall production, Argentina grows nearly a fifth of the world's soya beans, behind only the USA (35 per cent) and Brazil (27 per cent).[36] Most of Argentina's land used for arable crops – 18 million hectares of a total of 32 million – has now been turned over to genetically modified (GM) soya.[37] Cultivators churn out almost 50 million tonnes of the stuff every year,[38] much of it for the overseas market.

Argentina has established itself as the soya meal export capital of the world, accounting for nearly half of global exports.[39] Soya meal is the high-protein powder that is separated out from the oil when the beans are crushed. Although soya can make perfectly good nutritious food for people, much of it is destined for industrial animal feed. The UK is an eager customer – nearly half the soya meal imports used on British farms come from Argentina.[40] For Argentina, it's big business. Exports of soya meal alone were worth over US$7 billion in 2008.[41] With a 32 per cent export tax, it's a major money spinner for the government. For a handful of landowners and foreign speculators too, the returns have been spectacular.

Meanwhile the impact on the cattle-ranching industry has been far-reaching, with animals pushed off the land they used to graze and forced into intensive fattening systems: 'feedlots'. Corralled into grassless pens carpeted in manure, they are often sustained on a diet of concentrated feed and antibiotics and swiftly transformed into beef.

So Argentina offers a double window on the world of industrial farming. On the one hand, it is literally feeding factory farms in the UK and other parts of Europe, via shiploads of ground soya. On the other, it is a showcase for one of the most intensive farming systems in the world: feedlot farming, or what some call 'battery' beef. Already rife in South America and the US, these cattle feedlots could soon make their way to the UK and other parts of Europe. Meanwhile, in restaurants across the EU, diners continue to tuck into bargain-basement beef from Argentina thinking it is some kind of luxury product. Most are blissfully ignorant of the conditions in which it was produced, and know little of the true quality of the meat.

*

My journey to look at the transformation of Argentina's countryside had begun in the northeastern city of Rosario. With a population of 1.7 million, it is the third-largest city in the country. It lies at the heart of a major industrial corridor and is the hub of Argentina's soy industry, its sprawling grey port the dispatch point for soya exports.

The city is a 300-kilometre drive northwest from Buenos Aires through the pampas. With my journalist companion and camera crew in tow, my schedule and budget was tight. We landed in Buenos Aires mid-morning local time after an overnight flight from London, and with only a coffee and a rather leathery croissant from the airport, we picked up a hire car, met our local fixer and got straight on the road.

I was looking forward to the journey to Rosario and imagined a lush and varied landscape of eucalyptus trees, horses and haciendas. My heart sank as we broke out of the Buenos Aires suburbs and found ourselves in a pancake-flat landscape of endless soya. Though the iconic pampas grass still grew in abundance by the roadside there was precious little else to see from the car window but field after field of the scrubby little soya crop, either green or a dreary yellowish brown, depending on the ripeness. Farmers had turned the perimeters of their fields into rolling adverts for seed and pesticide companies, hanging ugly plastic posters from fences. There was little to break up the monotony: no villages, no churches, no farmhouses, and little sign of life except the odd stray dog lolloping along the verge.

It was an uninspiring introduction. Rosario wore a concrete tutu of slaughterhouses, meat-rendering operations, factories and soya-processing plants. All this industrial paraphernalia seemed to throttle what remained of the old town. A handful of fine nineteenth-century colonial-style houses and municipal buildings were eclipsed by more modern blocks of flats, offices and shops.

Overlooking the river was a clutch of sparkling new high-rise flats, apparently built with fortunes made from soy. Argentina remains haunted by the economic trauma of 1989, when inflation rates rocketed, and many entrepreneurs are still deeply mistrustful of leaving their money in the bank, preferring the security of bricks and mortar.

Rosario owes its status as an agro-economic hub to its location on the Paraná, the second-longest river after the Amazon in South America. It flows almost 5,000 kilometres through Brazil, Paraguay and Argentina before emptying into the Atlantic. In Tupi, a native Brazilian language that is now extinct, Paraná means 'as big as the sea', and at Rosario it is as wide as an estuary.

Since 1997, governments in the five countries of the Rio de la Plata Basin – Argentina, Brazil, Bolivia, Paraguay and Uruguay – have been plotting to transform the Paraná into an industrial shipping canal in a highly controversial scheme known as the Hidrovia project.[42] The river alterations outlined in the original plan, backed by the Inter-American Development Bank and the United Nations Development programme, included dredging, rock removal and structural channelling at hundreds of sites along the way, according to the organisation International Rivers. It could have had a devastating effect on the Pantanal, the world's largest tropical wetlands. The project was thrown out following an outcry by a wide coalition of environmental, social and indigenous organisations and various independent technical critiques, but is now back on the cards. The Andean Development Corporation is reported to have given the governments involved almost US$1 million for new studies, and there are fears that a revived scheme will involve even more intensive dredging and rock removal to guarantee the passage of barge convoys through twenty-three 'critical' river passes.[43]

If it goes ahead, the project will ease the flow of agricultural and other commodities through South America, to China and Europe – but at Rosario, it didn't look as if the export industry needed any help.

We arrived mid-afternoon, exhausted and bleary-eyed from the international flight and long drive. Next day we hired a boat to look at Rosario's many soya-processing factories from the water. At the small boatyard on the outskirts of the city there was a sickly meaty smell. The river was vast and appeared to be heavily silted, a great milk-chocolate flow punctuated by enormous tankers with romantic names like *Crimson Venus*, *Storm Ranger* and *Sea Honest*, flagged to Panama, Nassau and Limassol. There was nothing dreamy about the voyages they were about to undertake – no cargoes of coffee, wine, brightly coloured ponchos or other exotic Latin American goods. Just one product: soya, be it soya meal or soya beans. The vessels were magnificent in scale if not purpose, great hulking things the length of a small-town high street. There was little sign of life on board, though at one point a lone figure in an orange boiler suit appeared on a deck. Seeing us filming, he gestured at us to leave.

Soon it would be Easter, and the odd fisherman was trying his luck on the mud banks. On the riverbank, there were no trees or vegetation, only cracked brown mud, above which reared the dreary edifices of the soy-processing industry: enormous tangles of grey and brown metal, cranes and winches, funnels and chutes, pipes and ladder-like structures that looked like extended fire escapes. Huge pipes carrying waste water from the mills spewed their contents into the river.

The soya meal market is controlled by a handful of multinational operators. We sailed past a plant and watched an avalanche of soy pouring from a funnel jutting out from the factory into a ship container. Dust billowed over the boat: we were being sandblasted by particles of soya meal. The tiny beige flakes settled on our clothes.

On the other side of the river were verdant islands. Apparently they stretch for 70,000 square kilometres along the Paraná. During El Niño years, when the water is low enough, we heard that farmers drive cattle over the river to graze – but not before felling the trees, destroying a fragile ecosystem. The fact that cattle are on these islands at all has been blamed on the encroachment of soya, eating into grazing land. In 2009, the military were called in to help ranchers evacuate a million cattle off the islands for fear of the kind of flooding that claimed the lives of 300,000 cattle only two years earlier.[44]

The boat trip gave a stark impression of the sheer scale of the soya industry in Argentina: gargantuan factories and ships, industrial behemoths that feed factory farms all over the world. Who would live in such a place? The answer is: people who lived there before the industry arrived, and are stuck.

Rosario's soya factories have sprung up in the last decade or so, devastating what used to be peaceful suburbs. At a community centre in the neighbourhood of San Lorenzo, near the river, we met

Lillian Ober, a mother of two, in her forties. She moved to the area fifteen years ago after the old industries moved out, thinking it would be a nice place to bring up children. Today, no fewer than 1,000 trucks a day – she's watched and counted – thunder through her neighbourhood en route to the processing plants we saw from the water. It's a relentless, noisy, polluting caravan that is claimed to whip up coughs, asthma, and perhaps more sinister conditions.

A study by the Italiano Garibaldi Hospital in Rosario showed that in six towns in the region, the incidence of testicular and gastric cancer in males was three times higher than the national average; the incidence of liver cancer ten times higher; the number of cases of pancreas and lung cancer two times higher.[45] People who live in San Lorenzo believe it is the site of a cancer cluster. The dust is always bad, but what really gets them is the chemical spraying of soya as it arrives at the plants. To ensure the beans are insect-free when they are shipped overseas, we learned that the wagons are doused with chemicals before they are unloaded. The soy is sprayed again when it's dumped into storage containers, and sprayed a third time before being loaded onto the ship. I was told of local newspapers reporting that in the last decade as many as sixty truck drivers have dropped dead after being overcome by chemical fumes. It may only be anecdotal, but it's not hard to believe.

'When we moved to this area, my husband and I had no idea what was coming,' Ober told us. 'We thought it would be a lovely area to raise a family.' The community wants a proper assessment of the public-health risks associated with the industry. They have done their own informal research. It suggests that 90 per cent of health problems in the neighbourhood are respiratory or allergies. 'Everyone is complaining of the same sorts of conditions. We want an investigation. It seems obvious to people living here that the health pressures are linked to the soya industry, but we would like to see if there is scientific evidence.'

Six years ago, when a giant milling company decided to expand its plant in Rosario, Lillian and her husband thought about upping sticks and taking their two daughters, now eleven and fifteen, somewhere less polluted. After much soul-searching they decided to stay. They often wonder whether they did the right thing.

> My husband's elderly parents and family live here. You can't uproot an old tree, so while they are still alive, we won't move. It was also a principle for us – we wanted to teach our children that if you hit a problem, you don't just run away. You face up to it; tackle it. We can't change what's happened here, but now we are fighting to ensure the agro industry doesn't expand one more inch into San Lorenzo. But I do worry about my daughters' health.

Daniel Pablo, another local activist, in his early fifties, told us he had lost several members of his family to cancer. Perhaps it's just bad luck – after all, one in three people develop cancer at some point in life – but most of his relatives were relatively young, suggesting that something more is afoot. He told me:

> There's no history of cancer in my family. Yet since we moved here, my sister-in-law got a tumour; my brother got a brain tumour that killed him; and my brother-in-law got testicular cancer, for which he was successfully treated. Two of my cousins had premature babies, and my mother got a glandular condition. Two of my best friends died suddenly. All of them lived in this area. For the last four years, I've been asthmatic. Everyone here has allergies, particularly the kids. Soya is a business for the few and an epidemic for the masses.

The team and I left the community centre to look at the road where 1,000 or so trucks a day trundle to and from the factories. We stood on the verge, watching the wagons rumble along and churn up clouds of dust. Outside the plant nearest San Lorenzo a car park full of heavy vehicles waited to set off again. Behind barbed-wire fencing and a large sign saying *Prohibido* (Keep out) we saw the usual giant mesh of grey and brown metal: one factory, the size of a village.

With its apparent cancer clusters, nauseating smells and ugly industrial skirt, it was hard to see how anyone with a choice would hang around in Rosario. The following day we headed to San Jorge, 180 kilometres north, in the heart of the soya plantations. In 1996, Argentina became the first South American country to allow the use of genetically modified varieties.[46] Now the entire soya crop in Argentina is GM.[47] Initially, the new technology was a bonanza for farmers, increasing yields by 173 per cent.[48] It did not last. The weeds grow increasingly resistant to the chemicals, and farmers are having to use ever-stronger chemicals to produce the same harvest.[49]

The figures are startling. In 1990, before the arrival of GM in Argentina, 35 million litres of chemicals were used on crops per year. In 1996, the figure rocketed to 98 million litres. By 2000 it had soared again, to 145 million litres; and by 2010 the figure reached 300 million litres – almost ten times the amount of pesticides and herbicides used pre-GM.[50]

According to an organisation of concerned Argentinian doctors, known as Physicians in the Crop-Sprayed Towns, 12 million Argentinians are affected by the agrotoxins every year, as aerial and land-based sprayers douse houses, schools, parks, water sources and work areas. Incidences of serious public-health issues are on the rise, including rates of birth defects and stillbirths in such areas.[51]

One area that has been particularly badly affected is the poor Urquiza neighbourhood of San Jorge. Cancer rates in the suburb are reported to have spiked 30 per cent since 2000.[52] Our first stop was a press conference on chemical spraying at the municipal centre. A local politician, Esteban Roglich, was there along with Daniel Vezenasi, a doctor and one of Argentina's leading specialists in respiratory conditions. Roglich was unveiling a new bill he'd drafted that would create buffer zones around residential areas, over which aerial spraying would be banned. Local campaigners were also demanding that the few existing regulations governing pesticide spraying be properly enforced.

The doctor gave a powerful account of the health case. He talked of higher rates of miscarriage and birth defects in areas exposed to chemical spraying. He spoke of a research project he carried out with medical colleagues, involving eight communities with populations of under 10,000 in areas affected by crop spraying. In all, he and his colleagues surveyed a total of 45,000 patients. The research revealed that hypothyroidism is one of the top health issues in such areas – in stark contrast to the rest of the country.

Afterwards we went to visit a woman who had played a key role in exposing the human health risks associated with pesticide spraying. Viviana Peralta's story was sobering. The mother of six told us that she had been cooking tortillas at home in Urquiza when her baby nearly died. It had started out an ordinary day. Her husband was at work, selling furniture for a local carpenter, the older children were at school, and she was keeping an eye on the little ones while doing domestic chores. In the fields, soy cultivators were aerial-spraying the crops again. Then her four-year-old daughter Michaela burst in. 'Mum! Come quickly!' she shouted. 'The baby's not breathing. She's gone purple.' In her cradle, seven-month-old Aileen was having some sort of seizure. Peralta rushed the infant to the local medical centre, from where she was transferred to hospital, fighting for life. Later doctors told her that they had feared that a tracheotomy – radical throat surgery – would be the only way to save the infant.

Aileen, who had suffered from respiratory problems from birth, pulled through. The medics were in little doubt what was causing her problems: the remorseless aerial crop spraying in Urquiza. Peralta was advised to move out of the area and seek compensation.

So began a long campaign for justice: a quest not for money but for laws to stop the spraying. The day Peralta brought her baby back from hospital, she heard the familiar sound of a crop sprayer – this one a terrestrial 'mosquito' control vehicle – grinding its way towards the fields by Urquiza. She ran out of the house and stood in its path. The driver refused to turn back, so she hurled a brick at his machine. She chose to fight, not to move: she told us she and her husband had invested everything in their home.

'We built this place with our own hands and worked so hard for everything in it. It didn't seem right to me that we should be forced out, while the soy cultivators carry on their work.' Though her home was modest, there were signs of how hard she and her husband had worked: a fitted kitchen; a large TV and DVD player and an impressive hardwood dining table, large enough to seat twelve, with matching heavy wooden chairs. Outside was a pleasant yard where the children could play.

With Roglich's help, Peralta found a sympathetic lawyer in Santa Fe and took her fight to the provincial courts, having compiled enough medical evidence to prove beyond reasonable doubt the link between the pesticides and her daughter's near-fatal breathing difficulties. Local soy cultivators offered her money to shut up, and various other deals that she dismissed. 'At one point they offered to take me and my children to a hotel every time they were spraying. I didn't even consider it. They are so cynical.'

Eventually, her campaign paid off, but it was only a partial victory. In March 2009 a provincial judge banned cultivators from aerial crop spraying over her home, but absurdly the order only applied to her property. It means that theoretically the rest of Urquiza remains exposed. Aileen is now four and a half years old, an exceptionally cute little girl with long golden-brown hair swept up in a pony tail, dancing brown eyes and a cheeky smile. She made a full recovery from the seizure, and her health problems have largely disappeared since the spraying stopped, though she has been hospitalised on a number of occasions since with breathing difficulties. They appear to have been linked to drift from chemical spraying in the area. Some of Viviana's other children continue to suffer from respiratory problems. Her campaign goes on.

Our next stop was a provincial town outside Buenos Aires, where we hoped to find out more about how Argentinian beef is produced. It meant another long road trip. On the face of it the motorway network in Argentina is impressive: superhighways with toll booths, the road surface in impeccable condition. When the going's good, it can be great, as there are so few cars. The problem is grain lorries: there are so many of them that if there's an accident or roadworks, the motorway very quickly turns into a car park.

As we began a long drive southwest we found ourselves stuck on a slipway because of an overturned soya load. We were forced to leave the highway and take a scenic route. There was little to see. The countryside was featureless: nondescript soya fields, dusty villages, and the trappings of the agro industry. Somewhere along the way we passed a soy-processing complex the size of a town. Rows of rusty, dusty wagons were parked nose to tail in forty numbered lanes as if they were waiting to board a fleet of car ferries. Bored drivers loitered by their cabs. Beyond the rows of trucks we could see the plant itself, a grim grey monster. To the front were three enormous dark grey warehouses like aircraft hangars; behind, the usual giant tangle of funnels and chutes.

It turned out to be the edge of an agro-industrial estate. Half a kilometre away was another equally gargantuan plant, this one a huge grey block like a nuclear power station. Around the corner was a Monsanto factory with billboards outside advertising Roundup, the company's best-selling weedkiller.[53] From outside, with its innocuous green and red logos, it could have been a garden centre selling shrubs and plastic tables. Inside, brilliant minds were no doubt poring over new chemical solutions to nature's attempts to compete with monoculture.

The first feedlot we passed housed around 400 calves. By the road were tall conifers and clumps of trees, beyond which we could see maize fields. The countryside was richer, more interesting, than the usual soy, but in the corrals there was nothing for the animals to do except pick listlessly at their food. The temperature was pleasant, about 27 degrees. There was no shade for the cattle – not a serious problem in autumn but surely unbearable in summer.

I've seen many smaller versions of this – beef cattle crowded in one space – but this was something else. It was on a massive scale and very similar to the mega-dairies of California. I scrutinised the cattle: they were very young, and bored. Our arrival provided a brief distraction. The herd played grandmother's footsteps with us; as we stood looking at them from the road, they would inch towards us when we were still, retreating the second we advanced in their direction. I thought about the grass-fed cattle I was familiar with in places like the UK and felt glad this type of mega-farm has yet to arrive.

The town turned out to be a wealthy little place of coffee bars and plane-tree boulevards and what could almost be described as a boutique hotel, all mood lighting, low-slung sofas and wi-fi in the lobby. Its clientele seemed to be middle-aged businessmen from Buenos Aires, local landowners now rich enough to live in the city and pay someone else to do the hard work. After the grimness of Rosario, it was all quite pleasant.

We dumped our bags at the hotel and went to meet Pablo and Pilar Guerra (whose names have been changed to protect their identity), a couple who live by a feedlot on the outskirts of the town. Their home was a decent-sized, solid house with thick walls keeping it cool during the day and an extensive backyard. By the front door a skinny white cat lounged in a flowerbed, soaking up the afternoon sun. She was no ordinary family pet but one of a team of rat catchers, much needed around the Guerras' home since the feedlot was built ten years ago.

The couple's livelihood was a farm shop next to the house, where they sold home-cooked pastries, chicken and pork. They'd had the business since they bought the house twenty-six years ago. At that time it was in a lovely spot. Guerra told us he reckoned that the takings at his shop had halved since the feedlot arrived. The problem was the smell and the flies. Fighting to get the farmer to do something had proved hopeless.

For five years, I did everything I could to get the feedlot to clean up, or compensate us. I took my complaints everywhere I could – the local, provincial and national legislators; even the national watch-dog. We demanded that either the problems were tackled – the flies, the rats, the smells – or they closed down.

    I organised community meetings – we would get fifty or sixty people turning up, all unhappy about the feedlot – which is a very good turnout for a small place like this.

Despairing, Guerra and a handful of his neighbours sued the operators of the feedlot, winning a judicial order in 2008 to get the place shut down. It remained open pending an appeal, which the owners won. 'Gradually I realised I was knocking my head against a brick wall. Over the years, I must have discussed what was going on with 150 different politicians. They all fobbed me off with platitudes. Only one guy was honest. He told me: "This is your fate. Too bad. Accept it."' Guerra seemed a broken man.

    Though they gave up the battle years ago, he and his wife had not shrugged off their reputation as troublemakers in the eyes of local farming magnates. He told us that when he recently visited the local authority to renew his shop licence, out of the blue the official suddenly demanded to see the original plans for his house and shop. Guerra had never had them, and in twenty-six years had never needed them. Now, apparently there had been a 'complaint' about his property. 'Someone is making trouble for me. They'd be glad if I left the area,' he said sadly.

    When we met, he still had not obtained his permit and did not know how the situation was going to evolve. To make matters worse, he and his wife had just found out that a mega-piggery was being built over the road. Work had already begun. We saw the early signs of what was being built, all shiny aluminium. On the front was a bright orange sign saying 'Mega'.

    The value of Guerra's property had already fallen dramatically because of the feedlot. It must have felt like the last straw. The couple had spent the morning of our visit discussing whether to sell up, but like so many of the people we have interviewed for this book who have found themselves living next to factory farms, they seemed deeply reluctant to uproot.

    Later that day we met Miguel Martinez (whose name is changed for legal reasons), another man with a sad story about the feedlots. Approaching retirement, he was a civil servant in Buenos Aires, but spent weekends out here, where he grew up. He still had a little place near the town and some land, and once or twice a year he liked to head into the pampas to hunt wild boar. Dressed in his khaki hunting gear, he was clearly no sentimental animal lover. Yet he hated the feedlots, and what they had done to this area. He took us onto one of the fields he inherited from his grandparents, where he once hoped to build a house to retire. He abandoned the project when he discovered the neighbouring field had become a feedlot. 'I was going to build it right here, with a veranda looking out west,' he told us, gesturing to the plot he had in mind. 'There was a lovely little duck pond just over the hill, and woods behind. There was a fig tree my mum used to pick fruit from to make jam.'

The duck pond and fig tree had gone. In their place were thousands of cattle on mud. Around us was GM soy, interspersed by a lot of weeds and more mosquitoes than any of us had ever seen in one place. On Martinez's beige cap alone were at least eighty of the insects. They swarmed around our faces, attacking any bare flesh they could find. There was no stagnant water nearby; nothing that would obviously attract such a shockingly high concentration of flies. It seemed clear we were in the midst of an ecosystem out of balance.

Martinez seemed unfazed by the mosquitoes, but remembering his childhood and his retirement dream made him emotional:

> I was three months old when I first came here. This place is part of my life. It's where I learned to ride horses, and later to shoot, enough for dinner, never any more. There was always a strong sense of community; neighbours helped each other. My grandparents owned a thousand hectares, four hundred of which was divided between us grandchildren when they died. The rest was sold. Until the 1990s, all the farmers round here were local. They knew the area; had a connection to the place. Now it's just investors. One of the big land-owners round here owns car parks in central Buenos Aires. When I

came back here in 2005, after a while away, all the gates to properties in the area were padlocked. It was a shock. Some blighter who
bought the land from my grandparents' estate set up this feedlot.
When I saw it, there was the same feeling of terrible loss that I experienced when I had to clear out my grandparents' place, and when I
got divorced.

His reflections might have been dismissed as the misty-eyed nostalgia
of an old man, but Martinez made it clear that he did not simply
yearn for a bygone era:

> I understand that business is business. I am not against progress or
> anti-development. I don't mind living among cattle and horses. But
> four thousand cows on one field is too many, and the consequences
> are far-reaching. Small farmers cannot compete; the water supply is
> polluted; the air is bad. For investors, it's just money, but farming is
> not the same as working in the car industry; or owning parking lots.
> It's an art, and a responsibility.

The feedlot next to Martinez's land was owned by a successful
rancher. We knocked on his office door and told him about our
research. We handed over our business cards and after lengthy
consideration the rancher seemed satisfied, first ushering us inside
for an interview, and then accompanying us on a guided tour of the
feedlot. He told us that although he was brought up in this area,
these days he prefers the bright lights of Buenos Aires. In common
with many feedlot farmers who have made a success of their businesses, he now spends just three days a week on the farm; his home
is in the metropolis.

He was clearly proud of his business and spoke compellingly of his
drive to build a future for his children and grandchildren. He told us
he cared about his cattle. As we walked around the facility, I had spotted a dead cow abandoned at the edge of one of the corrals, swarming
with flies. It was a worrying sign, not least raising questions about

Equivalent area of global arable land dedicated to growing feed crops for farm animals

Cereal production

Other crops, including soya

If eaten directly, rather than fed to industrially reared livestock, the cereals alone could feed three billion people

How growing feed for industrial livestock increases pressure on finite arable land

Total land area suitable for rain-fed crop production worldwide: circa 30 million km²

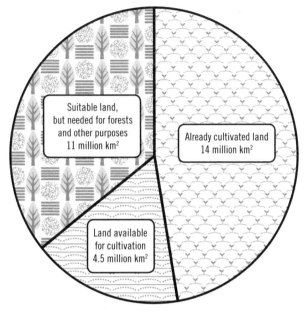

Suitable land, but needed for forests and other purposes
11 million km²

Already cultivated land
14 million km²

Land available for cultivation
4.5 million km²

'Ghost acres' farmed elsewhere to produce feed for industrially reared chickens

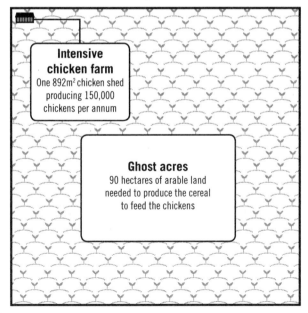

Intensive chicken farm
One 892m² chicken shed producing 150,000 chickens per annum

Ghost acres
90 hectares of arable land needed to produce the cereal to feed the chickens

First illustration based on OECD-FAO, *Agricultural Outlook 2009–2018. Highlights*, 2009 and K. Deininger, D. Byerlee, et al., *Rising Global Interest in Farmland: can it yield sustainable and equitable benefits?*, World Bank, 2010.

whether the rancher had the facilities to deal with the high mortality rate on feedlots.

Later that night, our last in the area, a local environmental group showed us film footage they'd taken of around two hundred dead cattle from a local ranch operation. They had been dumped, apparently using a digger, just outside the perimeter of the ranch, on what was thought to be public land. The corpses were in varying states of decay, some already little more than skeletons; others quite fresh, suggesting this was not some sort of one-off catastrophe.

I don't think the rancher we met was a bad man. Indeed, he was very courteous. Like so many of the people I have met in the factory-farming business, he struck me as just another enterprising but ultimately misguided individual trying to make money from a bad system.

12

Thicker than Water

Draining rivers, lakes and oil wells

TURNING OIL INTO FOOD

Northern Alaska is perhaps the most beautiful part of the United States. It is vast pristine tundra, illuminated at night by the dancing pinks, blues and greens of the Northern Lights and seared through the days by the dazzling Arctic sun. Almost a million caribou roam over this vast expanse, while the ice-bound coast is habitat for seals, polar bears and whales that fish beneath its freezing waters. This epic snowscape is also home to millennia-old native communities whose property is beginning to sag into the melting permafrost while their icy hunting grounds recede further offshore through global warming. Beyond the region's living beauty are treasures of our planet's evolutionary heritage, unique fossils of the dinosaurs and early mammals that first adapted to live in the cold.

However, the natural riches of this Arctic idyll go beyond what you see on the surface. The US Department of Energy estimates that about 10 billion barrels of oil lie beneath the tundra and frozen waters of Alaska's Arctic National Wildlife Refuge (ANWR) and its adjacent districts,[1] enough to feed US and EU domestic consumption for a year.[2] There is also an as yet unquantified natural gas reserve in the shale beneath whose rocks much of the oil is also trapped, complicating the process of extraction and increasing the potential for damage to the environment.[3]

Since 1980 there has been a Congressional moratorium on drilling in the area, reissued each year despite efforts by George W. Bush
to have it overturned during his presidency. In the wake of the 1989
Exxon Valdez disaster in Alaska's Prince William Sound, which was
the worst oil spill on record until the *Deepwater Horizon* catastrophe
in the Gulf of Mexico, it had seemed that the ANWR might be
spared the plundering of its natural resources. Indeed, President
Obama opposed exploiting Alaska's environmentally sensitive areas
during his first presidential election campaign, saying that he wanted
to reduce oil consumption and promote renewable energy.[4] His then
opponent, Senator John McCain, stated: 'As far as ANWR is
concerned, I don't want to drill in the Grand Canyon and I don't
want to drill in the Everglades. This is one of the most pristine and
beautiful parts of the world.'[5]

However, as high fuel prices continued to hurt the US consumer,
the president changed his position, announcing the issue of new leases
to oil companies in a vast region directly bordering the ANWR. Meanwhile Shell, which had shelved its Arctic drilling plans in the face of
opposition from environmental groups and regulatory hurdles, has
announced it is now considering pushing ahead again following positive signals from the government.[6]

Several other oil giants are heading in a similar direction. Total
wants to develop the Shtokman natural gas field off Russia, the largest
single potential offshore Arctic project, 560 kilometres into the
Russian-controlled part of the Barents Sea.[7] Meanwhile BP is planning to join a £10 billion venture to develop onshore oilfields in the
Yamal-Nenets Autonomous Area of Russia, in the Polar Circle.[8]

Such is the global hunger for oil that it seems no potential new
source, wherever it lies, remains off-limits to energy giants for long.
Factory farms are a big driver of the insatiable demand. While golden
fields of corn and cows in sheds may seem a world away from ugly
power stations and the plunder of precious habitats in the relentless
quest for more black stuff, farmers are among the fossil-fuel industry's
most important customers. Whereas traditional farms relied on

manual labour, modern agriculture is heavily dependent on oil- and gas-guzzling machinery and huge quantities of petrochemicals. That's why farmers are so often at the forefront of fuel protests. When oil prices rise, it hits them hard.

Most academic research into the amount of fossil fuel used by industrial farms has been carried out in America, where a study led by Professor David Pimentel, a renowned ecologist based at Cornell University in New York State, found that conventional crop production in America swallows up the equivalent of 6.3 barrels of oil per hectare. Of this, two-thirds is used for petrochemicals like fertilisers, pesticides and other inputs.[9]

One tonne of US maize, a staple feed crop for intensive livestock, takes a barrel of oil to produce,[10] while modern farming methods globally use two barrels of oil on average to produce enough fertiliser and pesticide for one hectare of crops.[11] Agriculture for food production is such a big oil eater that it accounts for 7 per cent of America's entire energy usage.[12] Oil and industrial farming are so tightly connected that Albert Bartlett, a physics professor at the University of Colorado, has described modern agriculture as 'using land to convert petroleum into food'.[13] This process is likely to become increasingly expensive as the era of cheap, easy oil draws to a close.

Conventional sources of crude oil and gas are running out and there is widespread consensus that energy is only going to get more expensive in future. This will have a knock-on effect on food prices. A doubling of oil prices, for example, could lead to US grain becoming about 20 per cent more expensive.[14] This would mean people paying more for staples like cereals. It would also increase the price of factory-farmed meat, for which feedstuffs like cereals form two-thirds of the production cost.

In 2007, a meeting of the National Petroleum Council in America heard evidence that 28 per cent of existing oilfields were in decline by 2005 and 40 per cent would be in decline by 2008–9.[15] This bleak forecast seems to have been right. In 2010, the International Energy Agency published figures showing that production from crude oilfields currently operational peaked sometime between 2006 and 2008. The IEA predicts that output from these fields will decline by as much as a third of 2010 production levels by 2035. At a press conference in London in November 2010 to unveil a report on the future of world energy supplies, the organisation declared: 'The age of cheap oil is over,' though policy action could bring lower international prices than would otherwise be the case.[16]

The Oil Depletion Analysis Centre believes the world has now consumed almost half the total amount of conventional oil that most experts estimate will ever be available for recovery. 'A dozen recent independent analyses all show global production reaching a natural peak within the coming decade [i.e. up to 2020],' the organisation has said.[17]

So-called 'peak oil' – the point at which the maximum rate of petrol extraction is reached, after which production falls into decline – was a big talking point a few years ago, but has now largely been replaced by discussion about a less drastic-sounding scenario – 'oil depletion'. The new language may have been adopted because oil companies are reluctant to admit they may not be able to meet demand.[18] Persistently high oil prices have made it worthwhile for companies to exploit more expensive and 'unconventional' fossil energy sources, such as shale gas, oil from deepwater platforms (like *Deepwater Horizon*), Canadian and Venezuelan tar sands and coalbed methane in Australia. 'Fracking', the hydraulic fracturing of rock to release natural gas, has become popular despite protests by those worried about the environmental consequences. Either way, demand for oil shows no sign of letting up, oil companies are having to work harder to maintain supplies, and the upward trend in prices is expected to continue, with serious implications for farmers and consumers.

The oil companies themselves share this view. A 2011 report by Shell International on future energy scenarios suggested that global demand for energy could triple in the next four decades compared with 2000 levels. They warned that this could leave a gap between supply and demand equal to the size of the whole industry in 2000.[19]

Higher prices are expected whether or not fossil fuels continue to be heavily used, because of the higher cost of exploiting unconventional sources and exploring new geographical fields. Against this backdrop, farmers and policymakers need to think about how to produce food in ways that use less of this more and more costly resource.

One town in Britain is already doing just that. I came across it by accident while I was on an August holiday. My wife and I were renting a cottage in the English countryside, and took a day trip to the pictur-esque town of Totnes, northeast of Plymouth. The town was in full-on tourist mode, with a medieval market under way. There were women wearing blue, beige and rust-coloured Elizabethan period costumes manning stalls, and it was all very cheerful. We walked along the steep high street and past the Norman castle built by invaders centuries ago as a supreme lookout. It's a place with a strong sense of history – a sign boasts that it has more listed buildings per head of population than any other town in the UK.

But it also seems to be a place with a strong sense of the future. People have been thinking seriously about how to prepare for a time when fossil fuels are in shorter supply. As we sat having lunch in a high-street café, something pinned on the noticeboard caught my eye. There was a poster about 'Transition town Totnes'. I discovered that Totnes is the first UK town to be preparing for peak oil – all the more impressive because it is a community-led initiative, not something forced on locals by a forward-thinking local authority.

The poster urged people to think about the amount of energy they use, adding that, properly planned, a town using much less energy would be 'more resilient, more abundant and more pleasurable than the present'. Among leaflets promoting Latin dance, a local auction and a myriad of local attractions, was an invitation to visit homes in Totnes and the nearby village of Dartington already making the tran-sition to lower-energy households.

Looking up at the cattle grazing on the hillside above the high street, it was difficult to imagine that much of our farming too needs to consider a future without cheap, easy oil. When animals are farmed as I could see them around Totnes, on land rather than inside industrial farms, they almost always use energy and other resources more efficiently. I was struck by a recent comment in the *Times* newspaper, which put it this way: 'Scientific agriculture has led us to a point where many times more energy goes into a field in the form of fuel, heavy machinery, pesticides and chemical fertilisers than is harvested from it.'[20] There is a range of alternatives to oil-hungry industrial agriculture. Perhaps the best-known is organic. Organic farming is considerably less oil-dependent. Researchers at Cornell University found that producing organic maize takes 31 per cent less energy than producing conventional crops. In a report published in 2006, they claim that if 10 per cent of all US maize (corn) were grown organically, it could save the USA the equivalent of 4.6 million barrels of oil a year.[21] And the huge quantity of oil used to produce crops pales into insignificance compared with the amount used to produce factory-farmed meat. Cornell has looked at the input of energy taken to produce maize and wheat relative to the output (calories) in the end product. Pimentel and his team carried out the same calculations for the production of beef, pigs and chicken meat, based on the amount of grain and forage consumed by the animals and the calories of animal protein they eventually produce.

The ratio for harvested maize was 4:1 and for harvested wheat 2:1, whereas for beef production it was 40:1, for pig production 14:1, and for chicken-meat production 4:1.[22] In other words, growing wheat and maize – and probably vegetables – is far more energy-efficient than producing meat.

In the UK, the Soil Association has studied the amount of fuel used in intensive meat production relative to the amount used to produce it organically. They found that organic meat production was generally far more energy-efficient, though organic chicken and eggs required more, because the birds live much longer and are allowed space to exercise. Their calculations, based on official government statistics on energy use in farming, are that organic milk production uses 38 per cent less energy than non-organic; organic beef uses 35 per cent less; organic lamb 20 per cent less, and organic pigmeat 13 per cent less.

From what I've learned, there are even greater energy savings to be had by moving away from the practice of feeding livestock copious cereals and soya – feeding them food waste for example.

The Soil Association also looked at crops and found that organic crops like wheat, oilseed rape and carrots use about a quarter less energy compared with conventional growing methods.[23]

At the moment, most businesses seem to assume that the answer to the challenge of peak oil simply lies in finding more. In April 2012, Lloyds of London, the world's biggest insurance market, became the first major business organisation to break ranks, voicing concerns about the huge potential environmental damage from oil drilling in the Arctic. The City institution estimates that US$100 billion of new investment is heading to the far north over the next decade. They have warned that the cost of cleaning up any spills in this remote and spectacular part of the world could be 'significantly greater' than anywhere else. A spokesman said: 'Given the Arctic's fragile ecosystem, it is vital that policy-makers and businesses take into consideration worst-case scenarios. Migration patterns of caribou and whales in offshore areas may be affected,'[24] he declared, and reeled off 'multiple ways in which ecosystems could be disturbed'.[25]

When a company like this voices such concerns, it does raise my hopes. What seems obvious is that we are reaching a tipping point.

INTENSIVE FARMING IS THIRSTY WORK

When equatorial winds sweep heavy rain clouds across the Pacific Ocean, they blow liquid gold to Fiji. As the clouds burst over the Yaqara Valley, drenching the tropical rainforest, they replenish the supply of water hundreds of feet beneath the canopy of leaves. After passing through layers of ancient volcanic sediment it eventually settles in a vast bed of porous rock – from where it is sucked up into bottles and transformed into one of the most sought-after and expensive drinks in the world. 'Untouched by man', according to the advertising blurb, Fiji Water is marketed as the purest mineral water on earth.[26]

The business is owned by Lynda and Stewart Resnick, entrepreneurs from California who shrewdly saw the way the world was going. The water is bottled in a totally sealed facility built directly above the aquifer in the rainforest. Apparently no human hand is allowed to touch it before it reaches the customer who breaks the seal. The company boasts that the taste is 'as unique as its creation'. They say their product has a 'unique mineral profile', and thanks to its special qualities and a highly sophisticated marketing campaign involving product placement on hit American TV shows like *Friends* and *Desperate Housewives*, it has become a celebrity favourite.[27]

In the UK it is highly sought after by well-heeled shoppers at Harrods and Selfridges, as well as reputedly being drunk by the Beckhams.[28] How much its extraordinary success relates to its supposedly distinctive taste (in ad-speak, its 'soft, smooth mouthfeel'[29]) is another question. At the end of the day, it's water: H2O.

Over the last forty years, bottled water, once a business that nobody took seriously, has become a multi-billion-dollar global industry. Seduced by clever marketing and beautiful packaging, wealthy consumers pay handsomely for a product that looks identical to what comes out of the tap and generally tastes pretty much the same. In what was derided at the time as a caricature of capitalism, in 2007 Claridge's Hotel in London introduced a water menu consisting of more than thirty varieties of bottled water from around the world. The Four Seasons Hotel in Sydney offers something similar – some two dozen options of still or sparkling – some of which are said to be shipped to the Antipodes all the way from the UK. It is difficult to square this booming industry with the vast quantity of water that is casually wasted, often by the same consumers who spend so much buying it in plastic bottles. For while people are prepared to pay top dollar for packaged water, ordinary water is undervalued and squandered wherever it is not obviously running out, especially by industrial farming.

Make no mistake, rearing animals is a thirsty business. Worldwide, around a quarter of freshwater use relates to producing meat and dairy.[30] On average meat needs around ten times the amount of water per calorie to produce as vegetables and other plants.[31] Just producing one kilo of beef requires the equivalent of nearly ninety bathtubs of water, while around thirty-three bathtubs are needed to produce a kilo of pork, and twenty-four tubs for a kilo of chicken.[32]

The water 'footprint' of the concentrated feed given to industrial livestock is more than five times greater than the footprint of the kind of food eaten by animals kept on pasture, such as the grass itself and silage.[33] In essence, factory farms are draining lakes and rivers to irrigate crops to feed to animals. Reared indoors in barns, the animals themselves drink and the sheds need to be hosed down. When animals are genuinely kept on a grazing system, much of the water is simple rain on grass – a natural process. In industrial rearing, water is often drawn from rivers and aquifers, thereby diverted from other useful purposes. Experts have calculated that grain-based animal feeds use forty-three times more irrigation water than pasture-based feeds.[34]

The perversities of the system are symbolised by an extraordinary business located deep in the Arabian desert. In the heat of the midday sun, temperatures in this part of the world reach a blistering 50 degrees Centigrade. There is precious little life save for a few scrubby bushes. But one species is defying the laws of nature: the American Holstein cow. Thanks to a complex irrigation system that pumps millions of gallons of water from deep under the sands, Al Safi mega-dairy in Saudi Arabia is flourishing.

In this most hostile environment, 29,000 listless cows are reportedly kept alive and functioning in open-sided sheds fitted with fans that waft a fine spray of water over the animals. The cooling equipment is imported from Arizona and enables them to survive the heat. According to a visiting journalist in 2002, they produce a phenomenal 549,000 litres of milk per day.[35] Of course the cows need to be fed, and Al Safi has found a way to make the desert oblige. Where there was once just hot sand, luxuriant green alfalfa now grows at the rate of a crop every three weeks. Fields are drenched by pivot sprinklers that suck water from sources up to a mile underground. It comes out close to boiling. Between drinking and cooling, each cow is said to use around 135 litres of water a day.[36]

The dairy uses sophisticated computer programming to monitor the milk output of every animal. Performance details are sent to a central database, where they are analysed and used to identify cows that are not coming up to scratch. The minute they run dry, it's off to the slaughterhouse.

Unpleasant though it is to see cows living like this – the *New York Times* reporter Craig Smith described the animals as 'so skinny that they look like a row of piebald dropcloths draped over scaffolding'[37] – this surreal operation is all the more disturbing for the vast amount of water it uses. After all, fresh water is a finite and diminishing resource, and the soaring global demand for meat is putting already dwindling supplies under increasing pressure. Factory farms in deserts expose the worst excesses of the system.

Many countries are already taking water from aquifers at well above the rate that nature can replenish them.[38] The UN warns that farming is already by far the dominant cause of water depletion globally.[39] And that simple equation, of taking more water out of the ground than the rain puts back in, is causing the oceans to rise, accounting for about a quarter of current sea-level rise.[40] Scientists report that global stocks of groundwater were shrinking more than twice as fast by the turn of the century as in 1960. If the USA's Great Lakes were being siphoned at the same rate, they would run dry after about eighty years.[41]

In wealthy countries, there is little public awareness of the real pressure on global water resources. Cynics often claim that water can't really be wasted because it is never destroyed: it evaporates, forms clouds, falls as rain, runs off mountains in rivers or seeps into the earth and emerges as springs that in turn feed rivers and lakes, in an endless cycle that never changes. But while the same amount of water exists on Earth today as it did millions of years ago – calculations put the total at roughly 1,620 quintillion litres – almost all those quintillions (97 per cent) are in the sea, where they're useless unless the salt can be removed.[42]

The hydrological engineer Michal Kravcik, who has studied water systems in Slovakia and neighbouring countries, has described how fresh water is being lost to the sea. According to the book *Blue Gold*, he describes how a drop of water first evaporates from a plant, earth surface, swamp, river, lake or sea, then falls back down to earth as rain. If the drop of water falls back onto a forest, lake, blade of grass, meadow or field, it 'cooperates with nature' to return to the hydrologic cycle.

However, if the earth's surface is paved over, stripped of forests and fields, or drained of natural springs and creeks, the drop will not go into rivers and lakes to be used by people and animals, but will head out to sea, where it will be stored. 'It's as if the rain is falling onto a huge, low-lying roof, or umbrella, of pavement and treeless areas: everything underneath stays dry, and the water runs off to the perimeter.' The result is rising sea levels.[43]

There is little doubt that rising pressure on global water supplies from agriculture, climate change and population growth, to name a few factors, is leading to critical shortages. Water is heavy and phenomenally expensive to transport, meaning that while parts of the world suffer catastrophic floods, there is no simple way of channelling their extra water to places that don't have enough. Up to 2 billion people in the world already suffer from water shortages, and scientists predict that the number will at least double, perhaps affecting as many as 7 billion people, the majority of the world's population, by 2050.[44] Since 70 per cent of the world's freshwater supply is used for agriculture,[45] any debate over water shortages must be a debate about the future shape of farming.

Many people mistakenly assume that this is only an issue for poor countries. This fallacy was exposed in 2012 when the UK government declared that London and the densely populated southeast of England were facing a drought. Reservoirs were said to be at an all-time low and a hosepipe ban was announced. A few days later it started raining – and barely stopped for six weeks. April 2012 was the wettest recorded since 1910, followed by the second-wettest summer for a hundred

years.[46] The supposed drought became a national joke. Yet the under-
lying supply problem was real, and it was not the first time the
government was forced to sound the alarm.

In 2006, water shortages became so serious in London that authorities considered bringing in supplies from Scotland and Scandinavia
by sea tanker.[47] Other desperate measures contemplated included
towing icebergs from the Arctic up the Thames Estuary, then breaking
them up to provide slush to pump into the water supply. Thames
Water, the company responsible for the capital's water supply, was also
reportedly looking into so-called cloud seeding, the creation of rain
clouds by dropping particles of silver iodide into the air.[48]

In the end they came up with a longer-term solution: the creation
of a £270 million desalination plant. Described by the city's former
mayor Ken Livingstone as 'technology more appropriate for the
desert', it is Britain's first foray into desalination, and opened in 2010.[49]
It is capable of providing enough water for 400,000 homes a day in
'seriously water-stressed' London, but given the vast amount of energy
required to strip salt water from the sea, will only be used in an emergency.[50] Worldwide, there are now more than 15,000 major desalination
plants, mostly in the Middle East. They are becoming increasingly
common in Spain and America.

Bitter political battles are already being fought over dwindling
freshwater supplies in other apparently rich countries. In some cases,
the combination of shortages caused by excessive draining of rivers
and the drastic measures taken by politicians to prevent the crisis esca-
lating is forcing people off their land and robbing them of homes and
livelihoods.

In Australia, the desperate state of the Murray–Darling, a major
river basin that drains a seventh of the continental land mass, domi-
nates politics. It is a hugely important source of water, irrigating
farmland that accounts for 30 per cent of the nation's agriculture. For
decades, the river was a free-for-all: dammed, diverted and piped off
all along its 3,375-kilometre course by whoever could afford to.
Nobody gave a thought to the consequences downstream as the river

was plundered to supply towns and cities and thousands of farms. The party went on until the early 1990s, when the catastrophic consequences of this haphazard overexploitation became all too evident. By 1994, human activity was consuming 77 per cent of the river's average annual flow and the mouth of the river was beginning to silt up.

Two developments propelled the issue to the top of the political agenda, where it has remained. City dwellers whose water comes from the Murray–Darling started noticing that it tasted salty. Around the same time a vile toxic bloom sprung up along a 1,000-kilometre stretch of the river, a result both of the dwindling flow and of pollution from farms. The hideous sight and smell killed fish, repelled tourists and devastated hundreds of businesses. People in Adelaide began to worry that their taps would run dry. Meanwhile farmers continued to siphon off unsustainable volumes, wasting as much as a third of what they took through leaks, seeps and evaporation.

Ever since there has been an almighty row over what to do, focused largely on the role of farmers. Dozens of contentious rescue plans and initiatives have been launched, some of which have helped but none of which have proven sufficiently robust, long-lasting or effective. Not until 2008 was a single intergovernmental body set up to monitor and manage the river. This Murray–Darling Basin Authority (MDBA) has ploughed hundreds of millions of taxpayer dollars into various schemes, capping the amount of water that could be taken from the river and keeping clear public records of water-use rights. A water-trading system was launched, under which farmers were given annual water allocations that they could sell. The reforms made a significant difference – the salty taste in tap water disappeared, fish began to return, and water levels in the river rose – but serious problems remain, and disputes over potential solutions are more bitter than ever. There is evidence that smaller farmers are slowly being driven out of business, as big operators flex their muscles to commandeer heavily restricted water supplies. In 2007, the late Peter Cullen, who was an academic and member of the Australian government's National Water Commission, predicted that investment and water will continue to gravitate towards big, professionally managed farms – ironically, the sort of operations that typically waste water – while small family-owned farms where animals are pasture-reared will decline.[51]

At the time of writing the MDBA was about to release yet another plan to save the river, after a previous scheme collapsed in acrimony. The original plan involved huge cuts in farmers' allocations but was shelved following furious protests by farmers and rural communities. The MDBA was ordered to come up with something else. Tellingly, some scientists walked out of the talks in disgust, believing that politicians were shirking the hard decisions needed to preserve the river.[52]

The plight of the Murray–Darling is far from unique. According to the World Economic Forum's 2009 report on water, seventy major rivers around the world are near maximum extraction levels, including the Colorado, the Ganges, the Nile and the Tigris-Euphrates.[53] In a joint report, the United Nations Environment Programme, the World Bank and the World Resources Institute have warned that water is likely to become 'one of the most pressing resource issues of the 21st Century'.[54]

In the Middle East, North Africa, parts of Asia and parts of Europe, water is being sucked out of aquifers at a far faster rate than they can be refilled. The problem is accelerating. Scientists have warned that there may soon come a point when groundwater levels are so low that 'a regular farmer with his technology cannot reach it anymore'.[55] According to the UN Food and Agriculture Organisation (FAO), water use for agriculture – arable farming as well as livestock – is almost entirely to blame. The World Economic Forum has described the livestock sector as a 'key player' in increasing water use, mostly for the irrigation of feed crops.[56]

With demand for food expected to soar between now and 2050, there needs to be a new approach. According to a 2009 joint report by the International Water Management Institute (IWMI) and the FAO on the future of irrigation in Asia, 'there are clear limits in most places on the amount of additional water that can be used for agriculture'.[57] IWMI's projections show that on current trends, South Asia is going to need 57 per cent more water for agriculture, and East Asia 70 per cent more, to meet demand. 'Given the existing scarcity of land and water, and growing water needs of cities, such a scenario is untenable,' the report concludes.[58]

A key factor in the mounting pressure on water in Asia is the region's greater taste for meat. Since the early 1960s, rising meat consumption has resulted in a 3.4-fold increase in the amount of water needed per person for food in China. Some experts have described this as the 'main cause of the worsening water scarcity' there. According to a contribution to the scientific journal *Nature*: 'If other developing countries follow China's trend towards protein-rich Western diets, the global water shortage will become still more severe.'[59]

Of course it's not only industrial agriculture that is to blame. Other sectors play their part – even innocuous-sounding businesses like growing flowers. Yet it is the industrialisation of farming in step with population growth that is likely to place the greatest strain on water supplies over the next four decades. And not only human population growth, but also the burgeoning number of factory-farmed animals. On UN FAO predictions the livestock population will almost double by 2050,[60] which is likely to mean a population explosion from 70 billion animals slaughtered a year to 120 billion. The greatest proportion of this increase is predicted in thirsty industrial systems reliant on vast areas given over to growing feed. Growing livestock feed is not a sustainable use of scarce water resources. It takes up good rainfed cropland, which itself is globally in short supply; and where it does not, it increases still further the use of irrigation. Both would be better served growing food directly for people.

A reduction in meat consumption, coupled with a shift to pasture-based rearing of livestock, could make a big difference. Outdoor grazing systems generally use far less fresh water than industrial systems. This is particularly true for genuinely pasture-based systems such as grass-fed cattle rearing, where the animals are not fed concentrates based on grain and soya. The disparity in water use soars where the crops used to make concentrated feed are irrigated and grown using large doses of fertiliser, which is common practice. Including the amount of water that is polluted by agrochemicals and waste products, the water footprint of concentrate feeds like cereals and soya can be up to sixty times higher.[61]

In places like Britain, water tends to be taken for granted. We're obsessed by the weather, and for us there's always too much rain. At least, that's how it's long been seen. But things are changing. I laughed along with everyone else at being drenched every day for weeks during the so-called drought. I stood mouth agape as the river that normally trickles past our front door swept by us in torrents, and cursed as every dog walk was accompanied by a thorough soaking. But warnings of drought alongside persistent rain show just how precious water really is, and how scarce it is becoming.

13

Hundred-dollar Hamburger

The illusion of cheap food

With just £23 a week to spend on food for herself and her husband, Annabel Abram has learned how to make every pound stretch. She's discovered that if she goes to the local supermarket after 8 pm there are bargains to be found as store managers discount fish and vegetables they failed to shift during the day. She buys 'just add water' dried mashed potato to thicken soups and make them more filling, though the price recently shot up from 18p to 28p a packet, and she makes good use of her 10 per cent discount at the café next door to the Peace and Justice Centre in Edinburgh where she works as a volunteer.

If it weren't for her husband, Annabel would probably be vegetarian, but David, formerly a long-distance lorry driver, likes his meat, so she occasionally buys it, especially as sausages and burgers can be cheaper than fresh vegetables and fruit. On the face of it, this couple are exactly the sort of people who should benefit from factory farming. They live in a council flat on a deprived estate in Edinburgh, and with David off work due to a heart condition, they depend on state benefits. They have to watch every penny, so should appreciate the opportunity to buy bargain-basement meat. David is particularly fond of sausages, bacon and ham, and doesn't really care about the conditions in which the pigs were reared.

Yet Annabel is as discerning as her budget allows, and would no sooner eat a £2 chicken than a tin of cat food. She is an intelligent woman with an interest in animal welfare, and the price tag would ring alarm bells. 'I would definitely think there was something suspect about it,' she says, and she is right to be suspicious, because that price tag is an illusion. It might only cost supermarket shoppers £2, but somewhere else in the world, people even poorer than her and her husband are paying the price.

Defenders of 'pile them high, sell them cheap' farming systems always wheel out economic arguments, claiming that it produces affordable meat for the masses. They talk as if industrial farming is some kind of driver of equality and suggest it's unreasonable – immoral even – for people who can afford the luxury of food produced in a gentler, kinder and healthier way to question the system.

So successfully have they propagated this myth that few people in rich countries ever pause to question it. When it's possible to buy an entire chicken – plucked, packaged and ready to pop into the oven – for £2 in a Tesco price-war promotion,[1] or snap up two litres of milk for a quid at Poundland, or get a packet of no-frills rump steak for less than the price of a cup of tea in a greasy spoon café, perhaps it's not surprising that consumers are taken in by this logic. Such bargains seem to show that factory farming delivers spectacular value.

Yet the truth is that factory farming drives up food prices, because of the vast quantity of grain and soya required to feed the animals. This is tipping the delicate balance of the supply-and-demand see-saw. So while factory farms may deliver low-cost (and lower-quality) meat for shoppers in developed countries, it is at the expense of people else-where. The irony is that the people who pay the real price for the production of the bargain chicken or steak have no choices and no welfare state to rely on. The result is that many starve.

Around the world, food prices are rocketing as global food produc-tion fails to keep pace with soaring demand. There is a direct link between this phenomenon and factory farming. In the UK, the cost of a typical basket of shopping rose by 6 per cent between 2010 and 2011,[2] but the price of certain products – such as pasta, butter, coffee – shot up by many times that figure. Food-distribution charities in Britain have reported a huge increase in the number of people going hungry.[3] As the economic downturn dragged on and the number of people out of work increased, the government instructed job centres to refer poor and hungry people to charity food banks for emergency food parcels.[4] Worldwide, the UN estimates higher food prices pushed a further 100 million people into poverty between 2007 and 2008, and nearly 50 million in the latter half of 2010.[5]

Weather conditions have played a role in this disaster. A blisteringly hot summer in 2010 ravaged 2 million square kilometres of wheat and cereal crops across Russia, Ukraine and Kazakhstan, sending world prices spiralling upwards. In 2011 France and Germany, Europe's biggest cereal exporters, suffered the driest spring for almost a century, affecting yields. This added to inflationary pressures. Droughts hit Australia, America and Africa. In Lusaka, Zambia, the price of bread soared by 75 per cent between September 2010 and April 2011.[6]

Extreme weather events that damage harvests, rising energy prices and financial speculation all play a role in food-price hikes. Yet the surging demand for cereal crops, corn (maize) and wheat, propelled by factory farming, and to a growing extent by biofuels, is exerting further pressure. The insatiable demand for grain and soya beans to feed the billions of animals being reared on industrial farms means that vast tracts of prime agricultural land are being used to grow feed instead of crops for human consumption. A third of the world's entire cereal harvest and 90 per cent of its soya now feeds industrially reared live-stock.[7] At the same time, millions of hectares of fertile land are being turned over to biofuels. Together, these pressures are limiting supply of cereal crops for human consumption, pushing prices beyond the reach of many. There is now a dangerous competition between crops for people, crops for industrial farms, and crops for cars.

Multiple organisations and experts have acknowledged this link. In 2009 an Oxfam report on sustainable UK consumption warned that increased demand for grain to feed livestock is likely to push food prices 'beyond the limits of affordability' for the world's poorest people: 'The recent rises in food prices have already caused misery for millions, but future price rises and pressures on food supplies are likely to be increasingly compounded by, perhaps even driven by, rising global demand for meat and dairy products.'[8]

It's a theme echoed by many other agencies. The 2011 report on agriculture produced by the Foresight unit at the UK government's Department for Business, Innovation and Skills warned that major jumps in meat consumption – 'particularly grain-fed meat' – will have serious implications for competition for land, water and other resources. It warned that soaring demand for grain-fed meat is likely to lead to 'substantially higher food prices'.

The outlook is grim. Most economists and agricultural experts who have examined the evidence believe that the era of food surpluses is over and that high food prices are here to stay. The Foresight report says there is a 'significant likelihood' that prices of major crops will rise, 'perhaps dramatically', over the next forty years.[9]

It's no exaggeration to say that the consequences of these food-price rises are already proving catastrophic. Hunger played a key role in the Arab Spring of 2011, with initial unrest in some places sparked by the rising price of bread.[10] Bread is a staple food in Arab nations, the key source of low-cost sustenance. In Egypt it is known as *aish*, meaning 'life', and the flat round variety called *baladi* is heavily subsidised by the government. Any dwindling of supply or sudden price hike raises the spectre of civil unrest.[11] According to *The Economist*, the food-price spike of 2008–10 was 'the final nail in the coffin of regimes that were failing to deliver their side of the social contract'. Bread riots in Bahrain, Yemen, Jordan, Egypt and Morocco in 2008 were followed by political uprisings three years later[12] and the fall of President Mubarak in Egypt. It seems clear that food scarcity will increasingly shape modern politics; even trigger wars.

Food-price rises threaten to negate progress made on the millennium goals on child poverty and malnutrition. Scientists at the International Food Policy Research Institute have warned that on current trends, the number of malnourished children in sub-Saharan Africa will be nearly the same in 2050 as it was in 2000 (even though it would be a smaller proportion of the overall population).[13]

Were all the cereals alone currently fed to factory-farmed animals offered directly to people instead of being converted into meat, it could feed a mind-boggling number – as many as 3 billion folk.[14] It would certainly be a far more efficient use of resources, considering just how much plant protein is required to create chicken, pork and beef: an average of 6 kg of plant protein such as cereals to make 1 kg of high-quality meat.[15] But not all this 'meat' is truly fit for people. Calculations by the University of Manitoba in Canada suggest that producing 1 kg of genuinely edible beef by industrial methods requires as much as 20 kg of feed. For pigmeat and chicken, it requires 7.3 kg and 4.5 kg of feed respectively.[16]

Chandran Nair, an Asian environmentalist who runs a think tank called the Global Institute for Tomorrow, believes that drastic measures are needed in relation to food pricing to avert a human and environmental catastrophe over the next four decades. He has voiced an argument that is almost impossible for politicians to make: that the price of factory-farmed meat will have to rise dramatically to correct the huge discrepancy between what consumers pay and the real cost of production. He argues that the true economic cost of a US$4 burger, if you factor in externalities (such as the cost of converting grain to meat, water and energy use), is 'something like US$100'.

Nair even goes further, bravely suggesting that the burgeoning populations of China and India will never be able to live like Americans 'simply because there isn't enough to go around'. 'A sort of intellectual subservience on the part of many Asian policymakers and economists has resulted in a denial of the scientific-based evidence that five billion Asians in 2050 cannot live like the average American,' he told the BBC. In the same interview he pointed out that Americans currently consume around 9 billion poultry a year. Asia, with around ten times America's population, currently gets through just under twice that. If Asian meat consumption increases as expected, in 2050 Asians will consume around 200 billion birds. 'This again is not going to be possible . . . [at] that level of consumption, we will see . . . collapse in ecological systems that we are very much dependent on,' Nair has said.[17]

At the moment, factory farms keep growing as if none of this matters. The economics of these outfits force the companies involved onto a desperate treadmill, on which they must run faster and faster just to stand still. If the only reason people buy your chicken as opposed to someone else's is that yours is cheaper, then you have to keep the price low or lose sales. As production costs rise because of energy prices and pressure on other resources, your profit margin per animal likely falls. Often, the only way to keep making money is to rear more animals. And so these farms expand and expand, multiplying the suffering, waste and environmental damage they cause.

That has not stopped developing countries trying to emulate the system. Impressed by the way factory farming has delivered artificially cheap meat in the West, governments in many developing countries are actively encouraging small farmers to adopt mass-production techniques. They're egged on by multinational food and biotech companies, often by organisations like the World Bank, and any number of others who spread the false gospel that intensive farming, with all its chemicals, its waste, its hideous animal-rearing methods, fills hungry bellies and makes farmers rich.

Yet the evidence suggests that factory farming is a dangerous export. In a number of countries, attempts to adopt Western-style industrial livestock production systems and arable farming have been little short of disastrous. It is becoming painfully apparent that factory farming is not the solution to poverty in the developing world.

Nowhere is this clearer than in India. The tragedy that has been quietly unfolding on the subcontinent offers a stark example of what can happen when governments and multinational companies try to foist intensive agriculture on farmers in developing countries. The story is encapsulated in the fate of an ordinary man called Shankara Mandaukar, reported in the British press.[18] The weapon he used to kill himself was a tool he once hoped would help make his farm more profitable.

For years, the Indian father-of-two had struggled to make ends meet as his crops fell victim to bad weather, weeds and pests. He was easy pickings for the biotech company salesman who dropped by one day with an enticing offer of 'magic' seeds with special powers to resist bugs. The price was high but Shankara was desperate and the salesman promised huge yields. With the help of the village moneylender, he scraped together the cash. But the genetically modified seeds failed twice running. Bankrupt and about to lose his farm to the loan sharks, Shankara could see no way out. One afternoon, he downed a bottle of insecticide, and died in agony in the dust outside his home. Though a crowd of villagers looked on as he moaned and vomited, they knew there was no point summoning medical help. They had seen it all before and knew he would be dead within an hour.[19]

In the state of Maharashtra, such scenes have become commonplace. Hundreds of farmers kill themselves every year, as they do in many other parts of the subcontinent. The statistics almost defy belief. Since 1995 more than a quarter of a million Indian farmers are reported to have taken this desperate step, leaving hundreds of thousands of wives and children destitute. It's equivalent to one suicide every thirty minutes, and is believed to be the largest wave of recorded suicides in human history.[20] And despite a number of interventions by the Indian government, there is little sign that the problem is going away. Maharashtra state, the area of the country worst affected, has become known as 'the suicide belt', consistently recording the highest number of cases.

It's impossible to imagine such a tragedy occurring in Europe or America without the whole world knowing. Yet this ghastly spectacle has played out against a backdrop of near-silence from the international community. Few people outside India are aware of the crisis, though the Prince of Wales briefly drew it to public attention in 2008 when he condemned the 'truly appalling' death rate and highlighted the role of GM crops in tipping thousands of small farmers over the edge.[21]

Every suicide has multiple causes, but a number of common themes have emerged from these deaths. Most of the suicides appear to be triggered by financial difficulties linked to attempts to adopt new farming methods, typically involving high quantities of expensive fertilisers, pesticides, herbicides or GM seeds. Palagummi Sainath, an award-winning journalist on *The Hindu* newspaper who has investigated the crisis in depth, has written about the 'predatory commercialisation of the countryside' in India, and the 'corporate hijack of every major sector of agriculture, including, and especially, seed'.[22]

A high proportion of deaths afflict cotton farmers, lured into borrowing money to pay for expensive GM varieties that have failed to yield the promised returns, leaving them heavily in debt and at the mercy of moneylenders. Yet agents working for biotech companies persuade farmers who can ill afford it to find the money. So far from proving pest-proof, a number of varieties of GM seed appear to have succumbed to parasites, leaving poor farmers with nothing. There are also reports of salesmen failing to warn farmers that the so-called magic seeds require up to double the amount of watering as traditional varieties – a life-or-death matter in areas prey to drought.

In 2005 the government of India commissioned a report from the Tata Institute of Social Sciences into the suicide crisis. The study was small – it looked in detail at just thirty suicide cases in the region – but it revealed the shameful vulnerability of struggling farmers to sales patter by biotech agents or government officials. Tata's report found that many of the farmers depended on fertiliser and pesticide company agents for advice on seeds and crop care. It concluded that they were peddled a 'false perception of prosperity', prompting them to take 'serious risks' such as abandoning traditional crop rotation. They were unable to meet the rising costs of production, spreading on yet more fertilisers even while crop performance was declining.[23]

Professor Joan Mencher has pointed out that as well as examining the circumstances under which farmers have killed themselves, it's also useful to look at the circumstances and practices of those farmers who have not: 'On the whole, they tend not to have taken such large loans for chemical pesticides, herbicides and seeds. They tend to continue to grow food crops to be eaten not only by their own families, but for local markets and nearby cities. They inter-crop, rotate their crops, and have a backup in case one particular crop fails.' She concludes that: 'Excessive commercialisation usually means growing for distant markets and ignoring soil regeneration.'[24]

Dil Peeling, whom we met in chapter 6, has spent most of his career working in developing countries and has seen how unhelpful it can be to promote agricultural intensification in poor places. It's a lesson he learned right at the start of his career, when he was working with Voluntary Service Overseas in Indonesia. He recalls trying – and failing – to teach Western production methods to farmers on the tropical island of Sulawesi.

'My Indonesian wasn't good,' he remembers. 'I was bellowing instructions through a megaphone. They were nodding respectfully and pretending to listen, but I knew they weren't taking much notice.' His audience was arranged by status – the richest farmers at the front, the poorer standing behind them, a straggle of women at the back. In front was a posse of government officials from the ministry of agriculture. They sat round a collapsible wooden table and oozed superiority.

Armed with his loudhailer, Peeling was doing his best to convey the received wisdom that if they moved into intensive livestock production they would get richer. His heart wasn't in it, and not just because he found the condescending attitude of the local government officials distasteful. He'd noticed that the standard line of impressing Western intensification on farmers in the developing world wasn't working and that his audience would go home and ignore everything he'd said. Most of the frustrated NGOs and government agricultural officials seemed to think this was because the farmers on Sulawesi were just too stupid. They could not understand why the men seemed so resistant to the message. Most likely, it was because they simply knew better.

Peeling stayed in Indonesia for a while, but a few months later, two of his colleagues who had been working with the UK's Overseas

Development Administration (ODA) returned to London. During their time in Indonesia, Sarah Holden and Peter Bazeley had likewise observed that foreign aid-funded schemes designed to help the poor by promoting livestock intensification weren't working. They wanted to get to the bottom of it. Once a Whitehall backwater, ODA was being transformed by Tony Blair's new Labour government. It had a shiny name – the Department for International Development (DFID) – and it was an exciting place to be. The new administration wanted to do foreign aid differently. Old norms were being torn up; Clare Short, the secretary of state at the time, was determined that taxpayers did not throw money at stuff that did not work.

Together with the agricultural economist Steve Ashley, Holden and Bazeley secured public funding to see whether the limitations of the projects they'd observed in Indonesia were evident elsewhere. They reviewed several hundred aid projects in developing countries geared towards moving poor farmers away from traditional practices.[25] Most of the livestock projects aimed to provide poor farmers with new technology and services designed to boost production. The results were damning: the projects were not helping. Peeling, who kept in close contact with his old friends while they were carrying out the review, told me:

> By encouraging poor farmers to increase production, projects were intended to help the poor by a number of routes. Firstly, it was assumed that increased production meant more access to meat for the producers. But the problem is that the poor generally chase calories. They may have access to more meat, but high levels of protein are an unaffordable luxury when your family is underfed, so they sell it for something that gives more energy, like sorghum.
>
> Secondly, the projects were based on a false assumption that if you intensify, you will boost jobs. That's not true. Whereas arable farming tends to be labour-intensive, livestock production is capital- and energy-intensive. Ironically, intensifying actually pushes people out of jobs – the employer needs money to buy stock and feed, and can't afford to pay staff.

Thirdly, the projects hoped to increase the supply of meat for the hungry, by boosting production, and therefore bringing prices down for consumers. It didn't work because it ignored two key facts. The first is that hunger is still, in the main, a rural phenomenon. Even if highly intensive production could generate plentiful and cheap animal protein at source, delivering those perishable products to remote and dispersed rural populations through poor transport links in hot countries is simply economically untenable.

When it comes to Third World poverty, Peeling believes that factory farming is the wrong answer to the wrong question. You have to ask why people are going hungry in the first place:

> People are hungry because they are poor. People who are not poor are not hungry. So the problem is one of access, and frustrated demand, in that the poor cannot access food even if it exists. But the prescription that governments and aid agencies have provided to address hunger focuses on the supply side – by stimulating increased production. Yet eighty per cent of the world's malnourished children live in countries that produce an agricultural surplus. So the key question is not 'How do we produce more food?' but 'Who produces it?'

Having spent most of his career working with small-scale farmers in developing countries, often for the UN, his experience suggests that it is women who tend to suffer most, because they have significantly less access to resources.

> In many societies, keeping poultry, goats and sheep remains one of the few areas where productive assets are controlled by women. This type of small-scale livestock rearing provides a rare and precious opportunity to target women and children through development initiatives. The frustration is that where production has been intensified and commercialised, men have tended to take over and a golden opportunity for poverty reduction is lost.

Peeling feels that many people who are pushing for developing countries to adopt Western farming techniques misunderstand the way the
poor use livestock. Out of 1.4 billion people in the world who are classified by the UN as 'extremely poor' (surviving on less than $1 a day),
the vast majority (between 700 million and 1 billion) live in rural
areas[26] and rely on their animals for a living.

> If you ask them what their best chance of getting out of poverty is,
> they say livestock. But if you ask them what their biggest source of
> income is, livestock only comes fifth or sixth on the list. Why the
> discrepancy? Because people in developing countries use livestock
> for things other than the market.
>
> There's an old Swahili expression that a man without a donkey is
> a donkey. People use their livestock as an asset, which reproduces
> faster than interest in a bank; or they use it for labour. They keep it
> as an insurance policy, perhaps to buy the right for their daughters
> to marry into a wealthy family. They keep their animals if they
> possibly can and only sell when they absolutely have to – something
> which goes some way to explaining the indifference of those Sulawesi
> farmers to my highly educated, strident but totally irrelevant advice
> on how they could commercialise their production.

In any case, deeply ingrained cultural values based on socio-economic
realities in poor rural communities are not possible to overturn or
shift quickly. The non-market services provided by farm animals are
not just a social construct: they underpin rural economies. Food
poverty is largely found in rural areas, whereas factory farming is
geared toward feeding cities. In developing countries, it presents the
poor with a double whammy, failing to provide them with affordable
food and denying them the opportunity to grow food to sell to their
urban cousins.

A number of factors are now starting to work against the approach
of rolling out industrial grain-fed livestock agriculture across the
world. These include falling water tables, degraded soil and rising

temperatures. Good arable land and the aquifers that produce irrigation water are both in decline. While the world's food production continues to increase, the rate of increase has slowed. From 1970 to 1990, world grain production grew by 64 per cent. From 1990 to 2009, it increased by only 24 per cent.[27] Since 2002, world grain stocks (measured in days of available consumption) have been lower than at any time since the early 1970s.[28] A growing human population is in a furious competition for food with a burgeoning farm animal population. The number of animals is on course to near-double between now and 2050, mainly on factory farms. The global livestock industry already contributes 14.5 per cent of human-produced greenhouse gas emissions[29] – more than all our cars, planes and trains put together.

As the effects of global warming take hold, the sea is likely to rise and flood farmland. In some of the poorest tropical regions crop yields will decrease as a result of heat, drought and salination of soil.[30] For food production alone, at least 2 million square kilometres of additional land will be needed by 2030[31] – an area eight times the size of the UK. But a similar area of land could be flooded by the middle or end of this century.

When world food prices were rising in 2008, the UK government warned: 'In the developing world, food price rises threaten to throw millions of people back into poverty and increase the number going hungry.'[32] Yet few governments are willing to tackle the hidden costs of 'cheap' industrial food exemplified by the hundred-dollar hamburger.

VI

TOMORROW'S MENU

It was 2011, the year that *The King's Speech* reigned over the British Academy Film Awards, winning seven BAFTAs, including Best Film and Leading Actor for Colin Firth. Five million people tuned in to watch Firth receive his award. At the British equivalent of the Oscars, Natalie Portman won Leading Actress for her portrayal of a tortured ballerina in *Black Swan* and J. K. Rowling was awarded a special BAFTA for her contribution to British films.

So it was with some excitement that I accepted an invitation to lunch at the prestigious BAFTA building in the heart of London's West End. The meal was hosted by two distinguished chefs, Paul Merrett and Anton Manganaro, who had taken on the challenge of imagining what the restaurant menu of the future might look like. Still dressed in their chefs' aprons, they weren't claiming to have the answers, but were hoping the meal would start a conversation about how, in a world with a rapidly growing population and diminishing resources, our choice of food might need to differ from a typical meal today. Would the answer prove tasty and enjoyable to eat?

That day, we dined on a choice that included apple and parsley salad, parsnip soup and cobnuts, local line-caught fish, slow-baked Cornish lamb or roasted vegetable crumble with sheep's milk and cheese dauphinoise, and beetroot carpaccio with spelt. The gathered throng agreed it was delicious!

The following chapters are inspired by that meal, and the challenge faced by a future world of more than 9 billion people. The UN has warned that global food supply needs to increase by 70–100 per cent by 2050. Yet today as much as half the food produced worldwide is squandered – binned, left to rot or fed to farm animals.

How do we tackle this situation to everyone's benefit, including the animals'? What might the future hold for technologies like GM? How will pressure on the global food system change as China establishes itself as a superpower, and people in other rapidly developing countries in Asia and South America demand a slice of the meat- and dairy-rich diets long taken for granted in the West? What new ingredients might we sample, and is there a recipe for how we might feed everyone in a way that is kind to animals and saves the planet too. That day at BAFTA, Merrett and Manganaro declared on their menu: 'It is time for change. It is time to think differently.' I hope these suggestions will give you a taste of the future. *Bon appétit.*

14

GM

Feeding people or factory farms?

GOLDEN RICE

Ingo Potrykus is elderly now, but is determined to live for at least another two years. Happily he is in robust health and he has a huge incentive to stay that way – because soon he expects to see his life's work fulfilled. The German scientist has spent more than a decade campaigning for his extraordinary invention to be delivered to the world's poorest children.[1] During the agonising wait, he believes that millions of people have died who would still be alive today if only they had been able to take advantage of his breakthrough.

It's called Golden Rice, and it is perhaps the best advert for genetically modified food. It is a variety of rice that has been adapted so that it contains high quantities of the nutrient beta-carotene, which the body converts into Vitamin A. It's a substance not found in ordinary rice. Potrykus's genetically modified version of this staple food looks as ordinary and appetising as the saffron-coloured rice served in Indian restaurants. Its supporters, including the billionaires Bill and Melinda Gates, the Rockefeller Foundation and the US Agency for International Development, believe it has the potential to prevent between 1 and 2 million deaths a year in the developing world, and to save as many as 500,000 children from going blind.[2]

Around 124 million people in 118 developing countries suffer from Vitamin A deficiency (VAD) and its potentially fatal side effects. In southeast Asia alone, more than 90 million children suffer from the condition.[3] By eating just one bowl of Golden Rice a day, there is a decent chance these people could be saved.[4]

Yet since 1999, when Potrykus and his collaborator Peter Beyer worked out how to alter rice genes so that they produce beta-carotene in the part of the plant eaten by people, rather than just in the husk, where it is found naturally, Golden Rice has been stuck in a laboratory. Potrykus, Beyer and many humanitarian organisations who support their work have spent the best part of this time campaigning for permission from governments all over the world to start production and distribution. However, the long wait has not been entirely worthless – the pair and their collaborators have also busied themselves engineering an even better version with much more beta-carotene than the original creation. It will mean people don't have to eat nearly as much to get the benefits.

Now, finally, Golden Rice is on the brink of clearing all its regulatory hurdles in a number of developing countries, a moment that promises to be the proudest of Potrykus's life. I rang him in Switzerland, where he lives these days, and he told me it would be the culmination of his life's work. 'I have devoted everything to Golden Rice. It has taken an awfully long time. I just need to live another two years, and then I will see it finally saving lives.'

Golden Rice raises hope that the answers to world hunger can be developed in science labs. Many people believe that if science can solve malnutrition, we have an absolute moral responsibility to let it get to work. Even the Vatican is on-side. In 2010, after a study week by a group of scientists, the Holy See put out a statement declaring that governments have a duty to make GM crops more readily available and to remove barriers to their development: 'There is a moral imperative to make the benefits of [this] technology available on a larger scale to poor and vulnerable populations who want them.' Supporters of Golden Rice even invoke human rights to their cause.

They cite Article 27 of the Universal Declaration of Human Rights, which states that everybody is entitled to 'share in scientific advancement and its benefits'.

That's certainly how Potrykus sees it. What's particularly attractive about Golden Rice is that it was developed for humanitarian reasons, and Potrykus, who is in his late seventies, remains adamant that there will be no role for profiteering. He and Beyer could have made a fortune by selling the patent, but they have given it away free. 'We have donated the technology,' he told me. 'Neither of us was ever tempted to make money from it. My entire career has been dedicated to this. It is all about food security, and nobody will have financial benefit.'

Throughout the long years in his laboratory and the battle to win regulatory approval, he has been spurred by the memory of what it's like to go hungry. Growing up in post-war Germany, he and his brother had to steal and forage for food. 'That's what it was like for me, between the ages of twelve and fourteen. It was a very difficult time. I was fighting to survive. That has been my motivation with Golden Rice.'

The first country likely to authorise Golden Rice is expected to be the Philippines, shortly followed by Bangladesh, then probably by India, Vietnam, China and Indonesia. Though he is philosophical now, perhaps because the end is in sight, Potrykus never imagined it would take so long. Yet there are good reasons for the delay. A number of scientists have raised questions about the safety of Golden Rice and regulators have been reluctant to give it the go-ahead until these questions have been answered.

Most of the critics of Golden Rice cite general fears relating to the unintended consequences of messing around with the genetic makeup of edible crops. The vagueness of these concerns has been a major source of frustration for the international organisation that campaigns for the adoption of Golden Rice.[5] Yet questions remain about whether it will achieve everything Potrykus believes. There are fears that it could actually exacerbate malnutrition by discouraging poorer people from taking their own steps to improve their diets by eating more leafy greens.

Professor Dr Klaus Becker, of the University of Hohenheim in Germany, has warned that it could 'encourage a diet based on a single industrial staple food rather than upon the reintroduction of many vitamin-rich food plants with high nutritional value that are cheap and readily available'.[6] Other scientists believe that very malnourished people may not be able to make use of the beta-carotene because their bodies do not contain enough fat and iron to absorb it. There are also concerns that compounds linked to beta-carotene could cause birth defects. The World Health Organization (WHO) argues that there are simpler solutions to vitamin A deficiency. Their strategy focuses on promoting breastfeeding (breast milk is a natural source of vitamin A) and supplying high-dose vitamin A supplements for deficient children, a policy the organisation says has proven a 'simple' and 'low-cost' intervention that has had 'remarkable results' – reducing mortality by 23 per cent overall. The WHO is also working to encourage poor families to grow vitamin A-rich vegetables in their gardens.[7]

DO GM CROPS DELIVER?

It seems strange and incongruous that Golden Rice has taken so long to reach the table. After all, other genetically engineered crops are now widespread. In 2008, 13.3 million farmers in twenty-five countries – 90 per cent of them smallholders in developing countries – were growing genetically modified crops, covering 125 million hectares.[8] The most common modifications are herbicide tolerance and insect resistance. By tinkering with the genetic makeup of crops it is possible to give them new traits that enable them to thrive despite being doused in powerful weed- or pest-killers. The trouble is that these 'broad-spectrum' pesticides are indiscriminate, wiping out helpful insects that prey on the bugs that destroy crops in the first place. In other words, they destroy natural biological controls that can work very well to prevent blight.

GM crops may seem like a quick-fix solution to challenges farmers have faced for millennia, but they create a new set of problems, if not for the farmer, for everyone else. Research into the environmental impact of herbicide-tolerant crops carried out in the UK and published by the government department Defra in 2003–5 showed that GM crops were linked to a dramatic fall in the number of butterflies, bees, weeds and seeds compared with traditional intensive production using conventional weedkillers and insecticides.[9] An obvious criticism of this study is that it compared one environmentally damaging method with an even worse one. A 2009 University of California report into the ecological impact of GM crops and conventional fertilisers and weedkillers concluded: 'The massive use of transgenic [GM] crops and agrochemical inputs, mainly fertilisers and herbicides . . . pose grave environmental problems.'[10]

Outside the European Union, which remains wary of the technology, GM crops are commonplace. Proponents argue that they are a vital weapon in the battle to feed the world. In truth, the crops that are most likely to be GM are also those most often destined for animal feed. Over the last two decades, the technology has become a vital component of the industrial farming juggernaut, boosting production of feed crops for factory farms. The 'big four' GM crops – corn (maize), soya, cotton and rapeseed – are all used for animal feed, with corn and soya far the most important. About half of the world's corn (maize),[11] and over 90 per cent of soya beans,[12] in the form of soya meal, are used for animal feed. GM feed production is highest in North America, the global leader in industrial animal production. The US feeds almost 40 per cent of its corn to farm animals,[13] and 85 per cent of it is GM.[14] Similarly, the vast majority of the world's soya harvest is GM.[15] The uptake of GM corn and soya is high among developing countries where factory farming, or growing associated feedstuffs, has taken off.[16]

The hype about GM feeding the world appears little more than rhetoric, especially given that factory farms waste more food than they make, GM or otherwise. Only about 30 per cent of the calories in terms of corn or soya used to feed incarcerated farm animals are returned in the form of meat or other livestock products.[17] In other words, 'world hunger' is a convenient cover for what can be a deeply dubious business, where profit comes before the efficient production of food for people.

Saving seeds is intrinsic to farming worldwide: seeds are sown, the resulting crops are harvested and the seeds are extracted for the next season's planting. That's how it's always been. But in 1980 the US Supreme Court agreed that GM seeds could be patented – a move that has distorted this natural cycle. It is now illegal for American farmers growing GM crops to save seeds: they have to buy a new set every year or run the risk of prosecution.

Eagleville, Missouri, population 321, is hardly a crime hotspot. A cluster of houses huddled around two church spires and a water tower, it boasts a sleepy town square and the quiet, white picket-fenced lanes of any American village. Its general store, The Square Deal, supplies groceries and other bits and pieces to the villagers and farmers. Grateful to be spared the drive to neighbouring towns, locals pop in to buy everything from hunting kit to ice cream, and perhaps swap some gossip with the store's owner, Gary Rinehart.

One day in 2002 a stranger marched into the shop and asked for Rinehart by name. His tone was officious. He was there to make a serious allegation: planting genetically modified soya-bean seeds in violation of a patent held by the designer, the US agribusiness giant Monsanto. Rinehart was puzzled. Of course he'd heard of Monsanto – their 'Round-up' herbicide is used all over America – but he personally didn't plant or even deal in soy seeds, and his only contact with farming was via the sharecropping his brother did in a few family fields.

Monsanto's private investigator was insistent, accusing him of breaking the law and warning that he would be made to pay. There were other customers in the shop. Angered, Rinehart refused to answer any more questions and the Monsanto man walked out. He had been in the shop for less than two minutes.

The scenes that took place in Eagleville are repeated daily across North America as Monsanto and its competitors dispatch their legions of private detectives to protect their revenues. Such is the culture of persecution that American farmers now talk of a climate of fear. The way firms like Monsanto see it, farmers who save seeds from expensive genetically modified crops and use them to grow another harvest for nothing are simply thieves, and that is how they treated Rinehart. After going to his shop and openly accusing him of breaking the law, Monsanto hit him with a federal lawsuit, accusing him of 'knowingly, intentionally and willfully' planting GM seeds in violation of the company's patent right.[18]

In the months that followed, Rinehart learned that Monsanto had drafted in a St Louis-based investigative agency called McDowell and Associates to put local farmers under surveillance after receiving an anonymous tip-off that someone was illegally saving patented seeds. According to documents filed to the courts, a private detective named Jeffrey Moore had seen Rinehart planting soya-bean seeds from plain brown bags. According to Monsanto, when he had finished he tossed the empty bags into a ditch and drove off. Moore retrieved the bags and sent a handful of beans left in the bottom for analysis. The results showed they were 'Roundup Ready'.

After much toing and froing during which Rinehart continued to protest his innocence, Monsanto finally dropped the lawsuit. It had been a case of mistaken identity. The real culprit turned out to be his nephew Tim. The case was finally settled when the younger man apparently agreed to pay for the seed he'd saved. Both sides remain sore about what happened. According to Monsanto's website, they have 'not collected one cent'.[19]

It didn't take biotech companies long to figure out that the legal hassle associated with pursuing farmers who save seeds could be avoided if there was a way of making saved seed useless. The result is so-called 'terminator seeds', designed to yield only one crop. And so a millennial model of sustainability, in which farmers plant their own seeds, is coming to an end in America – and where America leads, others follow.

It might not seem unreasonable for companies to find innovative ways of stopping people using goods they have not paid for, but consider the implications for farmers who cannot afford GM seed, or simply prefer to do things the old-fashioned way. If their property borders fields sown with GM seeds, a phenomenon known as 'genetic drift' can occur, resulting in the traditional farmer's fields being contaminated with plants from patented seeds. This effect could have devastating consequences for farmers in developing countries like India, which has begun to import and experiment with terminator seeds. What if poor farmers who are used to sustainably replanting their own seed have their crops contaminated and rendered sterile?

Growing a means to survive has never been easy. Droughts, insects and crop blights have caused countless famines and continue to kill millions despite technological advances. Naturally farmers are always looking for ways to reduce these risks – and companies like Monsanto seem to offer an easy solution. Around 80 per cent of all food consumed in America now contains material from GM crops. Monsanto argues its GM technology can double yields at the same time as reducing the resources required to complete the cycle from seed to harvest. The company claims it helps farmers 'produce more while conserving more'[20] – as long as that doesn't mean conserving Monsanto seeds, of course.

Beyond Eagleville lie North America's plains, vast fields of swaying crops that stretch as far as the eye can see. In the old days, these endless plains were sown with a variety of crops. Now large tracts of land are cultivated with just one crop, from GM seed owned by one company, engineered to be resistant to herbicide supplied by that company. It's known as mono-cropping. Inevitably, it means more power to the seed company and less to the farmers.

The inevitable damage to wildlife, biodiversity and farmers who prefer to do things differently would not jar so much if GM seed dramatically increased production, saved land, or reduced food prices for ordinary people. But there's not much evidence it does any of these things. Disturbing reports are emerging that in some places Monsanto's

GM corn has stopped doing what it's supposed to do. Bugs appear to be developing a resistance. There are serious concerns that the same will happen with weeds, creating an even worse problem for farmers than the one they faced in the first place.[21]

There are also concerns about Monsanto's Bt-corn, designed to kill a bug called rootworm. Many farmers in America's cornbelt consider this creature their number one enemy, especially in Minnesota, where the corn harvest is worth $7 billion. So there was an enthusiastic uptake of Monsanto's genetically engineered variety, which promised to eliminate the problem.

For a long time it worked wonders. Then farmers began noticing some of their plants were toppling over – the worm was back. The first scientific confirmation of a problem came in August 2011, when Iowa State University released the results of a study.[22] The university described the reappearance of rootworm as very significant, dismissing the notion that there were just a few isolated cases. Now, in half a dozen states stretching from Illinois to South Dakota, the bug appears to be outwitting the men in lab coats. Michael Gray, an agricultural entomologist at the University of Illinois in Urbana, says that replanting GM crops year after year increases the danger that the insects will develop a resistance to the substance designed to finish them off. Monsanto's share price dropped 4.5 per cent on the news.[23]

It seems that GM technology doesn't even reduce food prices. At a time when more GM maize and soy is being grown than ever before, cereal and soy prices are at a record high. And high prices are now begging serious questions for governments worried about reliable food supplies.[24] As a way to solve world hunger, it doesn't stack up.

Britain's dairy cows had a close shave with GM when Monsanto tried to get a licence to sell a GM milk-boosting hormone to farmers in the UK. The product, widely used in the US, involves giving cows regular jabs with an artificial version of natural growth hormones to boost milk production by 10–20 per cent. The trouble is that high-yielding dairy cows are already pushed to their limits, producing ten times more milk than the calf would naturally drink. The product, called Bovine Somatotropin (BST), is associated with serious health risks including painful udder infections, digestive disorders and lameness. At the time, I was working as campaigner for Compassion in World Farming. We led a campaign to get it banned on animal welfare grounds. We wrote reports, badgered Westminster and Brussels and kicked up a real fuss. My team went on tour with a white coat and giant syringe to jab a lifelike model cow up the back end in high streets up and down the country. The resulting press did its job. After twelve years of hard campaigning, BST, known in the US as bovine growth hormone, was banned for both sale and use across the European Union.

The EU has adopted a highly cautious approach to GM. The only GM crop grown commercially by member states is Bt maize (MON810). In 2009, France and Germany both suspended approval for the crop, which is also banned in Austria, Hungary and Greece.[25] By contrast, in 1992 the US government decided to classify GM crops as 'GRAS' – Generally Recognised As Safe. This means GM food no longer has to carry any special label. No particular tests are required before it is sold to consumers. Companies can even introduce new GM food to the market without telling the authorities.[26]

Yet we still know little of the potential health risks. Research by the Institute of Ecology and Evolution of the Russian Academy of Sciences and the National Association for Gene Security found that rodents fed GM-soy lost the ability to reproduce within three generations.[27] An international team of scientists found that rats fed GM corn eat more and grow fatter than those on a non-GM diet. The effects were repeated when rats were fed fish which, in turn, had eaten GM food. Talking about these findings, Professor Åshild Krogdahl, of the Norwegian School of Veterinary Science, asked the obvious question: 'If the same effect applies to humans, how would it impact on people eating this type of corn over a number of years, or even eating meat from animals feeding on this corn?'[28]

Perhaps even more disturbing were the results of the world's first long-term feeding trial of GM maize. Researchers at the University of

Caen reported that rats fed a lifelong diet of a strain of genetically modified corn developed breast tumours and severe disturbances in liver and kidney function.[29]

Meanwhile, though GM crops are banned in the UK, there is no law against giving farm animals GM feed. Since there's no requirement to say anything about that on meat and dairy product labels, shoppers simply never know.

CLONING

Like millions of pet owners, Duane Kraemer and his wife Shirley dote on their cat. Pretty brown and white CC and her mate Smokey are so pampered they have a custom-made two-storey kitty house in the yard with a screened front porch, air conditioning, heating, catwalks, lofts and an enclosed outdoor play area. Care has been taken over the interior decor, with a framed photograph of CC as a kitten hanging on the wall. CC's favourite spot is at an upstairs window where she spends much of the day sitting looking out for visitors while her offspring Tess, Tim and Zip scamper around. Those who come to see her are often surprised by how ordinary she looks. For CC – or Carbon Copy as she is officially known – was the world's first cloned cat and her birth on 22 December 2001 in a Texas laboratory made international headlines.[30]

She spent the first two months of her life at the College of Veterinary Medicine, Texas A&M University, being paraded for the cameras and television crews and monitored by scientists for any sign of abnormality or ill health. Then she was adopted by the Kraemers. After they took her home she largely disappeared from the public eye, but in 2011 she was wheeled out again to mark her tenth birthday.[31] She certainly seemed in excellent health. Despite her unique origins, she is said to have lived a pretty normal life, producing a litter of kittens with Smokey in 2006. Apparently, she proved a great mother, and still is, though she takes life gently these days.

Like CC, the Kraemers are also beginning to slow down a little, but though Duane is now in his seventies, he is far from ready to hang up his white lab coat. He was one of the research team that created CC and has devoted the last decade of his career to exploring how cloning technology can be put to use – particularly by the farming industry.[32] Ironically Kraemer himself originally planned to be a farmer. He grew up on a dairy in Wisconsin and left school intending to learn animal husbandry and take over the family business. But as a young student at Texas A&M, the sixth-largest university in the United States, he was bitten by the research bug. To his father's disappointment he decided on an academic career instead.

The research project that produced CC was known as Operation Copy Cat and was part of a project called Missyplicity which has all the makings of a Hollywood script.[33] Bankrolled by an eccentric American multi-millionaire named John Sperling,[34] the scheme was inspired by the creation of the world's first cloned mammal, Dolly the Sheep, born at the Roslin Institute in Scotland in 1996 to a worldwide fanfare.

Sperling and his partner Joan Hawthorne were fascinated by what the Roslin Institute had achieved and saw an immediate application for the groundbreaking technology in their home – creating a carbon copy of their beloved pet dog. Missy, a border collie and husky cross, was getting on a bit and the couple were prepared to spend whatever it took to immortalise her by creating a genetically identical replica who would make them feel as if she was still with them after she'd gone to the great kennel in the skies.

News of their unusual project spread quickly and they were soon contacted by wealthy people all over the world who also liked the idea of immortalising their four-footed friends. Scenting a business opportunity, they set up a company called Genetic Savings and Clone with a view to providing an international pet-cloning service. The company opened for business in February 2000, but cloning dogs proved trickier than anticipated. For a while, some of their resources were directed at cloning cats, which is how CC came to be.[35] By the time scientists cracked the technology for cloning dogs, Missy had died, but her DNA had been gene-banked for future research. In 2005, Korean scientists created the world's first cloned dog, named Snuppy,[36] and two years later Missy's owners had her DNA flown out to Seoul, where it was used to create three carbon copies of their late pet.

In the meantime, Kraemer and his team were moving on to other species of clone. Kraemer doesn't see a problem with rich people investing their money to create copies of their pets, though the technology can't guarantee that the clones look identical to the original donor or 'blueprint'. (CC's donor, Rainbow, who is now dead, was a different colour – white, brown and ginger – to CC, who has no orange markings.) Perhaps that's partly why it has never really taken off, though the huge sums of money involved must be the main reason.

Since CC was developed, a handful of individuals have used the technology to clone pets, including a colourful character from California called Bernann McKinney who spent US$50,000 commissioning a lab in South Korea to create identical copies of her dead pit bull terrier Booger.[37] She went to collect the five puppies in person, but refused to let them travel in the cargo space of the plane home. The airline would only let her carry one pup on her lap at a time, so she spent another US$20,000 making five separate trips to ferry each puppy in style.[38]

However, predictions of a vast commercial market for resurrected pets through cloning fell flat. BioArts, the leading US pet-cloning company, which was set up by Joan Hawthorne's son Lou, closed in 2009 after concluding that the market was too limited. And there was another, uglier, problem: the number of deformed animals that were being produced. Lou Hawthorne has described how one clone that was supposed to be black and white had 'greenish yellow' bits; others had skeletal malformations, which he has described as 'generally not crippling, though sometimes serious, and always worrisome'.[39]

However, all the scientific money and effort that had gone into developing the technology had not been wasted. While there were too few pet owners who were willing or able to spend tens of thousands of pounds cloning their dogs, the technology pioneered by Kraemer and other so-called embryo transfer scientists had already found another type of customer: agricultural animal breeders. Cloning is now an important tool in the deeply dubious and growing business of developing ever more unnaturally high-yielding beef cattle, dairy cows and pigs.

A superficially attractive aspect of this new branch of science is the creation of animals that are resistant to certain diseases. After helping to create CC, Kraemer took the technology one step further, using it to clone a bull resistant to a bunch of nasty conditions common in cattle: brucellosis, tuberculosis and salmonellosis. Nicknamed Bruce, the bull was the first animal in the world cloned specifically for disease resistance. He was created using genetic material from a long-dead animal named Bull 86, who had been identified as naturally resistant to those illnesses. At the time, Kraemer's team described the implications of their achievement as 'potentially monumental'.[40] Though the three cattle diseases have been virtually eradicated in the USA and Canada, brucellosis and tuberculosis are widespread in other parts of the world, so that the conditions could easily return.

Cloning is more commonly used in intensive farming to create animals that are more efficient money-making units. For the proud owners of pedigree beasts you can see the attraction: it offers a way of creating multiple copies of their prize animals, albeit at huge cost. The farm animals that merit the trouble and expense of cloning are the supermodels of the industry, themselves the product of highly sophisticated selective breeding techniques designed to make them ever more meaty and milky.

Selective breeding is all about controlling sexual reproduction, and has been going on since animal rearing began. Only the beefiest cows and the most productive milkers are allowed to mate, so that their superior genes are not mixed with those of flabbier, less impressive creatures. By picking out the animals with the most desirable characteristics, culling the rest, and using judicious inbreeding, it's possible to develop a bloodline that is even better than the original base stock. Naturally, these bovine and porcine Schwarzeneggers are worth a fortune, particularly for their superior ova and semen, but there's never any guarantee that their offspring will be as spectacular as the original – which is where cloning comes in. It offers a way to produce multiple 'twin' copies of top-producing animals.

As the US-based cloning company ViaGen boasts on its website, by having multiple animals that are genetically identical to your top performers you can 'greatly expand their reproductive potential'. There are other benefits too: it's a way to 'keep up with demand for offspring, embryos and semen' from top animals and insure against your prize bull being accidentally injured or killed. You can make sure your herd of animals is more consistently outstanding.

ViaGen, which offers an international cloning service for prime cattle, pigs and horses, makes it sound simple. All they need is a sample of an animal's genes. They provide a biopsy kit and a shipping container, the customer sends off a nick of the animal's flesh, and ViaGen's scientists do the rest. They culture the cells, transfer their DNA into eggs whose genetic material has been suctioned out, and put the resulting embryos into an incubator for a few days. Then they're transferred into a surrogate mother, and after the usual gestation period, the cloned calves, piglets or foals emerge. As soon as they're weaned and given a clean bill of health by a vet the youngsters are shipped off to the customer.[41]

Put like that it seems quite benign, but the truth is that cloning is a way of propagating breeds that have been pushed to their physical limits to produce ever more meat and milk. It threatens to accelerate the use of highly intensive genetics in farm animals, causing serious animal welfare problems. In short, cloning threatens to multiply animals that are genetically programmed to suffer. It is a way of locking in misery.

This is on top of the serious animal-welfare problems associated with the cloning process itself. ViaGen's website doesn't appear to mention it, but for every successfully cloned prize bull many others are likely to have died. From deformed hearts and other organs to being grossly oversized, cloned animals and their surrogate mothers suffer from a range of appalling health problems and deformities that are rarely seen otherwise.[42]

The scientists who created Dolly the Sheep implanted a total of 277 embryos in the process, from which only thirteen pregnancies resulted. Only one of these, Dolly, was a successful live birth. Despite years of research and efforts to perfect the technique, nature appears highly resistant to this contrivance and success rates remain incredibly low, at around one to thirty in every 1,000.[43]

One particularly nasty problem associated with clone pregnancies is hydroallantois (hydrops), a set of typically fatal conditions in which one of the foetal sacs swells with fluid to grotesque proportions. According to data from the US Food & Drug Administration (FDA), hydrops has occurred in 13–40 per cent of clone cow pregnancies; one study reports it in over half of cases. It's a condition that rarely occurs in pregnancies produced through normal artificial insemination or natural selective breeding.[44]

Late miscarriage is another major problem: studies in Europe show that most cloned embryos die during pregnancy.[45] Surviving the pregnancy is only the first hurdle. Cloned newborns are likely to suffer serious health issues, including deformities, lowered immune systems, and problems with their heart, lungs and other major organs. One reason Korean scientists won the race to produce the world's first cloned dog was that they had a ready supply of dogs of all shapes and sizes for experiments. In a culture that eats dogs for dinner and likely has few animal welfare restrictions, scientists had no difficulty sourcing canine guinea pigs and probably don't have to bother keeping a body count.

Establishing the scale of suffering is difficult: much of the information that is readily available is selective and biased, and long-term data is limited. However, when the European Food Safety Authority looked into the issue, it concluded that the health and welfare of 'a significant proportion' of clones was 'adversely affected, often severely and with a fatal outcome'.[46] Meanwhile the European Group on Ethics in Science concluded that the level of suffering and health problems experienced by surrogate dams and animal clones meant that it saw no 'convincing arguments to justify the production of food from clones or their offspring'.[47]

Encouragingly, New Zealand's leading farm-animal research centre, AgResearch, has abandoned its cloning research programme. Closure was blamed on unacceptable death rates. The catalogue of welfare concerns came to light only when reports were issued under the Official Information Act legislation, which gives the public a right to obtain certain previously secret data if it is felt to be in the public interest. The reports showed that animals had suffered from chronic arthritis, pneumonia, lameness and blood poisoning, and that only about 10 per cent of clones survived the trials.[48]

Whatever the research about suffering says, cloning animals for food is something I have always instinctively felt is wrong. The majority of the British public appears to agree. When Compassion in World Farming ran a campaign on the issue, some 2,000 of its supporters lobbied the government minister responsible in the UK. Nearly 3,000 also wrote to their MEPs, sending over 14,500 emails. Europe-wide polls show that nearly two-thirds of people see animal cloning as 'morally wrong'. Over half of those surveyed felt that cloning for food production was unjustifiable. Most said they would not buy meat or milk from cloned animals and eight out of ten said that it should be labelled if it ever became available in the shops.[49]

All the same, it managed to do so. In the UK, milk and beef from the offspring of cloned animals slipped into the food chain in 2010, unannounced and unauthorised. Its discovery caused a public furore. In August that year it emerged that beef from a bull whose mother was cloned had somehow found its way onto dinner tables. The bull was one of a pair produced by a cloned cow created using stem cells from the ear of a prize-winning dairy cow in America. Embryos produced by the clone and a normal bull were frozen and flown to the UK, where they were implanted in surrogates and born on a farm in Shropshire. Two of the animals ended up on a farm in Nairn in Scotland, where they sired ninety-six pedigree calves.

When this was exposed by the UK media, there was a public outcry.[50] David Cameron had been prime minister for just three months, but I was keen to make the most of the public reaction, so at

Compassion in World Farming we organised a stunt involving forty
Cameron lookalikes. Actors wearing identical suits, shirts, ties and
face masks were let loose in central London. They headed for
Downing Street so we could make our point. Passers-by pressed their
faces against car windows, stared out of buses and hailed the Cameron
army as it marched down Whitehall.

'One Cameron was enough!' a Londoner told me. 'Blinking cruel
to let forty of 'em loose at once.' If I'd had a pound for every person
who said something similar that day, I'd have gone home quids in.

Outside Downing Street, the lookalikes unfurled a giant white
banner condemning cloning as cruel. I was carrying a pile of petitions –
thousands of signatures we'd collected in just a few hours. I was ushered
through the gates to a security booth and on to the famous black door
of Number 10. I banged on it theatrically. A polite but not particularly
welcoming official opened it and listened dutifully as I said my piece.
He took the petitions. We shook hands, smiled for the cameras, and
then I left.

Next stop was the Houses of Parliament. The media took pictures
of forty mirror-image prime ministers on Westminster Bridge as Big
Ben chimed midday. Then we headed to the London Eye. I remember
thinking what a great picture it was going to be – all those clones
crammed into a glass pod high above the capital. Sadly, we weren't
allowed on. I wondered how many other smartly dressed but totally
innocent tourists would be turned away in error that day.

The stunt was fun, but the message was serious. Consumers had –
and still have – no way of knowing whether the food on their plate
had come from the offspring of cloned animals. We wanted government action, especially as there had been an overwhelming vote in
favour of banning food from clones and their offspring by the
European Parliament just a month earlier. Sadly, the complicated
world of European politics meant it didn't count for anything other
than an opinion; the vote was won but nothing changed.

'Frankenstein' food from imported descendants of cloned US
animals had all the hallmarks of a winnable issue. I genuinely thought

David Cameron would throw his weight behind us. Has there ever been a more colourful example of dishonesty in the food chain? Yet the prime minister did what governments usually do when they're in a hole: announce an investigation and let it drag on long enough for voters to lose interest. The Food Standards Agency looked into the issue on the basis that the sale of meat and milk from clones is unauthorised under a law called the Novel Foods Regulation. They eventually declared that there is no rule against the sale of meat and milk from the 'progeny' of cloned animals, and that it was, in their opinion, safe to eat.[51] The question left hanging is: how do they really know? And why ride roughshod over public and political opinion? It seemed to me an example of the weak leadership that is allowing our food system to drift into the abyss.

In America, the FDA approved in principle the sale of cloned food as safe for consumers in January 2008, despite widespread protests from consumer and animal welfare groups, environmental organisations, the public, the dairy industry and Congress.[52]

Cloning is just the most extreme example of the scientific wizardry being deployed by companies in the hope of creating farm animals that can produce even more for less. Shielded from the public eye, in laboratories all over the world, men and women in white coats are developing all sorts of weird artificial creatures they hope will be prototypes for future generations of farm animals.

Take broiler chickens. Cram thousands of chickens into a tiny space and you get all sorts of problems, not least the same issue you have if you crowd thousands of humans into a confined space: it gets hot. There are many solutions, ranging from the obvious one of keeping fewer birds in one place, or opening the doors and letting some out, to the more expensive alternative of installing air conditioning.

Boffins may have found a more grotesque solution: featherless chickens. Not only do they stay cooler in tropical climates, but without the inconvenient coats nature provided, they take up less room. And behold, that means you can cram even more into the same space.

There's a further selling point for naked birds: once slaughtered, you don't have to bother to pluck them.[53]

The featherless chickens were created using traditional selective breeding techniques, rather than through cloning or GM. The Israeli geneticist who created the bare-skinned prototype in 2002 believes they could represent the future of mass poultry production in warmer climates. They look just like the raw chickens you buy in the supermarket, only they still have their heads – and unfortunately for them, they're still alive.

They are not the only farming freak show in town. How about cows that have been genetically modified to produce 'human' milk? It sounds like an April Fool trick, but within the next ten years it's conceivable that some kind of hybrid cow/human milk will be available from supermarkets, sold alongside nappies and jars of baby food. At China Agricultural University, scientists have reportedly introduced human genes into 300 dairy cows, enabling them to produce milk with some of the key properties of human breast milk. Apparently it tastes stronger than the usual stuff, but it contains proteins that boost an infant's immune system, just as a mother's milk would. The research team performed various other tricks that gave the bovine milk other human qualities. According to newspaper reports, Professor Ning Li, the scientist who led the team, described the result as 'a possible substitute for human milk'.[54] The mind boggles at how many genetically modified cows would be needed if plans press ahead for commercial production, not to mention the unknown health implications of bringing up a baby on it.

No doubt most scientists involved in cloning and genetically modifying animals genuinely believe their work is for the greater good. Kraemer himself, one of the pioneers, is a wonderful advertisement for what is a highly questionable business, with a kindly air, softly spoken and looking like everybody's grandad. He is clearly passionate about his research and wholeheartedly believes he is making the world a better place. On his office wall is his motto: 'Ask not only what nature can do for you, but also what you can do for nature.'

These days, his research is devoted to preserving endangered species. But are wacky technofixes the right response to the coming food crisis? Or do they simply take factory farming to newer extremes, pushing already overworked animals ever further, to the detriment of their welfare and the quality of food they produce? Thankfully, you don't need a degree in genetics to work that out.

15

China

Mao's mega-farm dream comes true

No exposé of factory farming would be complete without travelling to China. The People's Republic is already a major player in global food production and will undoubtedly have a big say in the shape of things to come. I therefore wanted to see how the most populous country on Earth, the jaw of the fast-growing Asian tiger economies, was getting on with the business of developing its agriculture. After all, half the world's pigs are in China. Steamed, roasted, barbecued or minced in dim sum dishes, the Chinese are big on pork, devouring 34 kg of the stuff per person per year, compared with 25 kg a head in Britain.[1]

Although many pigs are still reared on traditional smallholdings, big players in China's food-production industry are eagerly importing the most intensive pig-rearing techniques they can find in the West, and see the UK and US as role models.

In 2011 the British government signed a multi-million-pound livestock trade agreement with China,[2] involving the live export of thousands of prime breeding pigs. After decades of selective breeding programmes, the British pig industry has production down to a fine art, with the average UK-bred sow producing twenty-two piglets a year, compared with fourteen in China. Chinese farmers want a slice of these supernatural fertility rates and have taken the direct approach of buying British pigs, chartering entire Boeing 747 planes (at a cost of £330,000 per trip) and flying them 9,000 kilometres east.

The *Daily Mail* reported this unusual new trade as if it were an amusing curiosity, making much of the style the animals travelled in. An article highlighted their extensive leg room and freedom to 'relax and stretch out' while in the air, contrasting the conditions with those endured by human passengers in economy seats. A spokesperson for the Yorkshire-based company involved, JSR Genetics, said they are 'targeting China as a major growth area in the coming years', using their 'advanced technology' breeding programmes to develop bloodlines like the company's 'faster-finishing' boar.[3] The piece did not question what conditions the animals were destined for, nor explore what lies behind the new Sino-British porcine relationship – China's rapidly growing appetite for meat. It is this huge surge in demand for meat to feed China's growing middle classes that makes the People's Republic so important to any debate about the future of farming.

Its appetite for large-scale pig farms is actually nothing new. It dates back to the middle of the last century and the Great Leap Forward, Chairman Mao's disastrous campaign to catch up with – even overtake – the Western world's economy in less than fifteen years. Between 1958 and 1961, in an attempt to boost industrial and agricultural productivity, he reorganised his country's vast population into large-scale rural communes. Private farming was banned and those who dared engage in it were persecuted as counter-revolutionaries. The Hong Kong-based historian Frank Dikötter has described how the chairman's grand plan included 'extravagant schemes for giant piggeries that would bring meat to every table'. One scheme, designed to mark the tenth anniversary of the Chinese Revolution of 1949, included a 'pig city'. According to Dikötter: 'Many hundreds of houses set back from the street were destroyed to make room for the project.'[4]

The Great Leap Forward was catastrophic. Despite the huge investment that went into the project, the overall increase in national production was negligible. The ban on private smallholdings ruined peasant life at the most basic level. Villagers simply could not make a living, because they were no longer able to exploit their own land. The result was huge-scale famine. Dikötter calculates that as many as 45 million people were 'worked, starved or beaten to death'.[5]

Sixty years on, China has become a fearsome superpower with the potential to usurp America as the mightiest nation in the world. Yet it still struggles to feed its people. A 2008 UN study found that while the developmental level in Beijing and Shanghai is comparable to Cyprus and Portugal, some provinces such as Guizhou are more like Namibia or Botswana.[6] Poverty in China remains a largely rural matter. There's a vast and growing gulf between those in urban areas and the rural poor. Around 10 per cent of the nation still lives in poverty: 130 million people.[7]

With such a huge job on its hands, it's easy to see why the government has been seduced into believing large-scale industrial farming is the future. The regime is importing factory-farming models sold enthusiastically by the West. The industrial farming system has many champions and powerful interests who are only too eager to cash in on the potential new business from agricultural trade deals with the East.

So far, there is little evidence that it's feeding the rural hungry. There may be a lot of extra meat, but much of it seems to be feeding cities, not poor country folk. The scale and investment needed means that the rural poor are pushed out of the equation and denied the opportunity to provide food for the cities, perpetuating the poverty trap. Bizarrely, I learned of considerable amounts of Chinese pigmeat being shipped to Japan. It doesn't add up.

In 2011, I set off with a journalist and a cameraman for the eastern side of China, to see some of the biggest pig farms in the world. It was October and we spent the first twenty-four hours in Beijing, where we hooked up with Jeff Zhou, Compassion in World Farming's man on the ground in China. It was not my first time in Beijing – I'd been to a conference in the city three years previously – so the smog that greeted us as we stepped off the plane was all too familiar. I was wearing my binoculars through sheer force of habit – there was little hope of seeing any birdlife through the thick beige blanket.

Compassion in World Farming has been trying to get a foothold in China for a decade. Our first trip out there revealed that there were no words for 'animal welfare' in the Chinese language. In the years that followed, a lot of our efforts met with official bemusement. But something has changed. As we embarked on a fifteen-hour train journey from Beijing to the heart of pig country, Jeff explained why. China is undergoing a food-confidence crisis. For years consumers have simply been told what they want to hear, whether they're buying grapes, pork or fish. Today, thanks to education, access to the Internet and irrepressible evidence, the public can no longer ignore the shady origins of much of China's food. Finally, officials are listening.

In September 2008, a major scandal propelled food safety to the top of the political agenda. It emerged that powdered baby milk had been illegally adulterated with the chemical melamine,[8] apparently to give the appearance of higher protein levels when tested. It was genius for the factories. They could sell watered-down milk and no one would know the difference. Mothers would happily feed it to their babies. But one after the other, children were developing kidney stones and acute kidney failure. Melamine – the chemical also used in plastics as a fire retardant – turned out to be a killer. Thousands of babies were affected and six died. Hundreds underwent treatment for kidney failure. The authorities showed no mercy to the bosses of the baby milk company, executing two of them by firing squad.[9]

Jeff said the tragedy had made people think about food in a new way: 'For the first time they wanted to know where it came from.' Of course it was bad news for all the legitimate milk farmers in China. Millions of people swapped from dairy to soya or insisted on buying imported milk. But perhaps more importantly for the Chinese government, it was a big international embarrassment, reported in the UK and elsewhere.

Not long after that, pig farming came under the spotlight, in what Jeff called the scandal of the 'work-out pig'. Today's Chinese consumers like lean meat. The problem for factory farmers is that pigs in cages don't have much space to exercise. In any case, factory farmers are reluctant to 'waste' expensive feed by allowing animals to use precious energy moving around rather than growing. As a result, their meat is fatty. Chinese pig farmers were keen to find a way of keeping a pig in a cage and making it grow fast without getting fat. They hit on a solution: feeding pigs a steroid called Clenbuterol, which is sometimes used (illegally) by body builders to build muscle without fat. They did it quietly, but two things gave the game away.

First, the pigs grew so big that their skinny legs couldn't support their enormous bodies (an all-too-familiar complaint on intensive chicken farms). Pictures began to circulate on the Internet of pigs that couldn't stand. Second, people started to get ill. Clenbuterol is illegal in most countries, including China, for a good reason: it has serious side effects, including palpitations and stiffening of the heart muscle.[10]

In April 2011 the 'work-out pig' scandal hit the headlines.[11] It was another dangerous breach of public trust in a country walking a tightrope between communism and modernity, echoing an incident five years earlier in which the Chinese newspaper *People's Daily* reported that over 300 people had been poisoned by meat contaminated with Clenbuterol.[12]

The new public concern about how food is produced may explain the surprisingly warm welcome I received from officials when I arrived for this trip. Whereas I used to struggle to get any kind of a hearing from the Chinese government, this time my colleagues and I were treated to an exquisite dinner with special wine. More importantly, we learned the exciting news that finally the government has set up an organisation to promote animal welfare. It's clear that public health and international reputations are at stake in China, and with them internal stability and international trading opportunities. As a CEO campaigning for international welfare standards, suddenly I matter more than I did a decade ago. The question is how long the new attitude of officialdom will take to change anything on the ground.

While most decision-makers are city-based, the animals are in the countryside, albeit often surrounded by concrete. And so we found ourselves bound for Henan Province, the cradle of Chinese civilisation and apparently the centre of China's pig-farming universe. I was not sure what we might actually see. The Muyuan pig farm we hoped to visit had declined our request to be shown around, and a run-in with local security guards did not appeal.

We took a night train from Beijing to Nanyang, a twelve-hour journey through mile upon mile of maize fields. They stretched along the length of the railway track for at least the last hour of our journey. The crop, I was told, was destined for animal feed and biofuel. I was struck by the sheer scale of land devoted to feeding factory farms and cars rather than people.

After a restless night on a hard berth, we piled out of the train wondering if we'd ever see blue sky again. Even 700 kilometres from Beijing, the pollution was thick and deadening. We drove through the busy streets of Nanyang. A scooter pulled up beside us with a small Pekinese dog riding at the owner's feet. Another scooter whizzed by, this time with live chickens dangling by their legs like feathery saddle bags. Their wings were burning on the hot metal and their legs must have been cracking with every jolt of the bike. A few minutes later we saw a black dog caged outside a restaurant. The world bustled by. At last we left the traffic of the city for the open road. We passed through more miles of maize. A couple of storks' nests sat atop telegraph poles, looking like little pyres.

We arrived at our destination, a small village next to a mega-pig farm with 5,000 breeding sows and their attendant progeny. I was eager to hear about life so close to so many industrially reared pigs. After a quick shower and a bite to eat at a local hotel we set off in the hope of finding the pigs. Our first stop was a village just a kilometre downwind from the second of the twenty-one Muyuan pig farms that dominate Henan Province today. This farm is also the company headquarters of one of China's biggest pig producers.[13] Since our request for an official visit had been declined we decided it would be more discreet to abandon the car and get as close as we could on foot.

Before setting off, we researched the company's background. It turned out to be supported by the International Finance Corporation

(IFC), the private lending arm of the World Bank.[14] Indirectly, therefore, it is subsidised by taxpayers around the world. The IFC website offered a bit of information about Muyuan farm company, talking about the firm having a biogas digester, a machine that takes the pig muck and turns it into energy for use on the farm. Not a bad idea, but our calculations indicate that at best this might only provide for about 6 per cent of the total energy required to raise the estimated 450,000 pigs a year that Muyuan used to rear at the time the investment proposal was written.[15] Now they produce a million. The Muyuan company is growing at a phenomenal rate. It has outgrown twenty farm sites and there are reports that IFC taxpayer money is contributing to yet another farm. This twenty-first site will take the twenty-first-century pig one step further from the natural world.

We drove through kilometre after kilometre of maize to a tiny village near the firm's headquarters, then parked and made our way to the farm gates, knowing we were unlikely to go unnoticed for long. We were just a few hundred metres away from thousands of pigs – the smell told us that – but all we could see was vast sheds, so we got close enough to take some photos and then retreated, anxious not to blow our chances so early on the first day in Henan.

Back in the village where we had parked, people seemed happy to talk. A man in his fifties, smoking a cigarette and leaning up against a crumbling village wall, struck up conversation – Jeff translating. He spoke with authority. He gave us his name, but it is changed here to Mr Chan to protect his identity. Life in China has got better, Chan told us, but the farm had done nothing for the locals. It was ruining the road that the community built themselves and destroying their water source. Whereas once they were able to dig individual wells by their homes, now pollution of the ground water makes it undrinkable. They have to fetch water from a tank at the edge of the village.

'We never used to get mosquitoes, but now they're everywhere,' he added. 'We need nets just to open our windows. We used to sleep and eat outside when the weather was hot. That's impossible now – we have to shelter in our houses.'

This particular farm was built on the villagers' communal land. I was told they had been given compensation, but it was a one-off payment, and nearly fifteen years later, as roads, the railway and the farm circled ever closer, the land left available to cultivate had been halved. With so little land there was no work for the locals. 'We tried to prevent the building of the road to the factory,' Chan explained, pointing at the route that cuts across their field. 'But someone hired mafia men to scare us off with knives and sticks.'

Other bits of land have been polluted with pig effluent. When the villagers complained the company paid out compensation and took the land, which was badly poisoned. Despite bearing all these environmental costs, none of the villagers was employed on the farm. 'They don't trust us,' the man claimed. 'They think we'll steal things.' I asked if they benefited from the meat it produced, and he told me they did not. It was destined for city markets, and they could not buy direct from the farm.

As we talked a crowd gathered and children approached to touch the car, which looked flashy and out of place surrounded by stray dogs and wandering ducks. People were smiling, but we knew we could not afford to hang around with our cameras and notebooks. Though we were breaking no laws, we were reluctant to draw attention to ourselves. So we said our goodbyes and headed off in the car, hoping to find out more elsewhere.

Then, about a mile from the village, I noticed something strange about the trees back towards the farm. While most of them were perfectly healthy, in one area the trunks were bare. As there was nobody in sight, we decided to investigate. We scrambled along the edge of a maize field and then up a steep bank, and there we saw the source of the problem: a huge lagoon of putrid watery muck. Poplar trees poked their way out of the slime, but they were drowning in the toxic soup. Already leaves and branches were wilting.

The lagoon was no accidental spillage. Someone had built flimsy mud banks around the edge. We were told the weather had been dry lately, but it was nearly full to the brim. It was painfully obvious that it could overflow at any point, yet it was surrounded by crops intended for consumption. This was the contaminated land the villagers had mentioned and the effluent came straight from the nearby farm. Off-site and out of sight, here was evidence that Muyuan – for all its fancy biogas digesters – wasn't coping with its pig muck.

Ironically, the farm had been accredited by the UN on the basis of its environmental record. The letters 'UN CDM' are emblazoned in red across its towering biogas funnels. Under the international carbon-trading scheme, this very farm is one of the places in the developing world in which international companies can invest to say 'sorry' for polluting too much in the rich world. By supporting Muyuan, under the Clean Development Mechanism (CDM), a Japanese factory can earn the right to keep pumping out fumes at home. Muyuan seemed to me to represent a double whammy: not only was it damaging the environment, but with its proud UN badge, it could be enabling pollution by another filthy friend, thousands of miles away. Our worst environmental suspicions had been confirmed – but we still had not seen a single pig.

While figuring out a game plan, we decided to have a look at a backyard farm. I was keen to see how it works at the other end of the scale, because I am all too aware that small isn't always beautiful.

Jeff easily charmed his way into a smallholding not far from Muyuan, where pigs were being reared. We stepped through a private home into a tiny courtyard divided into concrete pens. Until recently this is what farming across China looked like. The picture is chang-ing fast, but at the time of writing, around 70 per cent of all pigs in China are still kept in informal family farms like the one we were about to see.

Covered with a rickety roof, and drained by nothing more than a sloping floor, the pigpen was as low-tech as it gets. Ten growing pigs, one mother sow and her eleven piglets were rubbing themselves sore against the walls and gnawing at the concrete floor out of sheer bore-dom. Any water they had been given had run out. I was shocked – it was simple animal cruelty.

The only good thing about the farm was that the pigs were fed slops rather than mass-produced chemical-soaked feed, shipped across the world. Pigs can be fantastic at recycling if we let them. But it hardly compensated for the appalling conditions. Nor could the farm give us any clue about how Muyuan is run; its squalor belonged to another age.

Our next stop was a medium-sized farm down the road. We were delighted to hear that it was an eco-farm and curious about what we might find. It came as a huge disappointment. Tens of pregnant sows were kept in sow stalls (also known as gestation crates) – a system banned in the UK on grounds of animal cruelty. The narrow stalls are no bigger than the pig herself and sows are kept incarcerated in them for nearly four months before giving birth. Pregnant pigs housed in this type of accommodation can't turn round in their individual cages, let alone forage or root. For four months they have nothing more to do than stand or lie on a slatted floor ten centimetres above a pit of their own waste. When they are ready to give birth, they are moved to the farrowing crate, an even more restricting metal contraption that will confine them until their piglets are taken away. Their distress is painful to watch, but it is the reality of factory farming, large and small, in many countries. It started in the West and, from what we could see, has very much been sold to the East.

Keen to get out, we said our thank yous to the owners of the 'eco-farm', stripped off our overalls and returned to the car, to run into a nasty surprise. The driver had just been phoned by our hotel, to say that the police were interested in why we'd been filming. Jeff warned that they could be waiting for us when we got back. I had been well aware of the notion that the Communist regime in China still operates an ear in every village, no matter how remote. Now I knew it was true.

In the safety of the car we thrashed out a strategy. We planned to be upfront and honest about the purpose of our visit – to understand pig farming in China better – but to do whatever we could to protect our film footage. Jim, our cameraman, removed the memory card from the camera and hid it. Notebooks were stashed out of sight. We all had visions of a night in a Chinese cell on trumped-up charges of trespassing or spying – which we thought would hardly be unusual.

Drawing up to the hotel, we took a deep breath and did our best to adopt an air of nonchalance, but our nerves were not helped when the reception staff at once removed our passports. We were told the police wanted to check them and verify who we were. I was worried – to be this deep in China and this far into an investigation with no passport was not good. But there was little we could do.

An hour later we met for dinner in the hotel lobby. We left Jeff doing some administration, since he was the only Mandarin speaker, while the hotel looked after us impeccably, ushering us to a private dining room for dinner. We had only just sat down when Jeff burst into the room with a huge grin as if he'd won the lottery. 'Great news!' he exclaimed. 'We've got new friends for dinner! From Muyuan farm!'

Sure enough, just behind him was a middle-aged man who introduced himself as Mr Chen, Muyuan's Environmental Manager. He was accompanied by two young women. 'I've told them we've been trying to contact them for weeks and I persuaded them to join us for dinner!' Jeff beamed. Apparently the Muyuan officials had 'bumped into' him in the hotel lobby, where he'd been glad to invite them to join us.

With smiles and what I hoped were welcoming-looking gestures, I leapt to my feet. Taking Jeff's lead, we pulled up seats for our unexpected guests, and ushered them warmly to the table, hiding our bemusement. Our exaggerated displays of hospitality seemed to defuse the tension. I handed them my business card. Before we knew it, our informal dinner had turned into a full meeting, with beer and much outward joviality.

Behind the smiles however, the pig man and I were sizing each other up. His curiosity about what I was doing with a camera near his farm was as great as my need to know what actually went on behind those concrete walls. What both of us knew, but were too discreet to mention, was that the grapevine in this small town was clearly a match for the Internet. There were eyes and ears everywhere. It was no coincidence that the pig man was in the hotel lobby that night. Our presence had been noted.

I took the opportunity to tell our guests about Compassion's international work, not least with major food companies. I mentioned some of the household names that we work with, like McDonald's. I talked about how we support and encourage improvements in animal welfare and food-quality standards and how these things can benefit business and consumers. Chen smiled. He told us about environmental measures undertaken by his company. He seemed to have come with a message to deliver.

During dinner, he slipped out to make a phone call, presumably to update his colleagues or the police on the status of the foreigners who had been seen taking pictures of the farm. We could see a police car out of the window, and Chen at the hotel entrance, talking on his mobile. The police car switched on its flashing lights, and drove off into the night. Chen returned, seeming more relaxed.

He declined to speak directly about the work of his department, deferring instead to his junior colleagues to explain, but he seemed to know the pig numbers inside out. He told us Muyuan produced a million pigs for sale each year and insisted it dealt effectively with all its waste. Though we had observed shocking evidence to the contrary, with the police so close it was not the time to argue, so we just smiled and let him continue. 'By 2017, Muyuan will rear up to nine million pigs a year in five different regions,' he told us. If true – and there is no reason to disbelieve it – these figures are incredible: Muyuan alone will be producing the same number of pigs as the entire British pig industry.

So now we knew it: this pig company, already vast, has ambitions way beyond its current boundaries. Before too long, what we had witnessed during the day could be replicated, perhaps all over China. Lagoons of filth, mosquitoes, villagers deprived of land, and no doubt desperate pigs crushed into cages built with the help of Western technology and perhaps supported by the UK and US taxpayer through the World Bank and the UN.

By the end of the meal I was exhausted but elated. Without us even getting through the Muyuan door, the pig man had provided a wealth of information. At the end of the meal, Chen not only graciously paid the bill, he also invited us to visit the farm and meet the staff next morning. We all shook hands and our guests left. It had been an extraordinary evening. Apparently, our encouraging smiles and friendly toasts to UK–Chinese cooperation had paid off – we were going to see inside those sheds after all. And our passports were returned.

The following morning, we headed back to the farm, this time as official guests. Chen wasn't there – presumably his job had been done the night before. We were ushered into a sterile meeting room, but no matter how loudly they talked, our hosts could not disguise the horrible screaming of pigs being loaded into lorries nearby.

We spent two hours on the premises, and learned that 70 per cent of Muyuan's pigs are sold domestically to major towns in China, travelling in open-sided trucks for between twenty and thirty hours. The remaining 30 per cent are destined for Japan. Some of the breeding pigs are imported – most recently from Canada – because of the more commercially productive pig breeds available abroad. We were told that the pigs are fed on imported soya, fishmeal from Peru, Chinese wheat and added vitamins, minerals and amino acids. Despite its prolific local production, maize is not on the menu.

Our requests to see the pigs were turned down for reasons of 'infection control' and our offers to don the usual white overalls and walk through anti-infection spray fell on deaf ears. It was clear that Muyuan's management did not want us to see the animals. We used our meeting with the staff to find out as much as we could. Muyuan's lead spokesperson was its Deputy General Manager, Tian Fangping, who was friendly and helpful, drawing diagrams on a whiteboard of the different types of pig accommodation they have. He told us that Muyuan started twenty years ago with twenty-two sows, and since then they have experimented with all types of rearing processes, each time modifying the last to make it more efficient. Predictably, he confirmed that they use the same sow stalls and farrowing crates we saw at the small-holding the day before.

All this work has led to phenomenal success, he told us. In 2010, the company made over £8 million profit and in the first half of 2011 alone they had already hit the £10-million profit mark. I asked if there was anything to limit Muyuan's expansion. He replied that the main constraints were availability of land and the environment. 'For some companies money may be a problem, but thanks to profits and easily available loans, for us finance is not an issue,' Fangping said, explaining that Muyuan gets preferential loans from the Chinese government.

In fact the company is positively rolling in cash. In 2010, it received US$10 million investment from the International Finance Corporation.[16] So it's no surprise that they are building farm number 21 down the road, and that this one will be a dozen times bigger than the average industrial breeding herd in Britain.[17] To our surprise, the Muyuan management offered to take us there for a tour – perhaps because as yet there are no pigs on the premises. They seemed eager to do anything for us, except let us see the animals themselves.

We bundled into a Muyuan van with Fangping and pulled on the Muyuan-branded white wellies. The new farm looked like a post-apocalyptic holiday resort designed by someone with a sick sense of humour. Row upon row of white 'holiday cabins', half built, surrounded by diggers, mud and cement mixers, house thousands of empty steel pigpens. Inside we observed every imaginable bit of technology required to strip the humans out of pig farming. Pipes, tubes, nozzles, fans, wires and of course a slatted floor for pigs to sleep on – like bacon already on a grill pan – so their excrement can be conveniently collected below. It was so automated that a single stockman can 'take care' of 3,000 pigs. It was fashioned in the West; among equipment suppliers, Fangping listed companies from Europe. This is the ultimate factory farm, inhumane and utterly divorced from nature.

'Some small farms don't realise the importance of technology,' the Deputy General Manager mused, gazing at the series of tanks and filters for the gallons of muck this farm will produce. 'Small farms will have to expand or go out of business.'

So there we have it – and this man was in a position to know. Muyuan and its twenty-first-century factory farms are seen as the future for food production in China unless something's done fast. Remembering the appalling conditions I'd seen on some of the smaller farms, I couldn't help thinking that, for China's pigs, it's out of the frying pan, into the fire.

To top it all, with an almost touching naivety, Fangping admitted his meat isn't cheap. This is not food for the hungry masses. 'We're not really reducing the cost of meat for the average consumer because we're catering for the high end and export market,' he told us, rattling off the names of various fancy hotels in China's big cities. Average consumers don't give Muyuan the kind of profits they need.

I had heard enough: I doubt I will ever forget that building site. Stomping across it in my shirt, tie and wellington boots heavy with mud, I thought gloomily about the fifteen-hour train journey ahead to our next destination. At least we were getting out of Muyuan and its pig cities.

It was a relief to move on to Wuxi, a city on the shores of Lake Taihu, China's third-largest freshwater lake, which laps the shores of Jiangsu Province. Tourism is booming. For centuries, the city was the seat of the emperors, and it attracts swathes of Chinese day-trippers and holidaymakers. There are boat trips and guided garden tours as well as 3,000-year-old tombs from the Zhou Dynasty. We were due to visit just before a major Chinese holiday and the hotels and restaurants were taking on extra staff in anticipation. For the first time in days we were due to stay in a really comfortable hotel.

The purpose of our trip was to look at the lake; we had heard it was not as picturesque as it used to be. There were reports that muck was seeping out of some of the pig and poultry farms nearby and into the water, turning it bright green and making it smell of rotten eggs. We wanted to see this direct consequence of intensive agriculture for ourselves.

After careful questioning, our hotel receptionist let slip that in 2007 the water from Taihu Lake – which usually supplies water to millions of residents in Wuxi and beyond – became so polluted it was undrinkable, despite going through the usual urban water-purification processes. When you turned on the tap, she told us, it came out cloudy and smelled foul. The Chinese premier, Wen Jiabao, ordered a clean-up[18] and dashed to the city to drink a glass of Wuxi tap water in front of the media cameras.[19] Since then, despite further efforts, every now and then the water becomes undrinkable.

I set out to the lakeshore from our hotel with my binoculars slung around my neck, hoping to see some birdlife. The lake was misty with the usual Chinese smog and I could just make out the ghostly outline of high-rise flats on the other side. Nonetheless it was a beautiful spot. Before too long I spotted a flash of cobalt blue: a kingfisher. The lake may be polluted, but for the time being the birdlife is wonderful.

For a closer look at the state of the lake, we bundled onto a tourist boat along with hordes of Chinese visitors. From the top deck there was a glorious view of the many-masted fishing vessels, their chopping-board sails fading in and out of focus in the mist. For the first time on the trip our video camera didn't feel out of place. Aboard were hordes of glamorous young couples, old ladies and families, enjoying a trip to so-called Fairy Island, one of many islands on the 2,300-square-kilometre lake. Shaped like a turtle drifting quietly in the water, Fairy Island was covered in lush green trees, buildings and pavilions. Everyone was excited, and many had camcorders, so nobody batted an eyelid when we got our filming equipment out.

Nonetheless, the pollution is a sensitive issue, and we knew we would have to be careful about what we said and who was in earshot. In 2007 a Chinese environmental activist in this region, Wu Lihong, was arrested on charges of fraud and blackmail and jailed for three years,[20] where he alleged he was subjected to physical torture because of his outspoken views.[21] After that brush with the police in Henan Province we were in a cautious mood.

We docked at Fairy Island. Through the trees, we could see Taoist temples and statues, but they were not old. During the Cultural Revolution in the 1960s, temples that had stood on the island for over 700 years were torn down by youths under instruction to destroy all that was old about China. China does nothing by halves. Today's versions are gaudy replicas, and whereas our fellow tourists were keen to see them – and in some cases even kneel before them – we were more interested in looking for muck.

The other passengers left the boat and soon dispersed across the island following neatly scripted signposts that read 'Matchmaker God Temple', 'Enlightenment Bay' or 'Heavenly Street'. With so many heavenly options, it felt a bit mean to be following our own noses to the green stink, but we didn't have to look far. The moment we stepped off the boat we spotted the problem.

Where the water met the land it was thick as paint, tattooing the rocks and tree roots with a luminous halo. It looked like a classic case of algal bloom caused by nitrates from fertilisers and manure getting into the water system. The algae multiply rapidly, thanks to nutrient-rich pollution, before dying and giving way to more of the same. The decaying mass of dead algae strips the water of oxygen, killing fish and other aquatic life. The Chinese government's own figures show that in 2010 nearly ten Olympic-sized swimming pools worth of nitrates poured into these waters. No wonder the lake is dying.[22]

Just a few metres off the tourist trail, we found two old men standing by a motorised pump, jetting green water away from the water's edge. Their job, we discovered, was to prevent the algae from accumulating by the shore. If it is allowed to stagnate, they told us, the stink gets worse and puts off tourists. The tiny pump and two old men seemed a pathetic effort to tackle such an enormous problem, but we quickly discovered that the two pensioners were part of a small army of workers engaged in this absurdly labour-intensive cosmetic surgery. They told us that between May and October, when the problem is at its worst, the government employs a thousand or more people of all ages to keep the muck at bay. 'This is not bad,' one of them told us with a toothy grin, pointing at the green tidemark on the shore. 'In summer we go out on boats with machines to sieve out the algae. It gets pumped into lorries and sent off to a processing centre.'

Of course, China has unlimited human resources to deploy on such clean-up tasks, but the impact is only superficial. The fish are dying. The men told us prices have soared, rising by 20 per cent in the last year alone. The fishermen are forced to tie up their boats most of the year in a government attempt to preserve what is left of the wildlife. Meanwhile intensive farms continue to spew untreated manure into the rivers. The men and their pumps could be no match for it.

In a small way, however, the island also offered some hope. A crowd of young people thronged at the feet of an enormous gold statue of Lao Tse, the grand master of Taoism. Taoism is an important part of Chinese spiritual life and there were a number of smartly dressed youths wearing white uniforms and name badges who had been hired to explain the principles to tourists. We asked them about the green sludge. They would not acknowledge or condemn it – after all they want to promote this spiritual island as a tourist destination – but they were willing to quote Lao Tse on the importance of respect for nature: 'People follow the earth, the earth follows heaven, heaven follows Tao, and Tao follows nature.'

We used our final day in the countryside to investigate the source of the algae on Lake Taihu. Not all of it is from agriculture; the dumping of sewage and industrial waste is also blamed. But I wanted to see for myself whether pig farming was at least part of the problem. After all, there are said to be more than 2,000 intensive livestock farms around the lake.[23] So I set off to find out if effluent from these farms was definitely flowing into the Taihu River basin.

Once again we squeezed into a taxi and set off to find pigs. It was no surprise to find that we were not welcome at the biggest farms. Visitors are generally banned on the ground of disease control – which is not unreasonable – though I suspected there were other things to hide. So we opted for a smaller farm, near a river that feeds into the lake.

We bumped along a track lined with bright green rice fields. Although we were just minutes from the high-rise buildings of Wuxi, the ramshackle farm at the end of the road, where the nearest thing to a tractor was a bicycle wheelbarrow, could have been in deepest rural China. It was run by three families whose eyes widened as we stepped out of the car. We appeared to be the first foreigners they had ever met.

There were at least one hundred pigs on this farm, so although it was small it was a commercial operation, and according to the owners, a viable one. The pigs spanned three generations. We saw tiny piglets nuzzling at their mothers; medium 'growers' getting ready for market; and enormous sows, pregnant and ready to pop.

Sadly, as in all the other pig farms we had seen in China, the animals were living in a totally barren environment, in dark indoor sheds and even on the ground floor of one family's home – right next to their kitchen. It may have been a small-scale operation, but I would still define it as a factory farm, because the animals were being reared intensively, clearly treated as if they were simply another component in an industrial process of turning feed into meat. The sows were stuffed into tiny stalls, lined up as if they were sausages already in a packet. One was so large she could not fit into her crate. Her hind legs were resting on the back of the pig in the neighbouring stall and her own back was pressed hard against the bars. Every time she flinched she gave an involuntary kick to the pig beside her. The suffering was palpable.

I did my best to focus on the task in hand, looking for evidence that farms like this are responsible for fouling up one of China's most beautiful natural lakes. The bright green river at the back of the farmhouse suggested we'd come to the right place. One of the farmers spoke frankly about how things worked. 'The government has said we're not allowed to dispose of the pig waste in the river, but if we give the local officers some benefits they will close their eyes. Nobody bothers checking on us.' He told us that some manure went straight into the river, and the rest was used as fertiliser for crops. When it rains, that too would run off into the river.

As we turned to leave, we noticed one last horror. Next to the kitchen was a pile of old medicine and injection bottles, needles sticking out. They were antibiotics, clearly being administered in an entirely haphazard way in an attempt to prevent the pigs getting sick. 'We have no medical background,' the lady farmer admitted. 'We don't really use a vet, so for all diseases we just use antibiotics.' Surrounded by feed bags, sprays, buckets, medicines and flies, it was clear that this farmer in her jeans and gumboots had no idea about the wider implications of this sort of behaviour. Money is tight and she was willing to do anything to prevent her pigs from succumbing to disease.

Looking around, I admit I felt some sympathy. It was clearly not a wealthy household. The family toilet – which I used in desperation – was proof enough of that. It was a hole in the ground, dug under the house, and sited right next to a pig pen. The family was living cheek by jowl with their pigs. Nonetheless, what they were doing was dangerous. The widespread prophylactic use of antibiotics on factory farms all over the world has devastating public-health implications. It is a practice that is unchecked in China where, the farmer confirmed, there is no need for a licence or vet's prescription to buy antibiotics. They are readily available over the counter. Translate a policy like this into big farms like Muyuan and you are putting global human health at grave risk.

Factory farmers large and small are breeding disease while mortgaging the global medicine cupboard. To them, more pigs in more airless sheds means more money. For everyone else, one consequence is frightening diseases out of control.

By that point the stench of ammonia, the squealing and crashing of piglets fighting in the background and the discussion of medicines was making me feel nauseous. My colleagues were also looking pale. It was time to get out. As I left, I stood for a moment beside the river and nearby pig sheds. Listening to frantic pig squeals, I watched aghast as smelly brown liquid poured from a pipe, down the bank and into the water.

A few hours later we were on the train from Wuxi to Shanghai, heading for our flight back to the UK. We glided through a countryside beaten into industrial submission. For mile upon mile, all we could see were factories, mines, building sites, car parks, cranes and more green-looking rivers and canals. Sitting on the train, I reflected on our outward journey, from Beijing to pig country. Buoyed by the unexpected welcome I'd received in the capital when we set off, I had been full of optimism. Now that I have some insight into the scale of the challenge to stop factory farming taking hold across China, I am daunted.

It is hard to work out what is worse – millions of tiny pig farms that are almost impossible to regulate, many meting out cruelty on a small scale, or massive global climate-changing mega-pig farms, that are equally inhumane and where the profits and jobs go nowhere near the average rural family. It was a stark illustration that it's not necessarily the scale of farming that is at issue, but the nature of the operation: small isn't always beautiful.

In a country the size of China, you have to think big to make any difference. It makes sense to focus on the big operators like Muyuan. If they change for the better, it improves the lives of millions of pigs at once.

There was one ray of hope. During our discussions, Muyuan's representatives did tell me about trials they were undertaking into more humane ways to keep breeding pigs, in more spacious group accommodation instead of narrow crates. I vowed to return to do whatever I could to turn that tiny trial into the norm, just as we've already done in Europe. I remembered those earlier discussions with the new government-backed organisation keen to consider animal welfare as a way of ensuring better food safety.

As we approached Shanghai, a rainbow of neon lights on skyscrapers lit up the city skyline. We left the station feeling excited. The place was vibrant, throbbing with money, life and possibilities. Bang in the city centre, next to the iconic 'Oriental Pearl' building, was a circular pedestrian skyway, like a ring of pavement on stilts. It was lined with red flags ready for a public holiday the following day. Buzzing with night life, it was a great place to while away half an hour on our final evening and watch the world go by.

A young woman with high heels swung her Louis Vuitton bag over her shoulder and strolled slowly around the circuit. An old couple, hand in hand, followed closely behind. Tourists snapped away and touts offered to take our photo. A nearby McDonald's was packed. In a last burst of investigative enthusiasm, I wandered round the circuit to the golden arches. Through the window I could see a young couple, lovingly feeding their toddler chicken and chips.

There's no doubt that many of these people are enjoying better lives than their parents did eking out a living on small farms, but the countryside is bearing the cost of this seductive change. China's rural poor see furnaces and funnels and struggle to find drinking water as their rivers turn to pea soup. Meanwhile, China's elite and growing middle classes increasingly munch on American-style fast food and sip on Starbucks as they watch the city lights twinkle.

As the taxi whisked us to the airport I reflected that if only a fraction of the effort that went into Shanghai's beautiful skyline went into improving animal welfare in China, the world would have millions of happier pigs and healthier people.

Chinese consumers need to start flexing some economic muscle. The food scares have left them understandably nervous. My time in China convinced me that it is not green lakes or sow stalls that will force change here, but consumer demand for healthy food. The Chinese finally can afford to choose.

An unhappy pig is an unhealthy pig, and an unhealthy pig makes unhealthy food.

16

Kings, Commoners and Supermarkets

Where the power lies

Judging by the sign he has erected by the gate to his country seat, the future King of England has a wry sense of humour. Visitors approaching the driveway to Highgrove House in Gloucestershire are greeted by a notice warning them to beware: they are about to enter 'an old fashioned establishment'. It's an unexpected touch, all the stranger because it is next to another sign which adds rather incongruously that his Majesty's residence is a 'GMO Free Zone'.

There were certainly no genetically modified organisms when Prince Charles was a boy, but his evident pride in declaring that his Gloucestershire estate is GM-free suggests he's considerably more up to date than most of his subjects on a very modern issue. He may be old-fashioned about some things, but he has long been ahead of his time about others.

Highgrove House, the family home of Charles and Camilla, Duke and Duchess of Cornwall, lies in the heart of the Cotswolds and is a model of sustainability. There's a bespoke reedbed sewage system to process royal excrement; bottles, cans, newspapers, cardboard and shredded white office paper are all recycled; leftover scraps from breakfasts and banquets are churned into a composting system. The chandeliers run off energy-saving light bulbs, and the staff car parks are lit with solar power.

The nearest place is Tetbury, an old market town with medieval streets lined with gorgeous antique shops and boutiques full of beautiful things. There are bijou cafés serving Earl Grey from delicate china cups on gingham tablecloths, sweet shops with jars of old-fashioned lemon sherbets and bonbons, and bakeries offering organic honey cakes and piles of strawberry meringues that look like little pink and white puffy clouds.

This luscious corner of England has long had royal connections: Gatcombe Park, Princess Anne's country residence, is six miles to the north, while the international polo tournaments at nearby Westonbirt and the horse trials a few miles south of Tetbury at Badminton are a magnet for the rich and famous. Tetbury is also home to the Duke of Beaufort's Hunt, one of the oldest and largest fox-hunting packs in England and still going strong, even though hunting wild animals with packs of dogs has been declared illegal. But while hotels and restaurants in Tetbury rake it in from the well-heeled local clientele and coachloads of tourists, one business is struggling to make ends meet: the organic farm on the Prince of Wales's estate.

In an era when EU and US subsidies incentivise intensive farming, Home Farm at Highgrove illustrates the huge financial challenges faced by those who are repelled by factory farming and want to rear animals and manage land in a gentler, more natural way. The Prince of Wales can of course afford to shoulder losses. However, he is no Marie Antoinette dabbling in this business as a gentle distraction from the burden of royal duty. He is a champion of agricultural sustainability who uses his influence as heir apparent to the throne to press the case to policymakers, the food industry and philanthropists, both privately and on an international stage. He has learned the hard way how challenging it is to make 'doing the right thing' commercially viable.

The Prince decided to convert his farm to a completely organic system in the mid-1980s, hoping to showcase the environmental and commercial benefits. Almost three decades on, his website describes his operation as a successful and viable working farm – 'a flagship for the benefits of an organic and sustainable form of agriculture' – but it has not been easy.[1] The truth is that Home Farm does not always make a profit: some years, it is a struggle just to break even.

The farm is home to 180 dairy cows, 150 suckler cows, 130 breeding ewes that produce around 200–220 lambs a year, and a few rare-breed pigs. It works on a crop-rotation system, a seven-year cycle designed to maximise the richness of the soil. Organic mutton from Home Farm is sent to Calcot Manor, a luxury hotel near Tetbury, and to the Ritz in London. The Prince is enthusiastic about restoring mutton (meat from a two-year-old sheep) to the dinner tables of the nation after speaking to sheep farmers who found they could no longer get a decent price for older ewes. Other products are sold to Duchy Organics, now a partnership with Waitrose supermarket.

His Royal Highness may be selling to the luxury market, but he doesn't get fancy prices just because of his name. Like most small farmers he is having to diversify and is currently considering producing cheese. 'If you turn [milk] into cheese, it's worth three times as much. It doesn't cost three times as much to turn into cheese, so it's something we're looking at,' his farm manager says.

Three days a week, the Prince's farm sells vegetables to locals from an old cattle shed. Though he's yet to be seen manning the farm shop himself, behind the scenes he is surprisingly hands-on. I was lucky enough to be invited for a private tour of the farm, joining a small group of charities and business people with an interest in sustainable food. It was a fascinating day out, not least for little insights we gleaned into the Prince – like his passion for hedge laying, a highly specialised and intricate operation involving cutting and weaving branches. But the revelation that his organic farm faces an uphill battle to remain commercially viable, despite all the cachet and advantages of his name and status, was a sobering reminder of the extent to which the odds are stacked against farmers who refuse to intensify.

The US and European agricultural system has been geared towards intensification since the post-war years. The original motive was laudable, at least in part. Governments wanted to end the years of austerity, ration books and food shortages. The nightmare of German U-boats sinking vital food supplies was still fresh in the public mind. Post-war governments were determined to make national food production more self-sufficient, and quick to pass new legislation that would set the tone for decades to come. The new strategy was focused on increasing production. Vast amounts of public money were used to support and encourage farmers to maximise output, with little thought about longer-term consequences.

The 1947 Agriculture Act was a defining moment in British farming, kick-starting factory farming in the UK.[2] In the US, by then it was already evolving, thanks to Congress passing a subsidy package for farming known as the Farm Bill in 1933. In the UK, farmers were encouraged to make use of the latest chemicals, machines and techniques. Mixed farms with their varied patchworks of crops and animals were abandoned as farmers began specialising in particular crops or species of farm animal. The age-old natural cycle, where crops would be rotated with livestock whose manure would replenish tired soil, disappeared, as artificial fertilisers were used instead. Farming was now an industry, like producing cars or TV sets. Quality was sacrificed for quantity. An agricultural revolution was under way.[3]

Government policy and subsidies were lined up behind the new methods. Agricultural colleges taught the next generation of farmers the way and legions of advisers and salesmen fanned out across the countryside to spread the message to the farmers of the day: either get with intensive production or get out. One of those farmers was Peter Roberts.

Many other farmers took the advice, whether in relation to chickens or other livestock and crops. Roberts was unusual in that he shunned the new way, fearing for animal welfare and the environment. Many were seduced onto the intensive-farming treadmill and a lot fell victim, being forced out of business. Just after the Second

World War, the UK had around half a million farmers. By the 1980s, numbers had fallen by nearly two-thirds.[4] The figures continue to fall today.

Farming was now in the grip of agribusinesses, a raft of ancillary industries spawned to support the 'modern' farmer: tractor and equipment companies, fertiliser and chemical manufacturers, seed, feed and pharmaceutical suppliers. Small farmers who would not, or could not, embrace the new system became hard pressed, often forced to the wall. Between 1947 and 2002, figures from another rapidly industrialising nation, Canada, show that farm revenues nearly doubled, but the money in farmers' pockets – actual net farm incomes – fell by more than half.[5] The suppliers to industrial farming thrived; farmers did not.

In 1964 Ruth Harrison's book *Animal Machines* described how life on the factory farm revolves 'entirely round profits, and animals are assessed purely for their ability to convert food into flesh, or "saleable products"'.[6] There was now some public awareness of what intensive farming meant for animals behind closed doors. It was the trigger that would fire the conscience of perhaps the greatest campaigning champion for farm animal welfare – Roberts, who at that stage, was still on his Hampshire farm.

In founding the charity Compassion in World Farming, with its mission to 'abolish the needless misery of factory farmed animals' and 'establish kindness and compassion', he set the wheels in motion for a decades-long struggle against industrial farming.

At first, it was a real cottage charity, being run with his wife, Anna, from their kitchen table. Up against the might and money of a well-funded system, it was to be the ultimate David and Goliath battle. Changing farming systems for the better is a more and more complex process involving multiple power brokers based in different parts of the world. Though theoretically 'the consumer is king', eradicating cruel, unsustainable and environmentally damaging farming methods involves far more than persuading the public to turn their back on certain products.

When talking to people about how campaigning works, I often draw a 'power pyramid'. To achieve change, campaigns need to pressurise and ultimately persuade each part of the pyramid. At the summit is the person or body that has the ultimate say in the matter in hand. Up until 1992, Britain presented campaigners with a classic power pyramid. At the top was the minister of agriculture, who could propose profound change and push it through government, or conversely, block it. Moving down, you had the permanent secretary or chief civil servant, the 'Sir Humphrey' of the British TV comedy *Yes, Minister*. While ministers would come and go with reshuffles and changes of government, these powerful unelected mandarins would stick around for years, sometimes decades. That could mean entrenched attitudes and a bias towards the status quo. One level down in the pyramid were influential MPs, followed by rank-and-file backbenchers. At the base of the pyramid was a large segment, distant from direct power, but if mobilised in large enough numbers, greatly influential: ordinary people, or consumers – you and me.

The way to gain influence was to mobilise each successive layer of the power pyramid at Westminster. I remember one of Compassion in World Farming's early victories, in 1991. It was a mild January morning and I was walking down Whitehall with the actress Joanna Lumley, a senior MP and a retinue of media hacks. Lumley, one of the UK's best-known actresses, had joined forces with a Conservative backbencher, Sir Richard Body, to demand a ban on the use of chains and restraining collars on pregnant pigs. These instruments of torture, along with narrow gestation crates – sow stalls – were being used to confine expectant sows for months at a time. They were a way of keeping a lot of pigs in a very small space without the animals fighting. By chaining them up, or keeping them in such tiny stalls that they could not even turn around, let alone bite each other, they could be kept in rows like parked cars, without the inevitable aggression. It was bad enough for any pig, but for a heavily pregnant animal, not being able to move was particularly cruel.

We were clutching bundles of papers tied together with red and blue ribbons: petitions. Lumley was also carrying a chain and restraining collar to show people what they looked like. As she held them up to the press, I remember the camera shutters going into overdrive.

Sir Richard had been an MP for an East Anglian farming constituency for over twenty-five years. Farming was in his blood: he'd been a farmer himself, as well as a stock breeder, writer and critic of post-war farming. He was passionate about pigs. He had come second in the annual parliamentary lottery whereby twenty MPs drawn at random can propose a new law. We had urged him to take up this cause for pigs. I was a new campaigner back then and remember sitting in our tiny office above a health-food store in Petersfield, listening to my then boss, Joyce D'Silva, talking nervously to Sir Richard about whether he would stick with it. He had been inundated with requests for bills and was under pressure to choose another issue. Would he hold firm? I heard Joyce shriek with delight – it was game on.

Looking back, it was a fairly clinical campaign. We had a committed champion in Parliament, who happened to be from the governing party of the time. We had a glamorous and high-profile celebrity endorsing the campaign. Plus ultimately we only needed to persuade one person: the agriculture minister. We mobilised concerned voters to write to their MPs to build up a head of steam. Petitions were collected the hard way – with pens and paper on the street – in those pre-Internet days. Press releases and stunts were organised to catch media attention.

The day came for the debate and vote on Sir Richard's bill. We needed at least 100 MPs voting in the House that day. It may not sound many, but the turnout for so-called Private Members' Bills can be very low, with MPs rarely compelled to attend. The mood in the chamber was supportive, though some politicians, including William Hague, then at the beginning of his political career, were worried about Britain going it alone while other European countries continued to use the restraints. Hague was slapped down by a chorus of voices calling for immediate action.

The Tory MP Michael Brown drew on Britain's colonial past to illustrate the importance of taking a principled stand. He declared:

In the seventeenth and eighteenth centuries, when France and Britain both had empires and both had slavery to maintain those empires, this House unilaterally decided to abolish slavery. Does my honourable friend think that some honourable Members opposed that on the grounds of timing, and said that we should wait until France and other empires had abolished slavery?

Eventually, a vote was called. We were jubilant: 118 votes in favour; only two against. We had won – or so we thought. Sadly that was not entirely the end of it: the draft bill faced two more parliamentary hurdles, and like so many private members' bills, it eventually ran out of time. Its opponents used the highly undemocratic device of 'talking it out', deliberately wasting vital debating time by waffling. We were furious, and determined to find another way to implement what was by now a popular reform. In the end we pulled it off after convincing the agriculture minister himself. The government took up the bill, and it was passed into law.

Since 1993, changing agricultural policy has become a more complicated business. The establishment of the single European market has meant a new strategy, involving influencing power pyramids in key member states throughout the European Union. Influencing the power brokers is a bit like getting to a cherry in the middle of a cake. To get the cherry – Brussels – to vote the way you want, you have to influence as many of the power pyramid 'slices' of the cake as you can. There are now twenty-eight countries in the European Union, and likely to be more soon. Hence, it is much harder to get things done. The plus side is that when reform is achieved, it takes effect in all member states, not just one.

Perhaps the single biggest obstacle to a radical shift away from factory farming in Europe and America is the subsidy system. Agricultural subsidies are hugely powerful players in the food-production game and conspire against producers, like HRH Prince Charles, who eschew intensification. The Common Agricultural Policy (CAP) may make eyes glaze over, but it is central to any debate about factory farming. Ultimately, it underpins the system.

Designed to provide farmers with a reasonable standard of living, consumers with decent-quality food at fair prices, and to preserve rural heritage, the CAP's complex system of protections and incentives has driven the decline in traditional mixed farming and is partly to blame for the great disappearing act of animals from the land. Four out of five of Europe's farm animals are now reared on industrial farms.

Historically, the CAP paid farmers direct subsidies to produce more, benefiting larger arable farmers the most. The system was heavily criticised for producing surpluses – butter and grain mountains, milk and wine lakes – that were frequently dumped on export markets outside the EU, undercutting local producers. In recent years it was reformed to 'decouple' payments from production, instead making payments based on the area of farmland growing goods eligible for subsidy; but even with decoupling and a limit on maximum payments, larger farmers and landowners continue to receive the biggest handouts. It dates back to the beginnings of the Common Market, when France insisted on a system of agricultural subsidies in exchange for agreeing to free trade in industrial goods. Now it is the most expensive and controversial scheme in the EU, costing around £48 billion a year and accounting for almost half of the EU's entire budget. Handouts are supposed to be conditional on meeting environmental or animal welfare standards, but how well this is enforced is open to question.

America has its own subsidy system that props up industrial agriculture, the Farm Bill, a multi-billion-dollar programme of government support. The 2008 package approved nearly £300 billion of spending on agricultural policy over five years.[7] Through this programme, US farmers receive billions of dollars of subsidy.[8] The most heavily subsidised crop in the US is corn (maize), the key feed ingredient of the US 'cheap' meat culture, which accounted for US$77 billion of handouts between 1995 and 2010.[9] The resulting meat may seem good value at the point of sale, but it comes at a high price for the animals reared indoors in horrible conditions, on below-cost cereals and soya beans, thanks to generous taxpayer-funded subsidies.

Through my work at Compassion, I've been campaigning for CAP reform for over two decades. It's a slow process, especially with so many powerful vested interests involved across Europe. Real opportunities for change come along every five years. I remember joining forces with various other charities and organisations, including the RSPB and National Consumer Council, to take the message out to the public. We had someone dressed up as the Grim Reaper handing out money on street corners. Our message was that the CAP was handing out public money to support often damaging farming practices. I'd like to think we've made some progress, but getting Europe's mammoth subsidy system to support a wholesale move away from industrial farming is still a dim and distant goal. Today, just 0.1 per cent of the CAP budget is spent on improving animal welfare – a minuscule amount given the size of the budget and the scale of the problem.

In the battle for a new system, it is possible to achieve more immediate change by winning over retailers rather than regulators. The key players here are supermarkets, fast-food restaurants and the big food-manufacturing companies, because of their huge market share. The big five supermarkets in the UK – Tesco, Sainsbury, Morrisons, ASDA and the Co-op – control roughly 80 per cent of the country's grocery market. Globally, the American-based chain Walmart, which owns ASDA, is number one, France's Carrefour is second, and the UK company Tesco ranks third.[10]

There's a similar picture of big-name domination in the global restaurant market with McDonald's as the world's number one, followed by Yum! Brands, which owns KFC and Pizza Hut. These are followed by the coffee chain Starbucks, Burger King and the sandwich makers Subway.[11]

Such companies have huge influence over the food system. They are a force for good as well as for bad. By working with them, and other influential firms, it is possible to make a radical difference to the entire food and farming chain, from the way farmers rear their animals to the final product. If they decide to make a change, for example to stock only milk from pasture-based cows or cage-free eggs, they can do it far more swiftly and decisively than governments. In the UK, Sainsbury's, the Co-op, Waitrose and Marks & Spencer now stock only free-range eggs. They took a company-wide decision to sell only cage-free, and rolled it out without compromise. Thanks to corporate commitment, the battery-egg-free high street is not far away in the UK.

Contrast that with the EU's attempts to ban battery cages. When Brussels made the decision in 1999, producers were given twelve years to change – more than enough time to get their act together, or so you would think. Yet when the new legislation came into force on New Year's Day 2012, nearly half of the countries were not ready, and were still keeping tens of millions of hens in what were by then illegal cages.

In any case, the new law itself is far from perfect, allowing as it does so-called 'enriched' cages. The new legal variety gives each bird a picture postcard-sized area of extra space. The chickens must now have somewhere to perch and scratch, but they still never see daylight, and are forced to stand on or above a sloping wire floor. It makes egg collection easier, as the eggs roll away once laid, but remains very uncomfortable for the birds' feet. So while the legislation was a huge milestone, the reality is that hen welfare still has a very long way to go in Europe before we can be proud; and it took a very long time to bring about change this way.

When retailers decide what products to stock and how discerning they should be about how the food they sell is produced, consumer views are obviously a powerful lever. Shoppers and diners in most EU countries are becoming increasingly aware of farm animal welfare, and it influences their purchasing decisions. Research and polling suggest that most people believe the issue is important – roughly three-quarters of consumers in the UK and France believe it matters, and the figures are even higher in Hungary and Sweden (83 per cent) and Norway and Italy (84 and 87 per cent respectively).[12] As a result, leading food companies are more and more interested in stocking animal-friendly farm products.

Compassion in World Farming holds an annual awards ceremony to celebrate companies for making animal-friendly policy commitments. I gave my first opening address at our inaugural 'Good Egg Awards' ceremony in the House of Commons in 2007. Since then, we have recognised nearly 500 companies as having made serious commitments to improving the animal welfare standards of the food they sell. Companies like Subway, Starbucks, Sainsbury's, Unilever and McDonald's, have taken pledges to use cage-free eggs in the UK and Europe. ASDA, the Co-op and the ice-cream manufacturer Ben & Jerry's have been recognised for pledges to source milk from cows allowed on grass, instead of locked indoors, during the grazing season. We also give out an award to the overall 'most compassionate' supermarket in the UK, a title that has passed back and forth between Waitrose and Marks & Spencer for over a decade.

From time to time, I'm asked to speak at film screenings. One environmental film company asked me to introduce the US film *Food Inc*, which explores what it calls the 'highly mechanised underbelly' of the industrial farming system in the United States. It's a shocking exposé, but watching it, I could see that it was more than a critique of the system. There was also a message of hope, with examples of companies and producers switching to more humane and sustainable ways of farming. One interviewee described how the sustainable and organic food movement needs to move beyond being David and become Goliath. It needs to be championed by the biggest companies in the world. That's why Compassion develops partnerships with some of the greatest 'Goliaths' in the industry.

It's an approach that involves sticks as well as carrots, but making big companies change their ways doesn't have to mean aggressive confrontation, as our 'Hetty the hen' campaign showed in the 1990s – a protest aimed at the supermarket chain Tesco. It started on an ordinary day, in a supermarket aisle in a sleepy Cornish town. A young man in an in-store security uniform was helping customers with their queries. He was also keeping a watchful eye for light hands: shoplifting was a constant threat, but he knew how to deal with it. What happened next did not feature in his training manual. He turned towards the store entrance and came face to face with someone dressed up as a six-foot hen. The eye-catching costume was of a tatty battery bird, with raw pink skin, flapping arms and sad eyes. This forlorn-looking creature was pushing a shopping trolley round the aisles with a small group of protesters following behind, who in turn were followed by journalists.

Flustered, the security guard stepped in and asked them to leave, but the hen wasn't going anywhere until he'd spoken to the manager. The stunt was part of a nationwide effort to persuade the supermarket to label battery eggs more clearly as 'eggs from caged hens', instead of using weasel words like 'country fresh' or 'farm fresh', which implied something more pleasant.

Earlier that morning, I'd gone head to head on live radio with a Tesco spin doctor who claimed the company's labelling policy was perfectly clear. He was very silver-tongued and probably sounded convincing to listeners. What he didn't know was that Hetty was about to hit roughly thirty Tesco stores at random over a two-week period, complete with local media entourage. We were poking at the soft underbelly of the corporate giant, and it quickly grew clear that they didn't like it.

Within minutes of Hetty's first store appearance, the Tesco spin doctor was on the phone to me. 'Call it off! Call it off!' he appealed. 'We're going to change our label.' From then on, Tesco's battery eggs bore the label 'eggs from caged hens', and the company began stocking more free-range options. Several years later, the EU made it compulsory to label battery eggs with the new, clearer term.

Compassion in World Farming's founder, Peter Roberts, himself learned the power of consumer pressure in the 1980s, in a seminal campaign involving some monks. The Norbertine 'white canons' of Our Lady of England Priory in Storrington, West Sussex, had been generating income for the monastery by rearing veal calves using a 'crating' system. Taken from their mothers at birth, the animals were confined inside 60-centimetre-wide enclosures throughout their short lives. Often chained by the neck to the front of the stall, they could not turn around, stretch their limbs or lie down comfortably. They were reared on milk and nothing else, and by the time they were slaughtered at six months, often they were too weak even to walk to their death. The aim of this shockingly cruel system was to produce very tender white meat by making the calves borderline anaemic.

The monks of Storrington were doing nothing unusual: this was how veal was produced at the time, in the UK, Europe and America. However, Roberts rightly figured that the spectre of such cruelty being inflicted by religious ascetics would capture the public imagination, and decided that Compassion should bring a private prosecution. The monks were charged with nine counts of cruelty under the 1911 Protection of Animals Act and the 1968 Agricultural Act.

Compassion's day in court was a frustrating one. Though the ladies loved Roberts – a Richard Burton lookalike in a tweed jacket who drove to the hearing in a bright yellow Triumph Spitfire convertible – he lost, when the judge ruled that veal crates did not cause 'unnecessary suffering'. Compassion was ordered to pay £12,000 in costs, a huge sum for what was then a tiny charity.[13]

It was only a temporary setback, however. The media loved the story and people could see that the system caused huge suffering. As Roberts would often say: 'Even a damned fool can see it's cruel.' Horrified consumers made their feelings known and the offending meat was left on supermarket shelves. Veal became a dirty word. Not long after the court case, the monks announced they were selling the farm. Not only had it become uneconomic; it had turned into a public-relations disaster.

The then Conservative government began to feel the heat, and Roberts was invited to attend a ministerial meeting on the issue. That same day, the government announced that veal crates would be banned. By then, however, the move was almost academic. Such was the strength of popular disgust that only a handful of veal crate farms were left in the country. The rest had either changed their rearing systems or packed up for good. It was a shining example of consumer power.

The trouble is that consumer power is limited by lack of information, and vested interests work hard to keep people in the dark, shielding them from the often ugly truth about how meat and dairy products are produced. Of course many people prefer not to know, but an increasing number do want to be in a position to make an informed choice. That's why labelling remains such a big issue. While eggs in Europe now have to be labelled according to how they've been produced, there is no such law for meat and milk, allowing retailers and restaurants to use all sorts of ruses to make things sound more appetising.

Take The Ivy, one of the most exclusive eateries in London. Among the regular items on its menu is a dish described as 'corn-fed chicken' – as if 'corn-fed' were a virtue. The Adjournment restaurant in the House of Commons does the same. The truth is that just about all chickens are corn-fed – the vast majority of them on factory farms. So that fancy 'corn-fed' chicken is most likely just factory-reared, by another name.

Logos and symbols on meat designed to imply that it has been produced without needless cruelty can also be misleading. The UK's 'Red Tractor' symbol, for example (officially known as the 'Assured Food Standards' mark), boasts that it stands for 'choosing high animal welfare standards'.[14] In reality, it often guarantees little more than compliance with minimum legislation and government guidelines. In 2002, Compassion in World Farming analysed the scheme against the RSPCA's Freedom Food label and the standards of the leading organic certifier the Soil Association. The Red Tractor scheme's assurances on higher animal welfare were hollow, allowing mothering pigs to be kept in narrow crates, piglets to be mutilated and chickens to be crammed into factory farms. Ten years later on, the study was repeated. Little had changed. Red Tractor again ranked lowest on animal welfare.

The Soil Association logo is the gold standard for animal welfare, though the RSPCA Freedom Food also delivers a genuinely higher welfare choice for consumers shopping for meat, milk and eggs.

The case for better labelling of meat and milk products was under-lined for me when a nine-year-old boy got up in front of an invited audience of MPs and lobbyists to launch a film he'd made called 'How was this animal kept?' Dressed in a blue blazer and wearing a radio microphone, the grandson of the UK government's business secretary, Vince Cable, called for a new law that would see meat and dairy products labelled according to how the animals were reared. It heralded a new campaign, 'Labelling Matters', run by Compassion in World Farming, the RSPCA, the Soil Association and the World Society for the Protection of Animals (WSPA), that calls for mandatory labelling of meat and milk according to method of production in the UK and Europe, in much the same way as we've already achieved for eggs.

The cornerstone of consumer choice is knowing what we're buying. For too long, shoppers have been sold factory-farmed produce under misleading labels. Enough is enough. Labels should be in plain words, not potentially confusing symbols or logos, and there should be guide-lines about prominence, otherwise there will be a temptation to bury the facts in tiny print.

In the end, changing the system matches campaigners against immense vested interests, from the feed manufacturers who convert grain into easily stored and transported 'compound' food, to the equipment manufacturers who make money out of selling farmers the very latest kit; the chemical and fertiliser companies who make fortunes selling pesticides and weedkillers to farms on the intensive treadmill; the pharmaceutical companies and vets who peddle anti-biotics to ward off the diseases inevitable when so many animals are packed into such a small space; and lastly to the farmers themselves.

In between is the farming media, whose publications all too often rely on advertising from chemical, drug and equipment firms, so much so that they often seem to act as cheerleaders for intensification, branding anyone worried about the general direction of travel as 'anti-farmer'.[15] Throw in the constant barrage of advice farmers receive from salesmen keen to sell the latest product, and from government and industry agencies who all too often have got behind the factory-farm model as the only way to go, and it is little wonder that they feel pushed and cajoled, and become so doggedly defensive in the face of criticism. After all, they are only following the path that everyone who ever banged on their door told them was the way ahead. As a result, many invested so heavily in the system that they now feel well and truly stuck.

17

New Ingredients

Rethinking our food

It was my first visit to Hackney City Farm. A dozen hens and ducks stood in a courtyard surrounded by small stables with some sheep, goats and a solitary pig. The surroundings offer a haven amidst the slightly run-down if Bohemian setting of this part of London. Its rustic café was full of character and pleasant for lunch with its menu of buffalo mozzarella, Italian sausage and rabbit ragu. As far as a farm goes, the resemblance ended there; it's little more than a petting zoo.

Tristram Stuart is an author and advocate for reducing food waste. He arrived with fluorescent cycling jacket and helmet in hand and a bee buzzing round his head. I moved to help. 'Don't touch it!' he exclaimed. 'It might be one of mine!' He recently moved from the country to the capital and, missing rural life, consoles himself by keeping bees.

Tristram talked to me about the scale of the problem:

Clearly, we need to feed people, but at present one-third to a half of the world's food is wasted. At the same time, a billion people are hungry and we are extending the agricultural frontier further and further into the world's remaining forests in the quest to grow more and more food. Reducing food waste is one of the simplest

ways of reducing pressure on agricultural land and increasing food
availability globally in a way that involves little or no sacrifice.

Around the middle of the last century, very little food was wasted by
UK households. Now, about a quarter of our food gets tossed in the
bin.[1] In the US, it's even worse: consumers waste about 30 per cent of
their food.[2]

Food is now wasted all along the food supply chain, from farm to
processor to retailer to consumer. In industrialised countries, by far
the majority of this wastage is traceable to shops, catering and households.[3] Supermarkets waste food at their distribution centres, where it
can be trashed before it ever reaches the shelves, or at stores once it
passes its sell-by date. Stuart calculates that the irrigation water used
globally to grow wasted food would be enough for the domestic needs
of 9 billion people – the number expected on the planet by 2050. He
reckons it would be a far better use of the land, oil and water that went
into making the food in the first place to recycle it through pigs and
poultry. 'That's what we domesticated those animals for,' he says
emphatically. With the rise of industrial agriculture, 'we turned the
entire rationale of animal agriculture on its head by feeding them
foods that humans could eat and wasting the food waste that we
should be feeding to them instead.'

His book on the subject, *Waste*, looks at how our throwaway society affects the poor in faraway countries. As a staple food, wheat for
example is traded internationally on the commodity market at a
global price determined by supply and demand. When demand goes
up, so does the price. And with a third of the world's cereal harvest
already being fed to an increasing population of industrially reared
animals, there's little wonder that we are beginning to see food prices
rise worldwide. 'Putting food like this in the bin really is equivalent
to taking it off the world market and out of the mouths of the starving,' Stuart concludes.

The EU disposes of millions of tonnes of valuable food waste while
at the same time importing 40 million tonnes of livestock feed from

South America every year. Stuart argues: 'We need to take account of the economic and environmental costs of continuing with the present system of producing livestock.' Whichever way you look at it, reducing the mountain of food we currently throw away makes good sense. It would go some way to restoring the natural order in the way we produce food too.

In step with common sense, science has a role to play in the menu of the future. I met two 'forward-to-nature' brains at the University of Wageningen in the Netherlands: Willem Brandenburg and René Wijffels. They are exploring the possibility of growing seaweed and algae on a massive scale.

Dr Brandenburg, a fifty-nine-year-old plant scientist, showed me round his glasshouse. It was filled with gurgling, bubbling tanks full of seaweed. He plucked out some slimy strips to show me. 'We only need three hundred and sixty thousand square kilometres of seaweed farming to feed the protein requirements of ten billion people,' he told me. 'That's an area of sea four times the size of Portugal.' Given that 70 per cent of the planet's land surface is covered by ocean, that is a lot of food for not a lot of sea.

Brandenburg is in no doubt about the scale of the challenge we face: 'Over the coming four decades, we'll need to be producing twice as much food with half the inputs; that's why we're looking at plants, plants and plants as the way forward.' It was a pleasant surprise to learn that seaweed is easily digested and compares favourably with meat for protein.

In an interesting combination of tomorrow's technologies, Brandenburg has a vision of floating wind farms connected by a lattice of seaweed farms below the surface. He already has an experimental farm off the Dutch coast of Zeeland and talks enthusiastically about seaweed as the 'engine in doubling plant production', thereby boosting food supplies without taking over more land.

Wijffels, another plant enthusiast, heads up the university's 'Algae Park', a miniature industrial site where racks of glass tubes hum like long fluorescent light bulbs, some filled with green water, some clear.

He is looking into growing algae as a source of protein and biofuel. He believes it could be much more efficient than traditional land-based agriculture and could replace the soya currently being imported into Europe, largely as animal feed. Although his work is in its infancy, Wijffels estimates it could be scalable commercially by 2025.

Some years ago, I looked into free-range farming of fish like salmon, more usually reared in cages. One promising alternative was ocean ranching, where juvenile fish are hatched and reared in captivity before being released into the sea. The liberated fish then live naturally in the wild before returning to their imprinted release point as adults, where they can be caught for harvest. I was delighted then to learn that nearly half the salmon caught commercially in Alaska in 2010 were ocean-ranched.[4] Alaska has really embraced ranching since it banned cage-farming of fish, fearing damage to wild salmon runs from disease and escapees.[5]

Japan has traditionally been big on ocean ranching, and at least ninety species have been released either commercially or experimentally.[6] A wide range of other countries, among them Scotland, Sweden and Iceland, have actively looked at this form of farming the sea.[7]

The way meat is produced 'hasn't changed much' over the last hundred years, according to the Microsoft magnate Bill Gates. That could be about to change: in August 2013 the world's most expensive beefburger was cooked and eaten in London in front of massed ranks of press. The burger, made from *in vitro* – laboratory-produced – meat, was the work of Professor Mark Post of Maastricht University and cost about £200,000 to develop. It was funded by Google's co-founder Sergey Brin, and was made of about 3,000 tiny strips of artificial beef grown from the stem cells of a cow. Speaking after the public tasting, Brin was quoted as saying: 'It's really just a proof of concept right now, from there I am optimistic we can scale by leaps and bounds.'[8]

Bill Gates believes that innovation in meat production has 'tremendous market potential'. As it stands, the basic process remains unchanged, of relying on feeding plants to animals that then return a fraction of the calories and protein they consume in the form of meat, milk and eggs. The outlook is for a near-doubling of global demand for meat by 2050, placing a huge strain on the planet's already over-stretched resources. As Gates puts it, meeting that demand isn't sustainable: 'There's no way to produce enough meat for nine billion people' – the number expected on the planet by mid-century. In an online presentation, Gates describes how food scientists are 'reinvent-ing' meat and eggs, creating alternatives that are 'just as healthful, are produced more sustainably'. It's not about asking everyone to be vege-tarian, he explains, but looking at fresh options for producing 'planet-friendly' meat. He sees the future being in the 'perfect fake'.[9] He's in good company. Winston Churchill saw the potential when he said: 'Fifty years hence, we shall escape the absurdity of growing a whole chicken in order to eat the breast or wing by growing these parts separately under a suitable medium.'

'I couldn't tell the difference between Beyond Meat and real chicken,' says Gates enthusiastically in the presentation. He enlists the help of the best-selling author of *The Omnivore's Dilemma*, Michael Pollan, to further explain what they describe as 'three principal moti-vators' that make reducing meat consumption a good idea: health, environment and animal welfare:

> Health, because we know high consumption of red meat correlates with higher chances of certain cancers; and the environment, because we know that conventional meat production is one of the biggest drivers of climate change, as well as water and pollution; and ethics, since the animal factories that produce most of our meat and milk are brutal places where animals suffer needlessly.[10]

According to New Harvest, an organisation funding research into *in vitro* or 'cultured' meat in the US and Europe, a single cell could, in theory, produce enough meat to feed the global population for a year. New Harvest's Jason Matheny told me what it would taste like when it's fully developed. 'Well, it should taste the same as conventional meat because it's made out of the same stuff . . . we think we can match that same taste and texture by producing meat in culture in a way that's much safer, much more efficient and much healthier for the consumer.'

There is a long way to go before large-scale *in vitro* meat production is realistic – and a mountain to climb to overcome the 'yuck' factor. However, Matheny is confident that it is worth pursuing, not least for the potential health benefits:

> In cultured meat, you can precisely control the amount of fat so you can have more of the healthy fats like omega-3 and less of the unhealthy fats. So we can have hamburgers that actually prevent heart attacks rather than cause them. The yuck factor should really be focused on conventional meat and the way it's produced right now, which is simply unhealthy, unsafe and unsustainable.

18

The Solution

How to avert the coming food crisis

I was in the deep south of America, Georgia, staying at the home of fifth-generation farmers. They were proud of their heritage and upbeat about the future. Will Harris, my host, was an imposing character, a fifty-eight-year-old cowboy whose uniform of choice was a terracotta shirt, worn jeans, lace-up boots and a tattered Stetson. He was warm, determined and ambitious and spoke with a thick southern drawl, smooth as molasses. His family had been raising cattle on their farm, White Oak Pastures, since the American Civil War a century and a half ago.

'Nature abhors a monoculture,' he told me. 'That's why we have a rotational mix of species on this farm.' Harris farms 1,060 hectares of land and a lot of animals: 1,800 cattle, 50,000 chickens for meat, 1,000 laying hens, 800 sheep and various other species. He was big on manners and extremely hospitable. The previous night, he'd drained a bottle of wine into plastic cups as we set off round the farm. Now it was morning, and back to business. He was going to give me a proper tour of the farm in an open-topped jeep. After a quick coffee, we set off. We bumped along a track through pine trees and found ourselves in a sort of swamp, a series of small lakes teeming with wildlife.

'There's plenty of fish, snakes and turtles in there,' Harris said. An osprey flapped lazily overhead. A 2½-metre alligator glided silently across the surface of the still water on one of the lakes. My host told me how he and his siblings loved to camp in this spot when they were little. 'We used to swim in that pond, gators an' all,' he grinned. They breed them tough in Georgia.

The jeep took us on a grass safari across endless meadows. There was nothing monotonous about the scenery, and Harris saw all the greenery through the eyes of his animals, pointing out the different types of grass as if reading through a menu: 'That's crimson clover, the *crème brûlée* of grasses . . . that's ryegrass, rocket fuel for cattle . . . and this one's Smutt grass, the one cows and sheep like least . . .' Young black heifers with catlike whiskers snorted softly and ripped up the grass with their tongues.

The farm operated a wholesome type of rotational grazing system. It involved the animals moving round the pasture in succession: big animals (cattle) followed by smaller animals (sheep) followed by poultry, each of them fed and returning manure to the land in their own fashion. It's a way of doing things that is not only healthy for the land but also helps with disease control. Parasites and pathogens often differ between cattle, sheep and chickens. Rotate animals by species, and it's harder for them to build up.

We stopped to admire some chicks with newly sprouted feathers. They were zipping about like clockwork toys. The small huts they were housed in at night were moved every couple of weeks. 'When the cattle defecate, the chickens work it, eating the bugs,' Harris told me. The field we were in held around 10,000 chickens, but you'd never have guessed it – there was not a shed in sight.

As we drove along a dirt track through the meadow, other fruits of the rotational system were revealed. 'Dung beetles are God's gift to pasture!' Harris exclaimed as the jeep shuddered to a halt. We jumped out and before I knew it we were on our hands and knees, inspecting a cowpat. Never let it be said that I don't know how to have fun . . .

The cowpat was peppered with little blooms of red soil pushed up by busy dung beetles playing an important role aerating the soil. Harris dug around in the mess with a paper cup: 'They've riddled the soil with holes, even in this hard-assed track! A healthy dung-beetle population is an indicator of a healthy soil.' He gently lifted one out, a little coffee bean on legs: nature's seal of approval on White Oak Pastures.

The farm had not always been like this. Following the Second World War, Harris's father started farming industrially. 'It was all about pounds of beef produced and nothing about the quality,' he told me. He admitted he found the industrial way exciting and that he and his father had been good at it. They fed the cattle grain and used hormone implants to make them grow faster. Antibiotics were mixed in feed and pastures doused with chemicals. But Harris grew disenchanted with the artifice of it all. When he took over the business from his dad in his forties, he dispensed with the props of intensification, bringing the farm full circle.

Now it is a celebrated model of environmental sustainability, animal welfare and good food. His office walls were covered in newspaper cuttings, full of glowing references to the way he runs the farm and the quality of his produce. His clients include the catering giants Sodexo and the retailers Publix and Whole Foods Market. Later that day, a Publix store assistant showed me some White Oak Pastures beef. 'We can't keep it in the store, it sells so fast,' she said.

So what do these happy cattle, living in a land of plenty, looked after by friendly farmers and consumed by contented customers, have to do with feeding a growing population with diminishing natural resources? Certainly, Georgia is a million miles from Malawi or Ethiopia, where a good beef steak is the stuff of daydreams. Yet there are more answers here than there are on high-tech factory farms where cattle are crammed into sheds and plied with antibiotics. As I have argued throughout this book, factory farming is not feeding the world, because the grain-feeding of confined animals uses more food than it produces.[1] It's part of a highly resource-intensive and wasteful food system. By contrast, no ground-up fish meal from Peru is flown across continents to feed the cows on White Oak Pastures; no oil-based fertilisers are poured onto the land. This is farming as nature intended.

Could it be done on a big scale? Harris has no doubt. 'I know I could scale up tenfold,' he said. He already employs eighty people and has plans to expand.

However, when it comes to world food, there's big and there's global. The United Nations estimates that food supply needs to increase by 70–100 per cent by 2050.[2] To achieve this without factory farming we need a common-sense approach, based on three principles: putting people first, reducing food waste, and farming as if tomorrow matters.

HOW PUTTING PEOPLE FIRST HELPS ANIMALS

A third of the world's cereal harvest is fed to farm animals.[3] If it went directly to humans instead, it would feed about 3 billion people.[4] Cereals are a big deal. They're not just for breakfast: worldwide they provide around half of the total calories for humans, in bread, pastries, pasta, tortillas, pies, pizzas – you name it. So how can it make sense to shovel this human staple into factory farms? It's not only cereals: in Argentina we had a glimpse of how 90 per cent of the world's soya production is destined to feed industrially reared animals.[5] As we saw in Peru too, factory farming's seemingly insatiable hunger extends to plundering the oceans to feed farmed fish, pigs and poultry. Given the chance, those confined animals would convert things that people don't or won't eat into something suitable for human consumption. For example cows and sheep will turn grass – often growing on land that can't be used for anything else – into meat and milk. Chickens will search pasture, woodlands and orchards for food, producing meat and laying eggs. Along with pigs, they will recycle food waste with great enthusiasm.

Yet industrial animal rearing has thrown farm animals directly into competition with people for food – and we are not winners in the process. For every 6 kilograms of plant protein such as cereals fed to livestock, only 1 kilogram of animal protein on average is given back in the form of meat or other livestock products for humans.[6] Factory farms are food factories in reverse: they waste it, not make it, and squander valuable cropland in the process.

Reducing the amount of grains fed to farm animals by half would go a long way toward a saner food system. People don't have to choose between eating cereals or meat. Both can be produced far more effectively with the right kind of farming.

The Solution

Rear ruminants on pasture not in sheds. Food from ruminant animals, such as beef, mutton, lamb and milk, should be produced by grazing on mixed, rotational farms, permanent pastures or marginal lands. This converts plant life that humans can't eat into edible food. End the wasteful practice of feeding grain to confined cattle for intensively reared beef or milk.

Feed fish to people, not to livestock. Up to a third of the fish landed in the world is not consumed directly by people. It is used mostly as feed for farmed fish and other livestock.[7] Overfishing and the practice of throwing back dead or dying fish are now well documented. The plundering of our seas to feed confined farmed animals is less well known. Ending the practice would take pressure off our often overexploited seas.

Strong action from governments, consumers and corporations alike, in the form of legislation, subsidy incentives, purchasing policies, research and advice, is needed to achieve these two recommendations.

REDUCING FOOD WASTE

North America and Europe waste up to half their food – enough to satisfy the hunger of the world's billion undernourished people between three and seven times over.[8] It's a staggering statistic. Whether it be from shops, catering companies or tossed into our bins at home, food is wasted all along the food supply chain in industrialised countries.[9] Tristram Stuart's groundbreaking book on the subject, *Waste*, shows graphic images of a whole crop left to rot in the field after being rejected by a supermarket; of potatoes rejected for cosmetic reasons; of masses of 'imperfect' bananas dumped in a ditch. It is not just fruit and veg that gets thrown away; in the UK alone, householders waste the meat equivalent of 50 million chickens, 1.5 million pigs and 100,000 beef cattle every year.

Traditionally, rearing farm animals was a land-based business. They grazed or foraged for food or, in the case of pigs and poultry, ate scraps from the kitchen. The system was based on diversity, maximising resources, working with natural processes and avoiding waste. The animals provided manure and food as part of the natural rhythm of farm life. With the rise of industrial agriculture, Stuart argues, 'we turned the entire rationale of animal agriculture on its head by feeding them foods that humans could eat and wasting the food waste that we should be feeding to them instead.'

Could we be recycling waste food for farm animals? Is this practical on a significant scale? I went to Dagenham, East London's windswept 'waste corridor' and a hotbed of sustainable industries, to look at some relevant recycling projects. I watched as used drink cans leapt off conveyor belts streaming with plastic bottles. Metal paddles stirred silver-grey liquid. A giant washing machine separated plastics from other rubbish. A vast spaghetti junction of pipes, frames and clanking machines stood within a warehouse, reincarnating plastic bottles. Outside, great bales of squashed bottles waited their turn. The company running the place was called Closed Loop. It transforms 875 million discarded bottles a year into something usable. 'Ten years ago, we didn't have the technology to build a plant like this to convert rubbish into resources. That's where food waste is right now,' the company's Nick Cliffe told me.

In the EU, it is currently illegal to feed animal by-products to farm animals. The ban was a panic measure following the 2001 outbreak of foot-and-mouth disease. As a result, a lot of food waste ends up in landfill – and in the UK and many other countries, landfill space is running out. Sites in the densely populated southeast of England could be full within five years. Already, waste is travelling many miles simply to be dumped up north. As space diminishes to bury rubbish, there is a new impetus for more adventurous recycling.

Pure plant-based food waste that has undergone strict processing can already be fed to animals. Closed Loop is working with a major frozen-food manufacturer in England that processes waste vegetables for animal feed. About a million tonnes of industrial by-products like whey and vegetable leavings are said currently to go to pigs in the UK.[10] There is the potential to do much more.

There are also some smaller, more local schemes. In the village of Pince in northwestern France, householders are being offered chickens in an attempt to reduce the amount of food going to waste.[11] In the London borough of Tower Hamlets, there's a weekly food-waste collection. Since it is mixed waste, it goes for composting, which is better than sending it to landfill, though not as efficient as using it as animal fodder.[12] The fact that it is only collected weekly is also likely to deter many people, especially those without much space in their homes, from taking part.

The Japanese, South Korean and Taiwanese governments are all ahead of the game. They have grasped the fact that feeding food waste to livestock is the most efficient way of recycling it and have set up food-waste collection and recycling centres that ensure the leftovers are properly sterilised and safe for animals intended for human consumption.[13] If Britain and the EU made food recycling easier, the 40 million tonnes of livestock feed imported from South America every year could be reduced, there would be less pressure on landfill sites, and pigs would enjoy a more varied diet.

Waste is of course also linked to commercially driven food cultures that encourage people to eat far more meat than they need, with serious health implications, where profit comes before feeding people properly.

Developing countries have food-waste problems too. However,

their waste is more often caused by a lack of basic technologies and infrastructures than by profligacy. Losses of up to half of a staple crop are all too common simply for want of simple technologies like decent storage facilities, refrigeration and transport.[14] Improving food security for countries like these is as much about improving these basics as it is about growing more.

Worldwide, the UN suggests that about a third of food is wasted through being binned or left to rot.[15] It estimates that 28 per cent of the world's agricultural land is used to produce food that is wasted at an economic cost of about US$750 billion, equivalent to the GDP of Switzerland.[16] If this were reduced by half, it could provide enough food for an extra billion people.[17] Recycling as much of the remaining waste as possible by feeding it to pigs and poultry would add further efficiency savings.

As I set out in previous chapters, avoiding overconsumption of meat deserves serious consideration in developed countries, for our own good.

The Solution

Feed pigs and poultry on food waste and encourage foraging. Pigs and poultry are nature's great foragers and recyclers, the perfect recipients of food waste. The current practice of feeding them cereals and soya squanders vast amounts of food. They should no longer be factory-farmed. Instead, make them integral to mixed farms where they can forage and turn food waste into eggs and meat. Governments must play their part by ensuring there are legislation and policy incentives in place to enable this.

Invest in waste reduction. Governments, civil society and corporations should encourage a reduction in food waste at every level, from farmer to corporation to consumer, through incentives, purchasing policies and the provision of research and advice.

Avoid overeating meat. Rejecting copious junk food in favour of high-quality meat will benefit us and the planet. Research has shown that too much saturated fat from meat and dairy products can be harmful to health and may contribute to obesity, type-2 diabetes and heart disease.[18] Reducing consumption of these saturated animal fats by 30 per cent would lead to about a 15 per cent reduction in heart disease in the UK and Brazil.[19] Consumers, governments, corporations and civil society should work together to promote healthy, sustainable balanced diets that, in Western countries, avoid overconsumption and instead include better-quality meat from animals kept in higher-welfare conditions. This would both benefit human health in the West and reduce pressure on the environment.

FARM AS IF TOMORROW MATTERS

The Chinese philosopher Confucius said: 'For all Man's supposed accomplishments, his continued existence is completely dependent upon six inches of topsoil and the fact that it rains.'

As a result of intensive farming and climate change, that vital topsoil is disappearing – and so, in some places, is any guarantee of rain.

Over the last half-century, many farm animals have disappeared from fields and been confined in sheds, in an agricultural system that has become divorced from the land and separated from the so-called 'nutrient cycle'. The natural cycle in which sun and rain fed grass, which fed animals, whose manure enriched the soil, has been replaced by a new system dependent on fossil fuel-based synthetic fertilisers. Monocultures, heavily reliant on chemical pesticides and artificial fertilisers, are hammering the soil and the environment. The UN has warned that the world's farmland could decline in productivity by a quarter this century.[20] Soil erosion already affects almost a third of the world's cropland,[21] and is widespread in the EU.[22] Meanwhile land is being lost to urbanisation, contaminated by irrigation,[23] and becoming desert as fast if not faster than we're adding to it.[24] There is now also the added pressure from land use for biofuels and the continued growth of industrial livestock.

Much greater emphasis is needed on soil-healthy rotational farming with a mix of crops, pastures and farm animals, reducing reliance on artificial fertilisers, as well as providing better animal welfare. Measures such as crop rotation, green manure, reforestation and taking unsuitable land (such as steep slopes) out of production would help to reverse soil erosion and land degradation.

The Solution

Produce food from mixed farms of crops and animals to enhance soil sustainability. Mixed farms where animals are rotated with soil-enhancing crop rotations should be encouraged. Most pigs and poultry in Europe and the USA are currently confined on factory farms. Restoring the natural link between farm animals and the land needn't require huge amounts of extra space. The UK, for example, rears over 800 million meat chickens a year. Keeping them free-range would need an area around a third of the size of the Isle of Wight – less than one-thousandth of the nation's total farmland.[25] Integrating them within mixed farming systems would benefit animal welfare and soil quality and sustainability.

As a global society, we are wasting as much as half of all the food we produce, by feeding it to farm animals, throwing it away, or letting it rot for want of basic technology. Land is often being driven so hard that we are playing off tomorrow's sustainable harvests against today's short-term gains. With the prospect of 2 billion more people to feed by 2050, our food system needs to be 70–100 per cent more effective. That cannot mean simply doubling farm outputs in a business-as-usual fashion.

Just to double output from our current food system would be like a water company with badly leaking pipes simply laying down a second set of equally leaky pipes. Yes, it would increase the water to people's homes. It would also increase the waste. Far better to repair the pipes.

In the course of writing this book, I have travelled through Europe, North and South America, China and elsewhere. What I have seen and heard has only strengthened my belief that we need an urgent rethink about feeding the world. Of one thing I am certain: industrial farming is not the answer. The veneer of efficiency is no more real than the emperor's new clothes. The system actually wastes food rather than making it.

What I have also discovered is that the means to feed the world's population today and for the foreseeable future are already with us. Globally, enough food is produced to feed around 11 billion people, if only we didn't waste it. Future harvests will need a hefty dose of common sense in their production if we are to feed people properly and fairly. Ending the competition for food between people and farm animals seems a good place to start, along with reducing and recycling food waste and taking animals out of factory sheds and restoring them to the land in fields. With that, we have the recipe for truly sustainable food on an increasingly crowded yet shrinking planet.

Global food production (in calories), with estimated losses, conversion and wastage in the supply chain

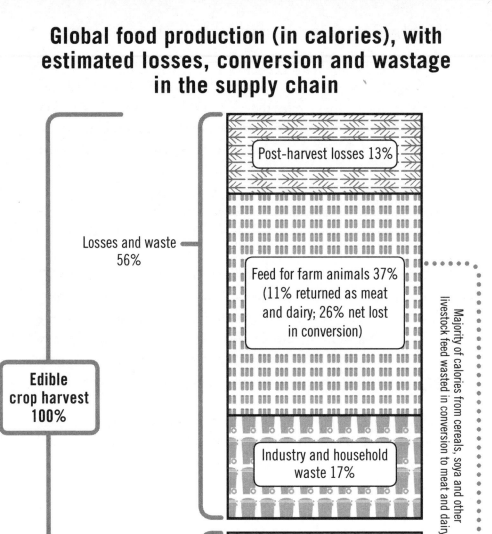

Losses and waste
56%

Edible
crop harvest
100%

Post-harvest losses 13%

Feed for farm animals 37%
(11% returned as meat
and dairy; 26% net lost
in conversion)

Industry and household
waste 17%

Majority of calories from cereals, soya and other
livestock feed wasted in conversion to meat and dairy

Meat and dairy produced 11%

Quantity available for
human consumption
44%

Remaining crop harvest 33%

Illustration based on Lundquist, 2008 in C. Nellemann et al., *The Environmental Food Crisis – The Environment's Role in Averting Future Food Crises*. A UNEP rapid response assessment, February 2009.

Wasted: farmed for food but thrown away

Amount of meat wasted worldwide each year in equivalent number of animals

11,600 million chickens wasted

Each icon represents 100 million chickens

270 million pigs wasted

59 million cattle wasted

Each icon represents
10 million pigs or cows

19

Consumer Power

What you can do

Bringing about a better food future is something that everyone can now get involved in. Each of us has three great opportunities a day to help make a kinder, saner food system through the choices we make.

The celebrity chef Hugh Fearnley-Whittingstall is a big champion of great cooking with integrity at his River Cottage on the south coast of England. 'I see the link between good animal welfare and good food all the time,' he told me. 'You see the difference on the plate, you taste the difference, and you feel the difference in your body.'

Like Hugh, I recognise that consumers have real power and believe the way we shop can change farming methods for the better, including animal welfare. Compassionate consumerism is a great way to choose wonderful food and save the world from Farmageddon. I advise: buy foods from the land – reared on farms, not factories; love leftovers, so as to reduce food waste; and choose a balanced diet without eating too much meat.

For food reared on the land, look out for products labelled free-range, pasture-raised, outdoor-reared or organic. Buying meat and milk from ruminants – sheep and cattle – is the most sustainable option, as these convert grass into food.

Free-range and organic pigs and poultry come with the drawback that, for now, they are largely reared on grain and soya. EU laws forbid the feeding of food waste to farm animals. As this inevitably changes, nature's great recyclers can roam the land once again, converting food that people won't eat into food that they will. But for the time being, buying pasture-raised pork, chicken and eggs will provide a better food choice for the consumer and a decent life for the animal, while speeding bigger changes in the future.

Avoid labels that just say things like 'farm fresh', 'country fresh', 'natural' or just 'fresh': it's probably from a factory farm. Labels that just say something like 'corn-fed' should be avoided too. In the UK, the ubiquitous 'Red Tractor' label means that the meat or milk has been produced to British standard and in itself is no guarantee of higher animal welfare.

In the UK, the RSPCA monitors the Freedom Food scheme to assure higher standards of animal welfare. In the Netherlands, look out for the Beter Leven (Better Life) scheme, and in the US, the Animal Welfare Assured (AWA) and Global Animal Partnership (GAP) label. A good choice in Australia is anything with the 'RSPCA approved farming' logo.

Lamb

Sheep usually spend more time in the great outdoors than most other farm animals. So, if in doubt about what to buy to assure grass-fed meat, then products from lamb and sheep are a good choice. But always check the label or ask the seller. Pasture-reared lamb is healthier than intensively reared lamb, having higher levels of the omega-3 essential fatty acids that are linked to reducing many chronic diseases.

Beef

Pasture-reared or grass-fed beef is a good choice, enabling animals to express their natural behaviours and feed in a more natural way. Beef raised this way has considerably less saturated fat and more vitamin E and healthy beta-carotene than intensively reared beef.

All too often, cattle are reared intensively, confined indoors on uncomfortable slatted floors or crowded into barren feedlots and fed grain or soya. In the US, unless the packaging says grass-fed or pasture-raised, cattle are likely to be finished on a confined feed-lot, which leads to severe welfare problems. So, again, really check the label.

Dairy

Milk has a wholesome natural image from cows left to gently graze in fields of green. In Britain, this is still largely the case in the summer-time. In the US and other countries, dairy cows are being 'zero-grazed': confined permanently indoors or in feedlot-style pens and never graz-ing a fresh blade of grass. Sadly, there isn't much on the labels to help shoppers choose. In the absence of decent pack descriptions, choose organic, or milk produced under one of the dedicated animal welfare schemes like Freedom Food.

In the US, look for Animal Welfare Approved standards. If unavailable, buy Certified Humane or USDA Organic. Or you could use dairy alternatives such as soy, coconut or almond milk, yogurts or desserts. Look for labels that say rBGH-free or rBST-free, which means that the cows were not dosed with genetically engineered milk-boosting hormones. While these are banned in the EU, they are still widely used in the US.

Don't forget to check the label on your cheese and yoghurt too! When you eat out, check whether the milk in your tea or the cheese in your sandwich is organic. If it doesn't say so on the menu, it prob-ably isn't.

But isn't organic milk the domain of the well-off and haute cuisine? In Britain, McDonald's restaurants offer only organic milk for their hot drinks.

Eggs

Many eggs are still produced from caged hens. Barren battery cages are commonly used worldwide, where several hens are crammed into tiny all-wire cages, unable to even stretch their wings for life.

Barren cages are now banned in the EU. However, a proportion of eggs are still produced using so-called 'enriched' cages, which have rudimentary features like perches and a bit more space, but still prevent hens from carrying out proper exercise or other natural behaviours.

In the EU, eggs are the exception in that they have to be labelled by law according to the way they are produced. Look out for free-range and organic; under these terms, the hens will have been given access to the outdoors. Free-range eggs often contain more healthy omega-3 fatty acids and antioxidants than cage eggs, and are a richer source of vitamin E. The general rule is that the more an animal is given access to the outdoors and able to eat grass and mixed foods, the healthier the resulting food.

'Barn' eggs will come from hens kept in big sheds and able to move around but not given access to the outdoors. Avoid eggs labelled 'eggs from caged hens' or 'enriched or colony cage' eggs; these are the rare example of the label telling you they are factory-farmed.

Outside the EU, in the absence of a recognised term denoting outdoor access, then the eggs are probably from battery caged hens. Again, avoid 'fresh' or 'natural'. The term is often confused with free-range, but means nothing of the kind.

In the US, most eggs still come from barren battery cages. Only buy cage-free eggs, those labelled pasture-raised, or eggs that meet animal welfare certification standards like Animal Welfare Approved and Certified Humane.

Remember that additional foods such as mayonnaise, cakes, cookies, pasta and quiches contain egg; unless the ingredients explicitly say 'cage-free' or free-range, they are likely from caged hens.

Chicken meat

By investing a little more in the chicken you choose you can make a big difference to its life. It can also give you a healthier product. Free-range and organic chicken contains up to 50 per cent less fat than its factory-farmed equivalent.

The chickens most commonly found on our supermarket shelves are bred and fed to reach their slaughter weight in around six weeks. Free-range chickens will usually be slaughtered at eight weeks and organic or pasture-raised at around twelve weeks.

Free-range, pasture-raised or organic chickens will have had access to the outdoors during their lives. In the US, look out for chicken certified Animal Welfare Approved (AWA), Global Animal Partnership (GAP), or Certified Humane. Avoid chicken that just says 'fresh' or 'farm-fresh', 'corn-fed', 'vegetarian-fed' or 'natural'. Some of the more outrageous labels found on factory-reared chickens include 'Fresh all natural' and 'cage-free'! Chicken is perhaps the meat most fraught with phony labels.

A good halfway house would be chickens that are reared indoors but to higher welfare standards, for example under the RSPCA Freedom Food scheme in the UK or the Certified Humane scheme in the US.

Turkey meat

As with chicken meat, look for labelling terms like free-range and organic. In the UK, also look for the RSPCA-monitored Freedom Food label. A good compassionate shopping tip is to look for slow-growing traditional turkey breeds like Norfolk Black, Black Wing Bronze and Cambridge Bronze.

Pork, bacon and sausages

Along with chickens, pigs have tended to be the most factory-farmed of animals. They are often kept in crowded indoor pens, bred in confinement crates and fed copious amounts of cereals, soya and other people-type food.

However, there has been a resurgence in recent decades of keeping pigs outdoors, at least for breeding, with some granted much of their lives outside. This is good news, as pigs are naturally inquisitive creatures and need to be able to root around and explore their world. As intelligent as the average dog, they can quickly become bored and suffer if their needs are denied.

In the EU, look out for free-range or organic – the pigs are born and reared in systems with outdoor space where they can roam outdoors. Free-range pigmeat is richer in vitamin E and iron than meat from intensively reared pigs.

'Outdoor reared' is another good choice – the pigs are born in systems with outdoor space and spend around half their life outdoors.

'Outdoor bred' means that the pigs will have been born outside – better for the breeding animals – but then reared indoors.

In the US, avoid pork or bacon from gestation-crate systems – cruel ways of confining pregnant pigs – and look for certifications that do not permit these. These include Animal Welfare Approved, Certified Humane, 5-Step Animal Welfare Rating Program, Organic and American Humane Certified.

As always, avoid general labels that sound good but are meaningless, like 'fresh'.

Farmed fish

This is a tricky area, as many wild fish species are increasingly threatened. Useful advice here is to avoid carnivorous species of farmed fish, such as salmon, trout, cod and halibut, as these are likely raised on feed made from wild fish – Peruvian anchovies and the like.

If sustainably caught, wild salmon and trout is by far the better purchase than their farmed cousins. Wild salmon has up to 60 per cent less fat than farmed.

If you do buy farmed fish, look out for those produced under an accredited scheme like organic or RSPCA Freedom Food.

Buy local

Choosing foods produced closer to home makes good sense. Of course, just being local doesn't mean that the food hasn't come from a factory farm. But buying from a supplier you know or a local farmers' market, or buying local produce from the supermarket, are all good ways to reduce your carbon 'footprint' – less transport needed to get the food to you. It also means you are more likely to strike up a rapport with the farmer, and perhaps even see for yourself how the food is produced. And it reinforces local food communities. It's naturally easier to find out what's going on with your food if it's produced close to home than if it is part of a global supply chain. As the British food writer Joanna Blythman points out, factory farms 'don't go out of their way to welcome us in for "Doors Open" days. So what chance do we have of knowing what's really going on in similar operations thousands of miles away?'[1]

Love leftovers, waste nothing

Avoiding wasting food is perhaps the simplest way to make a major contribution to a better food system. It will help reduce the amount of land, water and oil, not to mention animal suffering, that currently goes into feeding landfill. It cuts down your food bill too.

Avoid overeating meat

There is a growing body of evidence to show that people in the developed world are generally eating too much meat, eggs and dairy for their own health. Cutting down – going meat-free on Mondays for example – is a simple step towards avoiding factory-farmed produce and helping to balance your diet. One quick and easy way to eat well and be light on the planet is to have meat-, egg- and dairy-free meals.

Avoiding Farmageddon is easy. As long as we buy products from animals reared on the land (free-range, organic), favour local producers or retailers that we trust, eat what we buy and thereby reduce food waste, and avoid overeating meat, we can fill our plates in ways that benefit the countryside, our health and animal welfare.

Epilogue

Midsummer, and the garden looks amazing. Our little wildflower meadow has run riot; the poppies, cornflowers and hollyhocks have shot up and are now taller than I am. My wife and I planted them as ground cover for our hens, and to help preserve the butterflies and bees that need a helping hand.

In the cool of the morning, I open the coop and six reddish-brown bundles of feathers scurry out and start pecking and scratching as they busily go about their breakfast. Later, the sun gets the hens sunbathing; lying gently on their side, wings flicking, eyes bright and bulging with delight. They remind me every day that animals are individuals with their own wants and needs.

Black cattle with white faces graze the hill that looms over our village, so close it often sounds like they too are in the garden. Our small 200-year-old cottage nestles in the rural heart of the English South Downs National Park. This community and countryside has survived many changes, not least occupation by the Romans, then as King Alfred the Great's Royal Manor, before the Domesday Book and the iron grasp of William the Conqueror. Hitler's Luftwaffe tried hard to leave its mark, raining thousands of bombs on the area; the sole loss of life was a single unfortunate pig.

Despite the changes, and often because of them, the countryside looks stunning, shaped by history and stewarded by generations of farmers reaping harvests from the land. I listen to the trickle of the chalk stream and the low chatter of village folk drinking in the pub next door and reflect on two years of travel, of exploring the issues behind the brewing storm: the Farmageddon scenario that jeopardises food, the countryside and all of us.

Fifty years ago, Rachel Carson's *Silent Spring* delivered a stark warning of the perils of treating the countryside like just another industrial process. She revealed the realities of the new chemical era on the land, where pitched battles are fought with nature, using pesticide sprays as the weapon of choice. The mother of the modern environmental movement sparked controversy at the highest level – even the US president of the time, John F. Kennedy, was talking about it. She won some important reforms, but overall, her clarion call – that the industrial way was the wrong way – has been ignored.

While writing this book, I have seen what happens when we farm without proper care for nature; the far-reaching consequences of converting varied patchworks of fields into vast, monotonous food factories. From the grievous pollution facing the famous French beaches of Brittany, to the battle to preserve drinking water from toxic algal blooms in China, and the decline of the world-renowned Chesapeake Bay in the US, in each case intensive farming has been implicated. I remember the eerie feeling of looking down from a helicopter on a factory farm rearing three-quarters of a million chickens with not a bird in sight; of driving through a Mexican valley producing a million pigs without seeing a single animal. I've seen the tears of people driven from their land to make way for soya, or suffering ill-effects from the fumes of fishmeal plants, both to feed distant factory farms. I've wept too at the plight of a large-scale intensive dairy farmer, crippled by debt, who shot himself and left five children fatherless.

There is a story behind everything we eat. I've spoken to countless people involved; their personal stories are reflected in this book. Everyday meals like chicken and chips or bacon and eggs or just a glass of milk come with their very own cast of characters and consequences. Startling changes don't have to be accompanied by dramatic scenes. Sometimes, they can be as subtle as disappearing birds, bees and butterflies; as gradual as the erosion of the goodness of food and the quiet ebbing of our quality of life. Sometimes it has been difficult not to feel overwhelmed by the sheer scale of the problem, the Farmageddon scenario that threatens to engulf the countryside and society.

At the same time, I set out to find seeds of hope. I wanted to find better ways than the industrial ascendancy. I discovered they are often all around us; here small acorns in need of nurturing; elsewhere thriving oaks. I felt privileged to see the pasture plains of free-ranging animals in Georgia; uplifted by fields in Argentina dancing defiantly with butterflies in contrast to their lifeless pesticide-soaked GM neighbours. I learned a lot from watching chickens in China roaming woodlands and pigs living inquisitive, active lives on a model farm in Beijing. I've been inspired by extensive farms in Britain and Europe, taking care of their animals, looking after the environment, and producing great food to boot. I found so much more than the few scattered crumbs of comfort I was expecting – and on my own doorstep too.

At our annual village beer festival, it was heartening to listen to a local farmer speaking proudly of his award-winning mixed farm, combining the job of producing food with caring for wildlife. He is not alone. Close by, through leafy lanes and rolling hills, more animals are free-range, and it's a joy to see. Brown and white cattle with tiny calves afoot chomp on grass up to their knees. Pigs scamper amongst scattered huts resembling a holiday camp. Such scenes are far from unique, but not nearly common enough. In the industrialised nations where food factories replace countryside, these oases shine as beacons of hope.

With nearly a third of the planet's land surface devoted to rearing farm animals or growing their feed, perhaps I shouldn't have been surprised at how big the environmental impact can be. I was struck too by the link between how animals are kept and the quality of the food they produce. Generally, the more that animals are reared on the land with natural, varied diets, the healthier and tastier the food. We instinctively know this, which is why terms like 'natural' and 'free-range' are so attractive. It also explains why marketers all too often try to mask factory-farmed food behind labels showing false depictions of green fields, small farmhouses accompanied by comforting terms like 'farm fresh' and 'country fresh'. It speaks of the need for better labelling, to inform people how their food is produced; to remove the blindfold that hinders so many from truly exercising the consumer choice that is their right.

I also explored some of the big questions facing humankind: not least, how to feed the coming world of 9 billion people – 2 billion more than we have as I write. Surely, if we don't industrialise food production, some say, make it even more intensive – perhaps using a greenwash term like 'sustainable intensification' – then we are bound to starve? What I found is that this couldn't be further from the truth; that our planet already produces more than enough food for everyone, now and into the future, if only we didn't waste it. About 11 billion people could be fed on what the world currently produces, many more than today's 7 billion. The problem lies not with producing enough food, but with the extent to which it is wasted, from the simple act of throwing food away in our homes or at the supermarket, to letting it rot in developing countries for want of simple, low-tech assets like decent grain stores. What has become evident to me is the way that one of the biggest causes of food waste is so often overlooked: cereals, soya and fish fed to factory-farmed animals, who then return a fraction of the protein and calories in the form of meat, milk and eggs. If the animals were reared on the land instead, they would swell the global food basket, instead of pilfering from it.

The food system today is like a leaky bucket; it wastes half of what it produces. Simply churning out more without fixing the leaks will cause yet more waste and intensify pressure on already overstretched ecosystems. Of course, higher productivity in some parts of the world would be a good thing, particularly in some developing countries. But as a general strategy, it's likely to be a costly failure. Plugging the leaks seems a much more economic, more sensible way to go. But how much more food could be made available this way? Halving the amount dumped or rotting would free up enough food to feed an extra billion people. A further billion or more people could be fed by halving the amount of cereals destined for industrially reared animals.[1] In this way, enough food could be made available to feed future populations with little or no extra cost to the environment.

The industrial food system is geared towards producing food in volume, regardless of quality, in ways that rely on large amounts of finite resources, including land, soil, oil and water. What will happen when these essential ingredients for the agricultural machine start to run out? 'Man has lost the capacity to foresee and forestall,' said Albert Schweitzer. Avoiding Farmageddon will require us to revive this capacity. Through researching this book, I have seen how profits are often put before feeding people. I have seen compelling evidence of how, if something isn't done soon, warnings of a Farmageddon future could become a reality, one that brings with it a deeply diminished countryside, surging disease, unhealthy food, and growing world hunger. Thankfully, I have also found it doesn't have to be like this.

At a dinner party with representatives of leading businesses, I was asked, given three minutes with the US president or UK prime minister, what I would ask them. I would urge them to support food production that puts animals back on the farm instead of in factories; extensive farming connected to the land, providing more nutritious food in ways that are better for the countryside and animal welfare. Governments could help improve the health of their nation and safeguard future food supplies by building on natural resources: the pasturelands that cover a quarter of farmland worldwide, and two-thirds in Britain, for example. For a generation of consumers shielded from the realities of factory farming, brought up as they are on picture-book images of Old Macdonald and his small farmyard idyll, reinforced by advertising and often misleading labels, the truth often comes as a shock. Putting farm animals back on the farm could be a big vote-winner too, as many people believe that is where they are anyway.

As awareness grows, things are beginning to change. In Europe, some forms of factory farming, like veal crates that prevent calves from ever turning around, and barren hen cages where the birds can never flap their wings, are banned. Animals now have legal recognition as 'sentient beings', capable of feeling pain and suffering – a view long denied in some quarters. Major food companies in Europe – many household names – are increasingly moving to only cage-free eggs, higher-welfare chicken and the like.

During the course of my work as CEO of Compassion in World Farming, I always hoped that getting changes in Europe would lead to similar moves elsewhere. In the United States, where factory farming first emerged, changes are indeed afoot. Kindred spirits in the US, together with concerned citizens, consumers and policymakers, are bringing about reforms to some of the worst examples of factory farming. It was something that Compassion's founder, Peter Roberts, always dreamt of.

I remember vividly the day in late autumn 2006 when I visited Peter's bedside. Compassion's headquarters team had been rejoicing on hearing the news from the USA that Arizona had agreed to ban veal crates. For Peter, the cruel veal crate had been a cause célèbre, and a battle he had won in the UK two decades earlier. Peter was lying in a hospital bed and in a bad way. I hastily rearranged my schedule and rushed through the whitewashed hospital corridors, heart in mouth. He was in a side room surrounded by his wife and three daughters. For several days he had been unconscious and unresponsive. To see him lie so still, with his eyes firmly shut, choked me with emotion. After greeting his distraught family, I leant over, took Peter's hand and, trembling, began to deliver the news: that what he started in the UK had sent ripples across the Atlantic. As I did so, Peter's eyes opened, fixing mine with a listening attention as each sentence rolled into the next. When I stopped talking, his eyes gently closed. Shortly afterwards, he passed away.

Through writing this book, I have become convinced that we can all make a big difference. It has been a privilege to listen to so many people and to tell their stories. I have been left in no doubt about the tremendous power we have as consumers; the difference we can make three times a day with every meal. I have learned how choices we all make can have a real effect, not only on the people, animals and environments behind the food we eat, but on ourselves and our families. Simple measures like eating what we buy instead of throwing some away, and eating less but better meat, can make that difference, and when consumers choose alternatives to industrial factory farming – like free-range, pasture-raised, organic or the like – then supermarkets and policymakers take note. Things begin to change – from Farmageddon to a better future for people, animals and the planet.

Philip Lymbery
Hampshire, England
July 2013

Acknowledgements

When I first joined the animal welfare organisation Compassion in World Farming in the spring of 1990, I had no idea that I would be taking the first step on a journey of exploration that would span three decades. This book feels like the culmination of thoughts, observations and conversations with a vast number of people spanning all of that time. I owe a huge debt of gratitude to the late Peter and Anna Roberts, founders of Compassion in World Farming, for having the faith to employ me when I had little to offer except energy and enthusiasm. I am thankful that Peter saw through my initial failings, not least plummeting through his favoured glass coffee table just days before my trial period was up.

In those early days, I made it my goal to see as many farming systems firsthand as possible and to talk to the people involved, listening to their perspectives and looking for ways to improve things for everyone. This book feels like a natural extension of that early endeavour. I am grateful to all those, too numerous to mention individually, who have hosted me on their farm or business and taken the trouble to explain what they do. I appreciate the often lengthy discussions with colleagues in the animal welfare and environmental community that have informed my thinking and perspective.

When I set out to write this book in early 2011, I had no idea how much would be involved. Many people have given generously of their time and insights along the way, for which I am eternally grateful. I would like to give particular acknowledgement to my co-author and collaborator Isabel Oakeshott, for her hard work, her instinct for storytelling, for teaching me the value of crafting prose with 'colour', rather than just facts, and for enduring some pretty awful sights during our travels.

I owe a huge debt of thanks to our researcher, Jacky Turner, without whose thoroughness and commitment this book would have been much the poorer. Grateful thanks go too to Tina Clark for her endless patience, for reading and commenting on drafts time after time, planning field trips and providing essential support so reliably with unfaltering ease. To Veronica Oakeshott for documenting our trip through China so well, and to Jeff Zhou for seeing us through some difficult moments; thanks to Jim Wickens for his encyclopedic insight into the issues, where to go and who to talk to; to our camera crews and support: Alejandro Reynoso, Brian Kelley and Jim Philpott. Many thanks to Luke Starr for research related to our field trips, to Luke Oakeshott for additional research and to Laurence Stephenson for help in editing pictures and video arising from the trips. Thanks also to Pru Elliott for coming up with the initial graphic ideas that adorn this book.

Grateful thanks to all who kindly commented on drafts – Blake Lee-Harwood, Dil Peeling, Emily Lewis-Brown, Heather Pickett, Phil Brooke, Jeff Zhou, John Robins, Joyce D'Silva, Leah Garcés, Richard Young, Steve McIvor; to Sir David Madden and René Olivieri for spending so much time reading early drafts of the manuscript, providing invaluable advice; to Peter Stevenson for careful attention to detail and for stimulating discussions on how best to feed the world without cruelty to animals.

Special thanks to our editorial team at Bloomsbury, Bill Swainson, Elizabeth Woabank and Steve Cox, and to our literary agent, Robin Jones, for support and encouragement.

A special mention is due to Paul Blanchard for inspiring the book in the first place, for bringing the authors together, and for his boundless enthusiasm for the project. Invaluable help, advice and guidance has been received during our field trips from Alberto Villareal in Argentina; Maria Elena Foronda Farro from Natura, Chimbote; Ron Lane of the Food Animal Initiative; Stefan Austermuhle from Mundo Azul, Peru; Tom Frantz in California.

Grateful thanks to Valerie James, Jeremy Hayward, Sir David Madden, Reverend Professor Michael Reiss, Michel Vandenbosch, Rosemary Marshall, Sarah Petrini and Teddy Bourne for steadfast belief and support throughout.

Finally, huge thanks to my wife, Helen, for her support and understanding, particularly during long periods away from home so soon after our marriage.

Notes

PREFACE

1 R. Harrison, *Animal Machines*, Vincent Stuart, London, 1964.

2 M. Bittman, 'Don't End Agricultural Subsidies, Fix Them', *New York Times*, 1 March 2011, http://opinionator.blogs.nytimes.com/2011/03/01/dont-end-agricultural-subsidies-fix-them/.

INTRODUCTION: OLD MACDONALD

1 G. Dvorsky, 'China's worst self-inflicted environmental disaster', 2012, http://io9.com/5927112/chinas-worst-self+inflicted-disaster the-campaign-to-wipe-out-the-common-sparrow (accessed 8 May 2013).

2 Ibid.

3 Jonathan Leake, 'Farmers to be paid to feed starving birds', *Sunday Times*, 13 May 2012, http://www.thesundaytimes.co.uk/sto/news/uk_news/Environment/article1037693.ece (accessed 8 May 2013).

4 Defra, *Agriculture in the UK 2010*.

5 Ibid.

6 Government Office for Science, *Foresight Project on Global Food and Farming Futures Synthesis Report C1: Trends in food demand and production*, 2011; S. Msangi and M. Rosegrant, *World agriculture in a dynamically-changing environment: IFPRI's long term outlook for food and agriculture under additional demand and constraints*, paper written in support of Expert Meeting on 'How to Feed the World in 2050', Rome, FAO, 2009; H. Steinfeld et al., *Livestock's Long Shadow, environmental issues and options*, FAO, Rome, 2006, Introduction, p. 12.

7 FAO, *State of the World Fisheries and Aquaculture 2010*, UN Food and Agriculture Organization, Rome.

8 Calculated from FAOSTAT online figures for global grain harvest (2009) and food value of cereals. Based on a calorific intake of 2,500 kcalories per person per day.

9 WHO press release, 'World Health Day 2011, Urgent action necessary to safeguard drug treatments', 6 April 2011, http://www.who.int/media-centre/news/releases/2011/whd_20110406/en/index.html.

10 Food Safety Authority Ireland, press release, 'FSAI Survey Finds Horse DNA in Some Beef Burger Products', 15 January 2013, http://www.fsai.ie/news_centre/press_releases/horseDNA15012013.html (accessed 20 June 2013); http://www.guardian.co.uk/world/2013/feb/08/how-horse-meat-scandal-unfolded-timeline.

11 European Commission press release, 'Commission publishes European test results on horse DNA and Phenylbutazone: no food safety issues but tougher penalties to apply in the future to fraudulent labelling', 16 April 2013, http://europa.eu/rapid/press-release_IP-13-331_en.htm (accessed 20 June 2013).

12 BBC, 'Horsemeat in Tesco burgers prompts apology in UK papers', 17 January 2013, http://www.bbc.co.uk/news/uk-21054688 (accessed 20 June 2013).

13 Simon Neville, 'Frozen beefburger sales down 43% since start of horsemeat scandal', 26 February 2013, http://www.guardian.co.uk/uk/2013/feb/26/frozen-beefburger-sales-down-43-horsemeat (accessed 20 June 2013).

14 BBC, 'Horsemeat in Tesco burgers prompts apology in UK papers', 17 January 2013, http://www.bbc.co.uk/news/uk-21054688 (accessed 20 June 2013).

I RUDE AWAKENINGS

1 *Daily Telegraph*, 14 June 2012, Where do milk, eggs and bacon come from? One in three youths don't know, http://www.telegraph.co.uk/foodanddrink/foodanddrinknews/9330894/Where-do-milk-eggs-and-bacon-come-from-One-in-three-youths-dont-know.html (accessed 13 September 2013).

I CALIFORNIA GIRLS: A VISION OF THE FUTURE?

1 http://www.esri.com/mapmuseum/mapbook_gallery/volume23/agriculture1.html (accessed 13 July 2012).

2 http://www.nass.usda.gov/Statistics_by_State/California/Publications/ California_Ag_Statistics/2010cas-ovw.pdf (accessed 13 July 2012).

3 Calculated from formula; 200 dairy cows produce as much manure as a town of 10,000 people: *Animal waste pollution in America: an emerging national problem, 1997. Environmental risks of livestock and poultry production.* A report by the Minority Staff of the US Senate Committee on Agriculture, Nutrition and Forestry for Senator Tom Harkin.

4 http://www.farmland.org/programs/states/futureisnow/default.asp (accessed 13 July 2012).

5 http://www.sraproject.org/wp-content/uploads/2007/12/dairytalking-points.pdf.

2 HENPECKED: THE TRUTH BEHIND THE LABEL

1 *Guardian*, 'Why are we all keeping hens', 1 August 2011, http://www.guardian.co.uk/lifeandstyle/2011/aug/01/keeping-hens (accessed 2 October 2012); 'Your chickens', article, http://www.yourchickens.co.uk/home/ advertise (accessed 2 October 2012); *Daily Mail*, 'How to . . . keep hens and harvest your own eggs in the comfort of your garden', 15 February 2010, http://www.dailymail.co.uk/femail/article-1251042/How--hens.html (accessed 2 October 2012).

2 Defra, *Outbreak of Highly Pathogenic h5n1 Avian Influenza in Suffolk in January 2007: a Report of the Epidemiological Findings by the National Emergency Epidemiology Group*, 5 April 2007, http://archive.defra.gov. uk/foodfarm/farmanimal/diseases/atoz/ai/documents/epid_findings070405.pdf; Cabinet Office, UK Resilience, 2007, http:// webarchive.nationalarchives.gov.uk/+/http://www.cabinetoffice.gov.uk/ ukresilience/response/recovery_guidance/case_studies/grey1_bmatthews.aspx (accessed 2 October 2012); BBC *News*, 'Bird flu virus is Asian strain', 3 February 2007, http://news.bbc.co.uk/1/hi/uk/6328161. stm (accessed 2 October 2012).

II NATURE

1 http://www.macla.co.uk/nocton/index.php; http://www.allsaintsnocton .org.uk/history.htm; http://www.nocton.org/#today; http://en.wikipedia .org/wiki/Nocton.

2 http://www.youtube.com/watch?v=nnWb9WJ8anU&feature=related; http://www.youtube.com/watch?v=oht1741iqlM&feature=related.

3 Butterfly Conservation website: http://www.butterfly-conservation.org/

Butterfly/32/Butterfly.html?ButterflyId=15 (accessed 2 October 2012); Bumblebee Conservation Trust leaflet, Farms, crofts and bumbles, http://www.snh.gov.uk/docs/A463311.pdf (accessed 2 October 2012).

3 SILENT SPRING: THE BIRTH OF FARMING'S CHEMICAL AGE

1 Rachel Carson, *Silent Spring*, Penguin, London, 1962 (2000 reprint); Conor Mark Jameson, *Silent Spring Revisited*, Bloomsbury, London 2012.

2 W. J. L. Sladen et al., 'DDT residues in Adélie penguins and a crabeater seal from Antarctica', *Nature*, 210, 14 May 1966, pp. 670–3, http://www.nature.com/nature/journal/v210/n5037/abs/210670a0.html (accessed 10 May 2013).

3 *Baltimore Sun*, 'Geese's movie careers take flight: Scientist Dr. William J. L. Sladen is director of environmental studies at the Airlie Sanctuary in Virginia, home to several of the geese that star in the movie "Fly Away Home"', 6 September 1996, http://articles.baltimoresun.com/1996-09-06/news/1996250099_1_sladen-igor-swans (accessed 10 May 2013).

4 National Wildlife Federation, 'Chesapeake Bay', http://www.nwf.org/wildlife/wild-places/chesapeake-bay.aspx (accessed 7 August 2012).

5 http://www.chesapeakebay.net/issues/issue/agriculture#inline (accessed 7 August 2012).

6 US EPA, Chesapeake Bay Program, 'Health of Freshwater Streams in the Chesapeake Bay Watershed', www.chesapeakebay.net/status_stream-health.aspx?menuitem=50423.

7 Pew Environment Group, *Big Chicken: Pollution and industrial poultry production in America*, Pew, Washington, July 2011.

4 WILDLIFE: THE GREAT DISAPPEARING ACT

1 J. R. Krebs et al., 'The second Silent Spring?', *Nature*, 400, 12 August 1999, pp. 611–12.

2 British Trust for Ornithology (BTO), 'Breeding birds in the wider countryside 2010. Trends in numbers and breeding performance for UK birds', accessed July 2011, http://www.bto.org/about-birds/bird-trends; British Trust for Ornithology (BTO), 'Breeding birds in the wider countryside 2010, Trends in numbers and breeding performance of UK birds. Section 4.2, Latest long term alerts', http://www.bto.org/birdtrends2010/discussion42.shtml.

3   Defra, 'Wild bird populations: farmland birds in England 2009', news release 29 July 2010.

4   BirdLife International, 'Europe-wide monitoring schemes highlight declines in widespread farmland birds', 2008, presented as part of the BirdLife State of the world's birds website, available from http://www.birdlife.org/datazone/sowb/casestudy/62.

5   North American Bird Conservation Initiative, US Committee, *The State of the Birds 2011: report on public lands and waters, United States of America*, 2011.

6   North American Bird Conservation Initiative, US Committee *The State of the Birds 2009, United States of America*, 2009.

7   Defra statistical release, 'Wild bird populations in the UK [to 2009]', 20 January 2011, http://archive.defra.gov.uk/evidence/statistics/environment/wildlife/download/pdf/110120-stats-wild-bird-populations-uk.pdf.

8   Krebs et al., 'The second Silent Spring?'.

9   R. Watson, S. Albon et al., *UK National Ecosystem Assessment: Synthesis of the Key Findings*, 2011, National Ecosystem Assessment project, Defra, NERC, together with agencies in Scotland, Wales and Northern Ireland.

10 New World Encyclopedia, http://www.newworldencyclopedia.org/entry/earthworm (accessed 24 July 2012); Wikipedia, http://en.wikipedia.org/wiki/Earthworm (accessed 24 July 2012).

11 S. Kragten et al., 'Abundance of invertebrate prey for birds on organic and conventional arable farms in the Netherlands', *Bird Conservation International* (2011) 21, pp. 1–11.

12 BirdLife International, 'Grassland birds are declining in North America', 2004, presented as part of the BirdLife State of the world's birds website, www.birdlife.org/datazone/sowb/casestudy/63.

13 See F. Dikötter, *Mao's Great Famine*, Bloomsbury, London, 2010.

14 Bumblebee Conservation Trust, www.bumblebeeconservation.org.uk (accessed July 2011).

15 C. Carvell et al., 'Comparing the efficacy of agri-environment schemes to enhance bumble bee abundance and diversity on arable field margins', *Journal of Applied Ecology* (2007), 44, pp. 29–40.

16 'Colony Collapse Disorder and the Human Bee', 12 August 2008, http://www.articlesbase.com/environment-articles/colony-collapse-disorder-and-the-human-bee-519377.html (accessed 21 May 2013).

17 Ibid.

18 *Daily Mail*, 'Rescuers battle 17 million angry bees after flatbed trailer crashes in fatal U.S. accident', 25 May 2010, http://www.dailymail.

co.uk/news/article-1281226/Truck-carrying-17million-bees-crashes-Minnesota.html.

19 *Los Angeles Times*, 'Hives for hire', 3 March 2012, http://articles.latimes. com/2012/mar/03/business/la-fi-california-bees-20120304 (accessed 21 May 2013); *Slate* magazine, 'Rent-a-hive', 27 June 2008, http://www. slate.com/articles/news_and_politics/explainer/2008/06/rentahive.html (accessed 21 May 2013).

20 A. Benjamin and B. McCullum, *A World Without Bees*, Guardian Books, London, 2008.

21 Ibid.

22 *Los Angeles Times*, 'Hives for hire', 3 March 2012.

23 A. Manriquez, Apinews, 'China – hand pollination', 17 December 2010, http://www.apinews.com/en/news/item/12780-china-hand-pollina-tion/ (accessed 19 July 2012).

24 *Los Angeles Times*, 'Pesticides suspected in mass die-off of bees', 29 March 2012, http://articles.latimes.com/2012/mar/29/science/la-sci-bees-pesticides-20120330 (accessed 21 May 2013); *Natural News*, 'Confirmed: Common pesticide crashing honeybee populations around the world', 10 April 2012, http://www.naturalnews.com/035518_honey_bees_pesticides_ science.html (accessed 21 May 2013).

25 BBC, 'Bee deaths: EU to ban neonicotinoid pesticides', 29 April 2013, http://www.bbc.co.uk/news/world-europe-22335520 (accessed 21 May 2013).

26 Ibid.

27 D. Goulson, University of California website, 'David Goulson: Ecology and Conservation of Bumble Bees', 17 April 2013, http://entomology. ucdavis.edu/News/David_Goulson____Ecology_and_Conservation_ of_Bumble_Bees/ (accessed 21 May 2013).

28 Achim Steiner, quoted in 'Bees under bombardment: Report shows multiple factors behind pollinator losses', United Nations Environment Programme, Geneva/Nairobi, 10 March 2011, http://www. unep.org.

29 J. Simpson, 'Chasing butterflies: The Victorian hobby of entomology', 2010, http://suite101.com/article/chasing-butterflies-the-victorian-hobby-of-entomology-a222953 (accessed 27 July 2012).

30 http://www.monarchwatch.org/ (accessed 27 July 2012).

31 http://nationalzoo.si.edu/Animals/Invertebrates/News/monarchmigra-tion.cfm; http://www.sciencelatest.com/2011/12/the astounding monarch butterfly voyage/.

32 *The McGill Tribune*, 2010, 'Follow the butterflies: A monarch migration under threat' (updated 21 September 2010), http://www.mcgilltribune.

com/2.12327/follow-the-butterflies-a-monarch-migration-under-threat-1.1626302 (accessed 27 July 2012).

33 http://www.unityserve.org/butterfly/urquharts.html; http://www.science-latest.com/2011/12/the astounding monarch butterfly voyage/; http://www.ecology.info/monarch butterfly page 3.htm; http://www.monarch butterfly.com/monarch butterflies facts.html; http://www.worldwildlife.org/species/finder/monarchbutterflies/monarchbutterflies.html#; http://www.monarchwatch.org/news/urquhart.htm.

34 Butterfly Conservation, Natural England and FWAG, *Butterflies and Farmland*, http://www.butterfly-conservation.org/uploads/bc0011%20 Butterflies%20and%20Farmland(1).pdf, no date, bc0011.

35 UK Butterfly Monitoring Scheme (2010), UK Summary of changes table 2010, http://www.ukbms.org/docs/reports/2010/Summary.

36 http://news.bbc.co.uk/1/hi/sci/tech/3568321.stm (accessed 27 July 2012).

37 http://www.butterfly-conservation.org/article/9/103/large_blue_butter-flies_back_in_britain.html (accessed 27 July 2012).

5 FISH: FARMING TAKES TO THE WATER

1 'Mauritius Aquaculture Masterplan goes green', The FishSite.com, 17 April 2009, http://www.thefishsite.com/fishnews/9633/mauritius-aqua-culture-masterplan-goes-green (accessed 2 March 2012); Department of Environment: Ministry of Environment and national development unit, 2009. EIA guidelines for fish farming in the sea, Mauritius, http://environment.gov.mu.

2 IPS Inter Press News Service Agency, 'Our sea and lagoon are not for sale', 1 August 2007, http://ipsnews.net/africa/nota.asp?idnews=38753 (accessed 2 March 2012).

3 'Fish farms: Emerging threats coming ashore', The FishSite.com., 28 June 2007, http://www.thefishsite.com/fishnews/4615/fish-farms-emerging-threats-coming-ashore (accessed 2 March 2012).

4 P. Coppens, 'The sacred island of the moon', http://www.philipcoppens.com/lochmaree.html (accessed 1 August 2012); http://www.ovguide.com/isle-maree-9202a8c04000641f8000000006ecb0a0# (accessed 1 August 2012); http://www.ancientsites.com/aw/Post/1264229&authorid=238 (accessed 1 August 2012).

5 S. Millar, 'Last leap for the wild salmon', *Observer*, 11 June 2000, available from http://www.guardian.co.uk/uk/2000/jun/11/stuartmillar.theobserver (accessed 2 August 2012); Wester Ross Fisheries Trust, article, 'Sea trout:

River Ewe and Loch Maree', http://www.wrft.org.uk/fisheries/seatrout.cfm (accessed 2 August 2012).

6 H. Davis, L. Lamb and S. Frost, 'Fishing in the Gairloch area', http://www.gairloch-fishing.co.uk/maree.htm.

7 Wester Ross Fisheries Trust, article, 'Sea trout: River Ewe and Loch Maree', http://www.wrft.org.uk/fisheries/seatrout.cfm (accessed 2 August 2012).

8 Wester Ross Fisheries Trust Review (2011), available from www.wrft.org.uk/files/WRFT.

9 J. Owen, 'Sea trout loss linked to salmon farm parasite', *National Geographic* News, 22 October 2002, http://news.nationalgeographic.com/news/2002/10/1022_021022_seatroutfish.html (accessed 2 August 2012).

10 A. Mood, *Worse things happen at sea: the welfare of wild-caught fish*, 2010, www.fishcount.org.uk.

11 FAOSTAT online database, http://www.faostat.fao.org.

12 Lenfest Ocean Program (2008), 'Research series: global assessment of aquaculture impacts on wild salmon', Lenfest, www.lenfestocean.org/publication/global-assessment-aquaculture-impacts-wild-salmon.

13 A. G. J. Tacon and M. Metian, 'Global overview on the use of fish meal and fish oil in industrially compounded aquafeeds: Trends and future prospects', *Aquaculture*, 285 (2008), pp. 146–58.

14 R. L. Naylor et al., 'Feeding aquaculture in an era of finite resources', *PNAS*, 106(36) (2009), pp.15103–10; Tacon and Metian, 'Global overview'.

15 FAO, *State of the World Fisheries and Aquaculture*, 2010.

16 Ibid.; Henk Westhoek et al., *The protein puzzle: the consumption and production of meat, dairy and fish in the European Union*, PBL Netherlands Environmental Assessment Agency, The Hague, 2011.

17 Naylor et al., 'Feeding aquaculture'.

18 Seafish, Annual Review of the status of the feed grade fish stocks used to produce fishmeal and fish oil for the UK market, March 2012, http://www.seafish.org/media/publications/SeafishAnnualReviewFeedFishStocks_201203.pdf.

19 Naylor et al., 'Feeding aquaculture'.

20 Lenfest Ocean Program (2009), *Summary: Important protein sources for the world's impoverished in competition with aquaculture and animal feed.* Lenfest, September 2009 www. lenfestocean.org/publication/important-protein-source-world%E2%80%99s-impoverished-competition-aquaculture-and-animal-feed.

21 FAO, *State of the World Fisheries.*

22 B. A. Costa-Pierce et al., 'Responsible use of resources for sustainable aquaculture', *Global Conference on Aquaculture 2010*, 22–25 September 2010, Phuket, Thailand, Food and Agriculture Organization of the United Nations (FAO), Rome, Italy, 2011.

23 P. Stevenson, *Closed Waters: The welfare of farmed Atlantic Salmon, Rainbow Trout, Atlantic Cod and Atlantic Halibut*, WSPA/CIWF, London, 2007; P. Lymbery, *In Too Deep: The welfare of intensively farmed fish*, CIWF Trust, Petersfield, 2002.

24 FAO, *State of the World Fisheries*.

25 Atlantic Salmon Trust, 'Salmon farming in Scotland: economic success or ecological failure?', http://www.atlanticsalmontrust.org/concerns/salmon-farming-in-scotland-economic-success-or-ecological-failure.html (accessed 2 August 2012).

26 M. J. Costello, 'How sea lice from salmon farms may cause wild salmonid declines in Europe and North America and be a threat to fishes elsewhere', *Proc. R. Soc. B*, 276 (2009), pp. 3385–94; M. Krkošek et al., 'Epizootics of wild fish induced by farm fish', *PNAS*, 103(42) (2008), pp. 15506–10; M. Krkošek et al., 'Sea lice and salmon population dynamics: effects of exposure time for migratory fish', *Proc. R. Soc. B*, 276 (2009), pp. 2819–28.

27 SEPA, *Regulation and monitoring of marine cage fish farming in Scotland*, Annex H, Scottish Environment Protection Agency, May 2005.

28 The FishSite, 'Sea Lice: a Parasite of Fish and Farmers Alike', 6 February 2009, http://www.thefishsite.com/articles/616/sea-lice-a-parasite-of-fish-and-farmers-alike (accessed 2 August 2012).

29 Krkošek et al., 'Sea lice and salmon population dynamics'.

30 The FishSite, 'Sea Lice'.

31 Atlantic Salmon Trust, 'Salmon farming in Scotland: economic success or ecological failure?', http://www.atlanticsalmontrust.org/concerns/salmon-farming-in-scotland-economic-success-or-ecological-failure.html (accessed 2 August 2012).

32 D. Mackay, 'Perspectives on the Environmental Effects of Aquaculture', presented to the Aquaculture Europe Conference, Norway, August 1999, Scottish Environment Protection Agency.

33 M. Krkošek et al., 'Declining Wild Salmon Populations in Relation to Parasites from Farm Salmon', *Science*, vol. 318 no. 5857 (2007), pp. 1772–5.

34 BC Pacific Salmon Forum, *Final report and recommendations to the Government of British Columbia*, January 2009.

35 B. Harvey, *Sea lice and salmon farms: a second look*, prepared for the BC Pacific Salmon Forum, 2009.

36 A. A. Rosenberg, 'The price of lice', *Nature*, 451 (2008), pp. 23–4.

37 The FishSite, 'Salmon Escape ill-timed as Data Published on Global Incidents', 4 December 2007, http://www.thefishsite.com/fishnews/5834/salmon-escape-illtimed-as-data-published-on-global-incidents (accessed 2 August 2012).

38 FRS Marine Laboratory, *Scottish Fish Farms Annual Production Survey 2000*, Fisheries Research Services Marine Laboratory, Aberdeen, 2001.

39 Orr, 'The Way to Save the Salmon', *Independent*, 30 July 1999.

40 Mackay, 'Perspectives on the Environmental Effects of Aquaculture'.

41 *Orcadian*, 28 September 2000, cited in P. Lymbery, *In Too Deep: The welfare of intensively farmed fish*, CIWF Trust, Petersfield, 2002.

42 SSPO, 'Confirmed breaches of containment, 1st January – 1st Dec 2010', www.scottishsalmon.co.uk/userFiles/769/SSPO_breaches_of_containment_2010.pdf.

43 USDA Nutrient Database, 2011, USDA Agricultural Research Service, National Agricultural Library, Nutrient Database for Standard Reference, Release 24, Nutrient Data Laboratory Home Page: http://ndb.nal.usda.gov/ndb/foods/list (accessed 2 October 2012).

44 R. A. Hites et al., 'Global Assessment of Organic Contaminants in Farmed Salmon', *Science*, vol. 303 no. 5655 (2004), pp. 226–9, http://www.sciencemag.org/content/303/5655/226.short.

45 L. Madsen, J. Arnbjerg and I. Dalsgaard, 'Spinal deformities in triploid all-female rainbow trout (Oncorhynchus mykiss)', *Bull. Eur. Ass. Fish Pathol.*, 20 (5) (2000), pp. 206–8; R. Johnstone, *Production and Performance of Triploid Atlantic Salmon in Scotland*, Marine Laboratory, The Scottish Office Agriculture and Fisheries Department, 1992; S. Willoughby, *Manual of Salmonid Farming*, Fishing News Books, Blackwell Science, Oxford, 1999; A. E. Wall and R. H. Richards, 'Occurrence of cataracts in triploid Atlantic salmon (Salmo salar) on four farms in Scotland', *Veterinary Record*, 131 (1992), pp. 553–7.

46 BBC, 'Headless seals may have been shot', 20 May 2008, http://news.bbc.co.uk/1/hi/scotland/highlands_and_islands/7410701.stm (accessed 2 August 2012).

47 iWatch News, '"Free for all" decimates fish stocks in the South Pacific', http://www.iwatchnews.org/2012/01/25/7900/free-all-decimates-fish-stocks-southern-pacific (accessed 3 August 2012).

48 Institut de Recherche pour le développement, 'Scientists working for responsible fishing in Peru', scientific bulletin no. 349 – May 2010, http://www.en.ird.fr/content/download/17178/146692/…/4/…/

FAS349a-web.pdf; C. E. Paredes, 'Reforming the Peruvian anchoveta sector', Instituto del Peru, July 2010, http://www.ebcd.org/pdf/presentation/164-Paredes.pdf; Y. Evans and S. Tveteras, *Status of Fisheries and Aquaculture Development in Peru: Case Studies of Peruvian Anchovy Fishery, Shrimp Aquaculture, Trout and Scallop Aquaculture*, FAO, Rome, 2011, available from www.fao.org/.

49 Seafish, 'Seafish publishes comprehensive review of feed fish stocks used to produce fishmeal and fish oil for the UK market', 16 April 2012, http://www.seafish.org/about-seafish/news/seafish-publishes-comprehensive-review-of-feed-fish-stocks-used-to-produce-fishmeal-and-fish-oil-for-the-uk-market (accessed 3 August 2012).

50 Seafish, *Fishmeal and Fish Oil Facts and Figures*, 2011, www.seafish.org.

51 http://www.mapsofworld.com/peru/provinces-and-cities/chimbote. html; iWatch News, '"Free for all" decimates fish stocks in the South Pacific'; *New York Times*, 'In Mackerel's Plunder, Hints of Epic Fish Collapse', 25 January 2012, http://www.nytimes.com/2012/01/25/science/earth/in-mackerels-plunder-hints-of-epic-fish-collapse. html?pagewanted=all (accessed 3 August 2012).

52 J. Del Hoyo, A. Elliott and J. Sargatal (eds), *Handbook of the Birds of the World*, vol. 1, Lynx Edicions, Barcelona, 1992.

53 W. M. Mathew, 'Peru and the British guano market 1840–1870', The Economic History Review New Series, vol. 23, no. 1 (April 1970), pp. 112–28, Blackwell Publishing; http://is.gd/F1HbXg (accessed 3 August 2012).

54 I. Newton, *Population Limitation in Birds*, Academic Press, London, 1998.

55 *The Economist*, 'Fishing in Peru: The next anchovy coming to a pizza near you', 5 May 2011, http://www.economist.com/node/18651372 (accessed 3 August 2012).

56 Evans and Tveteras, *Status of Fisheries and Aquaculture Development in Peru*.

57 J. Jacquet et al., 'Conserving wild fish in a sea of market-based efforts', *Oryx*, 44(1) (2009), pp. 45–6.

58 The Goldman Environmental Prize, http://www.goldmanprize.org/ 2003/southcentralamerica (accessed 3 August 2012).

6 ANIMAL CARE: WHAT HAPPENED TO THE VET?

1 Defra website: http://www.defra.gov.uk/food-farm/animals/welfare/slaughter/premises/ (accessed 13 August 2012).

2   Food Standards Agency website: http://www.food.gov.uk/enforcement/
    monitoring/mhservice/workwithindustry/workforce (accessed 13 August
    2012).

3   Animal Aid, 'The "humane" slaughter myth', http://www.animalaid.org.
    uk/h/n/CAMPAIGNS/slaughter/ (accessed 13 August 2013).

4   Compassion in World Farming, 'Suffering at slaughter exposed by
    new film', http://www.ciwf.org.uk/news/factory_farming/suffering_
    exposed_by_film.aspx (accessed 13 August 2013).

5   British Veterinary Association, personal communication, 2012.

6   J. Mackey, *Conscious capitalism: Creating a new paradigm for business*,
    2007, http://www.wholeplanetfoundation.org/files/uploaded/John_
    Mackey-Conscious_Capitalism.pdf (accessed 13 August 2013).

7   http://thinkexist.com/quotation/i-hope-to-make-people-realize-how-
    totally/380118.html (accessed 13 August 2012).

                            III HEALTH

1   http://en.wikipedia.org/wiki/Guy's_Hospital; http://www.bbc.co.uk/his-
    tory/historic_figures/bevan_aneurin.shtml.

2   http://www.nhs.uk/NHSEngland/thenhs/about/Pages/overview.aspx.

       7 BUGS 'N' DRUGS: THE THREAT TO PUBLIC HEALTH

1   Hansard, 13 May 1953, 1327–43.

2   Chief Medical Officer's Annual Report, 2008, chapter: 'Antimicrobial
    resistance: up against the ropes'.

3   Dr Margaret Chan, Director-General World Health Organization
    (WHO), speaking on World Health Day, 7 April 2011.

4   *Case Study of a Health Crisis: How Human Health Is under Threat from
    Over-use of Antibiotics in Intensive Livestock Farming*, a report for the
    Alliance to Save Our Antibiotics, Godalming, 2011.

5   The Joint Committee on the use of Antibiotics in Animal Husbandry
    and Veterinary Medicine, chaired by Professor M. M. Swann, was
    appointed jointly by Health and Agriculture Ministers in July 1968. Its
    report was issued in November 1969.

6   J. Harvey and L. Mason, *The Use and Misuse of Antibiotics in UK Agricul-
    ture*, Part 1, *Current Usage*, Soil Association, Bristol, 1968.

7   *Case Study of a Health Crisis.*

8   C. Nathan, 'Antibiotics at the crossroads', *Nature*, 431 (2004), pp. 899–
    902; World Health Organization, 2011, 'World Health Day 2011.

Urgent action necessary to safeguard drug treatments', http://www.who.int/mediacentre/news/releases/2011whd_20110406/en/.

9 M. Mellon, C. Benbrook and K. L. Benbrook, 'Hogging It. Estimates of Antimicrobial Abuse in Livestock', Union of Concerned Scientists, 2001; K. M. Shea, 'Antibiotic resistance: what is the impact of agricultural uses of antibiotics on children's health?', *Pediatrics*, 112(1) (2003), pp. 253–8.

10 Committee for Medicinal Products for Veterinary Use, *Reflection Paper on the Use of Fluoroquinolones in Food-producing Animals in the European Union: Development of Resistance and Impact on Human and Animal Health*, 2006, www.emea.europa.eu/pdfs/vet/srwp/1846510en.pdf.

11 Naheeda Portocarero, 'Continued focus on food security and welfare', *World Poultry*, vol. 27, no. 5, online version 23 August 2011; X. Manteca, 'Physiology and disease', in M. C. Appleby et al. (eds), *Long Distance Transport and Welfare of Farm Animals*, CABI, 2008, pp. 69–76.

12 M. McKenna, 'Turning grief into action: Moms and antibiotic misuse', *Wired.com.*, 2011, available from http://www.wired.com/wiredscience/2011/05/grief-moms-antibiotics/#more-59108 (accessed 2 August 2011).

13 V. Jones, 'Deadly Bacteria (MRSA) Kill A Baby Boy, Part 1', *Revolution Health*, 2008, available from http://www.revolutionhealth.com/blogs/valjonesmd/deadly-bacteria-mrsa-15730 (accessed 2 August 2011).

14 Ibid.

15 *Huffington Post*, http://www.huffingtonpost.com/everly-macario-scd-ms-edm (accessed 21 May 2013).

16 IDSA (Infectious Diseases Society of America), March 2006, article: http://www.idsociety.org/Simon_Macario/ (accessed 21 May 2013).

17 http://www.wired.com/wiredscience/2011/05/grief-moms-antibiotics/#more-59108.

18 European Commission, *Staff working paper of the services of the Commission on antimicrobial resistance*, SANCO/6876/2009r6, 18 November 2009.

19 C. Nunan and R. Young, *MRSA in farm animals and meat: a new threat to human health*, Soil Association, 2007.

20 Ibid.

21 E. de Boer et al., 'Prevalence of methicillin-resistant Staphylococcus aureus in meat', *Int. J Food Microbiology*, 134(1–2) (2009), pp. 52–6.

22 EFSA Panel on Biological Hazards, 'Foodborne antimicrobial resistance as a biological hazard. Scientific Opinion', *EFSA Journal*, 765 (2008), pp. 1–87.

23 L. Garcia-Alvarez et al., 'Meticillin-resistant *Staphylococcus aureus* with a novel *mecA* homologue emerging in human and bovine populations in

the UK and Denmark: a descriptive study', *Lancet Infectious Diseases*, 2011.

24 Defra, *Zoonoses Report: UK 2010*, 2011.

25 EFSA-ECDC, 'The European Union Summary Report on Trends and Sources of Zoonoses, Zoonotic Agents and Food-borne Outbreaks in 2009', *EFSA Journal*, 2011, 9(3), 2090.

26 Defra, *Zoonoses Report: UK 2010*.

27 Chief Medical Officer's Annual Report, 2008, 'Antibiotic resistance'.

28 E. Scallan et al., 'Foodborne illness acquired in the United States—major pathogens', *Emerging Infectious Diseases,* 2011 (Epub ahead of print), DOI: 10.3201/eid1701.P11101.

29 *MeatPoultry* Staff, 'Salmonella Heidelberg infections rise to 107', 12 August 2011, http://www.meatpoultry.com/News.

30 B. Salvage, 'Salmonella Heidelberg infections rise to 119: CDC', Meat-Poultry.com, 15 September 2011, http://www.meatpoultry.com/News/.

31 FAWC, *Report on the welfare of laying hens*, 1997, Section: History, Table 1, http://www.fawc.org.uk/reports/layhens/lhgre007.htm.

32 Defra, *Egg Statistical Notice*, 4 August 2011.

33 Defra, *Zoonoses Report: UK 2010*.

34 C. Snow et al., 'Investigation of risk factors for Salmonella on commercial egg-laying farms in Great Britain, 2004–2005', *Veterinary Record*, 166 (2010), pp. 579–86.

35 Pew Commission on Industrial Farm Animal Production, *Putting Meat on the Table: Industrial Farm Animal Production in America*, 2008; http://www.pewtrusts.org/uploadedFiles/wwwpewtrustsorg/Reports/Industrial_Agriculture/PCIFAP_FINAL.pdf; M. Greger, 'The Human/Animal Interface: Emergence and Resurgence of Zoonotic Infectious Diseases', *Critical Reviews in Microbiology*, 33 (2007) pp. 243–99, DOI: 10.1080/10408410701647594.

36 FAOSTAT, http://fasotat.fao.org.

37 WHO (2010) Cumulative Number of Confirmed Human Cases of Avian Influenza A/(H5N1), reported to WHO, 9 August 2011, www.who.int/csr/disease/avian_influenza/country/cases_table_2011_08_09/en/index.html.

38 M. Du Ry van Beest Holle, 'Human-to-human transmission of avian influenza A/H7N7, The Netherlands, 2003', *Eurosurveillance* 10(12), 1 December 2005, pp. 264–8; http://www.eurosurveillance.org/em/v10n12/1012-222.asp.

39 D. MacKenzie, 'Five easy mutations to make bird flu a lethal pandemic', *New Scientist*, 24 September 2011, p. 14 (online article 21 September).

40 Editorial, 'The risk of an influenza pandemic is fact, not fiction', *New Scientist*, 24 September 2011, p. 3.

41 C. J. L. Murray et al., 'Estimation of potential global pandemic influenza mortality on the basis of vital registry data from the 1918–20 pandemic: a quantitative analysis', *Lancet,* 368 (2006), pp. 2211–18.

42 Oxford Centre for Animal Ethics, news release, 'Bird Flu Will Remain A Threat As Long As Factory Farms Exist', 17 February 2012, http://www.oxfordanimalethics.com/2012/02/news-release-bird-flu-will-remain-a-threat-as-long-as-factory-farms-exist/.

43 GCM website, http://www.granjascarroll.com/ing/ing_historia.php (accessed December 2011).

44 GCM website, http://www.granjascarroll.com/ing/ing_preguntas.php (accessed 27 July 2012).

45 GCM website, http://www.granjascarroll.com/ing/ing_preguntas.php (accessed 3 October 2012).

46 *Guardian*, 'La Gloria, swine flu's ground zero, is left with legacy of anger', 23 April 2010, http://www.guardian.co.uk/world/2010/apr/23/swine-flu-legacy-la-gloria (accessed 27 July 2012).

47 *Washington Post*, 'Mexicans blame industrial hog farms', 10 May 2009, http://www.washingtonpost.com/wp-dyn/content/article/2009/05/09/ (accessed 27 July 2012).

48 S. M. Burns, 'H1N1 Influenza is here', *Journal of Hospital Infection*, 17 July 2009, http://download.thelancet.com/flatcontentassets/H1N1-flu/epidemiology/epidemiology-76.pdf (accessed 27 July 2012).

49 World Health Organization, South East Asia Regional Office (SEARO), 'Message from the Regional Director', November 2009, http://www.searo.who.int/linkfiles/news_letters_nov2010.pdf (accessed 30 May 2012).

50 World Health Organization, 2010, http://www.who.int/csr/don/2010_05_14/en/index.html (accessed 30 May 2012).

51 *Guardian*, 'La Gloria, swine flu's ground zero, is left with legacy of anger'; Encyclopedia Britannica, 'Influenza pandemic (H1N1) of 2009', http://www.britannica.com/EBchecked/topic/1574480/influenza-pandemic-H1N1-of-2009#toc281756 (accessed 27 July 2012).

52 Ibid.

53 GCM website, http://www.granjascarroll.com/ing/ing_preguntas.php (accessed 27 July 2012).

54 Ibid.

55 Ibid.

8 EXPANDING WAISTLINES: FOOD QUALITY TAKES A NOSE-DIVE

1 *Daily Mail*, '58st and a £500,000 bill: But I deserve NHS support says world's fattest man', 14 February 2012, http://www.dailymail.co.uk/news/article-2100052/Worlds-fattest-man-Keith-Martin-lives-London-58-stone.html (accessed 5 October 2012).

2 News-Medical, 'World's "fattest man" needs an army of carers', 15 February 2012, http://www.news-medical.net/news/20120215/Worlde2 8099s-e2809cfattest-mane2809d-needs-an-army-of-carers.aspx (accessed 15 August 2012); *Daily Mail*, '"I ate 20,000 calories a day, had a 6ft waist . . . and last left my house on 9/11": Horrifying life of the blonde-haired little boy who grew into the world's fattest man', 6 May 2012; http://www.dailymail.co.uk/news/article-2140307/Keith-Martin-Horrifying-life-worlds-fattest-man.html#ixzz23b7wAYay; (accessed 15 August 2012); *Daily Mail*, 'Britain's fattest man who weighs 58 stone when he was a regular-sized 15st', 9 April 2012, http://www.dailymail.co.uk/news/article-2126848/Keith-Martin-Britains-fattest-man-weighs-58stone-regular-sized-15st.html#ixzz23b8aJom8; (accessed 15 August 2012); *Daily Telegraph*, 'Fire crews demolish walls to release Britain's fattest teen from house after she posted plight on Facebook', 25 May 2012, http://www.telegraph.co.uk/health/healthnews/9288612/ Fire-crews-demolish-walls-to-release-Britains-fattest-teen-from-house-after-she-posted-plight-on-Facebook.html (accessed 15 August 2012).

3 W. H. Dietz, 'Reversing the tide of obesity', *Lancet*, 378 (2011), pp. 744–6.

4 S. Friel et al., 'Public health benefits of strategies to reduce greenhouse-gas emissions: food and agriculture', *Lancet*, 374, 9706 (2009), pp. 2016–25.

5 G. L. Huber, 'Fats and the prevention of coronary heart disease', http://www.livingheartfoundation.org/fatscoronaryprevention.pdf (accessed 17 August 2012); *Lancet*, 'Plasma Lipid and Lipoprotein Pattern in Greenlandic West-Coast Eskimos', June 1971, http://www.thelancet.com/journals/lancet/article/PIIS0140-6736(71)91658-8/abstract (accessed 17 August 2012).

6 A. P. Simopoulos, 'The importance of the omega-6/omega-3 fatty acid ratio in cardiovascular disease and other chronic diseases', *Experimental Biology and Medicine*, 233 (2008), pp. 674–88.

7 C. A. Daley et al., 'A Literature Review of the Value-Added Nutrients found in Grass-fed Beef Products', June 2005, draft manuscript available at All Things Grass Fed: A cooperative project between California State University, Chico College of Agriculture and University of California

Cooperative Extension, http://www.csuchico.edu/grassfedbeef/; A. P. Simopoulos (2000), 'Human requirement for N-3 polyunsaturated fatty acids', *Poultry Science*, 79(7) (2000), pp. 961–70; A. P. Simopoulos, 'The Importance of the Omega-6/Omega-3 Fatty Acid Ratio in Cardiovascular Disease and Other Chronic Diseases'.

8   H. Pickett, 'Nutritional benefits of higher welfare animal products', 2012, http://www.ciwf.org.uk/includes/documents/cm_docs/2012/ n/nutritional_benefits_of_higher_welfare_animal_products_report_ june2012.pdf.

9   C. A. Daley et al., 'A review of fatty acid profiles and antioxidant content in grass-fed and grain-fed beef', *Nutrition Journal*, 9:10, 2010, http:// www.nutritionj.com/content/9/1/10.

10   J. D. Wood et al., 'Fat deposition, fatty acid composition and meat quality: A review', *Meat Science*, 78 (2008), pp. 343–58.

11   H. Pickett, 'Nutritional benefits of higher welfare animal products'.

12   Ibid.

13   Ibid.

14   Danyel Jennen, *Chicken fatness: from QTL to candidate gene*, PhD thesis, Wageningen University, The Netherlands, 2004, with summary in Dutch, ISBN 90-8504-069-8.

15   Jon Ungoed-Thomas, '"Healthy" chicken piles on the fat', *Times*, 3 April 2005, http://www.timesonline.co.uk/.

16   Richard Young, 'Does organic farming offer a solution?', *The Meat Crisis*, ed. Joyce D'Silva and John Webster, Earthscan, 2010, chapter 5.

17   Z. Hunchar, 'A Hard Story to Swallow: McDonald's Forced to Pay Employee for Weight Gain', *Technorati Blogging*, 2010, available from: http://technorati.com/blogging/article/a-hard-story-to-swallow-mcdon-alds/ (accessed 2 September 2011); http://www.neatorama.com/2010/ 10/30/man-sued-mcdonalds-for-making-him-fat-and-won/ (accessed 2 September 2011); Legal Zoom, 'McDonald's Manager in Brazil Wins Obesity Lawsuit', *Legal Zoom News Sources*, 2010, available from http://www.legalzoom.com/news/politics/international/mcdonalds-manager-brazil-wins (accessed 2 September 2011).

18   Veg Lawyer, 'McDonald's made me fat . . . revisited', *Veg Lawyer's Weblog*, 2007, available from http://veglawyer.wordpress.com/2007/11/23/mcdon-alds-made-me-fatrevisited-2/ (accessed 2 September 2011); S. Krum, 'It's fat, fat and more fat', *Guardian*, 27 August 2002, available from http://www. guardian.co.uk/world/2002/aug/27/usa.health (accessed 2 September 2011).

19   Veg Lawyer, 'McDonald's made me fat . . . revisited'.

20   J. Cloud, 'A Food Fight Against McDonald's', *TIME*, 2 December

2002, available from http://www.time.com/time/magazine/article/
0,9171,1003804,00.html (accessed 2 September 2011).

21 Ibid.

22 S. English, 'Judge pulls plug on teenagers' claim against McDonald's',
Daily Telegraph, 6 September 2003, available from http://www.telegraph.
co.uk/news/1440693/Judge-pulls-plug-on-teenagers-claim-against-
McDonalds.html (accessed 2 September 2011).

23 A. Freeman, 'Fast Food: Oppression Through Poor Nutrition', *California Law Review*, 2007, available from http://www.bfair. net/?p=1054
(accessed 4 September 2011).

24 Dietz, 'Reversing the tide of obesity'.

25 Anthony J. McMichael et al., 'Food, livestock production, energy, climate change, and health', *Lancet*, vol. 370, issue 9594 (2007), pp.
1253–63.

26 Reed Business Media, 'Meat-free drive is impacting consumer markets',
Euromonitor, news release 30 August 2011, http://www.foodand-
drinkeurope.com/Products-Marketing/Meat-free-drive-is-
impacting-consumer-markets-Euromonitor/.

27 World Poultry news online, 'Rabobank predicts sharp decline in meat and
poultry production', 30 September 2011, http://www.worldpoultry.net/
news/rabobank-predicts-sharp-decline-in-meat-and-poultry-production-
9428.html.

28 Meat & Poultry staff, 'Flexitarians will increase in 2012: study', M&P
news online, 28 December 2011, http://www.meatpoultry.com/News.

29 World Poultry news online, 'Rabobank predicts'.

IV MUCK

1 *Daily Telegraph*, 'Farmers warn Beckett over "EU manure mountains"', 12
March 2002, http://www.telegraph.co.uk/news/uknews/1387466/Farm-
ers-warn-Beckett-over-EU-manure-mountains.html# (accessed 1 October
2012).

2 Dairy Co, 2011, UK cow numbers, 13 December 2011, http://www.
dairyco.org.uk/market-information/farming-data/cow-numbers/uk-
cow-numbers/ (accessed 3 October 2012).

3 Natural England, website article 'Capital Grant Scheme', http://www.
naturalengland.org.uk/ourwork/farming/csf/cgs/default.aspx (accessed
3 October 2012).

9 HAPPY AS A PIG: TALES OF POLLUTION

1 *Independent*, 'Farmers and greens fight the war of the killer seaweed', 15 August 2011, http://www.independent.co.uk/environment/nature/farmers-and-greens-fight-the-war-of-the-killer-seaweed-2337803.html (accessed 6 August 2012); *The Connexion*, 'Brittany beaches after toxic fumes', 1 September 2011, http://www.connexionfrance.com/50-brittany-beaches-closed-after-toxic-fumes-kill-boar-13715-view-article.html (accessed 6 August 2012); *Daily Mail*, 'Holidaymakers warned of deadly seaweed on Brittany's popular beaches', 28 July 2011, http://www.dailymail.co.uk/travel/article-2019700/Brittany-seaweed-warning-Holidaymakers-told-beware-toxic-fumes-rotting-seaweed.html (accessed 6 August 2012); *Daily Telegraph*, 'Toxic seaweed on French coast sparks health fears', 22 July 2011, http://www.telegraph.co.uk/news/worldnews/europe/france/8655329/Toxic-seaweed-on-French-coast-sparks-health-fears.html (accessed 6 August 2012); *Guardian*, 'Brittany beaches hit by toxic algae', 27 July 2011, http://www.guardian.co.uk/environment/2011/jul/27/brittany-beaches-toxic-algae-boars (accessed 6 August 2012); *The Horse*, 'Horse Dies in Decomposing Seaweed; Toxic Gas Blamed', 6 August 2009, http://www.thehorse.com/ViewArticle.aspx?ID=14674 (accessed 6 August 2012); *Guardian*, 'Lethal algae take over beaches in northern France', 10 August 2009, http://www.guardian.co.uk/world/2009/aug/10/france-brittany-coast-seaweed-algae (accessed 6 August 2012); Science Ray, 'Green algae is fatal to men', 11 September 2011, http://scienceray.com/technology/green-algae-is-fatal-to-men/ (accessed 6 August 2012).

2 S. Heliez et al., 'Risk factors of new Aujeszky's disease virus infection in swine herds in Brittany (France)', *Veterinary Research*, 31 (2000), pp. 146–7, http://www.vetres.org/ (accessed 6 August 2012).

3 *BPEX Weekly*, 'French producers will go bust', 3 December 2010, http://www.bpex.org/bpexWeekly/BW031210.aspx (accessed 12 August 2012).

4 WattAgNet, 'French pig producers are determined to thrive in spite of new welfare, environmental regulations', 10 November 2011, http://www.wattagnet.com/French_pig_producers_are_determined_to_thrive_in_spite_of_new_welfare,_environmental_regulations.html (accessed 6 August 2012).

5 *Daily Telegraph*, 'Toxic seaweed on French coast sparks health fears', 22 July 2011, http://www.telegraph.co.uk/news/worldnews/europe/france/

8655329/Toxic-seaweed-on-French-coast-sparks-health-fears.html (accessed 6 August 2012).

6 *New York Times*, 'Cultivated environment French farmer pushes green methods', 28 May 1993, http://www.nytimes.com/1993/05/28/business/worldbusiness/28iht-farm.html (accessed 3 October 2012); *Central Brittany Journal*, website, André Pochon, http://www.thecbj.com/andre-pochon/ (accessed 3 October 2012).

7 Rodale Institute, extracts from Senate Testimony by Rick Dove, 2002, http://newfarm.rodaleinstitute.org/depts/pig_page/rick_dove/index.shtml (accessed 6 August 2012); *Waterkeeper* magazine, Summer 2004, http://www.waterkeeper.org/ht/a/GetDocumentAction/i/9899 (accessed 6 August 2012); *Waterkeeper* magazine, Fall 2005, http://www.waterkeeper.org/ht/a/GetDocumentAction/i/9903 (accessed 6 August 2012).

8 North Carolina State University website, http://www.ncat.edu/academics/schools-colleges1/saes/facilities/farm/swineunit.html (accessed 21 May 2013).

9 North Carolina in the Global Economy website, http://www.soc.duke.edu/NC_GlobalEconomy/hog/overview.shtml (accessed 21 May 2013).

10 Food and Water Watch website, http://www.factoryfarmmap.org/facts/ (accessed 21 May 2013).

11 Centre for research on globalisation, 'Pork's dirty secret', 4 May 2009, http://globalresearch.ca/index.php?context=va&aid=13479 (accessed 6 August 2012).

12 J. Trotter, 'Hogwashed', *Waterkeeper* magazine, Summer 2004, http://www.waterkeeper.org/ht/a/GetDocumentAction/i/9899 (accessed 6 August 2012).

13 J. Tietz, 'Boss Hog', *Rolling Stone*, 14 December 2006, http://regional-workbench.org/USP2/pdf_files/pigs.pdf (accessed 6 August 2012).

14 H. Steinfeld et al., *Livestock's Long Shadow, environmental issues and options*, FAO, Rome, 2006.

15 North Carolina Waterkeeper and Riverkeeper Alliance website, 'Hog pollution and our rivers', http://www.riverlaw.us/ (accessed 6 August 2012).

16 US Government Accountability Office, *Concentrated Animal Feeding Operations: EPA Needs More Information and a Clearly Defined Strategy to Protect Air and Water Quality*, statement of Anu K. Mittal, Director Natural Resources and Environment, 24 September 2008, highlights of GAO-08-1177T, a testimony before the Subcommittee on Environment and Hazardous Materials, Committee on Energy and Commerce, House of Representatives.

17 S. R. Carpenter and E. M. Bennett, 'Reconsideration of the planetary boundary for phosphorus', *Environmental Research Letters*, 14 February 2011.

18 D. Gurian-Sherman, *CAFOs Uncovered: the untold costs of confined animal feeding operations,* Union of Concerned Scientists, 2008.

19 Ibid.

20 European Commission, 'The EU Nitrates Directive', factsheet, January 2010, http://ec.europa.eu/environment/pubs/factsheets.htm.

10 SOUTHERN DISCOMFORT: THE RISE OF THE INDUSTRIAL CHICKEN

1 Georgians for Pastured Poultry, *Out of Sight, Out of Mind: The Impacts of Chicken Meat Factory Farming in the State of Georgia,* GPP, Decatur, 2012.

2 Red Earth Farm website, http://redearthfarm.weebly.com/ (accessed 7 August 2012).

3 2010 FAOSTAT:http://faostat.fao.org; FAO, *Livestock's Long Shadow: Environmental Issues and Options,* Rome, 2006 – proportion industrially reared.

4 Numbers indicate broiler chickens sold and farms with broiler chicken sales, taken from the USDA Census of Agriculture through 2007, Census information, www.agcensus.usda.gov/Publications/2007/Full_Report/Volume_1,_Chapter_1_US/st99_1_001_001.pdf.

5 Pew Environment Group, *Big Chicken: Pollution and industrial poultry production in America,* Pew, Washington, July 2011.

6 USDA, National Agriculture Statistics Service, 2010, 'Broilers: Inventory by State, US', http://www.nass.usda.gov/Charts_and_Maps/Poultry/brlmap.asp (accessed 1 December 2011); United States Department of Agriculture, *2007 Census of Agriculture – Georgia,* http://www.agcensus.usda.gov/Publications/2007/Full_Report/Volume_1,_Chapter_1_State_Level/Georgia/gav1.pdf (accessed 16 November 2011).

7 FAOSTAT data, 2010, http://faostat.fao.org.

8 The New Georgia Encyclopedia, http://www.georgiaencyclopedia.org/nge/Article.jsp?id=h-1811 (accessed 1 December 2011).

9 Ibid.; 'From Supply Push to Demand Pull: Agribusiness Strategies for Today's Consumers', available from http://www.ers.usda.gov/Amber-Waves/November03/Features/supplypushdemandpull.htm (accessed 2 December 2011).

10 The New Georgia Encyclopedia; Cagle's, Inc., History, http://www.

fundinguniverse.com/company-histories/Cagles-Inc-Company-History. html (accessed 2 December 2011).

11 *Today in Georgia History*, 'Jesse Jewell', http://www.todayingeorgiahis-tory.org/content/jesse-jewell (accessed 7 August 2012).

12 The New Georgia Encyclopedia.

13 Ibid.

14 Georgians for Pastured Poultry, *Out of Sight, Out of Mind*.

15 D. L. Cunningham, 'Contract Broiler Production: Questions and Answers', in Science UoGCoAaE, CAES, 2009; Poultry Workshop, Public Workshops Exploring Competition in Agriculture, 21 May 2010, Alabama A&M University, Knight Reception Center, Normal, Alabama, United States Department of Justice, 2010.

16 Ibid.

17 Cunningham, 'Contract Broiler Production'.

18 Knowles T. G., Kestin S. C., Haslam S. M., Brown S. N., Green L. E., et al. (2008) 'Leg Disorders in Broiler Chickens: Prevalence, Risk Factors and Pre-vention'. PLoS ONE 3(2): e1545, doi: 10. 1371/journal. pone. 0001545. http://www.plosone.org/article/info.

19 Pilgrim's Pride, http://www.turnaround.org/cmaextras/PilgrimsPride. pdf (accessed 16 December 2011).

20 D. L. Cunningham, 'Cash Flow Estimates for Contract Broiler Produc-tion in Georgia: A 30-Year Analysis', The University of Georgia College of Agricultural and Environmental Sciences, 31 January 2011, http:// www.caes.uga.edu/Publications/pubDetail.cfm?pk_id=7052 (accessed 5 December 2011).

21 Georgians for Pastured Poultry, *Out of Sight, Out of Mind*.

22 Interview conducted by Compassion in World Farming of Southern Poverty Law Center members who have worked with catchers, 2 Novem-ber 2011.

23 B. Kiepper, 'Poultry Processing: Measuring True Water Use', University of Georgia Cooperative Extension, 2011.

24 Bureau of Labor Statistics, Table SNR12, 'Highest incidence rates of total nonfatal occupational illness cases 2010', Bureau of Labor Statistics US Department of Labor, October 2011.

25 Georgia Education Agricultural Curriculum Office, 'Broilers: An over-view of broiler production in Georgia. Powerpoint presentation', 2006, http://www.powershow.com/view/108ba-YTFiY/Broilers_An_Over-view_of_Broiler_Production_in_Georgia_flash_ppt_presentation (accessed 15 December 2011); 'Injury and Injustice – America's Poultry Industry', United Food and Commercial Workers International Union,

cited in Southern Poverty Law Center, *Injustice on Our Plates: Immigrant Women in the US Food Industry*, 2010, p. 36; G. Guthey, 'The New Factories in the Fields: Georgia Poultry Workers', *Southern Changes*, vol. 19, no. 3–4, 1997, pp. 23–5.

26 Human Rights Watch, *Blood, Sweat, and Fear: Workers' Rights in US Meat and Poultry Plants*, New York, NY, 2004.

27 Wage and Hour Division, US Department of Labor, Poultry Processing Compliance Survey Fact Sheet, US Department of Labor, 2001.

28 T. Ashdown, 'Poultry Processing', in J. M. Stellman (ed.), *Encyclopaedia of Occupational Health And Safety* III, Geneva, Switzerland, International Labor Organization, 1998.

29 Human Rights Watch, *Blood, Sweat, and Fear*.

30 Ibid.

31 N. Stein and D. Burke, 'Son Of A Chicken Man. As he struggles to remake his family's poultry business into a $24 billion meat behemoth, John Tyson must prove he has more to offer than just the family name', from *Fortune* Magazine, quoted in Human Rights Watch, *Blood, Sweat, and Fear*.

32 *Independent*, 'The true cost of cheap chicken', 4 January 2008, http://www.independent.co.uk/news/uk/home-news/the-true-cost-of-cheap-chicken-768062.html (accessed 9 August 2012).

33 CIWF, 2010, press release, 'UK Consumers Vote for Higher Welfare Chicken and Eggs', 8 April 2010, http://www.ciwf.org.uk/includes/documents/cm_docs/2010/n/nr1009.pdf.

V SHRINKING PLANET

11 LAND: HOW FACTORY FARMS USE MORE, NOT LESS

1 BBC, 'Argentina's forest people suffer neglect', 27 September 2007, http://news.bbc.co.uk/1/hi/programmes/from_our_own_correspondent/7014197.stm (accessed 20 August 2012); University of Pennsylvania website, http://www.sas.upenn.edu/~valeggia/pdf (accessed 20 August 2012); Star of Hope website, http://www.starofhopeusa.org/component/myblog/argentian-some-history-regarding-toba-indians-565.html (accessed 20 August 2012); *Ethnologue*, Languages of Argentina, 2012, http://www.ethnologue.com/show_country.asp?name=AR (accessed 20 August 2012); http://intercontinentalcry.org/peoples/toba-qom/ (accessed 20 August 2012).

2 BBC, 'Argentina's forest people suffer neglect.

3 *Argentina Independent*, 'Qom indigenous leader hit by truck in alleged attack', 10 August 2012, http://www.argentinaindependent.com/tag/formosa/ (accessed 20 August 2012).

4 Calculation by Compassion in World Farming, 2012.

5 Thomas K. Rudel et al., 'Agricultural intensification and changes in cultivated areas, 1970–2005', *PNAS*, 106 (49) (2009), pp. 20675–80.

6 Calculation by Compassion in World Farming, 2011.

7 J. Lundqvist, C. de Fraiture and D. Molden, *Saving Water: From Field to Fork – Curbing Losses and Wastage in the Food Chain*, SIWI Policy Brief, 2008.

8 G. Borgstrom, *The Hungry Planet*, 2nd revised edition, New York, Collier Books, 1972.

9 R. K. Pachauri, 'Global warning! The impact of meat production and consumption on climate change', CIWF Peter Roberts Memorial Lecture, London, 8 September 2008, http://www.ciwf.org.uk/includes/documents/cm_docs/2008/l/1_london_08septo8.pps.

10 OECD-FAO, *Agricultural Outlook 2009–2018: Highlights*, 2009.

11 K. Deininger, D. Byerlee et al., *Rising Global Interest in Farmland: can it yield sustainable and equitable benefits?*, World Bank, 2010.

12 C. Vicente, GRAIN, Buenos Aires, personal communication, 2012.

13 Soybean and Corn Advisor website, http://www.soybeansandcorn.com/Argentina-Crop-Acreage (accessed 21 May 2013).

14 *Chicago Tribune*, 'ANALYSIS – Argentina's soy addiction comes back to bite farmers', 22 April 2013, http://articles.chicagotribune.com/2013-04-22/news/sns-rt-argentina-soy-analysisl2nod6135-20130422_1_soy-yields-corn-yields-pampas-farm-belt (accessed 21 May 2013).

15 Ibid.

16 Harvard Business School, from website, www.losgrobo.com (accessed 20 August 2012); Reuters, 'High yields boost Argentine soy outlook', 3 May 2010, http://www.reuters.com/article/2010/05/03/us-latam-summit-argentina-losgrobo-idUSTRE64259K20100503 (accessed 20 August 2012).

17 L. Cotula, S. Vermeulen, R. Leonard and J. Keeley, *Land Grab or Development Opportunity? Agricultural Investment and International Land Deals in Africa*, IIED/FAO/IFAD, London/Rome, 2009.

18 D. Headley, S. Malaiyandi and F. Shenggen, *Navigating the Perfect Storm: Reflections on the Food, Energy and Financial Crises*, August 2009, IFPRI (Online Resource) available at http://www.ifpri.org/sites/default/files/publications/ifpridpoo889.pdf.

19 Deininger, Byerlee et al., *Rising Global Interest in Farmland*.

20 'Global Land Grabbing: Update from the International Conference on Global Land Grabbing', ISS, 2011, http://www.iss.nl/fileadmin/ASSETS/iss/Documents/Conference_programmes/LDPI_conference_summary_May_2011.pdf (accessed 20 August 2012).

21 Chayton Africa website, http://www.chaytonafrica.com/ (accessed 20 August 2012).

22 'Chayton combines good land and secure water assets to grow its Atlas Agricultural operation', *HedgeNews Africa, Journal of the African Alternatives and Hedge Fund Community*, Second Quarter, 2011, vol. 1, 7, http://www.oaklandinstitute.org (accessed 20 August 2012).

23 Crowder, quoted in N. Nyagah, 'Zambia: Rich African farms draw international investors', 2 March 2011, http://allafrica.com/stories/201103021113.html (accessed 20 August 2012).

24 *Guardian*, 'Land deals in Ethiopia bring food self-sufficiency, and prosperity', 4 April 2011, http://www.guardian.co.uk/global-development/poverty-matters/2011/apr/04/ethiopia-land-deals-food-self-sufficiency (accessed 20 August 2012); *Ethiopian Times*, 'Land grab in Africa: demystifying large-scale land investments', 2 April 2012, https://ethiopiantimes.wordpress.com/2012/04/02/land-grab-in-africa-demystifying-large-scale-land-investments/ (accessed 20 August 2012).

25 Karuturi Global website, http://www.karuturi.com/ (accessed 20 August 2012).

26 Karuturi Global website, Welcome to Karuturi Global Limited, http://www.karuturi.com/index.php?option=com_frontpage&Itemid=1 (accessed 3 October 2012).

27 *Guardian*, 'Land deals in Ethiopia'.

28 Bloomberg, 'Ethiopian Government Slashes Karuturi Global Land Concession by Two-Thirds', 4 May 2011, http://www.bloomberg.com/news/2011-05-04/ethiopian-government-slashes-karuturi-global-land-concession-by-two-thirds.html (accessed 20 August 2012).

29 Bloomberg, 'Ethiopian farms lure Bangalore-based Karuturi Global Ltd. As Workers Live in Poverty', 30 December 2009, http://www.bloomberg.com/apps/news?pid=newsarchive&sid=aeuJT_pSE68c (accessed 20 August 2012).

30 Ibid.

31 M. Vermeer and S. Rahmstorf, 'Global sea level linked to global temperature', *Proceedings of the National Academy of Sciences*, 2009; DOI: 10.1073/pnas.0907765106; Potsdam Institute for Climate Impact Research (PIK), 'Sea level could rise from 0.75 to 1.9 meters this century', *ScienceDaily*, 8 December 2009.

32 *Stern Review on the Economics of Climate Change*, HM Treasury and Cabinet Office, 2006, part II, chapters 3 and 4.

33 Ibid.

34 The Rights and Resources Initiative (RRI), *Seeing People through the Trees: Scaling Up Efforts to Advance Rights and Address Poverty, Conflict and Climate Change*, Washington DC, RRI, 2008, http://www.rightsandresources.org/documents/files/doc_737.pdf.

35 *Stern Review on the Economics of Climate Change*, HM Treasury and Cabinet Office, 2006.

36 Soystats, 'World soybean production 2010', 2011, http://www.soystats.com/2011/page_30.htm (accessed 21 August 2012).

37 FAOSTAT: http://faostat.fao.org (accessed 8 September 2012); Soystats, 'Adoption of Bio-tech enhanced soyabean seedstock 1997–2010', 2011, http://www.soystats.com/2011/page_36.htm (accessed 21 August 2012).

38 Soystats, 'World soybean production 2010'.

39 Soystats 2012, http://www.soystats.com/archives/2012/no-frames. htm. (accessed 8 September 2012); USDA Economic Research Service, 'Soybeans and oil crops', 2012, http://www.ers.usda.gov/topics/crops/soybeans-oil-crops/trade.aspx (accessed 21 August 2012); Soystats, 'World soybean meal exports 2010', 2011, shows Argentina accounting for 49% of global exports, ahead of Brazil (23%) and USA (14%), http://www.soystats.com/2011/page_33.htm (accessed 21 August 2012).

40 'What's feeding our food? The environmental and social impacts of the livestock sector', http://www.foe.co.uk/resource/briefings/livestock_impacts.pdf (accessed 8 September 2012).

41 Alternet, 'Feedlot Meat Has Spurred a Soy Boom That Has a Devastating Environmental and Human Cost', 17 March 2011, http://www.alternet.org/story/150277/feedlot_meat_has_spurred_a_soy_boom_that_has_a_devastating_environmental_and_human_cost (accessed 21 May 2013).

42 International Rivers website, 'Paraguay-Paraná Hidrovia', 2012, http://www.internationalrivers.org/zh-hans/node/2348 (accessed 23 August 2012); *The South American Hidrovia Parana – Paraguay*, http://www.chasque.net/rmartine/hidrovia/Envxtrad.html (accessed 23 August 2012).

43 International Rivers website, 'Paraguay-Paraná Hidrovia', http://www.internationalrivers.org/campaigns/paraguay-paran%C3%A1-hidrovia (accessed 21 May 2013).

44 Reuters, 'Eyeing flood waters, Argentine ranchers move cattle', 30 October 2009, http://www.reuters.com/article/2009/10/30/idUSN30241232 (accessed 23 August 2012).

45 IPS, 'ARGENTINA: Countryside No Longer Synonymous with Healthy Living', 4 March 2009, http://www.ipsnews.net/2009/03/argentina-countryside-no-longer-synonymous-with-healthy-living/ (accessed 21 May 2013).

46 J. Richardson, 'Feedlot Meat Has Spurred a Soy Boom That Has a Devastating Environmental and Human Cost', *Axis of Logic*, 26 March 2011, http://axisoflogic.com/artman/publish/Article_62629.shtml (accessed 24 August 2012).

47 Soystats, 'Adoption of biotech-enhanced soybean seedstock 1997–2010', 2011, http://www.soystats.com/2011/Default-frames.htm (accessed 5 October 2012).

48 *Guardian*, 'GM soya "miracle" turns sour in Argentina', 16 April 2004, http://www.guardian.co.uk/science/2004/apr/16/gm.food (accessed 6 September 2012).

49 CAST (Council for Agricultural Science and Technology), Issue Paper 49, *Herbicide-Resistant Weeds Threaten Soil Conservation Gains: Finding a Balance for Soil and Farm Sustainability*, February 2012.

50 Faculty of Medical Sciences, National University of Cordoba, *Report from the 1st National meeting of Physicians in the Crop-Sprayed Towns*, 27 August 2010, http://www.reduas.fcm.unc.edu.ar/statement-from-the-1st-national-meeting-of-physicians-in-the-crop-sprayed-towns/ (accessed 21 May 2013).

51 Ibid.

52 Le Monde/World Crunch, 'Where Soy Is King: In Argentina, Local Health Costs Rise As Agro Booms', 15 August 2011, http://ww.worldcrunch.com/culture-society/where-soy-is-king-in-argentina-local-health-costs-rise-as-agro-booms-/c3s3581/ (accessed 6 August 2012).

53 Monsanto, Corporate Profile, 2012, http://www.monsanto.com/investors/pages/corporate-profile.aspx (accessed 6 August 2012).

12 THICKER THAN WATER: DRAINING RIVERS, LAKES AND OIL WELLS

1 Energy Information Administration, *Analysis of Crude Oil Production in the Arctic National Wildlife Refuge*, May 2008, http://www.eia.gov/oiaf/servicerpt/anwr/pdf/sroiaf(2008)03.pdf (accessed 7 September 2012).

2 CIA Factbook, https://www.cia.gov/library/publications/the-world-factbook/rankorder/2174rank.html (accessed 7 September 2012) (based on US daily consumption of 19.15 million barrels and EU, 13.68 million).

3   *Alaska Journal of Commerce*, 'USGS estimates on Slope shale oil, gas puts Alaska near top', 1 March 2012, http://www.alaskajournal.com/Alaska-Journal-of-Commerce/AJOC-March-4-2012/USGS-estimates-on-Slope-shale-oil-gas-puts-Alaska-near-top/ (accessed 7 September 2012).

4   *Time*, 12 November 2007, The Eco vote, http://www.time.com/time/2007/includes/eco_vote.pdf (accessed 7 September 2012).

5   National Review Online, 'The Campaign Spot', 16 January 2008, http://www.nationalreview.com/campaign-spot/10699/john-mccain-im-raising-hundreds-thousands-day-new-hampshire (accessed 7 September 2012).

6   *New York Times*, 'New and Frozen Frontier Awaits Offshore Oil Drilling', 23 May 2012, http://www.nytimes.com/2012/05/24/science/earth/shell-arctic-ocean-drilling-stands-to-open-new-oil-frontier.html (accessed 7 September 2012).

7   *Daily Telegraph*, 'Total insists Shtokman Russian Arctic gas project not delayed "indefinitely"', 31 August 2012, http://www.telegraph.co.uk/finance/newsbysector/energy/oilandgas/9512809/Total-insists-Shtokman-Russian-Arctic-gas-project-not-delayed-indefinitely.html (accessed 7 September 2012).

8   *Guardian*, 'Arctic oil rush will ruin ecosystem, warns Lloyd's of London', 12 April 2012, http://www.guardian.co.uk/world/2012/apr/12/lloyds-london-warns-risks-arctic-oil-drilling (accessed 7 September 2012).

9   D. Pimentel, *Impacts of Organic Farming on the Efficiency of Energy Use in Agriculture: An Organic Center State of Science Review*, The Organic Center, August 2006. This review cites findings in several other of the Pimentel group papers.

10 World Bank, *World Development Report 2008. Agriculture for Development*, 2008, chapter 2, 'Agriculture's performance, diversity and uncertainties', http://siteresources.worldbank.org.

11 FAO, *The energy and agriculture nexus*, Environment and natural resources working paper 4. Rome, 2000, chapter 2, 'Energy for agriculture', http://www.fao.org/.

12 Pimentel, *Impacts of Organic Farming*.

13 A. A. Bartlett, 'Forgotten Fundamentals of the Energy Crisis', 1978, http://www.npg.org/specialreports/bartlett_section3.htm (accessed 7 September 2012).

14 World Bank, *World Development Report 2008*, chapter 2.

15 National Petroleum Council, *Summary Discussions on Peak Oil*, working document of the NPC Global Oil & Gas Study, Topic Paper #15, July 2007,

http://downloadcenter.connectlive.com/events/npc071807/pdf-down-loads/Study_Topic_Papers/15-STG-Peak-Oil-Discussions.pdf.

16 International Energy Agency, *World Energy Outlook 2010*, presentation to the press, London, 9 November 2010.

17 Oil Depletion Analysis Centre, 'Peak Oil Primer', 24 November 2009, http://www.odac-info.org/.

18 D. Howden, 'World oil supplies are set to run out faster than expected, warn scientists', *Independent*, 14 June 2007, http://www.independent. co.uk/news/science/world-oil-supplies-are-set-to-run-out-faster-than-expected-warn-scientists-453068.html.

19 Shell International, *Shell Energy Scenarios to 2050: an era of volatile transitions*, 2011.

20 A. Coecup, letter to the editor, *The Times*, 30 May 2012.

21 Pimentel, *Impacts of Organic Farming*.

22 Ibid.

23 Soil Association, *Energy efficiency of organic farming: analysis of data from existing Defra studies*, published 31 January 2007.

24 Lloyd's, 'Investment in the Arctic could reach $100bn in ten years', 12 April 2012, http://www.lloyds.com/Lloyds/Press-Centre/Press-Releases/2012/04/Investment-in-the-Arctic-could-reach-USD100bn-in-ten-years.

25 *Guardian*, 'Arctic oil rush will ruin ecosystem'.

26 Fiji Water, official website, http://www.fijiwater.com/ (accessed 10 September 2012).

27 *Daily Telegraph*, 'Fiji Water accused of environmentally misleading claims', 20 June 2011, http://www.telegraph.co.uk/earth/earthnews/8585182Fiji-Water-accused-of-environmentally-misleading-claims.html (accessed 10 September 2012).

28 Ibid.

29 Fiji Water, official website, FAQ: About our water, http://www.fijiwater. com/company/faq/about-fiji-water/ (accessed 12 September 2012).

30 S. Parente and E. Lewis-Brown, *Freshwater Use and Farm Animal Welfare*, CIWF/WSPA, 2012, http://www.ciwf.org.uk/includes/documents/cm_docs/2012/f/freshwater_use_and_farm_animal_welfare_12_page.pdf.

31 World Economic Forum, 'The bubble is close to bursting: A forecast of the main economic and geopolitical water issues likely to arise in the world during the next two decades', draft for discussion at the World Economic Forum Annual Meeting 2009.

32 Based on a bathtub holding 175 litres of water, and published figures showing the total water footprint for a kilo of beef, pork and chicken

being 15,500, 5,900 and 4,300 litres consecutively; from Water Footprint Network, http://www.waterfootprint.org/?page=files/Animal-products (accessed 10 September 2012).

33 P. W. Gerbens-Leenes, M. M. Mekonnen and A. Y. Hoekstra, *A Comparative Study on the Water Footprint of Poultry, Pork and Beef in Different Countries and Production Systems*, University of Twente, September 2011.

34 Ibid.

35 C. S. Smith, 'Al Kharj Journal; Milk Flows From Desert At a Unique Saudi Farm', *New York Times*, 31 December 2002, http://www.nytimes.com/2002/12/31/world/al-kharj-journal-milk-flows-from-desert-at-a-unique-saudi-farm.html (accessed 10 September 2012).

36 Ibid.

37 Ibid.

38 2nd UN World Water Development Report, *Water, A Shared Responsibility*, chapter 4, 'The State of the Resource', UNESCO, WMO and IAEA, 2006., http://www.unesco.org/water/wwap/wwdr/wwdr2/pdf/wwdr2_ch_4.pdf.

39 H. Steinfeld et al., *Livestock's Long Shadow: environmental issues and options*, chapter 4, Food and Agriculture Organization of the United Nations, Rome, 2006, http://www.virtualcentre.org/en/library/key_pub/longshad/A0701E00.htm.

40 Y. Wada et al., 'Global depletion of groundwater resources', *Geophysical Research Letters*, vol. 37 (2010), L20402, doi:10.1029/2010GL044571; American Geophysical Union (AGU), 'Groundwater depletion rate accelerating worldwide', AGU Release No. 10–30, 23 September 2010, www.agu.org/news/press/pr_archives/2010/2010-30.shtml.

41 ibid.

42 *Wired* magazine, 'Peak Water: Aquifers and Rivers Are Running Dry. How Three Regions Are Coping', 21 April 2008, http://www.wired.com/science/planetearth/magazine/16-05/ff_peakwater?currentPage=all (accessed 10 September 2012); R. Courtland, 'News briefing, Enough water to go around?', *Nature*, published online 19 March 2008, doi:10.1038/news.2008.678, www.nature.com/news/2008/080319/full/news.2008.678.html.

43 M. Barlow and T. Clarke, *Blue Gold: The Battle against Corporate Theft of the World's Water*, Earthscan, London, 2002.

44 B. Bates et al., *Climate Change and Water*, IPCC Technical paper VI, IPCC, WMO and UNEP, 2008, http://www.ipcc.ch/pdf/technical-papers/climate-change-water-en.pdf.

45 Steinfeld et al., *Livestock's Long Shadow*.

46 BBC, 'Summer "wettest in 100 years" Met Office figures show', 30 August

2012, http://www.bbc.co.uk/news/uk-19427139 (accessed 11 September 2012).

47 *Guardian*, 'Drought tanker ships considered', 17 May 2006, http://www.guardian.co.uk/environment/2006/may/17/water.uknews (accessed 4 October 2012).

48 *Daily Mail*, 'Icebergs considered to help beat the drought', 17 May 2006, http://www.dailymail.co.uk/news/article-386582/Icebergs-considered-help-beat-drought.html (accessed 4 October 2012).

49 BBC, 'Salt water plant opened in London', 2 June 2010, http://www.bbc.co.uk/news/10213835 (accessed 11 September 2012); N. Larkin, 'London Mayor appeals Thames Water desalination plant (Update 2)', Bloomberg, 21 August 2007, http://www.bloomberg.com (accessed 4 October 2012).

50 Thames Water, 'Thames gateway water treatment works', 20 August 2012, http://www.thameswater.co.uk/your-water/9942.htm (accessed 4 October 2012).

51 *Economist*, 'Australia's water shortage: The big dry', 26 April 2007, http://www.economist.com/node/9071007 (accessed 8 May 2013).

52 ABC Riverland, 'Scientists quit flawed Murray-Darling process', 21 May 2011, http://www.abc.net.au/local/stories/2011/05/23/3223924.htm (accessed 8 May 2013).

53 World Economic Forum, 'The bubble is close to bursting'.

54 World Resources Institute, UN Environment Programme, UN Development Programme and the World Bank, *World Resources 1998–99: Environmental change and human health*, 1998, http://www.wri.org/publication/content/8261.

55 American Geophysical Union (AGU), 'Groundwater depletion rate accelerating worldwide'.

56 World Economic Forum, 'The bubble is close to bursting'.

57 A. Mukherji et al., *Revitalizing Asia's irrigation: to sustainably meet tomorrow's food needs*, Colombo, Sri Lanka, International Water Management Institute; Rome, Italy, Food and Agriculture Organization of the United Nations, 2009.

58 IWMI and FAO, 'IWMI-FAO report: Revitalising Asia's irrigation: to sustainably meet tomorrow's food needs', press release, 19 August 2009, http://www.fao.org/nr/water/docs/iwmi-fao-report-revitalizing-asias-irrigation-to-sustainably-meet-tomorrows-food-needs.pdf.

59 J. Liu, H. Yang and H. H. G. Saveniji, 'China's move to high-meat diet hits water security', *Nature*, 454 (2008), p. 397.

60 J. Bruinsma, *The resource outlook to 2050: by how much do land, water and*

crop yields need to increase by 2050?, Expert meeting on 'How to Feed the World in 2050', Rome, FAO, 24–26 June 2009.

61 Parente and Lewis-Brown, *Freshwater Use and Farm Animal Welfare*.

13 HUNDRED-DOLLAR HAMBURGER: THE ILLUSION OF CHEAP FOOD

1 *Independent*, 'Tesco hits a new low with arrival of the £1.99 chicken', 6 February 2008, http://www.independent.co.uk/life-style/food-and-drink/news/tesco-hits-a-new-low-with-arrival-of-the-163199-chicken-778672.html (accessed 12 September 2012).

2 *Guardian*, 'High food prices are here to stay – and here's why', 17 July 2011, http://www.guardian.co.uk/lifeandstyle/2011/jul/17/food-prices-rise-commodities (accessed 12 September 2012).

3 M. Cacciottolo, 'The "hidden hunger" in British families', BBC news, 7 October 2010, http://www.bbc.co.uk/news/magazine-11427207.

4 J. Owen and B. Brady, 'Jobcentres to send poor and hungry to charity food banks', *Independent*, 18 September 2011, http://www.independent.co.uk/news/uk/politics/jobcentres-to-send-poor-and-hungry-to-charity-food-banks-2356578.html.

5 UN Department of Social and Economic Affairs, *World Economic and Social Survey 2011*, United Nations, New York.

6 *Guardian*, 'High food prices are here to stay'.

7 Government Office for Science, *Foresight Project on Global Food and Farming Futures. Synthesis Report C1: Trends in food demand and production*, January 2011; S. Msangi and M. W. Rosegrant, *Agriculture in a dynamically-changing environment: IFPRI's long-term outlook for food and agriculture under additional demand and constraints*, paper written in support of Expert Meeting on 'How to feed the World in 2050', Rome, FAO, 2009, http://www.fao.org/wsfs/forum2050/wsfs-background-documents/wsfs-expert-papers/en/; H. Steinfeld et al., *Livestock's Long Shadow, environmental issues and options*, FAO, Rome, 2006, Introduction, p. 12.

8 Oxfam, *4-a-week: changing food consumption in the UK to benefit people and the planet*, Oxfam GB Briefing Paper, 2009.

9 Foresight, *The Future of Food and Farming: challenges and choices for global sustainability*, Final Project Report, The Government Office for Science, London, 2011.

10 *The Economist*, 'Food and the Arab Spring: Let them eat Baklava; Today's Policies are Recipe for Instability in Middle East', 17 March 2012, http://www.economist.com/node/21550328; UN, 'Soaring cereal tab

continues to afflict poorest countries, UN agency warns', UN News Centre, 11 April 2008, www.un.org/apps/news/story.asp?NewsID=2628 9&Cr=food&Cr1=prices.

11 *New York Times*, 'Bread, the (subsidized) stuff of life in Egypt', 16 January 2008, http://www.nytimes.com/2008/01/16/world/africa (accessed 12 September 2012).

12 *Economist*, 'Food and the Arab Spring: Let them eat Baklava'.

13 Msangi and Rosegrant, *Agriculture in a dynamically-changing environment*.

14 Calculated from FAOSTAT online figures for global grain harvest (2009) and food value of cereals, based on a calorific intake of 2,500 kcalories per person per day.

15 David Pimentel et al., 'Reducing energy inputs in the US food system', *Human Ecology*, 36 (2008), pp. 459–71.

16 Vaclav Smil, *Feeding the world: a Challenge for the Twenty-first Century*, MIT Press, 2000.

17 BBC, 'Hundred-Dollar hamburger?', 14 June 2011, http://www.bbc. co.uk/news/business-13764242 (accessed 12 September 2012).

18 *Daily Mail*, 'The GM genocide: Thousands of Indian farmers are committing suicide after using genetically modified crops', 3 November 2008, http://www.dailymail.co.uk/news/article-1082559/The-GM-genocide-Thousands-Indian-farmers-committing-suicide-using-genetically-modified-crops.html (accessed 12 September 2012).

19 Ibid.

20 Center for Human Rights and Justice, *Every Thirty Minutes: Farmer Suicides, Human Rights, and the Agrarian Crisis in India,* New York, NYU School of Law, 2011.

21 *Independent*, 'Charles: "I blame GM crops for farmers' suicides"', 5 October 2008, http://www.independent.co.uk/environment/green-living/charles-i--blame-gm-crops-for-farmers-suicides-951807.html (accessed 12 September 2012).

22 P. Sainath, 'Farm suicides: a 12-year saga', *The Hindu*, 25 January 2010, http://www.thehindu.com/opinion/columns/sainath/article94324.ece (accessed 12 September 2012).

23 Tata Institute of Social Sciences, *Causes of Farmer Suicides in Maharashtra: An Enquiry*, Final Report Submitted to the Mumbai High Court,15 March 2005, http://mdmu.maharashtra.gov.in/pdf/Farmers_suicide_TISS_report.pdf.

24 J. Mencher, commenting on online ISIS press release, 10 February 2010, http://www.i-sis.org.uk (accessed 12 September 2012).

25 S. Ashley, S. Holden and P. Bazeley, *Livestock in Poverty-Focused Development*, Livestock in Development, Crewkerne, UK, 1999, http://www.theidlgroup.com/documents/IDLRedbook_000.pdf.

26 IFAD, *Rural Poverty Report*, 2011, http://www.ifad.org/rpr2011/index.htm (accessed 12 September 2012).

27 L. R. Brown, *Plan B 4.0: Mobilizing to save civilization*, Earth Policy Institute, W. W. Norton, 2009.

28 Earth Policy Institute, *World grain consumption and stocks, 1960–2009*, supporting dataset for chapter 2 of Brown, *Plan B 4.0*, http://www.earth-policy.org/index.php?/books/pb4/pb4_data.

29 P. J. Gerber, H. Steinfeld, B. Henderson, A. Mottet, C. Opio, J. Dijkman, A. Falucci and G. Tempio, 'Tackling climate change through livestock – a global assessment of emissions and mitigation opportunities', Food and Agriculture Organisation of the United Nations (FAO), Rome, 2013.

30 *Stern Review on the Economics of Climate Change*, HM Treasury and Cabinet Office, 2006, part II, chapters 3 and 4, http://www.hm-treasury.gov.uk/sternreview_index.htm; Joachim von Braun, *The world food situation: new driving forces and required actions*, IFPRI, Washington DC, December 2007, http://www.ifpri.org/pubs/fpr/pr18.pdf; D. S. Battisti and R. L. Naylor, 'Historical Warnings of Future Food Insecurity with Unprecedented Seasonal Heat', *Science*, 323 (2009), pp. 240–4.

31 The Rights and Resources Initiative (RRI), *Seeing People Through The Trees*, RRI, Washington DC, 2008, http://www.rightsandresources.org/documents/files/doc_737.pdf.

32 Cabinet Office, *Food Matters: towards a strategy for the 21st century*, Strategy Unit, July 2008.

VI TOMORROW'S MENU

14 GM: FEEDING PEOPLE OR FACTORY FARMS?

1 I. Potrykus, 'The "Golden Rice" tale', Agbioworld: http://www.agbioworld.org/biotech-info/topics/goldenrice/tale.html (accessed 30 July 2012).

2 *New York Times*, 'Scientist at work: Ingo Potrykus; Golden Rice in a Grenade-Proof Greenhouse', 21 November 2000, http://www.nytimes.com/2000/11/21/science/scientist-at-work-ingo-potrykus-golden-rice-in-a-grenade-proof-greenhouse.html?

3   http://agropedia.iitk.ac.in/?q=content/golden-rice (accessed 30 July 2012).

4   Golden Rice Project, Golden Rice Humanitarian Board website, http://www.goldenrice.org/index.php (accessed 30 July 2012).

5   Golden Rice Project website, 'Frequently Asked Questions (2)', http://goldenrice.org/Content3-Why/why3a_FAQ.php#Pseudo-science (accessed 5 October 2012).

6   Greenpeace press release, 'Golden Rice is a technical failure standing in way of real solutions for vitamin A deficiency', 17 March 2005, http://www.greenpeace.org/international/en/press/releases/golden-rice-is-a-technical-fai/ (accessed 30 July 2012).

7   World Health Organization (WHO) website article 'Micronutrient deficiencies', http://www.who.int/nutrition/topics/vad/en/index.html (accessed 8 May 2013).

8   Golden Rice Project, Golden Rice Humanitarian Board website, http://www.goldenrice.org/index.php (accessed 30 July 2012).

9   Defra, 'Farm scale evaluations: Managing GM crops with herbicides: effects on farmland wildlife', 2005.

10 M. A. Altieri, 'The Ecological Impacts of Large-Scale Agrofuel Mono-culture Production Systems in the Americas', *Bulletin of Science Technology Society*, June 2009, 29(3), pp. 236–44, http://bst.sagepub.com/content/29/3/236.

11 FAO Food Outlook, May 2012, http://www.fao.org/giews/english/fo/index.htm.

12 H. Steinfeld et al., *Livestock's Long Shadow: environmental issues and options*, Food and Agriculture Organization of the United Nations, Rome, 2006.

13 National Corn Growers Association (NCGA), *Corn Facts*, 2011 (accessed 22 June 2011).

14 GMO Compass, Field areas 2009, 2010, www.gmocompass.org/eng/agri_biotechnology/gmo_planting/257.global_gm_planting_2009.html.

15 Ibid.

16 GMO Compass, 'Genetically modified plants: global cultivation area: Soybeans, Maize', 2010, www.gmo-compass.org/eng/agri_biotechnology/gmo_planting/342.genetically_modified_soybean_global_area_under_cultivation.htm; www.gmo-compass.org/eng/agri_biotechnology/gmo_planting/341.genetically_modified_maize_global_area_under_cultivation.html.

17 J. Lundqvist, C. de Fraiture and D. Molden, *Saving Water: From Field to*

Fork – Curbing Losses and Wastage in the Food Chain, SIWI Policy Brief, SIWI, 2008, figure 1.

18 D. L. Barlett and J. B. Steel, 'Monsanto's Harvest of Fear', *Vanity Fair*, May 2008, http://www.vanityfair.com/poli'cs/features/2008/05/mon-santo200805 (accessed 30 July 2012).

19 Monsanto, news & views, 'Gary Rinehart', http://www.monsanto.com/newsviews/pages/gary-rinehart.aspx (accessed 30 July 2012).

20 'Who We Are', http://www.monsanto.co.uk/.

21 Bloomberg, '"Mounting evidence" of bug-resistant corn seen by EPA', 5 September 2012, http://www.bloomberg.com/news/2012-09-04/-mounting-evidence-of-bug-resistant-corn-seen-by-epa.html (accessed 8 May 2013).

22 *Farm Industry News*, 'In-field resistance to Bt corn rootworm trait documented', 16 August 2011, http://farmindustrynews.com/corn-root worm-traits/field-resistance-bt-corn-rootworm-trait-documented (accessed 5 October 2012).

23 Bloomberg, 'Monsanto Corn Falls to Illinois Bugs as Investigation Widens', 2 September 2011, http://www.bloomberg.com/news/2011-09-02/monsanto-corn-is-showing-illinois-insect-damage-as-investigation-widens.html (accessed 8 May 2013).

24 OECD-FAO, *OECD-FAO Agricultural Outlook 2011–2020*, Summary and highlights, 2011.

25 BBC News online, 'Germany bans Monsanto's GM maize', 14 April 2009, http://news.bbc.co.uk/1/hi/world/europe/7998181.stm.

26 J. Smith, 'An FDA-Created Crisis Circles the Globe', October 2007, available at http://www.newswithviews.com/Smith/jeffrey17.htm (accessed 30 July 2012).

27 Institute for Responsible Technology, 'Genetically Modified Soy Linked to Sterility, Infant Mortality', 2010, http://www.responsibletechnology.org/article-gmo-soy-linked-to-sterility (accessed 30 July 2012).

28 Science Nordic, 'Growing fatter on a GM diet', 17 July 2012, http://sciencenordic.com/growing-fatter-gm-diet (accessed 30 July 2012).

29 G. F. Séralini et al, 'Long term toxicity of a Roundup herbicide and a Roundup-tolerant genetically modified maize', *Food and Chemical Toxicology*, volume 50, issue 11, November 2012, pp. 4221–31, http://www.sciencedirect.com.

30 My Sanantonio, 'First cloned cat is turning 10', 18 May 2011, http://www.mysanantonio.com/news/article/first-cloned-cat-is-turning-10-1383604.php (accessed 13 September 2012).

31 http://www.chron.com/life/article/First-cloned-cat-turns-10-1383844.php;

http://articles.nydailynews.com/2011-08-16/entertainment/29913126_1_
duane-kraemer-genetic-savings-and-clone-bioarts; http://en.wikipedia.org/
wiki/CC_(cat).

32 Texas A&M University website, http://vetmed.tamu.edu/rsl/faculty/
duane-kraemer (accessed 13 September 2012).

33 Yahoo voices, 'Dr. Duane Carl Kraemer: The Transfer Scientist', 2003,
http://voices.yahoo.com/dr-duane-carl-kraemer-transfer-scientist-
134787.html (accessed 13 September 2012); L. Hawthorne, 'A Project
to Clone Companion Animals', *Journal of Applied Animal Welfare Science*, 5(3) (2002), pp. 229–31, http://www.animalsandsociety.net/assets/
library/147_jaws050307.pdf; M. Warner, 'Inside the Very Strange World
of Billionaire John Sperling', 29 April 2002, Center for Genetics & Society, http://www.geneticsandsociety.org/article.php?id=108 (accessed 13
September 2012).

34 Yahoo voices, 'Dr. Duane Carl Kraemer'; Hawthorne, 'A Project to
Clone Companion Animals'; Warner, 'Inside the Very Strange World'.

35 BioTechnology, 'Genetic Savings and Clone forced to shut down', 2009,
http://biotechnology-industries.blogspot.co.uk/2009/01/genetic-sav-
ings-and-clone-forced-to.html (accessed 13 September 2012).

36 *National Geographic*, 'First Dog Clone', 28 October 2010, http://news.
nationalgeographic.com/news/2005/08/photogalleries/dogclone/
(accessed 13 September 2012).

37 Genome Alberta, 'Californian pit bull lives on in 5 cloned puppies', 5
August 2008, http://genomealberta.ca/connect-with-us/news-releases/
ge3ls08070801.aspx (accessed 13 September 2012); *Guardian*, 'Pet cloning service bears five baby Boogers', 5 August 2008, http://www.
guardian.co.uk/science/2008/aug/05/genetics.korea (accessed 13 September 2012); *Independent*, 'Saved by a pit bull, Californian owner
clones five more', 6 August 2008, http://www.independent.co.uk/news/
world/americas/saved-by-a-pit-bull-californian-owner-clones-five-
more-886108.html (accessed 13 September 2012).

38 *New York Post*, 'Adorable little abominations of nature', 14 May 2011,
http://www.nypost.com (accessed 13 September 2012).

39 L. Goldwert, 'First cloned cat nears 10 but pet replicating business
has not boomed due to money, ethical woes', *NY Daily News*, 16
August 2011, http://articles.nydailynews.com/2011-08-16/entertain-
ment/29913126_1_duane-kraemer-genetic-savings-and-clone-bioarts.

40 *Southwest Farm Press* staff, 'Disease resistant bull cloned at Texas A&M',
11 January 2001, Southwest Farm Press, http://southwestfarmpress.
com/disease-resistant-bull-cloned-texas-am.

41 Viagen website, http://www.viagen.com/ (accessed 13 September 2012).

42 H. Pickett, 'Farm Animal Cloning', Godalming, Compassion in World Farming, 2010, http://www.ciwf.org.uk/includes/documents/cm_docs/2010/c/compassion_2010_farm_animal_cloning_report.pdf.

43 University of Utah website, http://learn.genetics.utah.edu/content/tech/cloning/cloningrisks/ (accessed 13 September 2012).

44 FDA, *Potential Hazards and Risks to Animals Involved in Cloning*, http://www.fda.gov/animalveterinary/safetyhealth/animalcloning/ucm124840.htm (accessed 13 September 2012).

45 P. Loi, L. della Salda, G. Ptak, J. A. Modliński and J. Karasiewicz, 'Peri- and post-natal mortality of somatic cell clones in sheep', *Animal Science Papers and Reports*, 22 (Suppl. 1) (2004), pp. 59–70.

46 EFSA, 'Scientific Opinion of the Scientific Committee on a request from the European Commission on food safety, animal health and welfare and environmental impact of animals derived from cloning by somatic cell nucleus transfer (SCNT) and their offspring and products obtained from those animals', *EFSA Journal*, 767 (2008), pp. 1–49.

47 EGE, Opinion No. 23: 'Ethical Aspects of Animal Cloning for Food Supply', The European Group on Ethics in Science and New Technologies to the European Commission, 16 January 2008.

48 CIWF, 'Cloned animal suffering forces end to AgResearch programme', 23 February 2011, http://www.ciwf.org.uk/includes/documents/cm_docs/2011/n/nr1103.pdf (accessed 13 September 2012).

49 European Commission, 'Europeans' attitudes towards animal cloning', October 2008, http://ec.europa.eu/public_opinion/flash/fl_238_en.pdf.

50 *Daily Mail*, 'Clone beef's been on sale: After clone milk, now food watchdogs launch an investigation into illegal meat sold in British shops', 4 August 2010, http://www.dailymail.co.uk/news/article-1300097/Clone-beefs-sale-After-clone-milk-investigation-launched-illegal-meat.html (accessed 13 September 2012).

51 FSA, 'Cloned meat is safe – hypothetically speaking', 25 November 2010, http://www.food.gov.uk/news-updates/news/2010/nov/acnfcloned (accessed 13 September 2012).

52 FDA website: http://www.fda.gov/AnimalVeterinary/SafetyHealth/AnimalCloning/default.htm (accessed 13 September 2012).

53 The Poultry Site, 'Israeli scientists breed featherless chicken', 1 November 2011, http://www.thepoultrysite.com/poultrynews/24138/israeli-scientists-breed-featherless-chicken (accessed 13 September 2012); *New*

Scientist, 'Featherless chicken creates a flap', 21 May 2002, http://www.newscientist.com/article/dn2307-featherless-chicken-creates-a-flap.html (accessed 13 September 2012).

54 *Daily Telegraph*, 'Genetically modified cows produce "human" milk', 2 April 2011, http://www.telegraph.co.uk/earth/agriculture/geneticmodification/8423536/Genetically-modified-cows-produce-human-milk.html# (accessed 13 September 2012).

15 CHINA: MAO'S MEGA-FARM DREAM COMES TRUE

1 Nationmaster.com, http://www.nationmaster.com/graph/foo_por_con_per_cap-food-pork-consumption-per-capita (accessed 18 July 2012).

2 Defra press release, 'Vince Cable signs multi-million pound export deal to China', 8 November 2010, http://www.defra.gov.uk/news/2010/11/08/export-pig-china/ (accessed 18 July 2012).

3 V. Elliott, 'Why British pigs are flying in jumbo jets to China: Beijing snaps up our livestock to boost poor-quality herds', *Daily Mail*, 2 October 2011, http://www.dailymail.co.uk/news/article-2044201/China-ship-British-pigs-Beijing-boost-poor-quality-herds.html (accessed 18 July 2012); JSR Genetics, '900 high genetic merit JSR pigs delivered to China', 20 July 2012, http://www.jsrgenetics.com/news.php?sid=121 (accessed 4 October 2012).

4 F. Dikötter, *Mao's Great Famine*, Bloomsbury, London, 2010.

5 Ibid.

6 UNDP, China Human Development Report, 2007–2008, *Access for all: Basic public services for 1.3 billion people*, China Translation and Publishing Corporation, Beijing, 2008, http://hdr.undp.org/en/reports/national/asiathepacific/china/China_2008_en.pdf (accessed 23 July 2012).

7 A. Park, 'Still much to be done in fight against poverty', *China Daily*, 4 August 2009, http://www.chinadaily.com.cn/opinion/2009-04/08/content_7657358.htm (accessed 18 July 2012); CIA World Factbook, https://www.cia.gov/library/publications/the-world-factbook/fields/2046.html (accessed 23 July 2012).

8 BBC News, 'Chinese baby milk scare "severe"', 13 September 2008, http://news.bbc.co.uk/1/hi/world/asia-pacific/7614083.stm (accessed 18 July 2012).

9 Chinese milk scandal, http://en.wikipedia.org/wiki/2008_Chinese_milk_scandal (accessed 23 July 2012); SKY News, 'China Milk: Two sentenced to death', 22 January 2009, http://news.sky.com/story/663668/china-milk-two-sentenced-to-death (accessed 23 July 2012); *Daily Mail*, 'Two men

sentenced to death for roles in Chinese milk scandal which killed six babies', 22 January 2009, http://www.dailymail.co.uk/news/article-1126484/Two-men-sentenced-death-roles-Chinese-milk-scandal-killed-babies.html (accessed 23 July 2012); BBC News, 'Chinese baby milk scare "severe"'.

10 Clenbuterol side effects website, http://www.clenbuterolsideeffects.org/ (accessed 4 October 2012); Clenbuterol website, http://www.lenbuterol.tv/clenbuterol-side-effects/ (accessed 4 October 2012); *Independent*, 'Clenbuterol: The new weight-loss wonder drug gripping planet zero', 20 March 2007, http://www.independent.co.uk/life-style/health-and-families/health-news/clenbuterol-the-new-weightloss-wonder-drug-gripping-planet-zero-441059.html (accessed 4 October 2012).

11 *China Daily*, 'Who can guarantee China's pork is safe?', 6 April 2011, http://www.chinadaily.com.cn/china/2011-04/06/content_12281515.htm (accessed 18 July 2012).

12 *People's Daily*, 'Three arrested in pig meat food poisoning of 300 people in Shanghai', 4 November 2006, http://english.peopledaily.com.cn/200611/04/eng20061104_318172.html (accessed 18 July 2012).

13 International Finance Corporation, 'Muyuan Pig. Summary of proposed investment', 2010, http://www.ifc.org/ifcext/spiwebsite1.nsf/Project-Display/SPI_DP29089 (accessed 18 July 2012).

14 Ibid.

15 Calculation based on typical energy use in conventional pig production of 16–17 MJ energy per kg of pigmeat produced (Basset-Mens et al., 2005; Williams et al., 2006); annual production of 450,000 pigs slaughtered at average carcass weight for China of 76.7 kg (FAOSTAT, 2009); C. Basset-Mens and H. M. G. van der Werf, 'Scenario-based environmental assessment of farming systems: the case of pig production in France', *Agriculture, Ecosystems & Environment*, 105 (1–2) (2005), pp. 127–44; A. G. Williams, E. Audsley and D. L. Sandars, *Determining the environmental burdens and resource use in the production of agricultural and horticultural commodities*, Defra Project report ISO25, Bedford, Cranfield University and Defra, 2006.

16 International Finance Corporation (IFC) press release, 'IFC Equity Investment in Muyuan Food Supports Chinese Farming Sector', 18 August 2010, http://www.ifc.org/ifcext/agribusiness.nsf (accessed 18 July 2012).

17 The average commercial British pig farm has 500 sows, http://www.publications.parliament.uk/pa/cm200809/cmselect/cmenvfru/96/96.pdf; Muyuan farm #21 said to be set to house 6,500 sows.

18 CSRchina.net, 'China's economic engine forced to face environmental deficit', http://www.csrchina.net/page-1231.html (accessed 23 July 2012); http://factsanddetails.com/china.php?itemid=391&catid=10&subcatid=66.

19 *China Daily*, 'Wen urges cleanup of algae-stenched lakes', 1 July 2007, http://www.chinadaily.com.cn/china/2007-07/01/content_907145.htm (accessed 4 October 2012).

20 *Economist*, 'China: A lot to be angry about', 1 May 2008, http://www.economist.com/node/11293734 (accessed 23 July 2012).

21 AFP, 'China environmentalist alleges brutal jail treatment', 11 May 2010, http://www.google.com/hostednews/afp/article (accessed 23 July 2012).

22 Article: 'Development of organic agriculture in Taihu Lake region governance of agricultural nonpoint source pollution", http://eng.hi138.com/?i274195_Development_of_organic_agriculture_in_Taihu_Lake_region_governance_of_agricultural_nonpoint_source_pollution (accessed 23 July 2012). An Olympic-sized swimming pool holds 2,500 square metres of water.

23 Ibid.

16 KINGS, COMMONERS AND SUPERMARKETS: WHERE THE POWER LIES

1 The Prince of Wales website, http://www.princeofwales.gov.uk/personal-profiles/residences/highgrove/homefarm/ (accessed 14 September 2012).

2 BBC website, http://news.bbc.co.uk/onthisday/hi/dates/stories/december/1/newsid_3204000/3204279.stm (accessed 14 September 2012).

3 R. Body, *Farming in the Clouds*, Maurice Temple Smith, London, 1984.

4 4 January 1986. In R. Body, *Our Food, Our Land*, Rider, London, 1991.

5 Statistics Canada, *Agriculture Economic Statistics*, Cat. No. 21-603, and *Canadian Economic Observer*, Cat. No. 11-210. Cited in D. Qualman and F. Tait, *The Farm Crisis, Bigger Farms, and the Myths of 'Competition and Efficiency'*, Canadian Centre for Policy Alternatives, 2004, http://www.policyalternatives.org/documents/National_Office_Pubs /farm_crisis2004.pdf.

6 R. Harrison, *Animal Machines*, Vincent Stuart Ltd, London, 1964.

7 SNAP to health, website, US Farm Bill: Frequently asked questions, http://www.snaptohealth.org/farm-bill-usda/u-s-farm-bill-faq/ (accessed 14 September 2012); Wikipedia, http://en.wikipedia.org/wiki/Food,_Conservation,_and_Energy_Act_of_2008 (accessed 14 September 2012).

8 M. Bittman, 'Don't End Agricultural Subsidies, Fix Them', *New York Times*, 1 March 2011, http://opinionator.blogs.nytimes.com/2011/03/01/dont-end-agricultural-subsidies-fix-them/; J. Steinhauer, 'Farm Subsidies Become Target Amid Spending Cuts', *New York Times*, 6 May 2011, http://www.nytimes.com/2011/05/07/us/politics/07farm.html.

9 Environmental Working Group, National data from EWG farm subsidy database, 2011, http://farm.ewg.org.

10 Planet Retail, 'Global Retail Rankings, 2011', 2012, http://www.planetretail.net/Presentations/GlobalRetailRankings2011-Grocery.pdf (accessed 14 September 2012).

11 Planet Retail, 'Global Retail Rankings 2011; Food Service', 2012, http://www.planetretail.net.

12 U. Kjaernes, M. Miele and J. Roex, *Attitudes of Consumers, Retailers and Producers to Farm Animal Welfare*, Quality Report Number 2, EU 6th Framework Programme, Cardiff University, 2007, Welfare, March 2007, http://www.welfarequality.net/everyone/37097/7/0/22.

13 *Catholic Herald*, 'Monks of Storrington cease veal production', 27 September 1985, http://archive.catholicherald.co.uk/article/27th-september-1985/1/monks-of-storrington-cease-veal-production (accessed 14 September 2012); A. Johnson, *Factory Farming*, Blackwell, Oxford, 1991.

14 Assured Food Standards website, http://www.redtractor.org.uk/Why-Red-Tractor (accessed 14 September 2012).

15 *Farmers Weekly*, 'Farming under fire', 2011, http://www.fwi.co.uk/business/farming-under-fire/ (accessed 14 September 2012).

17 NEW INGREDIENTS: RETHINKING OUR FOOD

1 J. Parfitt, M. Barthel and S. Macnaughton, 'Food waste within food supply chains: quantification and potential for change to 2050', *Phil. Trans. R. Soc. B*, 365, 27 September 2010, pp. 3065–81.

2 C. Nellemann et al., *The Environmental Food Crisis – The Environment's Role in Averting Future Food Crises*, a UNEP rapid response assessment, February 2009, United Nations Environment Programme, GRID-Arendal, www.unep.org/pdf/foodcrisis_lores.pdf.

3 S. Fairlie, *Meat – a Benign Extravagance*, Permanent Publications, 2010, see pp. 46–50.

4 B. White, *Alaska Salmon Fisheries Enhancement Program Report 2010*, Annual Report, Alaska Department of Fish and Game, 2011, http://

www.adfg.alaska.gov/FedAidPDFs/FMR11-04.pdf (accessed 27 September 2012).

5   G. P. Knapp, 'Alaska Salmon Ranching: an Economic Review of the Alaska Salmon Hatchery Programme', in B. R. Howell, E. Moksness and T. Svasand (eds), *Stock Enhancement and Sea Ranching*, Fishing News Books, Blackwell Science, Oxford, 1999, pp. 537–56.

6   M. Kaeriyama, 'Hatchery Programmes and Stock Management of Salmonid Populations in Japan', in Howell et al., *Stock Enhancement and Sea Ranching*.

7   S. D. Sedgwick, *Salmon Farming Handbook*, Fishing News Books, Surrey, 1988.

8   ABC News, 'Google Co-founder: The man behind the $300k test-tube burger', 5 August 2013, http://abcnews.go.com/Technology/google-founder-sergey-brin-man-300k-test-tube/story?id=19872215 (accessed 16 August 2013).

9   B. Gates, *The Future of Food*, The Gates Notes, 2013, http://www.the-gatesnotes.com/Features/Future-of-Food (accessed 21 May 2013).

10 Ibid.

18   THE SOLUTION: HOW TO AVERT THE COMING FOOD CRISIS

1   UN Food and Agriculture Organization (FAO), *World Livestock 2011: Livestock in Food Security*, Rome, 2011.

2   J. Bruinsma, *The resource outlook to 2050: By how much do land, water and crop yields need to increase by 2050?*, FAO Expert Meeting on 'How to Feed the World in 2050', FAO, Rome, 24–26 June 2009; United Nations, *World Economic and Social Survey 2011: The great green technological transformation*, United Nations, New York, 2011.

3   Government Office for Science, *Foresight Project on Global Food and Farming Futures Synthesis Report C1: Trends in food demand and production*, 2011; S. Msangi and M. Rosegrant, *World agriculture in a dynamically-changing environment: IFPRI's long term outlook for food and agriculture under additional demand and constraints*, Expert Meeting on 'How to feed the World in 2050', Rome, FAO; H. Steinfeld et al., *Livestock's Long Shadow, environmental issues and options*, FAO, Rome, 2006, Introduction, p. 12.

4   Calculated from FAOSTAT online figures for global grain harvest (2009) and food value of cereals. Based on a calorific intake of 2,500 kcalories per person per day.

5   Steinfeld et al., *Livestock's Long Shadow*, p. 43.

6   David Pimentel et al., 'Reducing energy inputs in the US food system', *Human Ecology*, 36 (2008), pp. 459–71.

7   FAO, *State of the World Fisheries and Aquaculture*, 2010.

8   T. Stuart, *Waste: Uncovering the global food scandal*, Penguin, 2009.

9   S. Fairlie, *Meat – a Benign Extravagance*, Permanent Publications, 2010, see pp. 46–50.

10 Tristram Stuart, personal communication, 2 May 2012.

11 BBC, 'French village Pince to hand out chickens to cut waste', 28 March 2012, http://www.bbc.co.uk/news/world-europe-17540287 (accessed 17 September 2012).

12 Nick Cliffe, Project Manager, Closed Loop, Dagenham, London, personal communication, 2 May 2012.

13 Stuart, personal communication, 2 May 2012.

14 J. Parfitt, M. Barthel and S. Macnaughton, 'Food waste within food supply chains: quantification and potential for change to 2050', *Phil. Trans. R. Soc. B*, 365, 27 September 2010, pp. 3065–81; Institution of Mechanical Engineers, *Population: One planet, too many people?*, 2011.

15 J. Gustavsson, C. Cederberg, U. Sonesson et al., *Global Food Losses and Food Waste: extent, causes and prevention*, FAO, Rome, 2011, www.fao.org/fileadmin/user_upload/ags/publications/GFL_web.pdf.

16 UN FAO, 2013, Food wastage footprint: impact on natural resources, http://www.fao.org/docrep/018/i3347e/i3347e.pdf (accessed 13th September 2013).

17 P. Stevenson, 'Feeding nine billion: How much extra do we need to produce?', 13 June 2013, http://www.eating-better.org/blog/3/Feeding-nine-billion-how-much-extra-food-do-we-need-to-produce.html (accessed 25 July 2013).

18 K. Lock et al., 'Health, agricultural, and economic effects of adoption of healthy diet recommendations', *Lancet*, vol. 376, issue 9753 (2010), pp. 1699–1709.

19 S. Friel et al., 'Public health benefits of strategies to reduce greenhouse-gas emissions: food and agriculture', *Lancet*, vol. 374, issue 9706 (2009), pp. 2016–25.

20 Stuart, *Waste*.

21 Lester R. Brown, *Plan B 4.0: Mobilizing to save civilization*, Earth Policy Institute, W. W. Norton, 2009.

22 EEA, *The European environment – state and outlook 2010: synthesis*, European Environment Agency, Copenhagen, 2010.

23 European Commission, Joint Reseach Centre, http://eusoils.jrc.ec.europa.eu/library/themes/Salinization/ (accessed 17 September 2012).

24 N. V. Fedoroff et al., 'Radically rethinking agriculture for the 21st century', *Science*, 327 (12 February 2010), pp. 833–4.

25 Own calculation

19 CONSUMER POWER: WHAT YOU CAN DO

1 J. Blythman, *What to Eat*, Fourth Estate, London, 2012.

EPILOGUE

1 P. Stevenson, 'Feeding nine billion: How much extra do we need to produce?', 13 June 2013, http://www.eating-better.org/blog/3/Feeding-nine-billion-how-much-extra-food-do-we-need-to-produce.html (accessed 25 July 2013).

Index

A Note on the Author

Philip Lymbery is the CEO of leading international farm animal welfare organisation Compassion in World Farming and a prominent commentator on the effects of industrial farming. Under his leadership, Compassion's prestigious awards have included Observer Ethical Award for Campaigner of the Year and BBC Radio 4 Food and Farming awards for Best Campaigner and Educator. He is a lifelong wildlife enthusiast and lives in rural Hampshire with his wife and stepson.

Isabel Oakeshott is Political Editor at the *Sunday Times* and political commentator for BBC television and radio, Sky News and other channels. In 2012, she won Political Journalist of the Year at the UK Press Awards and she is the ghost writer for *Inside Out*, an explosive insider account of Gordon Brown's regime. She is a member of the parliamentary lobby and is based at Westminster. She lives in the Cotswolds with her husband and three young children.

A Note on the Type

The text of this book is set Adobe Garamond. It is one of several versions of Garamond based on the designs of Claude Garamond. It is thought that Garamond based his font on Bembo, cut in 1495 by Francesco Griffo in collaboration with the Italian printer Aldus Manutius. Garamond types were first used in books printed in Paris around 1532. Many of the present-day versions of this type are based on the *Typi Academiae* of Jean Jannon cut in Sedan in 1615.

A plea from the author, Philip Lymbery,
CEO of leading farm animal welfare organisation
Compassion in World Farming.

To join our campaign today,
please visit
ciwf.org

Registered Charity Number 1095050